809	T216e

Tate, Allen
AUTHOR

Essays of Four Decades
TITLE

89498

809   T216e
Tate, Allen
Essays of Four Decades
89498

ESSAYS OF FOUR

ESSAYS
OF FOUR
DECADES

BY *ALLEN TATE*

THE **SWALLOW PRESS** INC.
CHICAGO

This book is presented to
JOHN CROWE RANSOM
in his eightieth year

Contents

Preface

WHETHER THIS PREFACE will be a real preface, an easing of the reader's way into the book, or an attempt to bring order into opinions scattered in various essays over almost forty years, I cannot tell as I begin these observations. Of one thing only can I be certain. This meditation on a part of my own writings will be like those writings themselves; it will be an improvisation, or one thing leading to another. I have felt, for many years, serious though friendly envy of some of my contemporaries; for example, Mr. Kenneth Burke, a systematic thinker. Mr. Burke has an advantage over some systematic thinkers in having several systems, or a new system developing out of, or dovetailing with, an old one. When Dramatism would not quite expound the Book of Genesis, Mr. Burke stepped out of it into Logology, an extension of his meshed systems that permitted him to invent God. I am not being frivolous, or disrespectful; there is nobody in our "literary situation" for whom I have more respect. There is, simply, a large element of play in Mr. Burke's intellectual agility and terminological inventiveness (a phrase not unlike some of his own). I have profited by his Five Master Terms, without ever quite using them directly: years ago they sent me back to Aristotle's Four Causes, which like Mr. Burke's Five, are operative categories which help us to examine objects and/or persons, either as aggregates or as organic groups, whether in motion or at rest, with more than usual attention.

And I should hope, with more than usual order; but what one is trying to "order" is always difficult to decide when the putative order of one essay seems to have remote connections with the order of another, even if it doesn't contradict it outright. I cannot be sure that there is any consistency between "Tension in Poetry" (1938) and "The Point of Dying: Donne's 'Virtuous Men' " (1952). When I wrote the latter short essay I had been reading Dante for some years and it seemed inevitable that I should go to work on Donne with the Fourfold System, if only to see whether it could show me things in Donne that I had not seen before. I think it did; and that, of course, is the primary reason for writing any essay, the enlightenment of a possible reader always being the secondary reason. But even self-knowledge was not the immediate purpose of my little exercise on "A Valediction: Forbidding Mourning." A few years before 1952 Professor Douglas Bush had read an article at a meeting of the Modern Language Association, in which he said that most of the New Critics were ignorant, and that I in particular seemed to know nothing about Elizabethan literature except the habit of the poets of punning on the verb *to die* (*to die = to complete the act of love*). I had said somewhere that this pun was concealed in the two first stanzas of Donne's "A Valediction: Forbidding Mourning"; Professor Bush said it wasn't there. I wrote "The Point of Dying" to prove that it was, and I think I proved it.

Such are the occasions that prompt the essayist, but not the scholar or systematic critic, to run the hundred-yard dash and to leave to his colleagues of longer limb and wind the full-length book. Of the forty-two essays and six prefaces in this book, I can think of only two that I should like to rewrite, though I should like to alter phrases and clauses on almost every page. The two essays are "The Man of Letters in the Modern World" and "The Hovering Fly," neither of which is in any strict sense literary criticism; they are public debates with myself in which I was able to make my own ground rules and rig possible rebuttals to my own advantage.

I should be at a loss to say what may be original in my essays; that is, ideas and perceptions not entertained by critics in the past or by my friends of the present. I owe most to

John Crowe Ransom, some of my essays, like "Three Types of Poetry," being scholia on the essays that later appeared in his *The World's Body* (1938). I suppose I owe most of all to Coleridge, but just what it would be hard to say, beyond the general idea that poetry can be an undemonstrable form of knowledge. Nobody who read I. A. Richards' *Practical Criticism* when it appeared in 1929 could read any poem as he had read it before. From that time on one had to read poetry with all the brains one had and with one's arms and legs, as well as what may be inside the rib cage. What I owe to T. S. Eliot is pervasive. I think now of the relation of a young poet to certain traditions; I still believe that "novelty is better than repetition," that in novelty of a certain unpredictable kind a young poet finds his tradition. But novelty is not noise, or undressing on the public platform, or shouting bad metaphors from the printed page. The two first lines of "The Love Song of J. Alfred Prufrock" were the first gun of the twentieth-century revolution: the young Tom Eliot pulled the lanyard and quietly went back to his desk in a London bank. But it was a shot heard round the world. I also owe to Eliot, and perhaps not less to Herbert Read, gratitude for furnishing me a model of what the non-academic man of letters ought to be.

I am not alone in believing that "criticism" written by poets is "programmatic," and that criticism written by scholars is an effort to make the poets' intuited programs systematic and, further, to adjust all the programs of an age to one another and thus to reconstruct the "mind" of the age. But this is not the business of the poet-critic, who is not concerned with consistency and system, but merely with as much self-knowledge as he needs to write his own verse.

A. T.

I

The Man of Letters in the Modern World [1]

To THE QUESTION, What should the man of letters be in our time, we should have to find the answer in what we need him to do. He must do first what he has always done: he must recreate for his age the image of man, and he must propagate standards by which other men may test that image, and distinguish the false from the true. But at our own critical moment, when all languages are being debased by the techniques of mass control, the man of letters might do well to conceive his responsibility more narrowly. He has an immediate responsibility, to other men no less than to himself, for the vitality of language. He must distinguish the difference between mere communication—of which I shall later have more to say—and the rediscovery of the human condition in the living arts. He must discriminate and defend the difference between mass communication, for the control of men, and the knowledge of man which literature offers us for human participation.

The invention of standards by which this difference may be known, and a sufficient minority of persons instructed, is a moral obligation of the literary man. But the actuality of the difference does not originate in the critical intelligence as such; it is exemplified in the specific forms of the literary arts, whose final purpose, the extrinsic end for which they

1 The Phi Beta Kappa Address, University of Minnesota, May 1, 1952. Excerpts from this paper were read at the International Exposition of the Arts, under the auspices of the Congress for Cultural Freedom, Paris, May 21, 1952.

3

exist, is not the control of other persons, but self-knowledge. By these arts, one means the arts without which men can live, but without which they cannot live well, or live as men. To keep alive the knowledge of ourselves with which the literary arts continue to enlighten the more ignorant portion of mankind (among whom one includes oneself), to separate them from other indispensable modes of knowledge, and to define their limits, is the intellectual and thus the social function of the writer. Here the man of letters is the critic.

The edifying generality of these observations is not meant to screen the difficulties that they will presently encounter in their particular applications. A marked difference between communication and communion I shall be at some pains to try to discern in the remarks that follow. I shall try to explore the assertion: Men in a dehumanized society may communicate, but they cannot live in full communion. To explore this I must first pursue a digression.

What happens in one mind may happen as influence or coincidence, in another; when the same idea spreads to two or more minds of considerable power, it may eventually explode, through chain reaction, in a whole society; it may dominate a period or an entire epoch.

When René Descartes isolated thought from man's total being he isolated him from nature, including his own nature; and he divided man against himself. (The demonology which attributes to a few persons the calamities of mankind is perhaps a necessary convention of economy in discourse.) It was not the first time that man had been at war with himself: there was that first famous occasion of immemorial antiquity: it is man's permanent war of internal nerves. Descartes was only the new strategist of our own phase of the war. Men after the seventeenth century would have been at war with themselves if Descartes had never lived. He chose the new field and forged the new weapons. The battle is now between the dehumanized society of secularism, which imitates Descartes' mechanized nature, and the eternal society of the communion of the human spirit. The war is real enough; but again one is conscious of an almost mythical exaggeration in one's description of the combatants. I shall not condescend to Descartes by trying to be fair to him. For the battle is being fought, it has always been fought by men few of whom have heard of Descartes or any other philosopher.

Consider the politician, who as a man may be as good as his quiet neighbor. If he acts upon the assumption (which he has never heard of) that society is a machine to be run efficiently by immoral—or, to him amoral—methods, he is only exhibiting a defeat of the spirit that he is scarcely conscious of having suffered. Now consider his fellow-citizen, the knowing person, the trained man of letters, the cunning poet in the tradition of Poe and Mallarmé. If this person (who perhaps resembles ourselves) is aware of more, he is able to do less than the politician, who does not know what he is doing. The man of letters sees that modern societies are machines, even if he thinks that they ought not to be: he is convinced that in its intractable Manichaeism, society cannot be redeemed. The shadowy political philosophy of modern literature, from Proust to Faulkner, is, in its moral origins, Jansenist: we are disciples of Pascal, the merits of whose Redeemer were privately available but could not affect the operation of the power-state. While the politician, in his cynical innocence, uses society, the man of letters disdainfully, or perhaps even absentmindedly, withdraws from it: a withdrawal that few persons any longer observe, since withdrawal has become the social convention of the literary man, in which society, insofar as it is aware of him, expects him to conduct himself.

It is not improper, I think, at this point, to confess that I have drawn in outline the melancholy portrait of the man who stands before you. Before I condemn him I wish to examine another perspective, an alternative to the double retreat from the moral center, of the man of action and the man of letters, that we have completed in our time. The alternative has had at least the virtue of recommending the full participation of the man of letters in the action of society.

The phrase, "the action of society," is abstract enough to disarm us into supposing that perhaps here and there in the past, if not uniformly, men of letters were hourly participating in it: the supposition is not too deceptive a paralogism, provided we think of society as the City of Augustine and Dante, where it was possible for men to find in the temporal city the imperfect analogue to the City of God. (The Heavenly City was still visible, to Americans, in the political economy of Thomas Jefferson.) What we, as literary men, have been asked to support, and what we have rejected, is the action of society as *secularism,* or the society that substitutes means for ends. Although the idolatry of the means has been egregious enough in the West, we have not been willing to prefer the more advanced worship that prevails in Europe eastward of Berlin, and in Asia. If we can scarcely imagine a society like the Russian, deliberately committing itself to secularism, it is no doubt because we cannot easily believe that men will prefer barbarism to civilization. They come to prefer the senility (which resembles the adolescence) and the irresponsibility of the barbarous condition of man, without quite foreseeing what else they will get out of it. Samuel Johnson said of chronic drunkenness: "He who makes a beast of himself gets rid of the pain of being a man." There is perhaps no anodyne for the pains of civilization but savagery. What men may get out of this may be seen in the western world today, in an intolerable psychic crisis expressing itself as a political crisis.

The internal crisis, whether it precede or follow the political, is inevitable in a society that multiplies means without ends. Man is a creature that in the long run has got to believe in order to know, and to know in order to do. For doing without knowing is machine behavior, illiberal and servile routine, the secularism with which man's specific destiny has no connection. I take it that we have sufficient evidence, generation after generation, that man will never be completely or permanently enslaved. He will rebel, as he is rebelling now, in a shocking variety of "existential" disorders, all over the world. If his *human* nature as such cannot participate in the action of society, he will not capitulate to it, if that action is inhuman: he will turn in upon himself, with the common gesture which throughout history has vindicated the rhetoric of liberty: "Give me liberty or give me death." Man may destroy himself but he will not at last tolerate anything less than his full human condition. Pascal said that the "sight of cats or rats is enough to unhinge the reason"—a morbid prediction of our contemporary existential philosophy, a modernized Dark Night of Sense. The impact of mere sensation, even of "cats and rats" (which enjoy the innocence of their perfection in the order of nature)— a simple sense perception from a world no longer related to human beings—will nourish a paranoid philosophy of despair. Blake's "hapless soldier's sigh," Poe's "tell-tale heart," Rimbaud's nature careening in a "drunken boat," Eliot's woman "pulling her long black hair," are qualities of the life of Baudelaire's *fourmillante Cité,* the secularism of the swarm, of which we are the present citizens.

Is the man of letters alone doomed to inhabit that city? No, we are all in it—the butcher, the baker, the candlestick-maker, and the banker and the statesman. The special awareness of the man of letters, the source at once of his Gnostic arrogance and of his Augustinian humility, he brings to bear upon all men alike: his hell has not been "for those other people": he has reported his own. His report upon his own spiritual condition, in the last hundred years, has misled the banker and the statesman into the illusion that they have no hell because, as secularists, they have lacked the language to report it. What you are not able to name therefore does not exist—a barbarous disability, to which I have already alluded. There would be no hell for modern man if our men of letters were not calling attention to it.

But it is the business of the man of letters to call attention to whatever he is able to see: it is his function to create what has not been hitherto known and, as critic, to discern its modes. I repeat that it is his duty to render the image of man as he is in his time, which, without the man of letters, would not otherwise be known. What modern literature has taught us is not merely that the man of letters has not participated fully in the action of society; it has taught us that nobody else has either. It is a fearful lesson. The roll call of the noble and sinister characters, our ancestors and our brothers, who exemplify the lesson, must end in a shudder: Julien Sorel, Emma Bovary, Captain Ahab, Hepzibah Pyncheon, Roderick Usher, Lambert Strether, Baron de Charlus, Stephen Dedalus, Joe Christmas—all these and more, to say nothing of the precise probing of their, and our, sensibility, which is modern poetry since Baudelaire. Have men of letters perversely invented these horrors? They are rather the inevitable creations of a secularized society, the society of means without ends, in which nobody participates with the full substance of his humanity. It is the society in which everybody acts his part (even when he is most active) in the plotless drama of withdrawal.

I trust that nobody supposes that I see the vast populations of Europe and America scurrying, each man to his tree, penthouse or cave, and refusing to communicate with other men. Humanity was never more gregarious and never before heard so much of its own voice. Is not then the problem of communication for the man of letters very nearly solved? He may sit in a soundproof room, in shirt-sleeves, and talk at a metal object resembling a hornet's nest, throwing his voice, and perhaps also his face, at 587,000,000 people, more or less, whom he has never seen, and whom it may not occur to him that in order to love, he must have a medium even less palpable than air.

What I am about to say of communication will take it for granted that men cannot communicate by means of sound over either wire or air. They have got to communicate through love. Communication that is not also communion is incomplete. We *use* communication; we *participate* in communion. "All the certainty of our knowledge," says Coleridge, "depends [on this]; and this becomes intelligible to no man by the ministry of mere words from without. The medium, by which spirits understand each other, is not the surrounding air; but the *freedom* which they possess in common." (The italics are Coleridge's.) Neither the artist nor the statesman will communicate fully again until the rule of love, added to the rule of law, has liberated him. I am not suggesting that we all have an obligation of *personal* love towards one another. I regret that I must be explicit about this matter. No man, under any political dispensation known to us, has been able to avoid hating other men by deciding that it would be a "good thing" to love them; he loves his neighbor, as well as the man he has never seen, only through the love of God. "He that saith that he is in the light, and hateth his brother, is in darkness even until now."

I confess that to the otiose ear of the tradition of Poe and Mallarmé the simple-minded Evangelist may seem to offer something less than a solution to the problem of communication. I lay it down as a fact, that it is the only solution. "We must love one another or die," Mr. Auden wrote more than ten years ago. I cannot believe that Mr. Auden was telling us that a secularized society cannot exist; it obviously exists. He was telling us that a society which has once been religious cannot, without risk of spiritual death, preceded by the usual agonies, secularize itself. A society of means without ends, in the age of technology, so multiplies the means, in the lack of anything better to do, that it may have to scrap the machines as it makes them; until our descendants will have to dig themselves out of one rubbish heap after another and stand upon it, in order to make more rubbish to make more standing room. The surface of nature will then be literally as well as morally concealed from the eyes of men.

Will congresses of men of letters, who expect from their conversations a little less than mutual admiration, and who achieve at best toleration of one another's personalities, mitigate the difficulties of communication? This may be doubted, though one feels that it is better to gather together in any other name than that of Satan, than not to gather at all. Yet one must assume that men of letters will not love one another personally any better than they have in the past. If there has been little communion among them, does the past teach them to expect, under perfect conditions (whatever these may be), to communicate their works to any large portion of mankind? We suffer, though we know better, from an ignorance which lets us entertain the illusion that in the past great works of literature were immediately consumed by entire populations. It has never been so; yet dazzled by this false belief, the modern man of letters is bemused by an unreal dilemma. Shall he persist in his rejection of the existential "cats and rats" of Pascal, the political disorder of the West that "unhinges the reason"; or shall he exploit the new media of mass "communication"—cheap print, radio and television? For what purpose shall he exploit them?

The dilemma, like evil, is real to the extent that it exists as privative of good: it has an impressive "existential" actuality: men of letters on both sides of the Atlantic consider the possible adjustments of literature to a mass audience. The first question that we ought to ask ourselves is: *What do we propose to communicate to whom?*

I do not know whether there exists in Europe anything like the steady demand upon American writers to "communicate" quickly with the audience that Coleridge knew even in his time as the "multitudinous Public, shaped into personal unity by the magic of abstraction." The American is still able to think that he sees in Europe—in France, but also in England—a closer union, in the remains of a unified culture, between a sufficiently large public and the man of letters. That Alexis Saint-Léger Léger, formerly Permanent Secretary of the French Foreign Office, could inhabit the same body with St.-John Perse, a great living French poet, points to the recent actuality of that closer union; while at the same time, the two names for the two natures of the one person suggest the completion of the Cartesian disaster, the fissure in the human spirit of our age; the inner division creating the outer, and the eventual loss of communion.

Another way of looking at the question, *What* do we propose to communicate to *whom?* would eliminate the dilemma, withdrawal *or* communication. It disappears if we understand that literature has never communicated, that it cannot *communicate:* from this point of view we see the work of literature as a participation in communion. Participation leads naturally to the idea of the common experience. Perhaps it is not too grandiose a conception to suggest that works of literature, from the short lyric to the long epic, are the recurrent discovery of the human communion *as experience,* in a definite place and at a definite time. Our unexamined theory of literature as communication could not have appeared in an age in which communion was still possible for any appreciable majority of persons. The word communication presupposes the victory of the secularized society of means without ends. The poet, on the one hand, shouts to the public, on the other (some distance away), not the rediscovery of the common experience, but a certain pitch of sound to which the well-conditioned adrenals of humanity obligingly respond.

The response is not the specifically human mode of behavior; it is the specifically animal mode, what is left of man after Occam's razor has cut away his humanity. It is a tragedy of contemporary society that so much of democratic social theory reaches us in the language of "drive," "stimulus," and "response." This is not the language of freemen, it is the language of slaves. The language of freemen substitutes for these words, respectively, *end, choice,* and *discrimination.* Here are two sets of analogies, the one sub-rational and servile, the other rational and free. (The analogies in which man conceives his nature at different historical moments is of greater significance than his political rhetoric.) When the poet is exhorted to communicate, he is being asked to speak within the orbit of an analogy that assumes that genuine communion is impossible: does not the metaphor hovering in the rear of the word communication isolate the poet before he can speak? The poet at a microphone desires to sway, affect, or otherwise influence a crowd (not a community) which is then addressed as if it were permanently over *there*—not *here,* where the poet himself would be a member of it; he is not a member, but a mere part. He stimulates his audience—which a few minutes later will be stimulated by a news commentator, who reports the results of a "poll," as the Roman *pontifex* under Tiberius reported the color of the entrails of birds— the poet thus elicits a response, in the context of the preconditioned "drives" ready to be released in the audience. Something may be said to have been transmitted, or *communicated;* nothing has been shared, in a new and illuminating intensity of awareness.

One may well ask what these observations have to do with the man of letters in the modern world? They have nearly everything to do with him, since, unless I am wholly mistaken, his concern is with what has not been previously known about our present relation to an unchanging source of knowledge, and with our modes of apprehending it. In the triad of *end, choice,* and *discrimination,* his particular responsibility is for the last; for it is by means of discrimination, through choice, towards an end, that the general intelligence acts. The general intelligence is the intelligence of the man of letters: he must not be committed to the illiberal specializations that the nineteenth century has proliferated into the modern world: specializations in which means are divorced from ends, action from sensibility, matter from mind, society from the individual, religion from moral agency, love from lust, poetry from thought, communion from experience, and mankind in the community from men in the crowd. There is literally no end to this list of dissociations because there is no end, yet in sight, to the fragmenting of the western mind. The modern man of letters may, as a man, be as thoroughly the victim of it as his conditioned neighbor. I hope it is understood that I am not imputing to the man of letters a personal superiority; if he is luckier than his neighbors, his responsibility, and his capacity for the shattering peripeties of experience, are greater: he is placed at the precarious center of a certain liberal tradition, from which he is as strongly tempted as the next man, to escape. This tradition has only incidental connections with political liberalism and it has none with the power-state; it means quite simply the freedom of the mind to discriminate the false from the true, the experienced knowledge from its verbal imitations. His critical responsibility is thus what it has always been—the recreation and the application of literary standards, which in order to be effectively literary, must be more than literary. His task is to preserve the integrity, the purity, and the reality of language wherever and for whatever purpose it may be used. He must approach his task through the letter—the letter of the poem, the letter of the politician's speech, the letter of the law; for the use of the letter is in the long run our one indispensable test of the actuality of our experience.

The letter then is the point to which the man of letters directs his first power, the power of discrimination. He will ask: Is there in this language genuine knowledge of our human community—or of our lack of it—that we have not had before? If there is, he will know that it is liberal language, the language of freemen, in which a choice has been made towards a probable end for man. If it is not language of this order, if it is the language of mere communication, of mechanical analogies in which the two natures of man are isolated and dehumanized, then he will know that it is the language of men who are, or who are waiting to be, slaves.

If the man of letters does not daily renew his dedication to this task, I do not know who else may be expected to undertake it. It is a task that cannot be performed today in a society that has not remained, in certain senses of the word that we sufficiently understand, democratic. We enjoy the privileges of democracy on the same terms as we enjoy other privileges: on the condition that we give something back. What the man of letters returns in exchange for his freedom is the difficult model of freedom for his brothers, Julien Sorel, Lambert Strether, and Joe Christmas, who are thus enjoined to be likewise free, and to sustain the freedom of the man of letters himself. What he gives back to society often enough carries with it something that a democratic society likes as little as any other: the courage to condemn the abuses of democracy, more particularly to

discriminate the usurpations of democracy that are perpetrated in the name of democracy.

That he is permitted, even impelled by the democratic
condition itself, to publish his discriminations of the stag-
gering abuses of language, and thus of choices and ends,
that vitiate the cultures of Western nations, is in itself a
consideration for the second thought of our friends in
Europe. Might they not in the end ill prefer the upper
millstone of Russia to the nether of the United States? Our
formidable economic and military power—which like all
secular power the man of letters must carry as his Cross;
our bad manners in Europe; our ignorance of the plain fact
that we can no more dispense with Europe than almighty
Rome could have lived without a reduced Greece; our delusion that we are prepared to "educate" Europe in "democracy" by exporting dollars, gadgets, and sociology—to say
nothing of the boorish jargon of the State Department—
all this, and this is by no means all, may well tempt (in
the words of Reinhold Niebuhr) "our European friends
to a virtual Manichaeism and to consign the world of organization to the outer darkness of barbarism." But it
should be pointed out, I think, to these same European
brothers, that the darkness of this barbarism still shows
forth at least one light which even the black slaves of the
Old South were permitted to keep burning, but which the
white slaves of Russia are not: I mean the inalienable right
to talk back of which I cite the present discourse as an
imperfect example.

The man of letters has, then, in our time a small but
critical service to render to man: a service that will be in
the future more effective than it is now, when the cult of
the literary man shall have ceased to be an idolatry. Men
of letters and their followers, like the *parvenu* gods and
their votaries of decaying Rome, compete in the dissemi-

nation of distraction and novelty. But the true province of the man of letters is nothing less (as it is nothing more) than culture itself. The state is the mere operation of society, but culture is the way society lives, the material medium through which men receive the one lost truth which must be perpetually recovered: the truth of what Jacques Maritain calls the "supra-temporal destiny" of man. It is the duty of the man of letters to supervise the culture of language, to which the rest of culture is subordinate, and to warn us when our language is ceasing to forward the ends proper to man. The end of social man is communion in time through love, which is beyond time.

1952

To Whom Is the Poet Responsible?[1]

AND FOR WHAT? The part of the question that I have used as the title has been widely asked in our generation. I have seldom heard anybody ask the second part: *For what?* I shall have to assume, without elucidating it, a certain moral attitude towards the idea of responsibility which is perhaps as little popular in our time as the accused poetry that has given rise to the controversy. Thus I take it for granted that nobody can be held generally responsible, for if our duties are not specific they do not exist. It was, I think, the failure to say what the modern poet was responsible *for* that made it easy to conclude, from the attacks ten years ago by Mr. MacLeish and Mr. Van Wyck Brooks, that in some grandiose sense the poet should be held responsible to society for everything that nobody else was paying any attention to. The poet was saddled with a total responsibility for the moral, political, and social well-being; it was pretty clearly indicated that had he behaved differently at some indefinite time in the near or remote past the international political order itself would not have been in jeopardy, and we should not perhaps be at international loggerheads today. We should not have had the Second World War, perhaps not even the first.

The historical political suspicion of poetry is one thing;

[1] A brief version of this paper was read at Bennington College on April 16, 1950; present text, at a symposium of the American Committee for Cultural Freedom, May 10, 1951.

but the attacks that I have alluded to were by men of letters, one of them a poet—and this is another thing altogether. I do not know to what extent the Marxist atmosphere of the thirties influenced the attacks. In trying to get to the bottom of them one may dismiss too quickly the Communist party line as a perversion of the original Platonic rejection of poetry which holds that the arts of sensible imitation are a menace to the political order. One must dismiss it respectfully, because it contains a fundamental if one-eyed truth: that is to say, from Plato on there is in this tradition of thought the recognition that however useful poetry may be as a civilizing virtue, it should not be allowed to govern the sensibility of persons who run the state. One may scarcely believe that Sophocles *as poet* was appointed *strategos* in the Samian war, even though that honorific office followed upon the great success of the *Antigone* in the Dionysia of 440 B.C. What I am getting at here is that, were we confronted with an unreal choice, it would be better to suppress poetry than to misuse it, to expect of it an order of action that it cannot provide. (Stalinist Russia seems to do both: it suppresses poetry and supports party verse.) In any literary history that I have read there is no record of a poet receiving and exercising competently high political authority. Milton wrote Cromwell's Latin correspondence, and tracts of his own, but he was never given power; and likewise his successor, Andrew Marvell. We have read some of Shelley's more heroic assertions, in *A Defence of Poetry,* into the past, where we substitute what Shelley said ought to have been for what was. The claim that poets are "unacknowledged legislators" is beyond dispute if we understand that as legislators they should remain unacknowledged and not given the direction of the state. This limit being set, we are ready to understand what Shelley had really to say—which is the true perception that there is always a reciprocal relation between life and art, at that point at which life imitates art.

If poetry makes us more conscious of the complexity and meaning of our experience, it may have an eventual effect upon action, even political action. The recognition of this truth is not an achievement of our own age; it is very old. Our contribution to it I take to be a deviation from its full meaning, an exaggeration and a loss of insight. Because poetry may influence politics, we conclude that poetry is merely politics, or a kind of addlepated politics, and thus not good for anything. Why this has come about there is not time to say here, even if I knew. One may point out some of the ways in which it has affected our general views, and hence see how it works in us.

How does it happen that literary men themselves blame the poets first when society goes wrong? The argument we heard ten years ago runs somewhat as follows: The rise of Hitlerism (we were not then looking too narrowly at Stalinism) reflects the failure of our age to defend the principles of social and political democracy, a failure resulting from the apathy of responsible classes of society, those persons who have charge of the means of public influence that was formerly called language (but is now called "communications"). These persons are the writers, more particularly the poets or "makers," whose special charge is the purity of language and who represent the class of writers presumably at its highest. The makers, early in the nineteenth century, retired to a private world of their own invention, where they cultivated certain delusions—for example, their superiority to practical life, the belief in the autonomy of poetry, and the worship of the past. Some of them, like Baudelaire, actively disliked democracy. Their legacy to our tortured age turned out to be at once the wide diffusion and the intensification of these beliefs, with the result that we became politically impotent, and totalitarianism went unchecked.

This argument is impressive and we cannot wholly dismiss it; for directed somewhat differently it points to a true state of affairs: there was a moral and political apathy in the western countries, and there was no decisive stand against Nazism until it was too late to prevent war. Did the men of letters, the "clerks," have a monopoly upon this apathy? We may answer this question from two points of view. First, is there anything in the nature of poetry, as it has been sung or written in many different kinds of societies, which would justify putting so great a burden of *general* responsibility upon the man of imagination? Secondly, was there no other class of "intellectuals" in the modern world, scientists, philosophers, or statesmen, who might also be called into account?

If we address ourselves to the second question first, we shall have to observe that philosophers, scientists, and politicians have by and large assumed that they had no special responsibility for the chaos of the modern world. Mr. Einstein not long ago warned us that we now have the power to destroy ourselves. There was in his statement no reference to his own great and perhaps crucial share in the scientific progress which had made the holocaust possible. If it occurs, will Mr. Einstein be partly to blame, provided there is anybody left to blame him? Will God hold him responsible? I shall not try to answer that question. And I for one should not be willing to take the responsibility, if I had the capacity, of settling the ancient question of how much natural knowledge should be placed in the hands of men whose moral and spiritual education has not been impressive: by such men I mean the majority at all times and places, and more particularly the organized adolescents of all societies known as the military class.

Here we could meditate upon (or if we like better to do it, pray over) the spectacle, not military, widely reported in the newspapers, of the President of Harvard University congratulating his colleagues with evident delight when the first atom bomb was exploded in the desert. Among those present at Los Alamos on July 14, 1945, at five-thirty in the morning, were Mr. Conant and Mr. Bush. "On the instant that all was over," reported *The New York Times,* "these men leaped to their feet, the terrible tension ended, they shook hands, embraced each other and shouted in delight." We have no right to explore another man's feelings, or to say what should please him. Nobody then or since has said that Mr. Conant's emotions, whatever they may have been on that occasion, were irresponsible. Nor do I wish to use Mr. Conant or any other scientist, or administrator of the sciences, as a whipping boy for his colleagues. Yet it is a fact that we cannot blink, that the Renaissance doctrine of the freedom of unlimited inquiry has had consequences for good and evil in the modern world. This doctrine has created our world; insofar as we are able to enjoy it, we must credit unlimited inquiry with its material benefits. But its dangers are too notorious to need pointing out. An elusive *mystique* supports the general doctrine, which may be stated as follows: We must keep up the inquiry, come hell and high water.

One way to deal with this modern demi-religion is to say that a part of its "truth" must be suppressed. I am not ready to say that: I am only ready to point out that it is not suppression of *truth* to decline to commit wholesale slaughter even if we have the means of committing it beyond the reach of any known technique of the past. Is it suppression of truth to withhold from general use the means of exploiting a technique of slaughter? How might it be withheld, should we agree that it is both desirable and possible to do so? If we let government suppress it, government will in the long run suppress everything and everybody else—even democratic government. There is no just way of holding individuals and classes responsible for the moral temper of an entire civilization.

At this point the theologians and humanists, the men of God and the men of man, appear—or at any rate formerly appeared. The Christian religion, in its various sects, has been blamed for its historic conservatism in refusing to sanction the advances of science as they were made. It is my impression that this supposedly Christian skepticism is Arabic in origin. It was the followers of Averroës in Europe who upheld the secret cult of natural knowledge against the Thomists and the Scotists, who more than the disciples of Roger Bacon stood for the diffusion of scientific enquiry. It is significant that the one science of the ancient world that impinged directly upon the daily lives of men—medicine—was held to be esoteric; the school of Hippocrates hid the secrets of the "art" lest the uninitiate abuse them and pervert them to the uses of witchcraft. This is not the place, and I am not competent enough, to follow up this line of speculation. I have wished only to observe that before the Christian dispensation, and well into it, the professors of special knowledge tried to be responsible for the public use of their techniques. We have not, so far as I know, a record of any of their reasons for what we should consider an illiberal suppression of truth. But if we think of the Greek world of thought as having lasted about nine hundred years, down to the great pupils of Plotinus—Iamblichus and Porphyrius— we may see in it a sense of the whole of life which must not be too quickly disturbed for the prosecution of special scientific interests. Nature was investigated, but it was a nature whose destiny in relation to a transcendental order was already understood. The classical insight into this relation was, as usual, recorded very early in a myth—that of the brothers Prometheus and Epimetheus—which now gives signs of recovering the authority which in the modern world it had yielded to myths that science had created about itself.

The responsibility of the scientist has not, I am sure, been defined by this digression: I have merely suggested that if anybody have a specific responsibility, it may be the scientist himself. His myth of omnipotent rationality has worked certain wonders; but perhaps a little too rapidly. In Shelley's

Defence of Poetry there is a sentence that persons who press
the poet to legislate for us seldom quote: "Our calculations
have outrun conception; we have eaten more than we can
digest." Shall we hold the scientists responsible for this? Have
they made the child sick on green apples? I do not say that
they have. But the child is sick. If the scientist is not responsible, are philosophers, statesmen, and poets, particularly poets, responsible?

Before I return to the poet's responsibility, I shall consider briefly the possible responsibility of other persons, excluding this time the scientists, about whom it has become
evident that I know little; and I can scarcely do more than
allude to the other intellectual classes whose special disciplines might conceivably implicate them in care for the
public good. Of the philosophers, I likewise speak with
neither information nor knowledge. Like Mr. Santayana, I
might somewhat presumptuously describe myself as "an ignorant man, almost a poet." But one gets strongly the impression that the classical metaphysical question—What is
the nature of Being?—is semantically meaningless in our
age, a mere historicism reserved for the frivolous occasions
of lecture-room philosophy. Our going philosophy is reported to me as a curious, apostolic activity known as the
"philosophy of science," an attempt to devise a language for
all the sciences which through it would arrive at "unity."
This is no doubt a laudable program, unity being usually
better than disunity, unless the things to be joined do not
like each other, or, again, unless the union take place at a
level of abstraction at which certain things become excluded, such as human nature, of which the Nazi and the
Stalinist unities for some reason took little account. But
these are unities of the political order. What have the philosophers of unified science to do with them? They glanced at
them, I believe, in resolutions passed at philosophical congresses, or in interviews for the press, where we were told

that things will continue to go badly until men behave more rationally. Rationality usually turned out to be liberalism, or the doctrine that reason, conceived in instrumental terms, will eventually perfect us, even though our situation may be getting worse every day. This, it seems to me, was the contribution of certain philosophers to the Second World War. Was the contribution responsible or irresponsible? Common sense ought to tell us that it was neither; and common sense tells us that not all philosophers talked this way. Everybody knows that modern philosophers, like their brother scientists, and not unlike their distant cousins the poets, are pursuing specialisms of various kinds; and from the point of view of these interests, the investigation of the nature of being, with the attendant pursuit of the love of wisdom, is no more within their purview than it is within mine. In his extra-laboratory pronouncements the merged philosopher-scientist sounds uncomfortably like his famous creation in allegorical fiction, the "man in the street"—the man without specialisms who used to sit on the cracker barrel, and who, in all ages since hats were invented, has talked through his hat. Perhaps it was neither responsible nor irresponsible: it was merely dull to use the prestige of the philosophy of science as the stump from which to deliver commonplaces that were already at your and my command and that were doing us so little good that they might be suspected of having caused a part of our trouble. Reason—in the sense of moderate unbelief in difficult truths about human nature—and belief in the perfectibility of man-in-the-gross, were the great liberal dogmas which underlay much of our present trouble. The men in charge of nature never told me that I ought to try to perfect myself; that would be done for me by my not believing that I could do anything about it, by relying upon history to do it, by the invocation of ideals that many of us thought were democratic, by the resolutions of committees, conventions, and associations; and not least by condescending affirmations of faith in the Common Man, a fictitious person with whom neither the philosopher-scientist nor I had even a speaking acquaintance. Will it not be borne in upon us in the next few years that Hitler and Stalin *are* the Common Man, and that one of the tasks of democracy is to allow as many men as possible to make themselves uncommon?

Thus it is my impression that belief in a false liberal democracy was not lacking among certain classes of "intellectuals" in the period between the wars: the period, in fact, in which Mr. MacLeish and Mr. Brooks said that we had staggered into a war that might have been prevented had the men of letters not given us such a grim view of modern man from their ivory towers, or simply refused to be concerned about him. If the more respectable "intellectuals" were not heeded in the call to democratic action, would the mere literary men have been heeded? Was the poet's prestige so great that his loss of democratic faith (assuming he had lost it) set so bad an example that it offset the testimony to the faith of even the statesman?

By the statesman one means, of course, the politician, though one would like to mean more, whether he carry the umbrella or the infectious smile, the swastika or the hammer-and-sickle. It would seem to have been the specific duty of the politician to have kept the faith and forestalled the rise of Nazism, though it was not generally supposed that it was up to him to do anything about Soviet Russia, which was tacitly assumed, if not by you and me, then by the leaves in Vallombrosa, to be on our side. My own disappointment in the politician is somewhat mitigated by the excuse which his failure provides for the poet: if he could not baulk the enemy, whom he directly confronted, what chance had the poet?—the poet, whose best weapon in history seems to have been Shelley's fleet of toy boats, each bearing a cargo of tracts, which he committed to the waters of Hyde Park.

I am sorry to sound frivolous; I confess that the political responsibility of poets bores me. I am discussing it because it irritates me more than it bores me. It irritates me because the poet has a great responsibility of his own: it is the responsibility to be a poet, to write poems, and not to gad about using the rumor of his verse, as I am now doing, as the excuse to appear on platforms and to view with alarm. I have a deep, unbecoming suspicion of such talking poets: whatever other desirable things they may believe in, they do not believe in poetry. They believe that poets should write tracts, or perhaps autobiographies; encourage the public, further this cause or that, good or bad, depending upon whose political ox is being gored.

My own political ox was at least driven into a fence corner when Mr. Pound thumped his tub for the Axis; but what I cannot easily forgive him was thumping any tub at all—unless, as a private citizen, dissociated from the poet, he had decided to take political action at some modest level, such as giving his life for his country, where whatever he did would be as inconspicuous as his ejaculatory political philosophy demanded that it be. But on Radio Rome he appeared as Professor Ezra Pound, the great American Poet. Much the same can be said of Mr. MacLeish himself. It is irrelevant that I find his political principles (I distinguish his *principles* from his *views*), insofar as I understand them, more congenial than Mr. Pound's. The immediate *views* of these poets seem to me equally hortatory, quasi-lyrical, and ill-grounded. We might imagine for them a pleasant voyage in one of Percy Shelley's boats. If society indicted and condemned poets for the mixture and the misuse of two great modes of action, poetry and politics, we might have to indict Mr. Pound a second time, as it could conceivably be done in some Swiftian social order; and we should have in fairness to provide an adjoining cell for Mr. MacLeish.

The relation of poetry and of other high imaginative lit-

erature to social action was not sufficiently considered in the
attacks and counter-attacks of the past ten years. No one
knows precisely what the relation is; so I shall not try here
to define it, though what I am about to say will imply certain
assumptions. There is no doubt that poetry, even that of
Mallarmé, has some effect upon conduct, insofar as it affects
our emotions. To what extent is the poetry itself, even that
of Mallarmé, an effect? The total complex of sensibility and
thought, of belief and experience, in the society from which
the poetry emerges, is the prime limiting factor that the
poet must first of all be aware of; otherwise his language will
lack primary reality, the nexus of thing and word. The failure to consider this primary reality produces willed poetry
which usually ignores the human condition. The human condition must be faced and embodied in language before men
in any age can envisage the possibility of action. To suggest
that poets tell men in crisis what to do, to insist that *as poets*
they acknowledge themselves as legislators of the social order,
is to ask them to shirk their specific responsibility, which is
quite simply the reality of man's experience, not what his experience ought to be, in any age. *To whom* is the poet
responsible? He is responsible to his *conscience*, in the
French sense of the word: the joint action of knowledge and
judgment. This conscience has long known a severe tradition
of propriety in discerning the poet's particular kind of actuality. No crisis, however dire, should be allowed to convince
us that the relation of the poet to his permanent reality can
ever change. And thus the poet is not responsible to society
for a version of what it thinks it is or what it wants. *For
what* is the poet responsible? He is responsible for the virtue
proper to him as poet, for his special *arété* for the mastery
of a disciplined language which will not shun the full report
of the reality conveyed to him by his awareness: he must
hold, in Yeats' great phrase, "reality and justice in a single
thought."

We have virtually turned the argument of the attack around upon itself. For it was an irresponsible demand to ask the poet to cease to be a poet and become the propagandist of a political ideal, even if he himself thought it a worthy ideal. If the report of the imagination on the realities of western culture in the past century was as depressing as the liberal mind said it was, would not the scientist, the philosopher, and the statesman have done well to study it? They might have got a clue to what was wrong. They were, I believe, studying graphs, charts, and "trends"—the indexes of power—but not human nature. The decay of modern society is nowhere more conspicuous than in the loss of the arts of reading on the part of men of action. It was said at the beginning of the war that the traditions of modern literature represented by Proust had powerfully contributed to the collapse of Europe. It was not supposed that the collapse of Europe might have affected those traditions. If the politicians had been able to read Proust, or Joyce, or even Kafka, might they not have discerned more sharply what the trouble was and done something to avert the collapse? I doubt it; but it makes as much sense as the argument that literature can be a cause of social decay. If, for example, Mr. Churchill had been able to quote the passage about Ciacco from the *Inferno,* or the second part of *The Waste Land,* instead of Arthur Hugh Clough, might we have hoped that men would now be closer to the reality out of which sound political aspiration must arise?

I leave this subject with the observation that poetry had to be attacked for not having done all that men had expected of it at the end of the nineteenth century. "The future of poetry is immense," said Matthew Arnold. It had to be immense because, for men like Arnold, everything else had failed. It was the new religion that was destined to be lost more quickly than the old. Poetry was to have saved us; it not only hadn't saved us by the end of the fourth decade of this century, it had only continued to be poetry which was little read. It had to be rejected. The primitive Athenians, at the Thargelian festival of Apollo, killed two human beings, burnt them, and cast their ashes into the sea. The men sacrificed were called *pharmakoi:* medicines. We have seen in our time a powerful attempt to purify ourselves of the knowledge of evil in man. Poetry is one of the sources of that knowledge. It is believed by some classical scholars that the savage ritual of the *pharmakoi* was brought to Athens by barbarians. In historical times effigies made of dough were substituted for human beings.

1950

Is Literary Criticism Possible?[1]

THE QUESTIONS that I propose to discuss in this essay will
fall into two main divisions. I shall undertake to discuss,
first, the teaching of literary criticism in the university. Since
I am not able to *define* literary criticism, I shall be chiefly
concerned with the idea of a formal relation; that is to say,
supposing we knew what criticism is, what relation would it
have to the humanities, of which it seems to be a constituent
part? In the second division I shall try to push the discussion
a little further, towards a question that has been acute in
our time: Is literary criticism possible at all? The answer to
this question ought logically to precede the discussion of a
formal relation, for we ought to know what it is that we are
trying to relate to something else. But we shall never know
this; we shall only find that in teaching criticism we do not
know what we are teaching, even though criticism daily talks
about a vast material that we are in the habit of calling
the humanities. The mere fact of this witnesses our sense of
a formal relation that ought to exist between two things
of the nature of which we are ignorant.

I

Literary criticism as a member of the humanities I take to
be a problem of academic statesmanship inviting what we

1 Part I of this essay was read at a symposium on the humanities at Vanderbilt
University, October 20, 1950; Part II, at the Conference on the Philosophical
Bases of Literary Criticism at Harvard University, July 23, 1951. Both parts
have been amplified.

hopefully call "solutions" of both the theoretical and the practical sort. Is literary criticism properly a branch of humanistic study? That is the theoretical question, to which I shall avoid the responsibility of giving the answer. Without this answer, we cannot hope to understand the practical question: What is the place of criticism in the humanities program; on what grounds should it be there (if it should be there at all), given the kind of education that the present teachers of the humanities bring to their work?

The two questions, the theoretical and the practical, together constitute the formal question; that is to say, whatever criticism and the humanities may be, we should have to discuss their relation in some such terms as I am suggesting. But before we follow this clue we must address ourselves more candidly to the fact of our almost total ignorance.

The three grand divisions of higher education in the United States are, I believe, the Natural Sciences, the Social Sciences, and the Humanities. Of the first, I am entirely too ignorant to speak. Of the social sciences I know little, and I am not entitled to suspect that they do not really exist; I believe this in the long run because I want to believe it, the actuality of a science of human societies being repellent to me, apart from its dubious scientific credentials. Of the humanities, the division with which as poet and critic I am presumably most concerned, one must speak with melancholy as well as in ignorance. For into the humanistic bag we throw everything that cannot qualify as a science, natural or social. This discrete mixture of hot and cold, moist and dry, creates in the bag a vortex, which emits a powerful wind of ineffectual heroics, somewhat as follows: We humanists bring within the scope of the humanities all the great records—sometimes we call them the remains: poetry, drama, prescientific history (Herodotus, Joinville, Bede)—of the experience of man *as* man; we are not concerned with him as vertebrate, biped, mathematician, or priest. Precisely, reply the social scientists; that is just what is wrong with you;

you don't see that man is not man, that he is merely a
function; and your records (or remains) are so full of error
that we are glad to relegate them to professors of English,
poets, and other dilettanti, those "former people" who live
in the Past. The Past, which we can neither smell, see, taste,
nor touch, was well labeled by our apostle, Mr. Carl Sandburg, as a bucket of ashes . . . No first-rate scientific mind
is guilty of this vulgarity. Yet as academic statesmen, the
humanists must also be practical politicians who know that
they cannot stay in office unless they have an invigorating
awareness of the power, and of the superior footwork, of the
third-rate mind.

As for literary criticism, we here encounter a stench and
murk not unlike that of a battlefield three days after the
fighting is over and the armies have departed. Yet in this
war nobody has suggested that criticism is one of the social
sciences, except a few Marxists, who tried fifteen years ago
to make it a branch of sociology. History not long ago became a social science, and saved its life by losing it; and
there is no reason why sociology "oriented" toward literature
should not be likewise promoted, to the relief of everybody
concerned. And whatever criticism may be, we should perhaps do well to keep it with the humanities, where it can
profit by the sad example of Hilaire Belloc's Jim, who
failed "To keep ahold of Nurse / For fear of getting something worse."

It may not be necessary to know what criticism is; it may
be quite enough to see that it is now being written, that a
great deal of it was written in the past, that it is concerned
with one of the chief objects of humanistic study: literature.
And we therefore study it either as an "area" in itself—
that is, we offer courses in its history; or as a human interest
in some past age—that is, we use criticism as one way of
understanding the age of Johnson or the high Renaissance.
Guided by the happy theory of spontaneous understanding

resulting from the collision of pure intelligence with its object—a theory injected into American education by Charles W. Eliot—we expose the student mind to "areas" of humanistic material, in the confident belief that if it is exposed to enough "areas" it will learn something. If we expose it to enough "areas" in all three grand divisions, the spontaneous intelligence will automatically become educated without thought.

The natural sciences have a high-powered rationale of their daily conquests of nature. The social sciences have a slippery analogical [2] metaphor to sustain their self-confidence. The humanities modestly offer the vision of the historical lump. This lump is tossed at the student mind, which is conceived as the miraculous combination of the *tabula rasa* and innate powers of understanding. In short, the humanities have no rationale. We suppose that it is sufficient to show that a given work—a poem, a play, a critical "document"—came before or after some other poem, play, or critical "document," or was written when something else was happening, like Alexander's invasion of India or the defeat of the Armada. When these and other correlations are perceived, the result is understanding. But the result of correlation is merely the possibility of further correlation. Our modest capacity for true understanding is frustrated. For the true rationale of humanistic study is now what it has always been, even though now it is not only in decay, but dead. I allude to the arts of rhetoric.

By rhetoric I mean the study and the use of the figurative language of experience as the discipline by means of which men govern their relations with one another in the light of truth. Rhetoric presupposes the study of two prior disciplines, grammar and logic, neither of which is much pursued today, except by specialists.

[2] Analogous to the natural sciences.

These disciplines are no longer prerequisite even to the study of philosophy. An Eastern university offers a grandiose course in Greek philosophical ideas to sophomores who will never know a syllogism from a handsaw. A graduate student who, I was told, was very brilliant in nuclear physics, decided that he wanted to take a course in *The Divine Comedy*. (Why he wanted to study Dante I do not know, but his humility was impressive.) I was assured by the academic grapevine that he understood difficult mathematical formulae, but one day in class he revealed the fact that he could neither define nor recognize a past participle. At the end of the term he confessed that nobody had ever told him that the strategies of language, or the arts of rhetoric, could be as important and exacting a discipline as the theory of equations. He had thought courses in English a little sissified; he had not been told that it might be possible, after severe application, to learn how to read. He had learned to talk without effort in infancy, in a decadent democracy, and no doubt supposed that grammar came of conditioning, and that he would get it free.

Back of this homely exemplum stands a formidable specter whose name is Cultural Decay—at a time when men are more conscious of cultures than ever before and stock their universities and museums with lumps of cultures, like inert geological specimens in a glass case. I am far from believing that a revival of the trivium, or the three primary liberal arts, would bring the dead bodies to life: revivals have a fatal incapacity to revive anything. But unless we can create and develop a hierarchy of studies that can lead not merely to further studies but to truth, one may doubt that the accelerating decline of modern culture will be checked.

Without quite knowing what literary criticism is, let us assume again that we are teaching it within the humanities division, usually in the English Department, either because it ought to be there or because nobody else wants it. For convenience we may think of the common relations between the work of the imagination and the teaching activity under four heads, which I shall put in the form of rhetorical questions:

(1) Can a given work, say *Clarissa Harlowe* or "Kubla Khan," be "taught," in such a way as to make it understood, without criticism?

(2) Can the work be taught first, and the criticism then applied as a mode of understanding?

(3) Can the criticism be presented first and held in readiness for the act of understanding, which could thus be simultaneous with the act of reading the novel or the poem?

(4) Is the purpose of teaching imaginative works to provide materials upon which the critical faculty may exercise itself in its drive toward the making of critical systems, which then perpetuate themselves without much reference to literature?

These four versions of the relation by no means exhaust its possible variations. The slippery ambiguity of the word criticism itself ought by now to be plain. But for the purposes of this localized discussion, which I am limiting for the moment to the question of how to teach, we may think of criticism as three familiar kinds of discourse about works of literature. (We must bear in mind not only our failure to know what criticism is, but another, more difficult failure resulting from it: the failure to know what literature is.) The three kinds of critical discourse are as follows: (1) acts of evaluation of literature (whatever these may be); (2) the communication of insights; and (3) the rhetorical study of the language of the imaginative work.

I am not assuming, I am merely pretending that any one of the three activities is to be found in its purity. To the extent that they may be separated, we must conclude that the two first, acts of evaluation and the communication of insights, cannot be taught, and that the third, rhetorical analysis, has not been taught effectively in this country since the rise of the historical method in literary studies.

When I first taught a college class, about eighteen years

ago, I thought that anything was possible; but with every year since it has seemed a little more absurd to try to teach students to "evaluate" works of literature, and perhaps not less absurd to try to evaluate them oneself. The assumption that we are capable of just evaluation (a word that seems to have got into criticism by way of Adam Smith) is one of the subtler, if crude, abuses of democratic doctrine, as follows: all men ought to exercise independent judgment, and all men being equal, all are equally capable of it, even in literature and the arts. I have observed that when my own opinions seem most original and independent they turn out to be almost wholly conventional. An absolutely independent judgment (if such a thing were possible) would be an absolutely ignorant judgment.

Shall the instructor, then, set before the class his own "evaluations"? He will do so at the risk of disseminating a hierarchy that he may not have intended to create, and thus may be aborted, or at least stultified, the student's own reading. It is inevitable that the instructor shall say to the class that one poem is "better" than another. The student, in the degree of his intelligence, will form clear preferences or rejections that will do little harm if he understands what they are. But the teaching of literature through the assertion of preference will end up either as mere impressionism, or as the more sinister variety of impressionism that Irving Babbitt detected in the absorption of the literary work into its historical setting.

As to the communication of "insights," it would perhaps be an inquiry without benefit to anybody to ask how this elusive maid-of-all-work got into modern criticism. She is here, and perhaps we ought to be grateful, because she is obviously willing to do all the work. Insight could mean two things, separately or taken together: the perception of meanings ordinarily or hitherto undetected, and/or the synthetic awareness that brings to the text similar or contrasting qualities from other works. These awarenesses are the critical or receiving end of the Longinian "flash" proceeding from varying degrees of information and knowledge, unpredictable and largely unviable. They are doubtless a good thing for a teacher to have, but they cannot be taught to others; they can be only exhibited. If insight is like faith, a gift by the grace of God, there is no use in teaching at all—if insight-teaching is our only way of going about it. But if it is partly a gift and partly the result of labor (as Longinus thought), perhaps the teacher could find a discipline of language to expound to the class, with the hope that a latent gift of insight may be liberated.

Rhetoric is an unpopular word today, and it deserves to be, if we understand it as the "pragmatic dimension" of discourse as this has been defined by Charles W. Morris, and other semanticists and positivists. In this view rhetoric is semantically irresponsible; its use is to move people to action which is at best morally neutral; or if it is good action, this result was no necessary part of the rhetorician's purpose. The doctrine is not new; it is only a pleasantly complex and double-talking revival of Greek sophistry. But if we think of rhetoric in another tradition, that of Aristotle and of later, Christian rhetoricians, we shall be able to see it as the study of the full language of experience, not the specialized languages of method.[3] Through this full language of experience Dante and Shakespeare could arrive at truth.

This responsible use implies the previous study of the two lower, but not inferior, disciplines that I have already men-

---

[3] I hope it is plain by this time that by "rhetorical analysis" and the "study of rhetoric" I do not mean the prevailing *explication of texts*. If rhetoric is the *full* language of experience, its study must be informed by a peculiar talent, not wholly reducible to method, which I have in the past called the "historical imagination," a power that has little to do with the academic routine of "historical method." For a brilliant statement of this difference, see "Art and the 'Sixth Sense'" by Philip Rahv, *Partisan Review*, March–April, 1952, pp. 225–233. The "sixth sense" is the historical imagination.

tioned. One of these was once quaintly known as "grammar,"
the art that seems to be best learned at the elementary
stage in a paradigmatic language like Latin. I think of a
homely exemplum that will illustrate one of the things that
have happened since the decay of grammar. I had a student at the University of Chicago who wrote a paper on
T. S. Eliot's religious symbolism, in which he failed to observe that certain sequences of words in "Ash Wednesday"
are without verbs: he had no understanding of the relation
of the particulars to the universals in Eliot's diction. The
symbols floated, in this student's mind, in a void of abstraction; the language of the poem was beyond his reach. Is the
domination of historical scholarship responsible for the decline of the grammatical arts? I think that it may be; but it
would not follow from its rejection that these arts or their
equivalent would rise again. (One must always be prepared
for the rise of nothing.) My Chicago student was laudably
trying to read the text of the poem; he had nothing but a
good mind and good intentions to read it with. What he had
done, of course, was to abstract Eliot's symbols out of their
full rhetorical context, so that they had become neither
Eliot's nor anybody else's symbols. They were thus either
critically useless, or potentially useful in a *pragmatic dimension* of discourse where ideas may be *power:* as the full-
back is said to "bull" through the opposing line. The rhetorical disciplines, which alone seem to yield something like
the full import of the work of imagination, are bypassed;
and we bypass these fundamentals of understanding no less
when we read our own language. All reading is translation,
even in the native tongue; for translation may be described
as the *tact* of mediation between universals and particulars
in the complex of metaphor. As qualified translators we are
inevitably rhetoricians. One scarcely sees how the student
(like the Chicago student, who is also the Minnesota, the
Harvard, and the Cornell student) can be expected to begin

the study of rhetoric at the top, particularly if below it there is no bottom. If he begins at the top, as a "critic," he may become the victim of "insights" and "evaluations" that he has not earned, or he may parrot critical systems that his instructors have expounded or perhaps merely alluded to, in class. In any case, man being by nature, or by the nature of his language, a rhetorician, the student becomes a bad rhetorician. It is futile to expect him to be a critic when he has not yet learned how to read.

How can rhetoric, or the arts of language, be taught today? We are not likely to begin teaching something in which we do not believe: we do not believe in the uses of rhetoric because we do not believe that the full language of the human situation can be the vehicle of truth. We are not facing the problem when we circumvent it by asking the student to study the special languages of "criticism," in which we should like to believe. Can we believe in the language of humane truth without believing in the possibility of a higher unity of truth, which we must posit as *there*, even if it must remain beyond our powers of understanding? Without such a belief are we not committed to the assumption that literature has nothing to do with truth, that it is only illusion, froth on the historical current, the Platonic *gignomenon?* We languish, then, in the pragmatic vortex where ideas are disembodied into power; but power for what it is not necessary here to try to say. I turn now to literary criticism as it seems to be in itself, apart from any question of teaching it.

I I

We have reached the stage of activity in individual criticism at which we begin to ask whether what we severally do has, or ought to have, a common end. What has a common end may be better reached, or at any rate more efficiently pursued, if the long ways to it are bypassed for the short ways—if happily we can agree on a common methodology, or at worst a few cooperating methodologies. The image that this enticing delusion brings to mind is that of the cheerful, patient bulldozer leveling off an uncharted landscape. The treeless plain thus made could be used as a desert—by those who can use deserts—or as an airfield from which to fly somewhere else.

The notes that follow I have put in the form of propositions, or theses, which either I or some imaginable person might be presumed to uphold at the present time. Some will be found to contradict others; but this is to be expected when we try to distinguish the aims and habits of literary critics over a period so long as a quarter of a century. The ten theses will affirm, deny, or question a belief or a practice.

I. Literary criticism is in at least one respect (perhaps more than one) like a mule: it cannot reproduce itself, though, like a mule, it is capable of trying. Its end is outside itself. If the great formal works of literature are not wholly autonomous, criticism, however theoretical it may become, is necessarily even less so. It cannot in the long run be practiced apart from what it confronts, that gives rise to it. It has no formal substance: it is always *about* something else. If it tries to be about itself, and sets up on its own, it initiates the infinite series: one criticism within another leading to another criticism progressively more formal-looking and abstract; or it is progressively more irrelevant to its external end as it attends to the periphery, the historical buzz in the rear of literature.

II. The more systematic and methodical, the "purer," criticism becomes, the less one is able to feel in it the presence of its immediate occasion. It tends more and more to *sound* like philosophical discourse. There are countless degrees, variations, and overlappings of method, but everyone knows that there are three typical directions that method may take: (1) Aesthetics, which aims at the ordering of criticism within a large synthesis of either experimental psychology or ontology; from the point of view of which it is difficult to say anything about literature that is not merely pretentious. For example: Goethe's Concrete Universal, Coleridge's Esemplastic Power, Croce's Expression. (2) Analysis of literary language, or "stylistics" (commonly supposed to be the orbit of the New Criticism). Without the correction of a total rhetoric, this *techné* must find its limit, if it is not at length to become only a habit, in the extreme "purity" of nominalism ("positivism") or of metaphysics. (3) Historical scholarship, the "purest" because the most methodical criticism of all, offers the historical reconstruction as the general possibility of literature, without accounting for the unique, miraculous superiority of *The Tempest* or of *Paradise Lost.*

III. When we find criticism appealing to phrases like "frame of reference," "intellectual discipline," or even "philosophical basis," it is not improper to suspect that the critic is asking us to accept his "criticism" on the authority of something in which he does not believe. The two first phrases contain perhaps hidden analogies to mathematics; the third, a metaphor of underpinning. This is nothing against them; all language is necessarily figurative. But used as I have indicated, the phrases have no ontological, or substantive, meaning. The critic is only avoiding the simple word truth, and begging the question. Suppose we acknowledge that the critic, as he begs this question, gives us at the same moment a new and just insight into a scene in *The Idiot* or *King Lear.* Yet the philosophical language in which he visibly expounds the insight may seem to reflect an authority that he has not visibly earned. The language of criticism had better not, then, try to be univocal. It is neither fish nor fowl, yet both, with that unpleasant taste that we get from fishing ducks.

IV. Literary criticism may become prescriptive and dogmatic when the critic achieves a coherence in the logical and rhetorical orders which exceeds the coherence of the imaginative work itself in those orders. We substitute with the critic a dialectical order for the elusive, and perhaps quite different, order of the imagination. We fall into the trap of the logicalization of parts discretely attended. This sleight of hand imposed upon the reader's good faith invites him to share the critic's own intellectual pride. Dazzled by the refractions of the critic's spectrum, the reader accepts as his own the critic's dubious superiority to the work as a whole. He is only attending serially to the separated parts in which he worships his own image. This is critical idolatry; the idols of its three great sects are the techniques of purity described in Thesis II.

V. If criticism undertakes the responsibility and the privilege of a strict theory of knowledge, the critic will need all the humility that human nature is capable of, almost the self-abnegation of the saint. Is the critic willing to test his epistemology against a selfless reading of *The Rape of the Lock, War and Peace,* or a lyric by Thomas Nashe? Or is his criticism merely the report of a quarrel between the imagined life of the work and his own "philosophy"? Has possession of the critic by a severe theory of knowledge interfered with the primary office of criticism? What is the primary office of criticism? Is it to expound and to elucidate, with as little distortion as possible, the knowledge of life contained by the novel or the poem or the play? What critic has ever done this?

VI. A work of the imagination differs from a work of the logical intellect in some radical sense that seems to lie beyond our comprehension. But this much may be said: the imaginative work admits of neither progressive correction nor substitution or rearrangement of parts; it is never obsolete, it is always up-to-date. Dryden does not "improve" Shakespeare; Shakespeare does not replace Dante, in the

way that Einstein's physics seems to have "corrected" New-
ton's. There is no competition among poems. A good poem
suggests the possibility of other poems equally good. But
criticism is perpetually obsolescent and replaceable.

VII. The very terms of elucidation—the present ones, like
any others—carry with them, concealed, an implicated judgment. The critic's rhetoric, laid out in his particular grammar, is the critic's mind. This enables him to see much that
is there, a little that is there, nothing that is there, or something that is not there; but none of these with perfect consistency. We may ask again: to what extent is the critic ob-
ligated to dredge the bottom of his mind and to exhibit to an
incredulous eye his own skeleton? We might answer the
question rhetorically by saying: We are constantly trying to
smoke out the critic's "position." This is criticism of criticism. Should we succeed in this game to our perfect satisfaction, we must be on guard lest our assent to or dissent
from a critic's "position" mislead us into supposing that his
gift of elucidation is correspondingly impressive or no good.
If absolutely just elucidation were possible, it would also be
philosophically sound, even though the critic might elsewhere announce his adherence to a philosophy that we
should want to question.

VIII. If the implicated judgment is made overt, is there
not in it an invitation to the reader to dismiss or to accept
the work before he has read it? Even though he "read" the
work first? (Part of this question is dealt with in Thesis V.)
Is *a priori* judgment in the long run inevitable? What un-
formulated assumption lurks, as in the thicket, back of T. S.
Eliot's unfavorable comparison of "Ripeness is all" with
"E la sua voluntade é nostra pace"? Is Shakespeare's summation of life naturalistic, pagan, and immature? J. V. Cun-
ningham has shown that "Ripeness is all" is a statement
within the natural law, quite as Christian as Dante's statement within the divine law. The beacon of conceptual

thought as end rather than means in criticism is a standing menace to critical order because it is inevitable, human nature being what it is. One thing that human nature is, is "fallen."

IX. In certain past ages there was no distinct activity of the mind conscious of itself as literary criticism; for example, the age of Sophocles and the age of Dante. In the age of Dante the schoolmen held that poetry differed from scriptural revelation in its *historia,* or fable, at which, in poetry, the literal event could be part or even all fiction. But the other, higher meanings of poetry might well be true, in spite of the fictional plot, if the poet had the gift of anagogical, or spiritual, insight. Who was capable of knowing when the poet had achieved this insight? Is literary criticism possible without a criterion of absolute truth? Would a criterion of absolute truth make literary criticism as we know it unnecessary? Can it have a relevant criterion of truth without acknowledging an emergent order of truth in its great subject matter, literature itself?

X. Literary criticism, like the Kingdom of God on earth, is perpetually necessary and, in the very nature of its middle position between imagination and philosophy, perpetually impossible. Like man, literary criticism is nothing in itself; criticism, like man, embraces pure experience or exalts pure rationality at the price of abdication from its dual nature. It is of the nature of man and of criticism to occupy the intolerable position. Like man's, the intolerable position of criticism has its own glory. It is the only position that it is ever likely to have.

1951

The Function of the Critical Quarterly

IF THE quarterly journal has ceased forever to be our popular magazine, may it still be said that the specialized critical quarterly has a "use"? *Use* is a term too slippery to invite definition. Since the time I became aware of the literary magazine, nearly twenty years ago, the declining usefulness of the critical quarterly has been taken for granted. It now increasingly serves the end of acquainting unpopular writers with one another's writings. That is a "use" that I, for one, am not prepared to deride. But the reader is entitled to his own sense of usefulness. He is the cultivated layman who felt at one time, say a hundred years ago, that the high places of literature were not beyond his reach: he saw himself and the author in a communion of understanding in which the communicants were necessary to each other.

It is a communion lost to us. The weekly and the monthly, renovated for modern speed of the eye, have captured the intelligent layman entirely.[1] And for a good reason. At his best he likes his "theory," as he educatedly names ideas, mixed unobtrusively into the "practice" of his times: he likes to believe that the literary news of his period can bring him a sufficient criticism of it. And this was precisely what was procured for him, at a high level of excellence, by the British quarterlies in the day of Lockhart, Jeffrey, and Wil-

[1] Since this was written, in 1936, *Life, Look,* and many other picture magazines have appeared.

45

son. The layman found out what was happening at the same time that he was told what it meant.

Doubtless our own splitting off of information from understanding, this modern divorce of action from intelligence, is general, and not particular to the arts of literature. If it is a problem that on every hand confronts us, it must affect the policy of the critical review—and tremendously determine it. For the critical review stands for one-half of the modern dilemma, the purer half: the intelligence trying to think into the moving world a rational order of value.

The critical review, then, must severely define its relation first to a public and then to its contributors. The editor's attitude towards his contributors, his choice of contributors, and his direction of their work, depend upon the kind of influence that he has decided to exercise.

Our best quarterlies have readers but not enough readers to pay the "cost of production." The quarterly must be subsidized; it either runs on a subsidy or does not run. It cannot define its "use" in terms of the size of its public; and it assumes that the public needs something that it does not want, or—what is the same thing—that a minority wants what the greater public needs. The leading quarterlies are subsidized by universities or are backed, like the late *Hound and Horn,* by persons whose fortunes and interests may be expected to change. The fate of *The Symposium,* the best critical quarterly published in America up to its time (1929– 1933), offers timely warning to the founder of a review that cannot count upon a subsidy or a private fortune.

There is no record of success for a quarterly review that, in recent times, has tried to compete with the weekly or the monthly. The weekly reader gets the news of books and affairs while it is still, I imagine, hot; and if he asks for a little meditation upon the passing shadows, he will take not much more of this than he can get out of the pages of the monthly—regretting that the meditation is a month old and that something new to be meditated upon has, last week or yesterday, risen to invalidate the old meditation. Of course we ought to enjoin the reader to suspect the monthly meditation; it was perhaps not sufficiently considered and fundamental. We ought, in fact, to tell him that the critical quarterly, devoted to principles, can alone give him a meditation of such considered depth that it will illuminate the risen event of yesterday, or the rising event of tomorrow. But unfortunately the modern reader's synthesizing powers are limited, and nothing is applicable to nothing, and the gap between idea and event leaves the reader and the quarterly somewhat high and dry with respect to each other. The quarterly is always too late, even if its standards are not stubbornly too high. If the quarterly imitates the freshness of the weekly, its freshness is necessarily three months stale, refrigerated but not new; and if it tries for the liveliness of monthly commentary, its peril is the sacrifice of leisured thought. In either instance the quarterly sacrifices its standards only to attempt a work that it cannot hope to do.

But if the quarterly editor is not forced by poverty to run a monthly *manqué,* his problem at once becomes simpler and more difficult; simpler, because he does not need to find out by trial and error what a paying public will read; more difficult, because he must become himself a first-rate critic in the act of organizing his material, four times a year, into coherent criticism.

The critical performance of the quarterly lies no more in the critical essays than in the "creative" department; good creative work is a criticism of the second rate; and the critical department ought to be run for the protection of that which in itself is the end of criticism. If this observation be extended to society and social criticism, the complete function of the quarterly will emerge. For only the social criticism that instances the value of concrete social experience may be termed properly critical. Literature in this broadest sense tells us the meaning of experience, what it is and has been, and it is there that the political and aesthetic departments join.

It is a formidable union, and the difficulty of consummating it may well appal the stoutest editorial heart. Given the freedom to engage the difficulty, the editor is immediately assailed by a series of questions. Is there a critical task that might be done effectively by the quarterly? Can it be done at the present time? If it can, how can it best be done?

Though it would be untrue to say that good critical essays never appear in the monthly magazines, yet an effective critical program cannot, in that medium, be maintained. The monthly is too close to the weekly, the weekly to the newspaper, for any of these kinds of organ to maintain a critical program in the midst of the more pressing need to report the "scene." If one use of criticism is to make the reader aware of himself through the literature of his time, and aware, through this literature, of the literature of the past, the critical program must have an objective, and not be contented with partial glimpses or mere reports of points of view. The reader needs more than the mere news that a given point of view exists; he must be initiated into the point of view, saturated with it. The critical program must, then, supply its readers with coherent standards of taste and examples of taste in operation; not mere statements about taste. Mere reporting enjoins the editor to glance at all points of view. The reader gets a "digest" of opinion, not critical thought; he is encouraged to sample everything and to experience nothing.

A sound critical program has at least this one feature: *it allows to the reader no choice in the standards of judgment.* It asks the reader to take a post of observation, and to occupy it long enough to examine closely the field before him, which is presumably the whole field of our experience. This, one supposes, is dogmatism, but it is arguable still that dogma in criticism is a permanent necessity: the value of the dogma will be determined by the quality of the mind engaged in constructing it. For dogma is coherent thought in the pursuit of principles. If the critic has risen to the plane of principle, and refuses to judge by prejudice, he will, while allowing no quarter to critical relativity, grant enormous variety to the specific arts. For it must be remembered that prejudice is not dogma, that the one has no toleration of the other. If prejudice were dogma, *The New York Times Book Review* would be a first-rate critical organ. It allows the narrowest possible range of artistic performance along with the widest latitude of incoherent opinion and of popular success—simply because it uses, instead of principle, prejudice.

To deny the use of the critical quarterly today is to deny the use of criticism. It is a perilous denial. For criticism is not merely a way of saying that a certain poem is better than another; it gives meaning to the awareness of differences only insofar as it instructs the reader in three fundamentals of mounting importance: the exercise of taste, the pursuit of standards of intellectual judgment, and the acquisition of self-knowledge. If the reader is not encouraged in self-knowledge—a kind of knowing that entails insight into one's relation to a moral and social order that one has begun, after great labor, to understand—then taste and judgment have no center and are mere words.

If this is the task of criticism, and if the task of criticism can be accomplished only in the quarterly, what is to prevent its being carried out? There are obstacles. To distinguish cause and effect is neither easy nor, fortunately, obligatory: living evidence of the divorce of fact and understanding, of action and intelligence, is the mass-produced monthly. It is a kind of journalism that includes both the fashionable Hearst magazines and the "quality" group. The Hearst readers have always existed potentially; the "quality" readers number in their ranks many new recruits, but quite as many must surely be persons with an education that formerly qualified them to read the critical quarterly. Such readers have a certain sensibility, but not being actively critical themselves, they take what comes; and the monthly magazine, being efficiently because profitably distributed, is what they take. The inference to be studied here, if the inference were not already visible as fact, is that the quarterly must be heavily subsidized.

There is still another obstacle to successful quarterly publication: the task of getting suitable contributors. Or perhaps the obstacle is the effect of the monthly magazine on writers who might, but for its existence, be constantly available to the quarterly editor. The quality group, for example, can pay better rates for manuscripts than the most flourishing quarterly can ever pay. The monthly can command first choice of the work of writers who would otherwise put their best effort into the more considered, and to them more satisfactory, performance demanded by the more critical journal. If the quarterly pay five dollars a page, critics trying to set forth a program, and "creative" writers who wish to exhibit their work in terms of the coherent standards of those critics, will accept the five dollars a page— provided the lure of a bigger price does not meanwhile keep them from doing their better and more serious work. The menacing possibility of eight or ten dollars a page is, by writers of all sorts, gratefully embraced. The writer is offering a commodity for sale, and he, like every other producer, must get the highest price.

It is a law of "capitalism." There is no moral theory that can place a stigma upon this procedure. If it were possible for good writers deliberately to lower their quality, that would be a horse of another color; but the leveling comes from the market itself, which asks for a superficial, fragmentary performance that may, within the assigned limits, be excellent work. In the long run it is futile work, because it cannot be systematic and comprehensive. The writer, if he happen to be a critic, must begin his program over again with every essay, and journalize his thought out of existence: he cannot develop continuity of thought because he cannot count upon the attention of the same readers over a number of years: he is selling on the open market, and he cannot be sure that his product will be bought by the same *entrepreneur* a second time. He fidgets in this insecure, disorderly position because he must—or starve—seek the highest money reward for his work.

If the quarterly shall be less fragmentary than the monthly, it must maintain a policy that not only demands the leisured, considered performance; it has got to make the performance possible to its contributors. I suggest that the quarterly pay the highest rate it can—cheapening perhaps the quality of its paper and printing—but not that it try to compete in prices with the monthly. There is, I think, a compromise. And the compromise, a concession to the writer and an eventual benefit to the editor, consists in breaking the law of capitalism already referred to. One article of this law grows out of the merely cash nexus between producer and distributor—between writer and editor—and it urges the distributor to be as disloyal as possible—for a purpose— to the producer of the commodity which he sells. The distributor's purpose is to keep the producer insecure and humble, so that, should the strain of competition permit, he can give the producer the lowest possible price. For here it may be said that the monthly pays a better price than the quarterly, not because it is by good luck more prosperous and by nature more generous, but because competition forces it to pay ten dollars a page for work that might go to another editor for nine.

The quarterly must be loyal to its contributors in two indispensable ways, and both these ways involve another kind of "nexus" between writer and editor than the cash. A genuine critical objective cannot be attained if the editor waits on the market for what may arrive in the mail. If he has a mind, he must make up his mind what he wants and decide that there are certain contributors whom he would rather have than others. There will be perhaps a dozen of these and the editor has got to be loyal to them. If he is a second-rate man, and fears that, by giving rein over a long stretch to a talented group of men, he will be personally overshadowed, he had better write the entire contents of his magazine—a feat that, being a second-rate man, he will not be equal to.

Whether he be first- or second-rate, his first proof of loyalty is the highest price that he can pay. If the editor wants to enlist a regular staff of contributors whom he can call upon at a moment's notice, he should pay them a little more than he will pay for the casual manuscript, however good, that he found on his desk this morning. Authors are as responsive to kind treatment as other laborers. They will feel for this editor a corresponding loyalty. They will let him have for five dollars a page, for instance, a manuscript that, after a little blood-letting, they might easily sell for ten to a quality magazine. They will do this all the more eagerly if the editor is willing to let the writer continue the work in three or four more essays, or stories, or poems; if, in short, the writers are encouraged in their programs.

That, in fact, is the editor's second loyalty—to take most of the output of his selected, inner circle of contributors. He must assume, if he does not actually know, that his contributors are not men of independent income. He must take a responsible view of their welfare. If he does not, the lure of high prices will attract their work into the open market. If the quarterly editor's attitude is indistinguishable from that of the commercial editor, he is doomed to fail.

For, let his literary standards be the highest, his relation

to his contributors is still commercial, even if he is not trying "to make money." He is only a less effective part of a
system that the writer cannot afford to be loyal to. Both the
serious writer and the critical quarterly are thus defeated.
I could name a dozen leading writers, north and south, who
remember the quarterlies for manuscripts that they cannot
sell elsewhere at high prices. The quarterly review gets what
is left in the trunk.

There is no use blinking these facts. It is futile to discuss
the higher aims of the critical review without facing them.
There is, of course, a very small group of writers—the present
writer is doubtless one of them—whose aims are directed
towards the limited audience of the critical review. It is not
an exalted purpose that so confines them; it is only the accident of concentration. If the quarterly editor's attitude is the
same as his commercial colleague's, the performance of his
critical minority is not more effective than the scattered performance of the hack writer seeking the open market. The
minority suffers the restriction of audience without enjoying the satisfaction of taking part in a literature, and without getting the higher pay of competition.

Given the right relation between the editor and his contributors, what work may they together be expected to do?
The question is rhetorical; but I think it is clear that nothing
useful can be done without that right relation. Modern experiments in quarterly publication achieve moderate success; they win readers, a very few, year after year. The best
quarterlies indirectly affect the "quality" reader, for the
"quality" writer is often formed by the quarterly that his
public never sees. But the quarterly that would justify the
name of criticism must have a set purpose—not merely to
publish the "best" that drifts into its office; its internal organization and its outward policy must be sharply defined.

The great magazines have been edited by autocrats.

Within the memory of our time the great editors were Henley and Ford; in our own age, the late A. R. Orage and T. S. Eliot. Ford Madox Ford had notable success with *The English Review,* as early as 1909, because he knew what men to bring to the front: he gave concentration of purpose, the conviction of being part of a literature, to at least half of the distinguished writers who survived the War and who have deeply influenced our own age. He, more than any other modern editor, enrolled his contributors in the profession of letters—in a time when, under finance-capitalism, editors had already become employers who felt as little responsibility to their labor as manufacturers are able to feel towards theirs.

The Criterion under T. S. Eliot has been the best quarterly of our time.[2] It has become the fashion to deride it: its intellectualism, its traditionalism, its devotion to "lost causes," expose it to an attack that for my purpose here need not be discussed. The value of its critical program does not concern me at the moment. It has been important because it does have a critical program: the editor from the beginning set out to develop critical issues. For a brief period, around 1926 or 1927, *The Criterion* became a monthly; it soon reverted to quarterly appearance. In the reduced size of the monthly the editor could not print contributions long enough to carry considered critical discussion.

If the task of the quarterly is to impose an intelligible order upon a scattering experience that the monthly and the weekly may hope only to report, the task of the editor must be one of difficulty and responsibility. We must expect him to have power and influence. His power should be concentrated if—it is worth repeating again—he is not merely to do what the monthly can do better. There can be little doubt that the success of *The Criterion*—it has never, I

[2] It suspended publication with the January, 1939 issue.

believe, had more than two thousand subscribers [3]—has been due to concentrated editorship functioning through a small group of regular contributors. By group I do not mean the personal friends of the editor, or persons enlisted in some movement, for a movement is not always a program. By a group I mean a number of writers who agree that certain fundamental issues exist and who consent, under direction of the editor, to discuss them with a certain emphasis. The editor may not believe in Marxism or neo-Thomism, but he will see it as an issue, and he will seek discussion of Marxism or neo-Thomism from a point of view.

I have described the high aims of the critical quarterly as if financial backing were not a problem; as if the editor were at liberty to develop his program unhampered by the need of cash subscribers; as if his magazine were free to find whatever public may exist for it. All writing seeks an audience. But the editor has a responsibility that he must discharge as perfectly as the contingencies of backing and public will permit. He owes his first duty to his critical principles, his sense of the moral and intellectual order upon which society ought to rest, whether or not society at the moment has an interest in such an order or is even aware of a need for it. For the ideal task of the critical quarterly is not to give the public what it wants, or what it thinks it wants, but what—through the medium of its most intelligent members—it ought to have. At a time when action has become singularly devoid of intelligence, there could not be a "cause" more disinterested. The way to give the public what it resentfully needs is to discredit the inferior ideas of the age by exposing them to the criticism of the superior ideas.

1936

[3] After this essay appeared, Mr. Eliot told me that *The Criterion* never had more than 700 subscribers.

Tension in Poetry

I

MANY POEMS that we ordinarily think of as good poetry—
and some, besides, that we neglect—have certain common
features that will allow us to invent, for their sharper apprehension, the name of a single quality. I shall call that quality
tension. In abstract language, a poetic work has distinct
quality as the ultimate effect of the whole, and that whole
is the "result" of a configuration of meaning which it is the
duty of the critic to examine and evaluate. In setting
forth this duty as my present procedure I am trying to am-
plify a critical approach that I have used on other occasions, without wholly giving up the earlier method, which I
should describe as the isolation of the general ideas implicit in the poetic work.

Towards the end of this essay I shall cite examples of
"tension," but I shall not say that they exemplify tension
only, or that other qualities must be ignored. There are all
kinds of poetry, as many as there are good poets, as many
even as there are good poems, for poets may be expected to
write more than one kind of poetry; and no single critical
insight may impute an exclusive validity to any one kind.
In all ages there are schools demanding that one sort only
be written—their sort: political poetry for the sake of the
cause; picturesque poetry for the sake of the home town;
didactic poetry for the sake of the parish; even a generalized
personal poetry for the sake of the reassurance and safety of

numbers. This last I suppose is the most common variety, the anonymous lyricism in which the common personality exhibits its commonness, its obscure yet standard eccentricity, in a language that seems always to be deteriorating; so that today many poets are driven to inventing private languages, or very narrow ones, because public speech has become heavily tainted with mass feeling.

Mass language is the medium of "communication," and its users are less interested in bringing to formal order what is sometimes called the "affective state" than in arousing that state.

Once you have said that everything is One it is obvious that literature is the same as propaganda; once you have said that no truth can be known apart from the immediate dialectical process of history it is obvious that all contemporary artists must prepare the same fashionplate. It is clear too that the One is limited in space as well as time, and the no less Hegelian Fascists are right in saying that all art is patriotic.

What Mr. William Empson calls patriotic poetry sings not merely in behalf of the State; you will find it equally in a ladylike lyric and in much of the political poetry of our time. It is the poetry of the mass language, very different from the "language of the people" which interested the late W. B. Yeats. For example:

> What from the splendid dead
> We have inherited—
> Furrows sweet to the grain, and the weed subdued—
> See now the slug and the mildew plunder.
> Evil does overwhelm
> The larkspur and the corn;
> We have seen them go under.

From this stanza by Miss Millay we infer that her splendid ancestors made the earth a good place that has somehow gone bad—and you get the reason from the title: "Justice

Denied in Massachusetts." How Massachusetts could cause
a general desiccation, why (as we are told in a footnote to
the poem) the execution of Sacco and Vanzetti should have
anything to do with the rotting of the crops, it is never
made clear. These lines are mass language: they arouse an
affective state in one set of terms, and suddenly an object
quite unrelated to those terms gets the benefit of it; and this
effect, which is usually achieved, as I think it is here, without conscious effort, is sentimentality. Miss Millay's poem
was admired when it first appeared about ten years ago,
and is no doubt still admired, by persons to whom it communicates certain feelings about social justice, by persons
for whom the lines are the occasion of feelings shared by
them and the poet. But if you do not share those feelings, as
I happen not to share them in the images of desiccated nature, the lines and even the entire poem are impenetrably
obscure.

I am attacking here the fallacy of communication in poetry.
(I am not attacking social justice.) It is no less a fallacy in
the writing of poetry than of critical theory. The critical
doctrine fares ill the further back you apply it; I suppose
one may say—if one wants a landmark—that it began to
prosper after 1798; for on the whole nineteenth-century
English verse is a poetry of communication. The poets
were trying to use verse to convey ideas and feelings that
they secretly thought could be better conveyed by science
(consult Shelley's *Defence*), or by what today we call, in a
significantly bad poetic phrase, the Social Sciences. Yet possibly because the poets believed the scientists to be tough,
and the poets joined the scientists in thinking the poets
tender, the poets stuck to verse. It may scarcely be said that
we change this tradition of poetic futility by giving it a new
name, Social Poetry. May a poet hope to deal more adequately with sociology than with physics? If he seizes upon

either at the level of scientific procedure, has he not abdicated his position as poet?

At a level of lower historical awareness than that exhibited by Mr. Edmund Wilson's later heroes of the Symbolist school, we find the kind of verse that I have been quoting, verse long ago intimidated by the pseudo-rationalism of the Social Sciences. This sentimental intimidation has been so complete that, however easy the verse looked on the page, it gave up all claim to sense. (I assume here what I cannot now demonstrate, that Miss Millay's poem is obscure but that Donne's "Second Anniversarie" is not.) As another example of this brand of obscurity I have selected at random a nineteenth-century lyric, "The Vine," by James Thomson:

> The wine of love is music,
>   And the feast of love is song:
> When love sits down to banquet,
>   Love sits long:
>
> Sits long and rises drunken,
>   But not with the feast and the wine;
> He reeleth with his own heart,
>   That great rich Vine.

The language here appeals to an existing affective state; it has no coherent meaning either literally or in terms of ambiguity or implication; it may be wholly replaced by any of its several paraphrases, which are already latent in our minds. One of these is the confused image of a self-intoxicating man-about-town. Now good poetry can bear the closest literal examination of every phrase, and is its own safeguard against our irony. But the more closely we examine this lyric, the more obscure it becomes; the more we trace the implications of the imagery, the denser the confusion. The imagery adds nothing to the general idea that it tries to sus-

tain; it even deprives that idea of the dignity it has won
at the hands of a long succession of better poets going back,
I suppose, to Guinizelli:

> *Al cor gentil ripara sempre Amore*
> *Come alla selva augello in la verdura . . .*

What I want to make clear is the particular kind of failure, not the degree, in a certain kind of poetry. Were we
interested in degrees we might give comfort to the nineteenth century by citing lines from John Cleveland or Abraham Cowley, bad lyric verse no better than "The Vine,"
written in an age that produced some of the greatest English
poetry. Here are some lines from Cowley's "Hymn: to Light,"
a hundred-line inventory of some of the offices performed by
the subject in a universe that still seems to be on the whole
Ptolemaic; I should not care to guess the length the poem
might have reached under the Copernican system. Here is
one of the interesting duties of light:

> Nor amidst all these Triumphs does thou scorn
> The humble glow-worn to adorn,
> And with those living spangles gild,
> (O Greatness without Pride!) the Bushes of the Field.

Again:

> The Violet, springs little Infant, stands,
> Girt in thy purple Swadling-bands:
> On the fair Tulip thou dost dote;
> Thou cloath'st it in a gay and party-colour'd Coat.

This, doubtless, is metaphysical poetry; however bad the
lines may be—they are pretty bad—they have no qualities,
bad or good, in common with "The Vine." Mr. Ransom has
given us, in a remarkable essay, "Shakespeare at Sonnets" [1]

---

[1] His rejection of Shakespeare's sonnets seems to be a result of deductive necessity in his premises, or of the courage of mere logic; but the essay contains
valuable insights into the operation of the metaphysical "conceit."

(*The World's Body,* 1938), an excellent description of this kind of poetry: "The impulse to metaphysical poetry . . . consists in committing the feelings in the case . . . to their determination within the elected figure." That is to say, in metaphysical poetry the logical order is explicit; it must be coherent; the imagery by which it is sensuously embodied must have at least the appearance of logical determinism: perhaps the appearance only, because the varieties of ambiguity and contradiction possible beneath the logical surface are endless, as Mr. Empson has demonstrated in his elucidation of Marvell's "The Garden." Here it is enough to say that the development of imagery by extension, its logical determinants being an Ariadne's thread that the poet will not permit us to lose, is the leading feature of the poetry called metaphysical.

But to recognize it is not to evaluate it; and I take it that Mr. Ransom was giving us a true Aristotelian definition of a *genus,* in which the identification of a type does not compel us to discern the implied values. Logical extension of imagery is no doubt the key to the meaning of Donne's "A Valediction: Forbidding Mourning"; it may equally initiate inquiry into the ludicrous failure of "Hymn: to Light," to which I now return.

Although "The Vine" and "Hymn: to Light" seem to me equally bad poetry, Cowley's failure is somewhat to be preferred; its negative superiority lies in a firmer use of the language. There is no appeal to an affective state; the leading statement can be made perfectly explicit: God is light, and light is life. The poem is an analytical proposition exhibiting the properties inherent in the major term; that is, exhibiting as much of the universe as Cowley could get around to before he wearied of logical extension. But I think it is possible to infer that good poetry could have been written in Cowley's language; and we know that it was. Every term, even the verbs converted into nouns, denotes an object, and

in the hands of a good poet would be amenable to controlled distortions of literal representation. But here the
distortions are uncontrolled. Everything is in this language
that a poet needs except the poetry, or the imagination, or
what I shall presently illustrate under the idea of tension.

I have called "Hymn: to Light" an analytical proposition.
That is the form in which the theme must have appeared to
Cowley's mind; that is to say, simple analysis of the term
God gave him, as it gave everybody else in Christendom, the
proposition: God is light. (Perhaps, under Neo-Platonic influence, the prime Christian symbol, as Professor Fletcher
and others have shown in reducing to their sources the powers of the Three Blessed Ladies of *The Divine Comedy*.)
But in order to write his poem Cowley had to develop the
symbol by synthetic accretion, by adding to light properties
not inherent in its simple analysis:

> The Violet, springs little Infant, stands,
>   Girt in thy purple Swadling-bands: . . .

The image, such as it is, is an addition to the central figure
of light, an assertion of a hitherto undetected relation among
the objects, light, diapers, and violets—a miscellany that I
recommend to the consideration of Mr. E. E. Cummings,
who could get something out of it that Cowley did not intend us to get. If you will think again of "The Vine," you
will observe that Thomson permits, in the opposite direction, an equal license with the objects *de*noted by his imagery, with the unhappy results that we have already seen.

"The Vine" is a failure in denotation. "Hymn: to Light"
is a failure in connotation. The language of "The Vine"
lacks objective content. Take "music" and "song" in the
first two lines; the context does not allow us to apprehend
the terms in extension; that is, there is no reference to objects that we may distinguish as "music" and "song"; the
wine of love could have as well been song, its feast music.

In "Hymn: to Light," a reduction to their connotations of the terms *violet, swadling-bands,* and *light* (the last being represented by the pronoun *thou*) yields a clutter of images that may be unified only if we forget the firm denotations of the terms. If we are going to receive as valid the infancy of the violet, we must ignore the metaphor that conveys it, for the metaphor renders the violet absurd; by ignoring the diaper, and the two terms associated with it, we cease to read the passage, and begin for ourselves the building up of acceptable denotations for the terms of the metaphor.

Absurd: but on what final ground I call these poems absurd I cannot state as a principle. I appeal to the reader's experience, and invite him to form a judgment of my own. It is easy enough to say, as I shall say in detail in a moment, that good poetry is a unity of all the meanings from the furthest extremes of intension and extension. Yet our recognition of the action of this unified meaning is the gift of experience, of culture, of, if you will, our humanism. Our powers of discrimination are not deductive powers, though they may be aided by them; they wait rather upon the cultivation of our total human powers, and they represent a special application of those powers to a single medium of experience—poetry.

I have referred to a certain kind of poetry as the embodiment of the fallacy of communication: it is a poetry that communicates the affective state, which (in terms of language) results from the irresponsible denotations of words. There is a vague grasp of the "real" world. The history of this fallacy, which is as old as poetry but which towards the end of the eighteenth century began to dominate not only poetry, but other arts as well—its history would probably show that the poets gave up the language of denotation to the scientists, and kept for themselves a continually thinning flux of peripheral connotations. The companion fallacy, to which I can give only the literal name, the fallacy of mere denotation, I have also illustrated from Cowley: this is the poetry which contradicts our most developed human insights insofar as it fails to use and direct the rich connotation with which language has been informed by experience.

I I

We return to the inquiry set for this discussion: to find out whether there is not a more central achievement in poetry than that represented by either of the extreme examples that we have been considering. I proposed as descriptive of that achievement, the term *tension*. I am using the term not as a general metaphor, but as a special one, derived from lopping the prefixes off the logical terms *ex*-tension and *in*tension. What I am saying, of course, is that the meaning of poetry is its "tension," the full organized body of all the extension and intension that we can find in it. The remotest figurative significance that we can derive does not invalidate the extensions of the literal statement. Or we may begin with the literal statement and by stages develop the complications of metaphor: at every stage we may pause to state the meaning so far apprehended, and at every stage the meaning will be coherent.

The meanings that we select at different points along the infinite line between extreme intension and extreme extension will vary with our personal "drive" or "interest" or "approach": the Platonist will tend to stay pretty close to the end of the line where extension, and simple abstraction of the object into a universal, is easiest, for he will be a fanatic in morals or some kind of works, and will insist upon the shortest way with what will ever appear to him the dissenting ambiguities at the intensive end of the scale. The Platonist (I do not say that his opponent is the Aristotelian) might decide that Marvell's "To His Coy Mistress" recommends immoral behavior to young men, in whose behalf he would try to suppress the poem. That, of course, would be one "true" meaning of "To His Coy Mistress," but it is a meaning that the full tension of the poem will not allow us to entertain exclusively. For we are compelled, since it is there, to give equal weight to an intensive meaning so rich that, without contradicting the literal statement of the lover-mistress convention, it lifts that convention into an insight into one phase of the human predicament—the conflict of sensuality and asceticism.

I should like to quote now, not from Marvell, but a stanza from Donne that I hope will reinforce a little what I have just said and connect it with some earlier remarks.

> Our two soules therefore, which are one,
>   Though I must goe, endure not yet
> A breach, but an expansion,
>   Like gold to aiery thinnesse beate.

Here Donne brings together the developing imagery of twenty lines under the implicit proposition: the unity of two lovers' souls is a nonspatial entity, and is therefore indivisible. That, I believe, is what Mr. John Crowe Ransom would call the logic of the passage; it is the abstract form of its extensive meaning. Now the interesting feature here is the logical contradiction of embodying the unitary, nonspatial soul in a spatial image: the malleable gold is a plane whose surface can always be extended mathematically by one-half towards infinity; the souls are this infinity. The finite image of the gold, in extension, logically contradicts the intensive meaning (infinity) which it conveys; but it does not invalidate that meaning. We have seen that Cowley compelled us to ignore the denoted diaper in order that we might take seriously the violet which it pretended to swathe. But in Donne's "A Valediction: Forbidding Mourning" the clear denotation of the gold contains, by intension, the full meaning of the passage. If we reject the gold, we reject the meaning, for the meaning is wholly absorbed into the image of the gold. Intension and extension are here one, and they enrich each other.

Before I leave this beautiful object, I should like to notice two incidental features in further proof of Donne's mastery. "Expansion"—a term denoting an abstract property common to many objects, perhaps here one property of a gas: it expands visibly the quality of the beaten gold.

> . . . endure not yet
> a breach . . .

But if the lovers' souls are the formidable, inhuman entity that we have seen, are they not superior to the contingency of a breach? Yes and no: both answers are true answers; for by means of the sly "yet" Donne subtly guards himself against our irony, which would otherwise be quick to scrutinize the extreme metaphor. The lovers have not endured a breach, but they are simple, miserable human beings, and they may quarrel tomorrow.[2]

Now all this meaning and more, and it is all one meaning, is embedded in that stanza: I say more because I have not exhausted the small fraction of significance that my limited powers have permitted me to see. For example, I have not discussed the rhythm, which is of the essential meaning; I have violently isolated four lines from the meaning of the whole poem. Yet, fine as it is, I do not think the poem the greatest poetry; perhaps only very little of Donne makes that grade, or of anybody else. Donne offers many examples of tension in imagery, easier for the expositor than greater passages in Shakespeare.

But convenience of elucidation is not a canon of criticism.

---

[2] Mr. F. O. Matthiessen informs me that my interpretation here, which detaches the "yet" from the developing figure, is not the usual one. Mr. Matthiessen refers the phrase to the gold, for which in his view it prepares the way.

I wish now to introduce other kinds of instance, and to let them stand for us as sorts of Arnoldish touchstones to the perfection that poetic statement has occasionally reached. I do not know what bearing my comment has had, or my touchstones may have, upon the larger effects of poetry or upon long poems. The long poem is partly a different problem. I have of necessity confined both commentary and illustration to the slighter effects that seemed to me commensurate with certain immediate qualities of language. For, in the long run, whatever the poet's "philosophy," however wide may be the extension of his meaning—like Milton's Ptolemaic universe in which he didn't believe—by his language shall you know him; the quality of his language is the valid limit of what he has to say.

I have not searched out the quotations that follow: they at once form the documentation and imply the personal bias from which this inquiry has grown. Only a few of the lines will be identified with the metaphysical technique, or, in Mr. Ransom's fine phrase, the metaphysical strategy. Strategy would here indicate the point on the intensive-extensive scale at which the poet deploys his resources of meaning. The metaphysical poet as a rationalist begins at or near the extensive or denoting end of the line; the romantic or Symbolist poet at the other, intensive end; and each by a straining feat of the imagination tries to push his meanings as far as he can towards the opposite end, so as to occupy the entire scale. I have offered one good and one bad example of the metaphysical strategy, but only defective examples of the Symbolist, which I cited as fallacies of mass language: Thomson was using language at its mass level, unhappily ignorant of the need to embody his connotations in a rational order of thought. (I allude here also, and in a quite literal sense, to Thomson's personal unhappiness, as well as to the excessive pessimism and excessive optimism of other poets of his time.) The great Symbolist poets, from Rimbaud to

Yeats, have heeded this necessity of reason. It would be a hard task to choose between the two strategies, the Symbolist and the metaphysical; both at their best are great, and both are incomplete.

These touchstones, I believe, are not poetry of the extremes, but poetry of the center: poetry of tension, in which the "strategy" is diffused into the unitary effect.

> Ask me no more whither doth hast
> The Nightingale when *May* is past:
> For in your sweet dividing throat
> She winters, and keeps warm her note.

* * *

> O thou Steeled Cognizance whose leap commits
> The agile precincts of the lark's return . . .

* * *

> That time of year thou mayst in me behold
> When yellow leaves, or none, or few do hang
> Upon those boughs which shake against the cold,
> Bare ruined choirs where late the sweet birds sang.

* * *

> Beauty is but a flower
> Which wrinkles will devour;
> Brightness falls from the air,
> Queens have died young and fair,
> Dust hath closed Helen's eye.
> I am sick, I must die.
>   Lord, have mercy upon us!

* * *

> And then may chance thee to repent
> The time that thou hast lost and spent
>   To cause thy lovers sigh and swoon;
> Then shalt thou know beauty but lent,
>   And wish and want as I have done.

* * *

We have lingered in the chambers of the sea
By seagirls wreathed with seaweed red and brown
Till human voices wake us and we drown.

* * *

I am of Ireland
And the Holy Land of Ireland
And time runs on, cried she.
Come out of charity
And dance with me in Ireland.

* * *

And my poor fool is hanged! No, no, no life!
Why should a dog, a horse, a rat, have life
And thou no breath at all? Thou'lt come no more,
Never, never, never, never, never!—
Pray you undo this button; thank you, sir.—
Do you see this? Look on her,—look,—her lips,—
Look there, look there!

* * *

'Tis madness to resist or blame
The force of angry heavens flame:
　　And, if we would speak true,
　　Much to the Man is due,
Who, from his private Gardens, where
He liv'd reserved and austere,
　　As if his highest plot
　　To plant the Bergamot,
Could by industrious Valour climbe
To ruin the great Work of Time,
　　And cast the Kingdome old
　　Into another Mold.

* * *

Cover her face; mine eyes dazzle; she died young.

I I I

There are three more lines that I wish to look at: a terzina from *The Divine Comedy*. I know little of either Dante or his language; yet I have chosen as my final instance of tension—the instance itself will relieve me of the responsibility of the term—not a great and difficult passage, but only a slight and perfect one. It is from a scene that has always been the delight of the amateur reader of Dante; we can know more about it with less knowledge than about any other, perhaps, in the poem. The damned of the Second Circle are equivocally damned: Paolo and Francesca were illicit lovers but their crime was incontinence, neither adultery nor pandering, the two crimes of sex for which Dante seems to find any real theological reprobation, for they are committed with the intent of injury.

You will remember that when Dante first sees the lovers they are whirling in a high wind, the symbol here of lust. When Francesca's conversation with the poet begins, the wind dies down, and she tells him where she was born, in these lines:

> *Siede la terra dove nata fui*
> *Sulla marina dove il Po discende*
> *Per aver pace co' seguaci sui.*

Courtney Landon renders the tercet:

> The town where I was born sits on the shore,
> Whither the Po descends to be at peace
> Together with the streams that follow him.

But it misses a good deal; it misses the force of *seguaci* by rendering it as a verb. Professor Grandgent translates the third line: "To have peace with its pursuers," and comments: "The tributaries are conceived as chasing the Po down to the sea." Precisely; for if the *seguaci* are merely followers, and not pursuers also, the wonderfully ordered density of

this simple passage is sacrificed. For although Francesca has
told Dante where she lives, in the most directly descriptive
language possible, she has told him more than that. Without
the least imposition of strain upon the firmly denoted natural setting, she fuses herself with the river Po near which
she was born. By a subtle shift of focus we see the pursued
river as Francesca in Hell: the pursuing tributaries are a new
visual image for the pursuing winds of lust. A further
glance yields even more: as the winds, so the tributaries at
once pursue and become one with the pursued; that is to
say, Francesca has completely absorbed the substance of her
sin—she is the sin; as, I believe it is said, the damned of the
Inferno are plenary incarnations of the sin that has put them
there. The tributaries of the Po are not only the winds of
lust by analogy to visual images; they become identified by
means of sound:

> . . . *discende*
> *Per aver pace co' seguaci sui.*

The sibilants dominate the line; they are the hissing of the
wind. But in the last line of the preceding tercet Francesca has been grateful that the wind has subsided so that
she can be heard—

> *Mentre che il vento, come fa, si tace.*

After the wind has abated, then, we hear in the silence, for
the first time, its hiss, in the susurration to the descending
Po. The river is thus both a visual and an auditory image,
and since Francesca is her sin and her sin is embodied in this
image, we are entitled to say that it is a sin that we can both
hear and see.

1938

Literature as Knowledge

Comment and Comparison

I

MATTHEW ARNOLD'S war on the Philistines was fought, as everybody knows; but nobody thinks that it was won. Arnold conducted it in what he considered to be the scientific spirit. The Philistines had a passion for "acting and instituting," but they did not know "what we ought to act and to institute." This sort of knowledge must be founded upon "the scientific passion for knowing." But it must not stop there. Culture, which is the study of perfection and the constant effort to achieve it, is superior to the scientific spirit because it includes and passes beyond it. Arnold was, in short, looking for a principle of unity, but it must be a unity of experience. There was before him the accumulating body of the inert, descriptive facts of science, and something had to be done about it.

Yet if it is true, as T. S. Eliot said many years ago, that were Arnold to come back he would have his work to do over again, he would at any rate have to do it very differently. His program, culture added to science and perhaps correcting it, has been our program for nearly a century, and it has not worked. For the facts of science are not inert facts waiting for the poet, as emblematic guardian of culture, to bring to life in the nicely cooperative enterprise of scientist and poet which the nineteenth century puts its faith in. In this view the poet is merely the scientist who achieves completeness. "It is a result of no little culture," Arnold says, "to attain to a clear perception that science and religion are two wholly different things." Religion had yielded to the "fact" of science, but poetry on a positive scientific base could take over the work of religion, and its future was "immense." The "fact" had undermined religion, but it could support poetry.

Although Arnold betrayed not a little uneasiness about this easy solution, it was his way of putting literature upon an equal footing with science. If Arnold failed, can we hope to succeed? Whether literature and science considered philosophically, as Coleridge would phrase it, are the same thing, or different but equal, or the one subordinate to the other, has become a private question. It does not concern the public at large. While Arnold's poet was extending the hand of fellowship to the scientist, the scientist did not return the greeting; for never for an instant did he see himself as the inert and useful partner in an enterprise of which he would not be permitted to define the entire scope. He was not, alas, confined to the inertia of fact; his procedure was dynamic all along, and it was animated by the confident spirit of positivism which has since captured the modern world.

Had he been what Arnold thought he was, how conveniently the partnership would have worked! For what was Arnold's scientist doing? He was giving us exact observation and description of the external world. The poet could give us that, and he could add to it exact observation and description of man's inner life, a realm that the positivist would never be so bold as to invade. But the poet's advantage was actually twofold. Not only did he have this inner field of experience denied to the scientist, he had a resource which was his peculiar and hereditary right—figurative language and the power of rhetoric.

If the inert fact alone could not move us, poetic diction could make it moving by heightening it; for poetry is "thought and art in one." This is an injustice to Arnold; he was a great critic of ideas, of currents of ideas, of the situation of the writer in his time; and from this point of view his theory of poetry is of secondary importance. But since I am now interested in the failure, ours as well as his, to understand the relation of poetry and science, it has been necessary to put his poetic theory in terms that will bring out its defects. On one side it is an eighteenth-century view of poetic language as the rhetorical vehicle of ideas; and it is connected with Arnold's famous definition of religion as "morality touched with emotion." Poetry is descriptive science or experience at that level, touched with emotion.

If Arnold had taste, he had very simple analytical powers, and we are never quite convinced by his fine quotations from the poets. Why is this so? Because he admires good things for bad reasons; or because at any rate his reasons invariably beg the question. In the famous passage on Dryden and Pope in "The Study of Poetry" these poets are not poetic because they are not *poetic*. (Arnold himself is responsible for the italics.) And he looks to us for immediate assent to a distinction between a "prose" classic and a "poetic" classic that has not been actually made. He cites his "touchstones" for the purpose of moving us, and the nice discrimination of feeling which awareness of the touchstones induces will permit us to judge other passages of verse in terms of feeling. The "high seriousness" is partly the elevated tone, a tone which is a quality of the poet's feeling about his subject: it is the poet's business to communicate it to the reader.

This attitude, this tone, centers in emotion. But its relation to what it is about, whether it is external to the subject or inherent in it, Arnold refuses to make clear. The high seriousness may be said to reflect the subject, which must have Aristotelian magnitude and completeness. Arnold had a shrewd sense of the disproportions of tone and subject which he developed into a principle in the Preface to the 1853 edition of his poems. He was suppressing the very fine "Empedocles on Aetna" because, he said, it has no action; it is all passive suffering; and passive suffering is not a proper subject for poetry. (A view that has been revived in our time by the late W. B. Yeats.) Action, then, is the subject of the greatest poetry. This conviction is so strong—who will question its rightness, *as far as it goes?*—that he actually puts into quotation marks words which are not quoted from anybody at all but which represent for him the consensus of the ancients on the importance of action: " 'All depends upon the subject; choose a fitting action, penetrate yourself with the feeling of its situations; this done, everything else will follow.' " But will everything else follow? Does a great style follow? To a gift for action Shakespeare "added a special one of his own; a gift, namely, of happy, abundant, and ingenious expression. . . ." I think we should attend closely here to the words "added" and "ingenious," for they reveal Arnold's view of the function of language. And suppose you have lyric poetry which may be, like Arnold's own fine lyrics, more meditative than dramatic, and more concerned with the futility of action than with action itself? It has never, I believe, been pointed out that the Preface of 1853 cuts all the props from under lyric poetry. The lyric at its best is "dramatic," but there is no evidence that Arnold thought it so; for the lyric, though it may be a moment of action, lacks magnitude and completeness; it may be the beginning, or the middle, or the end, but never all three. What, then, is the subject of the lyric? Is it all feeling, nothing but feeling? It is feeling about "ideas," not actions; and the feeling communicates "power and joy."

This gross summary of Arnold's poetics omits all the sensitive discriminations that he felt in reading the poets; it omits all but the framework of his thought. Yet the framework alone must concern us on this occasion. Arnold is still the great critical influence in the universities, and it is perhaps not an exaggeration of his influence to say that debased Arnold is the main stream of popular appreciation of poetry. It would be fairer to say that Arnold the critic was superior to his critical theory; yet at the distance of three generations we may look back upon his lack of a critical dialectic—he even had a certain contempt for it in other critics—as a calamity for that culture which it was his great desire to strengthen and pass on.

His critical theory was elementary, and if you compare him with Coleridge a generation earlier, he represents a loss. His position is nearer to the neoclassicism of Lessing, whom he praises in *Culture and Anarchy* for humanizing knowledge, a leveling-off of distinctions of which Lessing as a matter of fact was not guilty. He shares with Lessing the belief—but not its dialectical basis—that the language of poetry is of secondary importance to the subject, that it is less difficult than the medium of painting, and that, given the action, all else follows.

This remnant of neoclassicism in Arnold has been ably discerned by Mr. Cleanth Brooks in *Modern Poetry and the Tradition*. I go into it here not to deny that action is necessary to the long poem; for Arnold's view contains a fundamental truth. But it is not the whole truth; asserted in his terms, it may not be a truth at all. The important question goes further. It is: What is the relation of language to the "subject," to the dramatic and narrative subject as action, or to the lyrical subject as "idea"? The question may be pushed even further: Is it possible finally to distinguish the language from the subject? Are not subject and language one?

For Arnold the subject is what we commonly call the prose subject; that is to say, as much of the poetic subject as we can put into ordinary prose. The poet takes it up at the level at which the scientist—or Arnold's simulacrum of him—takes it: the level of observation and description. The poet now puts it into language that will bring the inert facts to life and move us. The language is strictly what Mr. Richards calls the "vehicle"—it does not embody the subject; it conveys it and remains external to it.

For what are action and subject? The positivists have their own notion of these terms; and their language of physical determinism suits that notion better than the poet's. The poet's language is useless.

I I

Is it not easy to see how such a poetics gives the case for poetry away to the scientist? Not to Arnold's straw scientist, who politely kept to his descriptive place and left to literature man's evaluation of his experience; but to the scientist as he is: a remarkably ingenious and dynamic fellow whose simple fanaticism brooks no compromise with his special projects. Whatever these on occasion may be, he demands an exact one-to-one relevance of language to the objects and the events to which it refers. In this relevance lies the "meaning" of all terms and propositions insofar as they are used for the purpose of giving us valid knowledge. It is, of course, knowledge for action; and apart from this specific purpose, the problem of meaning is not even a real problem.

"Meaning" has been replaced by a concept of "operational validity"—that is to say, the "true" meaning of a term is not its definition; it is the number of statements containing it which can be referred to empirically observed events. Along with meaning and definition, universals also disappear; and with universals, cognition. A proposition does not represent an act of knowing by a knower—that is, a mind; it is, in a chemical metaphor, the expression of an interaction among certain elements of a "situation."

This advanced position in the philosophy of science has been set forth in the new *International Encyclopedia of Uni-*

fied Science, which is being published serially at the University of Chicago. Of great interest from the point of view of literary criticism are the brilliant studies of "semiosis," or the functioning of language as "signs." Mr. Charles W. Morris's "Foundations for the Theory of Signs," [1] is a model of exact exposition in a field of enormous complication. This field is popularly known as "semantics," but semantics in any exact sense is only one "dimension" of semiosis. In this brief glance at the aesthetic and critical implications of Mr. Morris's writings, his theory as a whole cannot be set forth.

Semiosis is the actual functioning of language in three dimensions which are located and described by means of the science of "semiotic." Semiotic, then, is the study of semiosis. The three dimensions in which all language, verbal, or mathematical, functions are: (1) the semantical, (2) the syntactical, and (3) the pragmatical; and the respective studies in these dimensions are semantics, syntactics, and pragmatics. It must be borne in mind that in semiosis the three dimensions are never separate; in semiotic they are distinguished abstractly for study. Semiotic looks towards the formation of rules which will govern the use of all language (signs), and it lays claim to an ultimate unification of all "knowledge."

That need not concern us here. Let us take a simple declarative sentence: "This county has an annual rainfall of fifty-one inches." From the semantical point of view the sentence designates certain conditions, or a situation: it is the "sign-vehicle" for that designation. If upon investigation we find that the situation actually exists, then it has not only been designated; it has also been *denoted.* From the syntactical point of view we are not concerned with what the sign-vehicle points to; for syntactics deals with the formal struc-

---

[1] *International Encyclopedia of Unified Science,* Vol. I, No. 2.

ture of the sentence, the relations of the words. From the pragmatical point of view the meaning of the sentence is the effect it has upon somebody who hears it or reads it. If I am about to buy a farm in this county, and learn that "this county has an annual rainfall of fifty-one inches," I may go elsewhere; at the moment I hear the sentence I may light a cigarette, or look the other way, or laugh, or swear. All this behavior would be the functioning of the sign in the pragmatic dimension.

The complex possibilities of semiotic may not be evident in this crude summary. Mr. Morris says: "The sign vehicle itself is simply one object." It is an object that may function in other sign-vehicles; it may be designated, denoted, or reacted to; and the process is infinite. The identification of signs and their relations is equally complex. There are, for example, a characterizing sign, a symbolic sign, an indexical sign, and an iconic sign; and any of these, in certain contexts, may function as any other. I shall return to them presently.

The only philosophic criticism of this system that I have seen is Howard D. Roelofs's article in the symposium on the "New Encyclopedists," published in *The Kenyon Review* (Spring, 1939). Mr. Roelofs is concerned with Mr. Morris's rejection of the problem of universals and of cognition. It ought to be plain from my brief exposition of the pragmatic dimension of semiosis that the significant factor is what I *do*, not what I *think* leading to what I do; and that thus the bias of the science of semiotic is pragmatic in the ordinary sense, and even behavioristic. For Mr. Morris says: "A 'concept' [i.e., a universal] may be regarded as a semantical rule determining the use of characterizing signs." Mr. Roelofs's comment is interesting:

Morris has no trouble with this problem [i.e., the problem of universals]. It is simply a rule of our language that such a term as "man" can be used as often as the conditions stated in its definition are fulfilled. That makes the term a universal. If we then ask how it happens those conditions are in fact frequently fulfilled, we are informed, "It can only be said the world is such." And those who are tempted by this fact to believe that universals are somehow objective, functioning in nature, are silenced with a threat: to talk as if universals were entities in the world is "to utter pseudo-thing sentences of the quasi-semantical type." . . . the heart of the problem is dismissed with a phrase and a language rule offered as a solution.

The bearing of Mr. Roelofs's criticism will be plainer in a moment. Now Mr. Morris, in discussing the syntactical dimension, says: "Syntactics, as the study of the syntactical relations of signs to one another *in abstraction* from the relations of signs to objects or to interpreters [persons], is the best developed of all the branches of semiotic." Exactly; because syntactics comes out of traditional formal logic and grammar, and because it "deliberately neglects what has here been called the semantical and the pragmatical dimensions of semiosis."

The role of syntactics in the semiotic science remains somewhat obscure; it seems to consist in a number of "transformation rules"—that is, in formulas by which given expressions in words, numbers, or symbols can be changed into equivalent but formally different expressions. What power of the mind there may be which enables us in the first place to form these expressions nowhere appears. (I daresay this statement is of the quasi-semantical type.) But Mr. Morris tells us how we are to think of the rules of the three dimensions of semiotic:

Syntactical rules determine the sign relations between sign vehicles; semantical rules correlate sign vehicles with other objects; pragmatical rules state the conditions in the interpreters under which the sign vehicle is a sign. Any rule when actually in use operates as a type of behavior, and in this sense there is a pragmatical component in all rules.

If we imagine with Mr. Roelofs a situation in which semiosis is functioning, we shall see pretty clearly the behavioristic tendency of the science of semiotic; and we shall also see in what sense "there is a pragmatical component in all rules." A simplified process of semiosis, or the actual functioning of signs, is very easy to state. There is first of all the sign, which we get in terms of a sign-vehicle. It looks two ways; first, it points to something, designates something; and, secondly, what is designated elicits a response from persons who are present. The thing pointed to is thus the *designatum;* the response is the *interpretant.* By implication there is an interpreter, a person, a mind; but Mr. Morris is consistently vague about him: he is not a technical factor, he is a superfluous entity, in semiosis. That is to say, not only is he not needed in order to explain the functioning of signs; he would embarrass the explanation. Mr. Roelofs makes this clear, as follows:

The innocent reader will take the analysis of the use of signs to be the analysis of a cognitive process. The correctness of the analysis as far as it goes conceals the fact that cognition itself has been eliminated. Consider this illustration. A maid enters the room and says to the three persons present, "The doctor called." One person thereupon takes a pen and writes a line in a diary; the second goes to a telephone and makes a call; the third says, "Did he?" According to the analysis offered by Morris, the words uttered by the maid are the sign-vehicle. The actual call of the doctor is the denotatum.[2] The three persons are the interpreters, and their three different actions are the interpretants, the responses of the interpreters to the denotatum via the sign-vehicle. No one is likely to deny these factors are present. It should be noted that the interpretants, to the extent that they are a sequence of physical actions, can be perceived. It should also be noted that

[2] *Denotata* are real things; *designata* may be pointed to, but they are not necessarily real. For example, the Phoenix's "spicy nest." The doctor's call is a *designatum* which is also a *denotatum*—it's "real."

such sequences of action are not cognitions . . . they are "interpretants," but their being such depends upon the cognitions of the interpreters. These responses are not themselves knowledge. They do depend upon knowledge, and that is precisely what Morris leaves out. . . . Morris objects to the term "meaning." This is not surprising. His analysis leaves out meaning in the primary sense of meaning. This is not to say that meanings are "like marbles" [Morris's phrase]. Meanings, indeed, like knowledge in general, are a unique kind of thing. There is literally nothing like knowledge except knowledge itself.

I have quoted Mr. Roelofs at length because what he has to say about the problem of cognition bears directly upon the semiotic version of the aesthetic problem. He sums up his argument:

The procedure culminates in eliminating not only universals, but cognition itself. Just as the answer to the problem of universals is that they do not exist [that is, they are only a semantical rule], the answer to the problem of knowledge is that there is no such thing. There are responses, but no cognition; there is a language, but not knowledge. Knowledge cannot be reduced to exclusively perceptual terms. Therefore it does not exist. This is not empiricism. *It is positivism.* [Italics mine.]

In this positivist technique for the analysis of language, the interpreting mind, the cognizing intelligence, is lost in the perceptual account of its external behavior. Mr. Morris says: "In general, from the point of view of behavior, signs are 'true' insofar as they correctly determine the expectations of the users, and so release more fully the behavior which is implicitly aroused in the expectation or interpretation."

In Mr. Morris's aesthetics there is an aesthetic sign. Does it implicitly—or explicitly—arouse expectations in terms of behavior? Does it correctly determine our expectations? Is the aesthetic sign "true" in that it is a determinant of our behavior? Mr. Morris is not unequivocal in his answers to these questions.

I I I

No—and yes, replies Mr. Morris, in two essays [3] the cunning and scholastic ingenuity of which make even the beautiful essay on the general theory of signs look amateurish. No, he says, because the aesthetic sign is a special sort of sign: it is *iconic*. It does not correctly determine our behavior. Yes, because it bears the formidable responsibility of showing us what we ought to try to get out of our behavior. The function of the aesthetic sign is nothing less than the "vivid presentation" of *values*, a presentation that is not only vivid, but *immediate*—without mediation—for direct apprehension. The iconic sign, in other words, designates without denoting; or if it does denote anything its *denotatum* is already in its own "properties." "In certain kinds of insanity," writes Mr. Morris, "the distinction between the designatum and the denotatum vanishes; the troublesome world of existences is pushed aside, and the frustrated *interests* [italics mine] get what satisfaction they can in the domain of signs. . . ." Likewise *designata* and *denotata* become in aesthetics the same thing; but in this logical shuffle, worthy of a thirteenth-century *doctor subtilis*, the aesthetic sign is never confused "with the object it designates." It is that alone which saves it from the ignominy of insanity.

The difficulties of this theory must already be apparent. First, the difference between insanity and art is the hairsbreadth line, in the interpreter's response to the sign, between substituting the sign for reality and maintaining the distinction between sign and reality. The first question that one must ask, then, is this: With what does the interpreter make this distinction? If the distinction is not inherent in the nature of the sign, does the interpreter not perform an act

[3] "Esthetics and the Theory of Signs," *The Journal of Unified Science,* VIII, 1–3, pp. 131–150; and "Science, Art and Technology," *The Kenyon Review,* Autumn, 1939, pp. 409–423.

of cognition? If the distinction is a mere interpretant, a behavioristic response, why do we not respond to a work of art uniformly; and why is that uniform response in every case not insane *unless we are capable of a primary act of knowledge,* of simply knowing the difference?

Secondly, if art is the realm of values—that is, if the peculiar nature of the aesthetic sign is that it shall convey values—the values must be inherent in the aesthetic sign, and must therefore compel in the interpreter the distinction between value and insanity; so that there is no possibility that the interpreter, who is incapable of cognition, will confuse the mere sign with reality. For the nature of the sign must determine the interpretant, or response.

There must therefore be a special "differentia" for the aesthetic sign that distinguishes it from all other signs whatever. "Lyric poetry," Mr. Morris says, "has a syntax and uses terms which designate things, but the syntax and the terms are so used that what stand out for the reader are values and evaluations." [4] Does not Mr. Morris confess his difficulty when he uses the vague metaphorical expression, "stand out," and the even more vague "so used"? Just what is this use? It is significant that in Mr. Morris's two articles on aesthetics, in which the word poetry frequently appears, there is no actual analysis of a passage or even of a line of verse; and not even a quotation from any poem in any language. He contents himself with assertions that the future of semiotic in the field of poetry is immense, and that only the work has to be done.

Now, if the contradiction that I have pointed out in general terms exists, we may see its origin if we examine further Mr. Morris's idea of the aesthetic sign. It is a special variety of the iconic sign. To illustrate this it will be sufficient to relate the iconic to the characterizing sign, and to distinguish the icon from the symbol.

[4] "Foundations for the Theory of Signs," *op. cit.,* p. 58.

A characterizing sign [he says] characterizes that which it can denote. Such a sign may do this by exhibiting in itself the properties an object must have to be denoted by it, and in this case the characterizing sign is an *icon;* if this is not so, the characterizing sign may be called a *symbol.* A photograph, a star chart, a model, a chemical diagram, are icons, while the word "photograph," the names of the stars and of chemical elements are symbols.

The terminology is quite special. Icon is the Greek (εἰκών) for a sculptured figure. Ordinarily a symbol is what Mr. Morris claims for the icon: it exhibits in itself the qualities it stands for—like Christ on the Cross—or it represents by convention something other than itself, like 2πr for the circumference of a circle. But here the terms are roughly equivalent, icon to image, symbol to concept; but only roughly, since in Mr. Morris's list of symbols "photograph" is not any particular photograph, while the name of a star must be the name of a particular star. There is a fundamental obscurity, that we shall have to pass over, in attributing to verbal language a thoroughly *iconic* property. In the list of icons, there are *a* photograph, *a* star chart, *a* model, *a* chemical diagram—all of them spatial and perceptual objects—but while language is always used in a spatial setting, words appear in temporal sequence and have only the spatial character of their occasion. We cannot *see* the properties of words in the words. We have simply got to know *what* the words convey. The phrase "a star chart" is not a star chart itself. Mr. Morris appears to have found in the term *icon,* at any rate so far as it pertains to aesthetics, merely a convenient evasion of the term *image;* for image would doubtless have held him to the old ontological aesthetics.

The essay, "Esthetics and the Theory of Signs," deals with the specific problem "of stating the differentia of the esthetic sign." Mr. Morris is constantly reminding us that iconic signs appear in all discourse, and that all discourse is by no means aesthetic discourse. Yet the special function of the iconic sign makes it possible for us to use it as the aesthetic sign; and that function is stated in a "semantical rule":

The semantical rule for the use of an iconic sign is that it denotes any object which has the properties (in practice, a selection from the properties) which it itself has. Hence when an interpreter apprehends an iconic sign-vehicle he apprehends directly what is designated; here mediated and unmediated taking account of certain properties both occur; [5] put in still other terms, every iconic sign has its own sign-vehicle among its denotata.

This is a difficult conception; perhaps it can be illustrated with a few lines of verse:

That time of year thou mayst in me behold
When yellow leaves, or none, or few do hang
Upon those boughs which shake against the cold . . .

According to Mr. Morris, the sign-vehicle here would be the leaves hanging on the boughs. This verbal sign-vehicle has the "properties" of the natural objects which it designates; and that which it denotes is in the designation itself. That is, leaves-bough does not point to a definite situation or condition beyond itself: we get "directly what is designated" because it is of the nature of the iconic sign to contain its own *denotatum.* (I have simplified this analysis by ignoring "That time of year," which I believe would make it impossible to apply Mr. Morris's terms coherently.)

The treatment of the iconic sign in semiotic is mysterious. If any generalization about it is legitimate, we may surmise that certain terms, which Mr. Morris calls "primary terms," are untranslatable; that is to say, they cannot be handled by any principle of reduction; they have a certain completeness and finality. They denote themselves; certain iconic signs seem to be such terms. They are sign-

[5] There seems to be evidence in this clause that Mr. Morris is not interested in syntactics.

vehicles for images, and our apprehension of them is direct. For while the iconic sign may denote something beyond itself, its specific character as an iconic sign is that part of what it denotes is the sign itself. "These facts," says Mr. Morris, "taken alone, do not delimit the esthetic sign, for blueprints, photographs, and scientific models are all iconic signs—but seldom works of art." He continues in a passage of great interest:

If, however, the designatum of an iconic sign be a *value* [italics mine] (and of course not all iconic signs designate values), the situation is changed: there is now not merely the designation of value properties (for such designation takes place even in science), nor merely the functioning of iconic signs (for these as such need not be esthetic signs), but there is the direct apprehension of value properties through the very presence of that which itself has the value it designates.

There are thus three steps in the "delimitation" of the aesthetic sign: First, it is an iconic sign; secondly, it is an iconic sign which designates a value; thirdly, it is an iconic sign which designates a value in the sign itself, so that our "apprehension" of that value is unmediated, that is, *direct.*

The difficulties created by this aesthetic doctrine are slippery and ambiguous. We may, for convenience, see them in two ways. The first set of problems lies in the term "apprehension"; the second, in the term "value."

The primary meaning of apprehension is a grasping or a taking hold of. What does Mr. Morris mean? If it means taking hold of by means of perception, we are asked to see ourselves *perceiving a value;* but a value cannot be an object of perception. If, however, apprehension means a direct, unmediated knowledge of a value, then there is an act of evaluation involved which implies the presence of a knowing mind. For the implied "semantical rule" for the aesthetic sign obviously forbids us to check the value wholly in terms of a situation external to the properties of the sign itself.

We have got to *know* the value in itself; and only in an act
of cognition can we know it. But if Mr. Morris means by
apprehension the response, or mere "interpretant," of semiosis, it is difficult to see how a mere response can be semantically correct unless the sign-vehicle points to a situation
outside itself in terms of which the response is relevant. If
there is no such situation, is not the interpretant a piece
of insanity?

I cannot see how there can be any direct apprehension
unless there is an agency to do the apprehending; and the
interpretant is not an agent, it is a response. "One additional
point may be noted to confirm the sign status of the work of
art: The artist often draws attention to the sign-vehicle in
such a way as to prevent the interpreter from merely reacting
to it as an object and not as a sign. . . ." Mr. Morris's
phrases, "in such a way," "so used that," remain painfully
evasive. What is that way? Now, if the preventive factor is
inherent in the work of art, why did not the birds refrain
from trying to eat the grapes in Zeuxis's picture? The citizens
of Athens did not mistake the sign-vehicle for an object.
Why? Because they *knew* the difference.

Mr. Morris's theory of value will further illuminate his
difficulty. It is an "interest" theory of value for which he
acknowledges an indebtedness to the pragmatic tradition of
Mead and Dewey. Objects, according to this ancient theory,
have value in relation to interests. "Values," says Mr. Morris,
"are consummatory properties of objects or situations which
answer to the consummation of interested acts." If I satisfy
my hunger by eating a banana, the banana has value in relation to the specific interest, hunger. Does it follow that we
have similar aesthetic interests, which we similarly satisfy?
No specific aesthetic interest appears in semiosis. The aesthetic satisfaction proceeds from the frustration of "real" interests, from the blockage of interests as they drive onward
to real "consummations." The aesthetic sign is a value that

has not been consummated. Art is the expression of what men desire but are not getting.

There are two passages in "Esthetics and the Theory of Signs" which reveal the fundamental ambiguity in Mr. Morris's conception of the aesthetic sign as a "value." We shall be struck, I believe, by the remarkable parallel between Mr. Morris's view of the aesthetic medium and the neoclassical view, which we saw in Matthew Arnold.

Even though the complexity of the total icon is so very great that no denotatum (other than the esthetic sign vehicle itself) can in actuality be found, the work of art can still be considered a sign—for there can be designation without denotation.

But can the aesthetic sign—and this is the center of the problem—designate an interest "value" if it does not point to an interest? It seems to me that it cannot be a value in any "interest" theory of value whatever. And when the aesthetic sign is so complex that it does not lead to denotation, is not this complexity a semantical failure so great that Mr. Morris actually ought to take it to an institution for the insane?

The traditional prestige of the arts is formidable; so, rather than commit himself to his logic of the aesthetic sign as a designation of a value which cannot be located and which thus cannot be an interest value, he offers us the ordinary procedure of positivism; that is to say, he shows us how we may reduce the aesthetic sign to a *denotatum* after all.

Since a statement must say something about something, it must involve signs for locating what is referred to, and such signs are ultimately indexical signs [i.e., "pointing" signs]. An iconic sign in isolation cannot then be a statement, and a work of art, conceived as an iconic sign, cannot be true in the semantical sense of the term. Nevertheless, the statement that a work of art is "true" might under analysis turn out to be an elliptical form of syntactical, semantical, or pragmatical statements. Thus semantically it might be intended to affirm that the work in question actually is iconic of the value structure of a certain object or situation. . . .

The work of art is elliptical and iconic; that is, it is an image from which the semantical dimension is omitted, or in which it remains vague. By translating the icon, by expanding it and filling it in with a *denotatum*, we construct a situation external to the work of art: a situation which replaces it. In the usual terms of literary criticism, this situation is the "subject" which exists outside the language of the poem. For the language is merely "iconic of" this ordinary prose subject.

So a neoclassical theory of poetic language not only gave the case for poetry away to the scientist; it has become the foundation of the scientists' theory of poetry. When Mr. Richards remarked, in *Science and Poetry,* that we were now getting on a large scale "genuine knowledge" which would soon reduce poetry to the level of the "pseudo-statement," we could not see how right he was: right—from the point of view of neoclassical theory. So long as the scientific procedure was observation, description, and classification, it was not very different from the procedure of common sense and its feeling for the reality of ordinary experience. As late as the first edition (1892) of *The Grammar of Science,* Karl Pearson said: "The aesthetic judgment pronounces for or against the interpretation of the creative imagination according as that interpretation embodies or contradicts the phenomena of life, which we ourselves have observed." But from the point of view of Unified Science, this principle of common-sense observation will no longer serve; it does not go far enough. And so we have a dilemma. Since the language of poetry can be shown to be not strictly relevant to objects and situations as these are presented by the positivist techniques, poetry becomes either nonsense or hortatory rhetoric.

The semiotic approach to aesthetics "has the merit of

concreteness"; yet we have seen that Mr. Morris never quite gets around to a specific work of art. In "Science, Art, and Technology," he distinguishes three primary forms of discourse and relates them to the three dimensions of semiosis:

(1) Scientific discourse: semantical dimension.

(2) Aesthetic discourse: syntactical dimension.

(3) Technological discourse: pragmatical dimension.

We have seen that the iconic sign is semantically weak; so the aesthetic sign, a variety of iconic sign, must function primarily at the syntactical level; that is, if we look at it "indexically" it "points" first of all to itself. Looking at the aesthetic sign from this point of view, we are forced to see that it wholly lacks cognitive content, and it is subject to the operation of "transformation rules." Does the "concreteness" of the semiotic approach to art consist in this? Again, is the syntactical dimension that in which direct apprehension of the aesthetic sign is possible? Once more it must be said that this direct apprehension seems impossible unless there is an agency of apprehension—a knowing mind; without this we get only an "interpretant," which is conceivable only at the pragmatic level; and if the interpretant is intelligible, it is so in terms of semantical relevance, or of the scientific form of discourse. For Mr. Morris himself confesses: ". . . in so far as the knowledge of value which art gives is the more than the having of value [i.e., is the *knowing* of value] there is no reason to suppose that this knowledge is *other than scientific in character.*"

It is significant here that Mr. Morris conceives the character of poetry in the relation of pragmatics and semantics. What is our response to poetry and how do we behave when we read it: what, in a word, does it lead to? There is a certain uneasy piety in the extravagant claim that poetry is the realm of values; and there is no way, I think, to get around the conclusion that, since the values are not attached to reality, they are irresponsible feelings. They are, in fact, rhetoric.

And it is also significant that for Mr. Morris the study of rhetoric is a branch of pragmatics; it is even a kind of technological instrument. For, in the essay, "Science, Art, and Technology," poetry seems to acquire its main responsibility in the technological function of telling us what we *ought* to want and do. Here again neoclassical didacticism appears in terms of a rigorous instrumentalism.

Does the language of poetry mean what it says, or does it mean the "situation" that we get from it in a process of reduction? Although we have seen Mr. Morris's bias, we have also seen that he has not made up his mind: he would like to have it both ways. The origin of this dilemma is remote. But there is always "the sad ghost of Coleridge beckoning from the shades."

I V

The famous Chapter XIV of *Biographia Literaria* has been the background of the criticism of poetry for more than a hundred years. Its direct influence has been very great; its indirect influence, through Poe upon Baudelaire, and through the French symbolists down to contemporary English and American poets, has perhaps been even greater. This chapter is the most influential statement on poetry ever formulated by an English critic: its insights, when we have them, are ours, and ours too its contradictions. Yet the remarkable "definition" of poetry, which I shall now quote, is not, as we shall presently see, the chief source of the aesthetic dilemma that we inherit today. (That source is another passage.) Here is the definition:

A poem is that species of composition, which is opposed to works of science, by proposing for its *immediate* object pleasure, not truth; and from all other species—(having this object in common with it)—it is distinguished by proposing to itself such delight from the *whole,* as is compatible with a distinct gratification from each component *part.*

Much of the annoyance and misunderstanding caused by this passage has not been Coleridge's fault; but is rather due to the failure of literary men to observe the accurate use of *species*. For Coleridge is giving us a strict Aristotelian definition of a *species* within a given *genus*. It is not a qualitative statement, and it does not answer the question: *What* is poetry? The *whatness* of poetry does not come within the definition; and I believe that nowhere else does Coleridge offer us an explicit qualitative distinction between poetry and other "species of composition" which may be "opposed" to it.

For what is Coleridge saying? (I have never seen a literal reading of the passage by any critic.) There is the generic division: composition. A poem is a species within the genus; but so is a work of science. How are the two species distinguished? By their immediate objects. It is curious that Coleridge phrases the passage as if a poem were a person "proposing" to himself a certain end, pleasure; so for *object* we have got to read *effect*. A poem, then, differs from a work of science in its immediate effect upon us; and that immediate effect is pleasure. But other species of composition may aim at the effect of pleasure. A poem differs from these in the relation of part to whole: the parts must give us a distinct pleasure, moment by moment, and they are not to be conceived as subordinate to the whole; they make up the whole.

If there is an objective relation of part to whole, Coleridge does not say what it is; nor does he distinguish that relation in terms of any specific poetic work. It is strictly a quantitative analogy taken, perhaps, from geometry. And the only purpose it serves is this: in the paragraph following the "definition" he goes on to say that "the philosophic critics of all ages coincide" in asserting that beautiful, isolated lines or distichs are not a poem, and that neither is "an unsustained composition" of uninteresting parts a *"legitimate* poem."

What we have here, then, is a sound but ordinary critical insight; but because it is merely an extension of the pleasure principle implicit in the "definition," we are not prepared by it to distinguish objectively a poem from any other form of expression. The distinction lies in the effect, and it is a psychological effect. In investigating the differentia of poetry—as Mr. Morris would put it—we are eventually led away from the poem into what has been known since Coleridge's time as the psychology of poetry.

The difficulties of this theory Coleridge seems not to have been aware of; yet he illustrates them perfectly. In the second paragraph after the famous definition he writes this remarkable passage:

The first chapter of Isaiah—(indeed a very large portion of the whole book)—is poetry in the most emphatic sense; yet it would be no less irrational than strange to assert, that pleasure, not truth, was the immediate object of the prophet. In short, whatever specific import we attach to the word, Poetry, there will be found involved in it, as a necessary consequence, that a poem of any length neither can be, nor ought to be, all poetry. Yet if an harmonious whole is to be produced, the remaining parts must be preserved in keeping with the poetry; and this can no otherwise be effected than by such a studied selection and artificial arrangement, as will partake of one, though not a peculiar property of poetry. And this again can be no other than the property of exciting a more continuous and equal attention than the language of prose aims at, whether colloquial or written.

This is probably the most confused statement ever uttered by a great critic, and it has probably done more damage to critical thought than anything else said by any critic. Isaiah is poetry in "the most emphatic sense," although his immediate object (effect) is truth. It will be observed that, whereas in the definition our attention is drawn to a species of composition, a poem, we are here confronted with the personage, Isaiah, who does have the power of proposing an object; and Isaiah's immediate object is truth. But are we to suppose that the effect of the poem and the object of the prophet are to be apprehended in the same way? Is our experience of truth the same as our experience of pleasure? If there is a difference between truth and pleasure, and if an immediate effect of pleasure is the specific "property" of poetry (how a property can be an effect it is difficult to see), how can the first chapter of Isaiah be poetry at all? It cannot be, looked at in these terms; and as a matter of fact Coleridge rather slyly withdraws his compliment to Isaiah when he goes on to say that a "poem of any length neither can be, nor ought to be, all poetry." Isaiah is not all poetry; he is partly truth, or even mostly truth. And the element of truth, while it is strictly speaking insubordinate and unassimilable, can be used by means of an artificial arrangement—meter. There is no doubt that meter does on the whole what Coleridge attributes to it: it demands a "continuous and equal attention." Does he mean to say that the insubordinate element of truth—insubordinate to the immediate effect of pleasure—should be given such conspicuous emphasis? Or does he perhaps mean that the attention will be fixed upon the metrical pattern, so that the nonpoetic element will be less conspicuous?

Coleridge's theory of meter is not quite pertinent here: in the later and more elaborate discussion of meter in *Biographia Literaria* there is the general conclusion that meter is indispensable to poetry. In Chapter XIV, now being examined, he speaks of meter as "an artificial arrangement . . . not a peculiar property of poetry."

There is, then, in Coleridge's poetic theory a persistent dilemma. *He cannot make up his mind whether the specifically poetic element is an objective feature of the poem, or is distinguishable only as a subjective effect.* He cannot, in short, choose between metaphysics and psychology. His general emphasis is psychological, with metaphysical ambiguities.

The distinction between Fancy and Imagination is ultimately a psychological one: he discusses the problem in terms of separate faculties, and the objective poetical properties, presumably resulting from the use of these faculties, are never defined, but are given only occasional illustration. (I have in mind his magnificent analysis of "Venus and Adonis," the value of which lies less perhaps in the critical principles he supposes he is illustrating, than in the perfect taste with which he selects the good passages for admiration.) When Coleridge speaks of the "esemplastic power" of the Imagination, it is always a "faculty" of the mind, not an objective poetic order. When he says that a poem gives us "a more than usual state of emotion with more than usual order," we acknowledge the fact, without being able to discern in the merely comparative degree of the adjective the fundamental difference between the poetic and the philosophic powers which Coleridge frequently asserts, but which he nowhere objectively establishes. The psychological bias of his "system" is perfectly revealed in this summary passage of Chapter XIV:

My own conclusions on the nature of poetry, in the strictest use of the word, have been in part anticipated in some of the remarks on the Fancy and Imagination in the early part of this work. What is poetry?—is so nearly the same question with, what is a poet?—that the answer to the one is involved in the solution to the other. For it is a distinction resulting from the poetic genius itself, which sustains and modifies the images, thoughts, and emotions of the poet's own mind.

There can be little doubt that Coleridge's failure to get out of the dilemma of Intellect-or-Feeling has been passed on to us as a fatal legacy. If the first object of poetry is an effect, and if that effect is pleasure, does it not necessarily follow that truth and knowledge may be better set forth in some other order altogether? It is true that Coleridge made extravagant claims for a poetic order of truth, and it is upon these claims that Mr. I. A. Richards has based his fine book, *Coleridge on Imagination:* Mr. Richards's own testimony is that the claims were not coherent. The coherent part of Coleridge's theory is the fatal dilemma that I have described. Truth is only the secondary consideration of the poet, and from the point of view of positivism the knowledge, or truth, that poetry gives us is immature and inadequate. What of the primary consideration of the poet—pleasure?

Pleasure is the single qualitative feature of Coleridge's famous definition; but it is not *in* the definition objectively. And with the development of modern psychology it has ceased to be qualitative, even subjectively. It is a *response.* The fate of Coleridge's system, then, has been its gradual extinction in the terminology of experimental psychology. The poetry has been extinguished in the poet. The poetic "effect" is a "response" to a "stimulus"; and in the early works of Mr. Richards we get for the first time the questions, rigorously applied: Is the poetic response relevant to the real world? Is it relevant to action? Poetry has come under the general idea of "operational validity." So we must turn briefly to Mr. Richards.

V

In *Science and Poetry* (1926) Mr. Richards condensed in untechnical language the position that he had set forth in detail earlier, in *The Principles of Literary Criticism.* The positivist side of Mr. Richards's thought at that time is plainly revealed in a passage like this:

You contrive not to laugh [in church]; but there is no doubt about the activity of the impulses in their restricted form. The much more subtle and elaborate impulses which a poem excites are not different in principle. *They do not show themselves as a rule, they do not come out into the open, largely because they are so complex.* [Italics mine.] When they have adjusted themselves to one another and become organized into a coherent whole, the needs concerned may be satisfied. *In a fully developed man a state of readiness for action will take the place of action when the full appropriate situation for action is not present.*[6] [Mr. Richards's italics.]

The mere state of readiness for action is the poetic experience in terms of value and relevance. The readiness points to the "direct apprehension" of an interest value in Mr. Morris's sense; but the failure of the action to come off, the lack of the "full appropriate situation for action," indicates the absence of a *denotatum*. We receive the designation of a value without being provided with a situation in which we can act upon it. The remarkable parallel between Mr. Richards's early theories of poetry and the recent theories of Mr. Morris need not detain us. It is enough to point out that Mr. Richards anticipated fifteen years ago everything that Mr. Morris's science of semiotic has to say about the language of poetry.

I have italicized a sentence, in the quotation from Mr. Richards, for two reasons: first, the vagueness of the language is significant; secondly, the idea of the coherent whole into which the "impulses" are organized has no experimental basis in terms of impulses. Mr. John Crowe Ransom remarks that Mr. Richards never shows us *how* this ordering act of poetry upon our minds takes place, and then proceeds to discern the reason for Mr. Richards's vague statements about the conduct of poetic stimulation and response:

Most readers will retort, of course, that in the very large majority of cases the spiritual happenings are the only happenings we have observed, and *the neural happenings are simply what the be-*

6 *Science and Poetry*, pp. 28–29.

haviorists would like to observe. [Italics mine.] At present the mental datum is the fact and the neural datum is the inference.[7]

In throwing out the mental fact Mr. Richards in his early writings preceded Mr. Morris in his rejection of the cognitive powers of the mind. I do not suggest any direct influence from Mr. Richards upon Mr. Morris, although Mr. Morris has acknowledged the work of his predecessor: it is easier to relate these men to a much wider movement. That movement is positivism, and it is more than a strict scientific method.

It is a general attitude towards experience. If it is not, why should Mr. Richards have attempted in his early criticism to represent the total poetic experience and even the structure of poetry in one of the positivist languages—experimental psychology? It was representation by analogy. The experimental basis for such a representation was wholly lacking. Mr. Richards, had we listened hard enough, was saying in *The Principles of Literary Criticism* and *Science and Poetry* that here at last is what poetry would be if we could only reduce it to the same laboratory technique that we use in psychology; and without warning to the unwary reader, whose credulity was already prepared by his own positivist *zeitgeist,* Mr. Richards went on to state "results" that looked like the results of an experiment; but the experiment had never been made. It had been inferred. The "impulses" that we feel in response to a poem, says Mr. Richards, "do not show themselves as a rule." There is no scientific evidence that they have ever shown themselves to Mr. Richards or to anybody else. Mr. Richards like a good positivist was the victim of a deep-seated compulsive analogy, an elusive but all-engrossing assumption that all experience

---

[7] "A Psychologist Looks at Poetry," *The World's Body,* p. 147. This essay is the most searching examination of Mr. Richards's position—or positions—that I have seen; but it does somewhat less than full justice to Mr. Richards's insights.

can be reduced to what is actually the very limited frame of reference supplied by a doctrine of correlation, or of the relevance of stimulus to response. This early procedure of Mr. Richards's was not even empiricism, for in empiricism the cognitive intelligence is not eliminated in the pursuit of verifiable facts. Mr. Richards, like Mr. Morris after him, eliminated cognition without demonstrating experimentally the *data* of his behavioristic poetics. So this doctrine was not empiricism: it came out of the demireligion of positivism. The poetry had been absorbed into a pseudo-scientific jargon, no more "relevant" to poetry than the poetic pseudo-statement was relevant to the world: the net result was zero from both points of view.

I have put this brief commentary on Mr. Richards's early poetics in the past tense because it is no longer his poetics. From 1926, the year of *Science and Poetry,* he has come a long way. It is perhaps not an extravagant claim to make for Mr. Richards's intellectual history, that it will probably turn out to be the most instructive, among critics, of our age. His great intellectual powers, his learning, his devotion to poetry—a devotion somewhat frustrated but as marked fifteen years ago as now—are qualities of an intellectual honesty rare in any age. In exactly ten years, from 1926, he arrived, in *The Philosophy of Rhetoric* (1936), at such a statement as this:

So far from verbal language being a "compromise for a language of intuition"—a thin, but better-than-nothing, substitute for real experience—language, well used, is a *completion* and does what the intuitions of sensation by themselves cannot do. Words are the meeting points at which regions of experience which can never combine in sensation or intuition, come together. They are the occasion and means of that growth which is the mind's endless endeavor to order itself. That is why we have language. *It is no mere signalling system.* [Italics mine.] It is the instrument of all our distinctively human development, of everything in which we go beyond the animals. [pp. 130–131.]

These words should be read and reread with the greatest care by critics who still cite the early Richards as the continuing head of a positivist tradition in criticism. There is, in this passage, first of all, an implicit repudiation of the leading doctrine of *The Principles of Literary Criticism*. The early doctrine did look upon poetic language as a "substitute for real experience," if by experience is meant responses relevant to scientifically ascertained facts and situations: this early doctrine, as I have indicated, anticipated in psychological terms Mr. Morris's poetic doctrine of designation without *denotatum*, of value without consummation of value, of interpretant without an interpreter. Mr. Richards's more familiar equivalents of the semiotic terms were: pseudo-statement without referents; poetry as the orderer of our minds, as the valuer, although the ordering mysteriously operated in fictions irrelevant to the real world; a response, a behavioristic "readiness for action," without a knowing mind.

Language, says Mr. Richards, "is no mere signalling system." With that sentence the early psychological doctrine is discreetly put away. Is it too much to assume that the adjective "signalling" may indicate the relation of Mr. Richards's present views to the pragmatic bias of Mr. Morris's aesthetics? He speaks of the inadequacy of "sensation" and "intuition," and of the equal inadequacy of "intuitions of sensation." Is not the mere sensation Mr. Morris's interpretant, the intuition of sensation his iconic sign? What is the "completion" which language "well used" can achieve beyond sensation and intuition?

It is doubtless knowledge of a kind that we can discuss only if we assume the action of a knowing mind. Of what is it the completion? In the paragraph following the passage that I have just quoted, Mr. Richards cites Coleridge:

Are not words parts and germinations of the plant? And what is the law of their growth? In something of this sort I would destroy the old antithesis of Words and Things: elevating, as it were, Words into Things and living things too.

This attribution to the language of poetry of a special kind of "life" goes back to Mr. Richards's *Coleridge on Imagination* (1935), the most ambitious attempt of a modern critic to force into unity the antithesis of language and subject, of pleasure and truth. It is an antithesis which, as we have seen, has harassed critical theory since the time of Coleridge. Mr. Richards's book may be looked upon as an effort to finish Coleridge's own uncompleted struggle with this neoclassical dilemma. This is not the place to describe the entire nature and scope of his effort, or to estimate it. A single chapter of the book, *The Wind Harp,* contains the clearest presentation of the antithesis that I have seen by a modern critic.

There are "two doctrines," he says, which have tended to flourish independently—"And yet, neither is intelligible, apart from Imagination." He continues:

The two doctrines can be stated as follows:

　1. The mind of the poet at moments . . . gains an insight into reality, reads Nature as a symbol of something behind or within Nature not ordinarily perceived.

　2. The mind of the poet creates a Nature into which his own feelings, his aspirations and apprehensions, are projected.

Now the positivist sciences have denied all validity to the first doctrine: as a proposition, in the many forms in which it may be stated, it is strictly meaningless. For the sole effective procedure towards nature is the positivist. The second doctrine is the standard poetics of our time: projection of feeling. The confusion and contradiction that we saw in Mr. Morris and in the early Richards came of trying to square a theory of interest value with a theory of emotional projection which was not firmly based upon positivist knowledge. That contradiction is the clue to the "unintelligibility" of the doctrines if held separately. If you take the first alone, eliminating the second, you eliminate the "mind," and you get pure positivism: in thus eliminating cognition you lose "everything in which we go beyond the animals." If you take the second alone, and eliminate the external world in any of the four meanings [8] that Mr. Richards gives to the phrase, you have a knowing mind without anything that it can know.

Before the development of the positivist procedures towards nature, the pressure of this dilemma was not seriously felt. We have seen in Matthew Arnold (the determined anti-dialectician) the belief that the subject is external to the language—a merely common-sense view inherited from neo-classical theory. The poetic subject was the world of ordinary experience; but as soon as the subject—Nature—became the field of positivism, the language of poetry ceased to represent it; ceased, in fact, to have any validity, or to set forth anything real. (The world of positivism is a world without minds to know the world; and yet Mr. Morris does not hesitate to assert that his Unified Science will save the world. For whom will it be saved?)

What is this Imagination which Mr. Richards says will make the two doctrines intelligible? No doubt it becomes in his hands something different from Coleridge's conception of it: it closely resembles an Hegelian synthesis, which joins the opposites in a new proposition in which their truths, no longer contradictory, are preserved.

They are [says Mr. Richards of the two doctrines] neither consequences of *a priori* decisions, nor verifiable as the empirical statements of science are verifiable; and all verifiable statements are independent of them. But this does not diminish in the least their interest, or that of the other senses in which they may be true.

With that we are almost ready to leave Mr. Richards, who offers no final solution of the problem of the unified imagination. "It is the privilege of poetry," he says finely, "to preserve us from mistaking our notions either for things or for

[8] *Coleridge on Imagination*, pp. 157–8.

ourselves. *Poetry is the completest mode of utterance."* [9] It is
neither the world of verifiable science nor a projection of
ourselves; yet it is *complete*. And because it is complete
knowledge we may, I think, claim for it a unique kind of
responsibility, and see in it at times an irresponsibility
equally distinct. The order of completeness that it achieves
in the great works of the imagination is not the order of
experimental completeness aimed at by the positivist sciences, whose responsibility is directed towards the verifica-
tion of limited techniques. The completeness of science is
an abstraction covering an ideal of cooperation among specialized methods. No one can have an experience of science,
or of a single science. For the completeness of *Hamlet* is not
of the experimental order, but of the experienced order: it
is, in short, of the mythical order. And here Mr. Richards
can give us a final insight. Myths, he says,

. . . are no amusement or diversion to be sought as a relaxation
and an escape from the hard realities of life. They are these hard
realities in projection, their symbolic recognition, co-ordination
and acceptance. . . . The opposite and discordant qualities in
things in them acquire a form. . . . Without his mythologies
man is only a cruel animal without a soul . . . a congeries of
possibilities without order and aim.[10]

Man, without his mythologies, is an interpretant. Mr.
Richards's books may be seen together as a parable, as a
mythical and dramatic projection, of the failure of the modern mind to understand poetry on the assumptions underlying the demireligion of positivism. We do not need to
reject the positive and rational mode of inquiry into poetry;
yet even from Mr. Morris we get the warning lest we substitute the criticism for the poem, and thus commit ourselves to a "learned ignorance." We must return to, we must

9 *Ibid.*, p. 163.
10 *Ibid.*, pp. 171–2.

never leave, the poem itself. Its "interest" value is a cognitive one; it is sufficient that here, in the poem, we get knowledge of a whole object. If rational inquiry is the only mode of criticism, we must yet remember that the way we employ that mode must always powerfully affect our experience of the poem. I have been concerned in this commentary with the compulsive, almost obsessed, application of an all-engrossing principle of pragmatic reduction to a formed realm of our experience, the distinction of which is its complete knowledge, the full body of the experience that it offers us. However we may see the completeness of poetry, it is a problem less to be solved than, in its full import, to be preserved.

1941

The Hovering Fly[1]

A Causerie on the Imagination and the Actual World

I

OF THE THREE great novels of Dostoevsky *The Idiot* has perhaps the simplest structure. In the center of the action there are only three characters. The development of the plot is almost exclusively "scenic" or dramatic; that is to say, a succession of scenes with episodic climaxes leads, with more than Dostoevsky's usual certainty of control, to the catastrophe at the end. There is very little summary or commentary by the author; here and there a brief lapse of time is explained, or there is a "constatation," a pause in the action in which the author assumes the omniscient view and reminds us of the position and plight of the other characters, who are complicating the problem of the hero. I emphasize here the prevailing scenic method because at the catastrophe the resolution of the dramatic forces is not a statement about life, or even about the life that we have seen in this novel: the resolution is managed by means of that most difficult of all feats, a narrow scene brought close up, in which the "meaning" of the action is conveyed in a dramatic visualization so immediate and intense that it cre-

[1] This essay was read as one of the Mesures Lectures at Princeton University, on April 8, 1943. The general subject of the series was "The Imagination and the Actual World."

ates its own symbolism. And it is the particular symbolism of the fly in the final scene of *The Idiot* which has provided the springboard, or let us say the catapult, that will send us off into the unknown regions of "actuality," into which we have received orders to advance.

What is *The Idiot* about? In what I have said so far I have purposely evaded any description of the novel; I have not tried to distinguish the experience which it offers, a kind of experience that might start a wholly different train of speculation upon actuality from that which will be our special concern in these notes. But now, before we get into the last scene, where the three main characters find themselves in a dark room, alone for the first time, we must drop them, and go a long way round and perhaps lose our way on a road that has no signs at the forks to tell us which turn to take.

II

When we say poetry *and* something else—poetry and science, poetry and morality, or even poetry and mathematics—it makes little difference in dialectical difficulty what the coordinate field may be: all problems are equally hard and in the end they are much the same. The problem that I shall skirt around in these notes is a very old one, going back to the first records of critical self-consciousness. Aristotle was aware of it when he said that poetry is more philosophical than history. Although the same quagmire awaits us from whatever direction we come upon it, the direction itself and the way we tumble into the mud remain very important. Perhaps the crucial value of the critical activity— given the value of the directing mind, a factor that "systematic" criticism cannot find—will be set up or cast down by the kind of tact that we can muster for the "approach," a word that holds out to us a clue.

Armies used to besiege towns by "regular approaches"; or they took them by direct assault; or they maneuvered the enemy out of position, perhaps into ambuscade. These strategies are used today, for in war as in criticism the new is usually merely a new name for something very old. When Caesar laid waste the country he was using a grand tactics that we have recently given a new name: infiltration, or the tactics of getting effectively into the enemy's rear. When you have total war must you also have total criticism? In our time critics are supposed to know everything, and we get criticism on all fronts. Does this not outmode the direct assault? When there are so many "problems" (a term equally critical and military) you have got to do a little here and a little there, and you may not be of the command that enters the suburbs of Berlin.

At any rate the world outside poetry, which continues to disregard the extent that it is also *in* poetry, resists and eludes our best understanding. When and why did it begin to behave in this way? When we had the Truce of God for three days a week, we attacked, with a great deal of military rhetoric and pageantry, the enemy, on the fourth day, and the attack was a frontal assault; both sides knew the rules. But we do not know them. And in the critical manual of war there has been nothing comparable to the rules since Arnold's doctrine of the "criticism of life" could still engage the non- or antipoetic forces of the world head on.

But suppose there isn't an enemy? Suppose the war figure is misleading? Henry James (one of the great critics) wrote to Stevenson in 1891 that "No theory is kind to us that cheats us of seeing." What did he mean? In this instance he meant Stevenson's refusal to visualize his scene. "It struck me," says James, "that you either didn't feel—through some accident—your responsibility on this article quite enough; or, on some theory of your own, had declined it." We know that Stevenson did have a theory that made him generalize his scenes.

It is not necessary to find out here what Stevenson missed,

or what, missing that, he did actually succeed in seeing. Every imaginative writer has a theory, whether he recognize it or not; it may operate for him at some dynamic level where it can liberate all that writer's power; but in so far as it participates in the exclusive nature of theory, it must entail upon some phase of his work very great risks, even perils. "Thus Hardy," says William Empson, "is fond of showing us an unusually stupid person subjected to very unusually bad luck, and then a moral is drawn, not merely by inference but by solemn assertion, that we are all in the same boat as this person whose story is striking precisely because it is unusual." The "solemn assertion" in Hardy and in many other writers, critics no less than novelists and poets, must always either limit or somehow illegitimately extend what the writer has actually seen.

What I want to end these beginning remarks with is an observation that has been too little acknowledged. The art of criticism must inevitably partake of the arts on which it lives, and in a very special and niggling way. I refer to the "approach," the direction of attack, the strategy; and in terms of the strategy of this occasion, I mean the "point of view," as Percy Lubbock understands that phrase when he tells us that very nearly the whole art of fiction is in it. From what position shall the critic, who is convinced that the total view is no view at all, the critic not being God, and convinced too that even if (which is impossible) he sees everything, he has got to see it from somewhere, like the painter Philippoteaux who placed himself under a tree in his picture of the Battle of Gettysburg to warn you that what you see is only what he sees, under that tree: under what tree, then, or from what hill, or under what log or leaf, shall the critic take his stand, which may be less than an heroic stand, to report what he sees, infers, or merely guesses? Merely to ask this question is enough to indicate something of the post which I am trying to find and hold.

You may locate it far to the sinister side of the line which divides the arts and the sciences. Even if this spectator succeeds in holding his ground, you may be sure that he will not be able to give you a scientific report.

III

Suppose we take two terms and relate them. The two terms for this occasion are, first, Poetry, and, second, the Actual World. Do we mean then by the actual world a world distinguished from one which is less actual or not actual at all? I suppose we mean both things; else we should say: Poetry and the World. We might again alter the phrase and get: Poetry and Actuality, which by omitting the world would give us a clue to its bearing in the preceding phrase; that is, world might then mean region, realm, field of observation or experience. So I take it that the bearing of the phrase "actual world" is towards something outside us, something objective, whose actuality is somehow an empirical one which tends to look after its own affairs without consulting us, and even at times resisting whatever it is in us which we like to call by names like subjective, private, human as opposed to nonhuman, although even the human and the subjective lie ready for objective scrutiny if we change our vantage point and let them stand opposite us rather than let them oppose a third thing, a world, beyond them. It is, in fact, no mere quibble of idealism if we decide to call this subjective field not only the world but the actual world, taking our stand on the assumption that it sufficiently reflects or gathers in or contains all that we can ever know of any other world or worlds that appear to lie beyond it.

Are we prepared to take this stand? Perhaps we are if we are philosophers of a certain logical stubbornness; but as poets our zeal for subjectivism might seem to be good only

at times, at certain places and moments. And are we, here
in this kind of enquiry, either philosophers or poets? To ask
that question is to diminish or perhaps to reduce to zero any
degree of confidence that we may have enjoyed in trying
to sort out, however provisionally, some of the bearings of
our phrase "actual world." When we are sorting them out
are we outside them, or inside, or partly inside and partly
outside?

If we go back for another glimpse of a suggestion that I
merely threw down at the outset of this discussion, we shall
drop to a degree somewhere below zero in our confidence of
certainty in this enquiry. From what position is the critic
looking at the object of his enquiry? That was our suggestion,
but we have now identified the critic's object as the actual
world, whatever that is, as that world is related to poetry,
whatever that is.

If I seem to be making this matter obscure, let me plead
my ignorance, and if you will, add your own ignorance to my
plea; or if you like it better, add your skepticism to mine;
and we shall examine together our riddle, so far as we can,
as if nobody had seen it before: which, I take it, is the
action of skepticism as distinguished from the mere feeling of the skeptic.

I suppose the easiest and, for all I know, the best way to
establish our post of observation to look at the actual world,
under our given condition, is to look at it through poetry.
But here again we encounter difficulties as harassing as those
we almost had to give up when we plumped ourselves down
into the actual world. Even if we knew what poetry is, we
should have to find it in particular poetic works: you see in
that abstract phrase—"particular poetic works"—how difficult it is to face the paralyzing simplicity of our problem at
this stage. We should have to find poetry in poems. Does
not that make it look easier? It does, until we remember that

even the man who may have read five thousand poems, an anthologist, for example, could lay claim to real mastery of not more than a few hundred.

What, then, is poetry? The innocence of the question ought to excuse it. Were we German idealists of the past century, or their disciples of today, we might easily begin poetry with a capital P, and putting initial capitals before actual and world, start Poetry and the Actual World off on their historic merry-go-round; or perhaps Poetry could pursue the Actual World as the Lord, in the Gullah sermon, chased Adam and Eve "round and round dat Gyarden, round and round"; or again there are the standard clowns in the bestiary of the animated cartoon that chase each other's tail until at last all that is left on the screen is a whirling vortex. Any of these similes will do that testify to our helplessness before the fenced-in apriorism of the merely philosophical approach: its conclusions are impressive and are usually stated at length, but I have never seen one of them that increased my understanding of the XXVIIIth Canto of the *Paradiso,* or even of "Locksley Hall."

But if we cannot say philosophically what poetry is, or even how it functions, how shall we know from any point of view what post of observation we are taking when we decide to look at the actual world through poetry? From now on this is what I shall be trying to get at. We shall certainly not be looking on as a spectator who has no stake in the scene; and yet to say that as a man who has written verse I have a special tact which will lead me to the right hill and turn my eyes in the right direction smacks a little of our national reliance upon expert testimony. For even if a poet, some other poet, seems in his verse to have given us flashes of what we may provisionally call actuality, he is not, as he talks about poetry, inside his verse, but outside it; and his report is as much under the obligation to make good as yours.

I V

I am sorry to introduce another complication before we go further. I must introduce a broader term, and the broader term usually lifts the spirits for a brief span, until somebody reminds us that it may be an evasion of the harder distinctions enjoined by the narrower term. The broader term is Imagination. If we say that we are trying to discover the relation between the Imagination and the Actual World, we find ready to run to our aid a host of comforting saws that could easily turn this vacillating discourse into an oration—and may actually do so before we are done. The Imagination is superior to Reality. Imagination is the rudder, Fancy the sails. Imagination is the esemplastic power. There are others as good, perhaps even better; and I do not deny the probability that before I am through I shall have spoken in substance one of these doctrines.

Yet I have brought in the Imagination for a more empirical reason. The great prose dramatists and novelists are makers and thus poets, and they give us something that is coherent and moving about human life which partakes of actuality but which is not actuality as it is reported to me by my senses as I look about me at a given moment. How does their report differ from mine? How does it differ from the report of the poet who writes, either lyrically or dramatically, in verse? Perhaps we had better take the risk and decide that the two reports seem to differ, verse being the occasion of the difference but not its explanation; and yet bearing in mind a few of the examples and comparisons which I shall produce or refer to in a few minutes, I make a large reservation about a categorical difference between the imagination in prose and the imagination in verse: Whether verse be expressive or formal in its function, it nevertheless becomes a sort of medium through which the poet may convey a deeper and wider heterogeneity of material than the prose vehicle will ordinarily carry. My reservation about this difference simply acknowledges the probability that it may be only a difference of degree, of intensity, of scope, with respect to the material; or if it is a real distinction, it cannot be said to hold all the time, but only as a rule. I admire, for example, the late Robert Bridges's poetry, but I see in it a failure or, if you will, a refusal to go all the way for as much of the richness of image as his magnificent control of verse-technique would have justified. On the other hand, if you will recall the cutting up of the whale in *Moby Dick* you will see at once the long reach of a prose style that is probably richer and more fluent than any verse style of its century, and far more dynamic than the style of *Dawn in Britain,* which perhaps alone in nineteenth-century poetry equals *Moby Dick* in rhetorical ambition. Bridges and Melville, then, might be seen as the exceptions in their respective mediums; and yet, in order to see them that way, we should have to establish a middle point at which the prose imagination and the verse imagination pass each other on the way to their proper extremes; and no such point exists except in books on the differential calculus.

But if we look at this matter empirically, not claiming too much for any differences or for our more confident distinctions, we may succeed in taking up an attitude towards a very real problem; for I take it that nobody denies the value of what seems to go on in sound works of the imagination. In what respects does this value belong to an actual world? In that spirit, we may phrase the question more narrowly, even finically, and ask it in terms of motion or process, or as Mr. Kenneth Burke would have it, of drama. In what ways, then, does an actual world *get into* the imagination?

Thus I turn to another line of speculation, with an observation that ought to arrest some of the vacillation of my opening trial flights, and at the same time fix our point of view. If we think of the actual world as either a dead lump or a whirling wind somewhere outside us, against which we bump our heads or which whirls us around, we shall never be able to discover it: we have got to try to find it in terms of one of our chief interests. Let us call that interest the imagination.

V

There is now raging in one of our best journals a controversy about a human crisis which the editors of that journal call "The Failure of Nerve." [2] The full implications of the controversy are irrelevant to the end of my discussion; yet there is one issue, perhaps the central issue, of that controversy which may instruct us, or at any rate prepare us for what follows. Professors Dewey, Hook, and Nagel are anxious and at moments even a little angry about the disorderly rebirth of certain beliefs about man that tend to reject scientific positivism and the reliance upon what they, in their tradition of thought, are pleased to call reason. The answers to these challenging blasts are scarcely developed; the editors of *Partisan Review* have so far relegated them to their correspondence columns; and I do not know whether or not there will be more considered replies. As an old antipositivist I cannot do less than to point out a standard objection to the positivist program, reminding its adherents that our supposed "failure of nerve" might actually turn out to be the positivists' failure to allow for all that our nerve ends are capable of taking in.

The positivist program for the complete government of man may perhaps be a form of what Scott Buchanan has called "occultation," a term that I should apply to positivism somewhat as follows: Positivism offers us a single field of discourse which may be briefly labeled as physicalism; and it pretends that this is the sole field of discourse, all the others being illusion, priestcraft, superstition, or even Nazism. Now as this single field of discourse is directed towards works of the imagination, it carries with it a certain test of validity, which is usually the semantical test; and I hold that when this test becomes the pragmatic test and usurps the business of other tests, from other fields of discourse, pretending to be the sole test, it is performing an act of occultation upon these tests—a hiding away, an ascription of dark motives, even an imputation of black art.

Is there failure of nerve in a recognition of the failure of positivism even at its subtlest level to deliver all the goods? Are men the victims of a failure of nerve if, standing on a precipice from which there is no retreat, they prepare to make the best jump possible, and refuse to mumble to themselves that their fall will only exemplify the laws of gravity? There is no doubt that the fall will offer this confirmation of positivism; for positivism is a highly efficient technique of our physical necessities; it is the creation of the practical reason which organizes our physical economy, without which we cannot live. But under the rule of a positivism which has become a group of self-sufficient sciences, the organization has grown exclusive. What is it that is excluded? What is *occulted?*

There are two answers to this question which are two ways of giving the same answer. But before I try to give this single-double answer I ought to say that my purpose here is not to berate the sciences but only the positivist religion of scientists. I am even more concerned with what it leaves out, or at least to "point" towards that omitted thing, as one nods in the direction of a good landscape which one might have missed, driving by it at seventy miles an hour.

What is excluded, what is occulted? First, the actual world; second, Dostoevsky's hovering fly: I shall be saying presently that in terms of the dramatic imagination the world and the fly are the same thing. Our skepticism—and as I say it I have my own doubt—our doubt of this identification proceeds from what we ordinarily call our common sense, a good thing to have, but not good enough if it is all we have. Let me put the matter somewhat differently. We may *look* at the hovering fly; we can to a degree *know* the actual world. But we shall not know the actual world by looking at it; we know it by looking at the hovering fly.

I am sorry that this sounds a little gnomic; and it is time to remember James's remark again: No theory is kind to us that cheats us of seeing. But it is also time to amend James: No theory is kind to us that cheats us of seeing what path we ought to be on. What is our path? When we do not know, we may get a vision, and then hope that all visions appear on the road to Damascus. Before we may build our hope so high we had better confront Pascal: "We run carelessly to the precipice, after we have put something before us to prevent us seeing it."

V I

The fly appears out of nowhere in the last scene in *The Idiot:* out of nowhere, but only if we limit our apperception of place to the scale of the human will. There are, as I have said, three persons in the scene, but one of them is dead, and her place is taken by the hovering fly. Nastasya Filippovna has appeared less directly in the action than other women characters of the story; but she is the heroine, for it is she who creates for the hero his insoluble problem. She is a beautiful and gifted orphan of good family who has been seduced by her guardian, a libertine of high political and social connections at the court. There is Rogozhin, who, as the story opens, has just inherited a fortune; he is in love with Nastasya and he offers her the worldly solution of money and marriage, a solution that she will not accept; and it is he, of course, who murders her at the end, since in no other way may he possess her. From the beginning Prince

Myshkin, our hero, has been in his special way in love with Nastasya. He is the "idiot," the man whom epilepsy has removed from the world of action. I am not prepared to add to our critical knowledge of Myshkin. He has a marvelous detachment and receptivity, and a profundity of insight into human motives which I believe nobody but Dostoevsky has ever succeeded so perfectly in rendering dramatically. (It is always easy for the novelist to *say* that a character is profound; it is quite another matter to dramatize the profundity, to make it *act*.) Nastasya's agony of guilt, the conviction of sin, mirrors an almost Christ-like perception of the same potentialities on the part of Myshkin; and it is Nastasya who creates Myshkin's problem. Nastasya is tortured by those oscillating extremes, personal degradation and nobility of motive; and Myshkin alone in his world knows that she is not a "bad woman." But she will not marry Myshkin either. Marriage to Myshkin would be the symbolic signal that the pressure of her conflict had abated, and that Myshkin's problem had found solution in Nastasya's solution of her own. She cannot marry Rogozhin because she is too noble; she cannot marry Myshkin because she is too degraded. Thus we get in Rogozhin's murder of Nastasya the deeply immoral implications of Rogozhin's character, and the dramatically just irony of the good in her being destroyed by the lover who was indifferent to it. When the murder is done, Myshkin feels no resentment: he can accept that too. The lovers stand over the dead body of the murdered girl:

[Myshkin's] eyes were by now accustomed to the darkness, so that he could make out the whole bed. Someone lay asleep on it, in a perfectly motionless sleep; not the faintest stir, not the faintest breath could be heard. The sleeper was covered over from head to foot with a white sheet and the limbs were vaguely defined; all that could be seen was that a human figure lay there, stretched at full length. All around in disorder at the foot of the bed, on chairs beside it, and even on the floor, clothes had been flung; a rich white silk dress, flowers, and ribbons. On a little table at the head of the bed there was the glitter of diamonds that had been taken off and thrown down. At the end of the bed there was a crumpled heap of lace and on the white lace the toes of a bare foot peeped out from under the sheet; it seemed as though it had been carved out of marble and it was horribly still. Myshkin looked and felt that as he looked, the room became more and more still and death-like. Suddenly there was the buzz of a fly which flew over the bed and settled on the pillow.

I assume that the minimum of exposition is necessary; it is one of the great and famous scenes of modern literature; and I hope that seeing it again you recalled the immense drama preceding it and informing it and stretching the tensions which are here let down, eased, and resolved for us. I am not sure that the power of the scene would be diminished by the absence of the fly; but at any rate it is there; and its buzz rises like a hurricane in that silent room, until, for me, the room is filled with audible silence. The fly comes to stand in its sinister and abundant life for the privation of life, the body of the young woman on the bed. Here we have one of those conversions of image of which only great literary talent is capable: life stands for death, but it is a wholly different order of life, and one that impinges upon the human order only in its capacity of scavenger, a necessity of its biological situation which in itself must be seen as neutral or even innocent. Any sinister significance that the fly may create for us is entirely due to its crossing our own path: by means of the fly the human order is compromised. But it is also extended, until through a series of similar conversions and correspondences of image the buzz of the fly distends, both visually and metaphorically, the body of the girl into the world. Her degradation and nobility are in that image. Shall we call it the actual world?

Or is there another adjective that we could apply to this world? There doubtless is; but I cannot, for my purpose, find it short of an adjectival essay, which this essay largely is, of another sort. With some propriety we might call it *an* actual world, which resembles other worlds equally actual, like Dante's or some of Shakespeare's, in its own final completeness, its coherence, depth, perspective. Yet I suspect that this side of the very great men we seldom get magnitude with actuality. We get magnitude in Thackeray and actuality in James; but not both in either. We get both in Tolstoy; but I take it that we accept his magnitude because it is actual, not because it is large. Thackeray's hurly-burly over the Battle of Waterloo is pleasant, empty, and immemorable; Prince André lying wounded under the infinite sky is all the world so lying; and we suspect that Tolstoy's magnitude is only a vast accumulation of little actualities—young Rostov on his horse at the bridgehead, the "little uncle" serving tea to the young people, Natasha weeping over Anatol in her room.

Whither do these casual allusions take us? They might take us far, on some other occasion, at a time when we had the heart for the consideration of actual worlds. But now we are in an occult world, from which actualities, which in their nature are quiet and permanent, are hard to find. As we face the morning's world we see nothing, unless we have the peculiar though intermittent talent for it, so actual as Dostoevsky's fly or Prince André's empty heavens. For if the drift of this essay have anything of truth in it, then our daily suffering, our best will towards the world in which we with difficulty breathe today, and our secret anxieties, however painful these experiences may be, must have something of the occult, something of the private, even something of the willful and obtuse, unless by a miracle of gift or character, and perhaps of history also, we command the imaginative power of the relation of things.

VII

It is a gift that comes and goes; its story is so long that neither time nor understanding has permitted me to tell it here. Yet I think that the risk, the extreme risk that I have so far faced, of some general commitments concerning the function of the imagination as a black art will be worth taking, if only to challenge a fierce denial. It ought to be plain to us, who share a common experience of two conflicts in a single war and who continue to wonder at the ingenious failure of our time, that although human powers are by no means depleted, something has gone wrong with their direction. No man but acknowledges this commonplace; yet how shall we imbed it, ground it, in some conceivable knowledge of the actuality of a world?

It must be plain also that the very instruments of our daily economy have more and more dictated our ends, or at best have suggested to an obscure power within us how we shall conduct our lives. The possibilities latent in our situation must make us falter. The obscure power within us we have made into an occult power; we are no longer conscious of its limits, its function, its purposes. Is that not the meaning of an occult power? One that we sway under but cannot know?

Here again I come up against formidable hazards, and I feel as if I had gone round the flank only to lose direction and to be cut off; but these perils will be plain enough although I shall not describe them. This occult power that seems to overwhelm us must, in times past, have enjoyed the fullness of light; but even underground it will not be gainsaid. If it does not have the privilege of its rational place in the order of human experience, it will take irrational toll of that order. Human violence is an historical constant; yet how shall we come to terms with a violence that is rationally implemented, an efficient, a total violence? It seems to me that the answer of our time to this problem is at present the historical answer of the dead end, of the stalemate, of the facile optimism of decay. In a time like ours you may be sure of this: that men will be easy and hopeful, and will try a little of the medicine of the bridge expert along with the elixirs of the innumerable Gerald Heards. Why? Because, although historically man may be a social being before he is a religious being, he is, after he achieves society, primarily religious, and remains incurably so. If he is told that mere "operational techniques" will see him through, whether these are put to work in society, or in the laboratory, or in industry, or in the arts, he may believe it for a while, and try to realize it; but like a child after the game is over and the fingers are uncrossed, he will return to the real world, unprepared and soon to be overwhelmed by it because he has been told that the real world does not exist.

Or perhaps you would prefer to call it merely another world, after the analogy of *an* actual world; not *the* other world and *the* actual world. For there must be a great many of these worlds, all actual, all to be participated in, all participating in us; yet I prefer the frank Platonism of *the* actual world, as Socrates himself preferred it when he told Ion that "poetry is one." And the impulse to reality which drives us through the engrossing image to the rational knowledge of our experience which, without that image, is mere process, must also be one. Once more the professed skeptic of thirty minutes ago reaches an immoderate deduction beyond any preparation that he has been able to ground it in.

For I should be chagrined could I feel that I have carried you, as well as myself, beyond known depths: are we not committed to the affirmation that actuality and poetry are respectively and even reciprocally one? If we are so committed, we must not affirm otherwise of humanity, which has been one from the beginning. And we cannot allow any novelty to our attempted insights.

Are we not saying something very old when we assert that we may know an actual world in the act of seeing the hovering fly? We are saying that our minds move through three necessities which, when in proper harmony and relation, achieve a dynamic and precarious unity of experience.

Now that our oration is over I may say quite plainly that the three necessities—necessities at any rate for Western man— are the three liberal arts. And any one of them practiced to the exclusion of the others retires a portion of our experience into the shadows of the occult, the contingent, the uncontrolled. The grammarians of the modern world have allowed their specialization, the operational technique, to drive the two other arts to cover, whence they break forth in their own furies, the one the fury of irresponsible abstraction, the other the fury of irresponsible rhetoric. The philosopher serves the operational technique, whether in the laboratory or on the battlefield. The poet—and the poet is the rhetorician, the specialist in symbol—serves the operational technique because, being the simplest mind of his trinity, his instinct is to follow and to be near his fellow men.

In a last glance at the last scene of *The Idiot* let us imagine that Myshkin and Rogozhin do not appear. The body of Nastasya Filippovna lies indefinitely upon the narrow bed, the white toe exposed, the fly intermittently rising and falling over the corpse. The dead woman and the fly are a *locus* of the process of decomposition. But, of course, we cannot imagine it, unless like a modern positivist we can imagine ourselves out of our humanity; for to imagine the scene is to be there, and to be there, before the sheeted bed, is to have our own interests powerfully affected. The fiction that we are neither here nor there, but are only spectators who, by becoming, ourselves, objects of grammatical analysis, can arrive at some other actuality than that of process, is the great modern heresy: we can never be mere spectators, or if we can for a little time we shall probably, a few of us only, remain, until there is one man left, like a solitary carp in a pond, who has devoured all the others.

1943

Techniques of Fiction

THERE MUST BE many techniques of fiction, but how many? I suppose a great many more than there are techniques of poetry. Why this should be so, if it is, nobody quite knows, and if we knew, I do not know what use the knowledge would have. For the great disadvantage of all literary criticism is its practical ignorance, which in the very nature of its aims must be incurable. Even the aims of criticism are unknown, beyond very short views; for example, in the criticism of the novel, Mr. Percy Lubbock tells us that the secret of the art is the strategy of "point of view"; Mr. E. M. Forster that the novelist must simply give us "life," or the illusion of "bouncing" us through it—which looks like a broader view than Mr. Lubbock's, until we pause to examine it, when it turns out to be worse than narrow, since to look at everything is to see nothing; or again Mr. Edwin Muir holds that "structure" is the key to the novelist's success or failure. There is no need here to explain what these critics mean by "point of view," or "life," or "structure"; but they all mean something useful—in a short view, beyond which (I repeat) critics seem to know little or nothing.

What the novelists know may be another thing altogether, and it is that knowledge which ought to be our deepest concern. You will have to allow me the paradox of presuming to know what the novelists know—or some of them at any rate—while as a critic I profess to know nothing. The presumption might encourage us to predict from the very nature of the critic's ignorance the nature and quality of the knowledge possible to good writers of fiction. The novelist keeps before him constantly the structure and substance of his fiction as a whole, to a degree to which the critic can never apprehend it. For the first cause of critical ignorance is, of course, the limitations of our minds, about which we can do little, work at them as we will. It is the special ignorance by which we, as critics, are limited in the act of reading any extended work of the imagination. The imaginative work must always differ to such a great degree as almost to differ in kind from philosophical works, which our minds apprehend and retain almost as wholes through the logical and deductive structures which powerfully aid the memory. Who can remember, well enough to pronounce upon it critically, all of *War and Peace,* or *The Wings of the Dove,* or even *Death in Venice,* the small enclosed world of which ought at least to do something to aid our memories? I have reread all three of these books in the past year; yet for the life of me I could not pretend to know them as wholes, and without that knowledge I lack the materials of criticism.

Because Mr. Lubbock seems to know more than anybody else about this necessary ignorance of the critic, and for other important reasons, I believe him to be the best critic who has ever written about the novel. His book, *The Craft of Fiction,* is very nearly a model of critical procedure. Even in so fine a study as Albert Thibaudet's *Gustave Flaubert* there is nothing like the actual, as opposed to the merely professed, critical modesty of numerous statements like this by Lubbock: "Our critical faculty may be admirable; we may be thoroughly capable of judging a book justly, if only we could watch it at ease. But fine taste and keen perception are of no use to us if we cannot retain the image of the book; and the image escapes and evades us like a cloud." Where, then, does Lubbock get the material of his criticism? He gets as much of it as any critic ever gets by means of a bias which he constantly pushes in the direction of extreme simplification of the novel in terms of "form," or "point of view" (after James's more famous phrase, the "post of observation"), or more generally in terms of the controlling intelligence which determines the range and quality of the scene and the action. It is the only book on fiction which has earned unanimous dislike among other critics (I do not know three novelists who have read it), and the reason, I think, is that it is, in its limited terms, wholly successful; or, if that is too great praise, it is successful in the same sense, and to no less degree than the famous lecture notes on the Greek drama taken down by an anonymous student at the Lyceum in the fourth century B.C. The lecture notes and *The Craft of Fiction* are studies of their respective arts in terms of form; and I think that Lubbock had incomparably the more difficult job to do. The novel has at no time enjoyed anything like the number and the intensity of objective conventions which the drama, even in its comparatively formless periods, has offered to the critic. The number of techniques possible in the novel are probably as many as its conventions are few.

Having said so much in praise of Mr. Lubbock, I shall not, I hope, seem to take it back if I say that even his intense awareness of what the novelist knows fails somehow, or perhaps inevitably, to get into his criticism. Anybody who has just read his account of *Madame Bovary* comes away with a sense of loss, which is the more intense if he has also just read that novel; though what the loss is he no more than Mr. Lubbock will be able to say. Yet no critic has ever turned so many different lights, from so many different directions, upon any other novel (except perhaps the lights that are called today the social and the historical); and yet what we get is not properly a revelation of the techniques of *Madame Bovary* but rather what I should call a marvelously astute chart of the operations of the central intelligence which

binds all the little pieces of drama together into the pictorial
biography of a silly, sad, and hysterical little woman, Emma
Bovary. It is this single interest, this undeviating pursuit of
one great clue, this sticking to the "short view" till the last
horn blows and night settles upon the hunting field, which
largely explains both the greatness of Mr. Lubbock's book
and the necessary and radical ignorance of criticism. We
cannot be both broad and critical, except in so far as knowledge of the world, of ideas, and of man generally is broadening; but then that knowledge has nothing to do specifically
with the critical job; it only keeps it from being inhuman.
That is something; but it is not criticism. To be critical is to
be narrow in the crucial act or process of judgment.

But after we gather up all the short views of good critics,
and have set the limits to their various ignorances, we are
confronted with what is left out or, if you will, left over:
I have a strong suspicion that this residue of the novel or
the story is what the author knew as he wrote it. It is what
makes the little scenes, or even the big ones, "come off." And
while we no doubt learn a great deal about them when,
with Mr. Muir, we study the general structure, or the relation of scenes, or, with Mr. Lubbock, follow the godlike
control of the mind of Flaubert or of James through all the
scenes to the climax—while this knowledge is indispensable,
I should, myself, like to know more about the making of the
single scene, and all the techniques that contribute to it; and
I suspect that I am not asking the impossible, for this kind
of knowledge is very likely the only kind that is actually
within our range. It alone can be got at, definitely and at
particular moments, even after we have failed, with Mr.
Lubbock (honorable failure indeed), to "retain the image of
the book."

It sounds very simple, as no doubt it is essentially a simple
task to take a scene from a novel apart, and to see what
makes it tick; but how to do it must baffle our best inten-

tions. Suppose you want to understand by what arts Tolstoy, near the beginning of *War and Peace,* before the ground is laid, brings Peter, the bastard son of old Count Bezuhov, into the old Count's dying presence, and makes, of the atmosphere of the house and of the young man and the old man, both hitherto unknown to us, one of the great scenes of fiction: you would scarcely know better than I where to take hold of it, and I have only the merest clue. Suppose you feel, as I do, that after Rawdon Crawley comes home (I believe from jail—it is hard to remember Thackeray) and finds Becky supping alone with Lord Steyne—suppose you feel that Thackeray should not have rung down the curtain the very moment Becky's exposure was achieved, but should have faced up to the tougher job of showing us Becky and Rawdon alone after Lord Steyne had departed: is this a failure in a great novelist? If it is, why? The negative question, addressed to ourselves as persons interested in the techniques of an art, may also lead us to what the novelists know, or to much the same thing, what they should have known. And, to come nearer home, what is the matter with Ty Ty Walden's philosophical meditations, towards the end of *God's Little Acre,* which freezes up our credulity and provokes our fiercest denial? It is surely not that Ty Ty is merely expressing as well as he can the doctrine of the innate goodness of man in the midst of depravity. That doctrine will do as well as any other in the mouth of a fictional character provided his scene and his experience within the scene entitle him to utter it; but before we can believe that Ty Ty is actually thinking anything whatever, we have got in the first place to believe that Ty Ty is a man —which is precisely what Mr. Caldwell evidently did not think it important to make us do.

How shall we learn what to say about particular effects of the story, without which the great over-all structure and movement of the human experience which is the entire novel cannot be made credible to us? The professional critics pause only at intervals to descend to these minor effects which are of course the problems without which the other, more portentous problems which engage criticism could not exist. The fine artists of fiction, I repeat, because they produce these effects must understand them. And having produced them, they are silent about the ways they took to produce them, or paradoxical and mysterious like Flaubert, who told Maupassant to go to the station and look at the cab drivers until he understood the typical cab driver, and then to find the language to distinguish one cab driver from all others in the world. It is the sort of *obiter dicta* which can found schools and movements, and the schools and movements often come to some good, even though the slogan, like this one, means little.

I suppose only the better novelists, like Defoe, Madame de La Fayette, Turgenev, Dickens, Flaubert, many others as great as these, some greater, like Tolstoy and Dostoevsky, knew the special secrets which I am trying, outside criticism, so to speak, to bring before you. There is almost a masonic tradition in the rise of any major art, from its undifferentiated social beginnings to the conscious aptitude which is the sign of a developed art form. Doubtless I ought to repeat once more that for some reason the moment the secrets of this aptitude come within the *provenance* of formal criticism, they vanish. They survive in the works themselves, and in the living confraternity of men of letters, who pass on by personal instruction to their successors the "tricks of the trade." The only man I have known in some twenty years of literary experience who was at once a great novelist and a great teacher, in this special sense, was the late Ford Madox Ford. His influence was immense, even upon writers who did not know him, even upon other writers, today, who have not read him. For it was through him more than any other man writing in English in our time that the great

traditions of the novel came down to us. Joyce, a greater
writer than Ford, represents by comparison a more restricted
practice of the same literary tradition, a tradition that goes
back to Stendhal in France, and to Jane Austen in England,
coming down to us through Flaubert, James, Conrad, Joyce,
Virginia Woolf and Ernest Hemingway.

It is a tradition which has its own secrets to offer; yet in
saying that I am not claiming for it greater novelists than
some other school can produce or novelists greater than those
who just happen. There is Meredith (for those who, like
Ramon Fernandez, can read him); there is Thomas Hardy,
there is even the early H. G. Wells. But there is not Arnold
Bennett; there is not John Galsworthy; not Hugh Walpole
nor Frank Swinnerton. This is prejudice, not criticism. And
these are all Britons, not Americans. I have no desire to play
'possum on the American question. Yet I am convinced that
among American novelists who have had large publics since
the last war, only Dreiser, Faulkner, and Hemingway are of
major importance. There are "good" popular novelists who
have done much to make us at home physically in our own
country; they have given us our scenes, our people, and
above all our history; and these were necessary to the pre-
liminary knowledge of ourselves which we have been a little
late in getting and which must be got and assimilated if we
are going to be a mature people. Possibly the American
novel had to accomplish the task that in Europe had been
done by primitive chronicle, memoir, ballad, strolling player.
The American novel has had to find a new experience, and
only in our time has it been able to pause for the difficult
task of finding out how to get itself written. That is an old
story with us, yet beneath it lies a complexity of feeling that
from Hawthorne down to our time has baffled our best
understanding. The illustration is infinite in its variety.
At this moment I think of my two favorite historians, Herodotus and Joinville, and I am embarrassed from time to

time because Herodotus, the pagan, seems nearer to my experience than Joinville, the Christian chronicler of St. Louis. It is perhaps easier for us to feel comfortable with the remote and relatively neutral elements of our culture. Those experiences of Europe which just precede or overlap the American experience bemuse us, and introduce a sort of chemical ambivalence into our judgment. Joinville is both nearer to me than Herodotus, and less immediate. What American could not be brought to confess a similar paradox? To our European friends who are now beginning to know us, and who in all innocence may subscribe to the popular convention of The Simple American Mind, I would say, if it is not too impolite: Beware.

But the American novel is not my present subject, nor, thank heaven, the American mind. My subject is merely the technique of fiction which now at last I feel that I am ready to talk about, not critically, you understand, but as a member of a guild. Ford used to say that he wrote his novels in the tone of one English gentleman whispering into the ear of another English gentleman: how much irony he intended I never knew; I hope a great deal. I intend none at all when I say that these remarks are set down by an artisan for other artisans.

Gustave Flaubert created the modern novel. Gustave Flaubert created the modern short story. He created both because he created modern fiction. I am not prepared to say that he created all our fictional forms and structures, the phases of the art of fiction that interest Mr. Lubbock and Mr. Muir. He did not originate all those features of the short story which interest historians and anthologists. These are other matters altogether. And I do not like to think that Flaubert created modern fiction because I do not like Flaubert. It was the fashion in France, I believe, until the Fall, to put Stendhal above Flaubert. I am not sure but I suspect that a very tired generation felt more at ease with a great writer whose typical heroes are persons of mere energy and whose books achieve whatever clarity and form that they do achieve as an accident of the moral ferocity of the author. But without *Le Rouge et Le Noir,* or without what it put into circulation in the French literary *milieu* after 1830, Flaubert could not have written *Madame Bovary.* I do not like to think that Stendhal did this because I do not like Stendhal. Both Stendhal and Flaubert had the single dedication to art which makes the disagreeable man. Doubtless it would be pleasanter if the great literary discoveries could be made by gentlemen like Henry James, who did make his share, and who, of course, was a greater novelist than either of these Frenchmen; or by English squires; but we have got to take them, as Henry James would not do in the instance of Flaubert, as they come, and they often come a little rough.

A moment ago I introduced certain aspersions upon a few English novelists of the recent past, but it was with a purpose, for their limitations, sharply perceived by the late Virginia Woolf in her famous essay *Mr. Bennett and Mrs. Brown,* will make quite clear the difference between the novelist who, with Mr. Forster, merely bounces us along and the novelist who tries to do the whole job, the job that Flaubert first taught him to do. Mrs. Woolf is discussing Hilda Lessways, Arnold Bennett's heroine, and she says:

But we cannot hear her mother's voice, or Hilda's voice; we can only hear Mr. Bennett's voice telling us facts about rents and freeholds and copyholds and fines. What can Mr. Bennett be about? I have formed my own opinion of what Mr. Bennett is about—he is trying to make us imagine for him. . . .

"Trying to make us imagine for him"—the phrase erects a Chinese wall between all that is easy, pleasant, and perhaps merely socially useful in modern fiction, and all that is rigorous, sober, and self-contained. Mrs. Woolf, again, in speaking of the novels of Galsworthy, Bennett and Wells, says: "Yet what odd books they are! Sometimes I wonder if we are right to call them books at all. For they leave one with a strange feeling of incompleteness and dissatisfaction. In order to complete them it seems necessary to do something —to join a society, or, more desperately, to write a cheque."

That is very nearly the whole story: the novelist who tries to make us imagine for him is perhaps trying to make us write a check—a very good thing to do, and I am not sure that even the socially unconscious Flaubert was deeply opposed to it, though I shall not attempt to speak for him on the question of joining societies. Let us see this matter as reasonably as we can. All literature has a social or moral or religious purpose: the writer has something that he has got to say to the largest public possible. In spite of Flaubert's belief that he wrote only for himself, this is as true of *Madame Bovary* as of *Uncle Tom's Cabin*. Is there a real difference between these books that might justify us in setting apart two orders of literature? Perhaps; for the difference is very great between getting it all inside the book and leaving some of it irresponsibly outside. For even though the check be written in a good cause it is the result of an irresponsible demand upon the part of the novelist. But the distinction is not, I think, absolute, nor should it be. And I am sure that Sainte-Beuve was right when he wrote in his review of *Madame Bovary* that not all young married women in Normandy were like Emma: was there not the case of the childless young matron of central France who, instead of taking lovers and then taking arsenic, "adopted children about her . . . and instructed them in moral culture"? Very good; for it is obvious that persons who join societies and write checks for moral culture are proper characters of fiction, as indeed all human beings of all degrees of charity or misanthropy are. But that is not the point at issue.

That point is quite simply that Flaubert, for the first time consciously and systematically, but not for the first time in the history of fiction, and not certainly of poetry—Flaubert taught us how to put this overworked and allegorical check *into* the novel, into its complex texture of scene, character and action: which, of course, is one way of saying that he did the complete imaginative job himself, and did not merely point to what was going on, leaving the imaginative specification to our good will or to our intellectual vanity. (I pause here to remark the existence of a perpetual type of critic who prefers inferior literature, because it permits him to complete it. Flaubert understood the critics who, committed to the public function of teacher, resent being taught.) This completeness of presentation in the art of fiction was not, I repeat, something new, but I gather that it had previously appeared only here and there, by the sheer accident of genius: I think of Petronius; a few incidents in Boccaccio; half a dozen scenes by the Duke of Saint-Simon (the memorialists shade imperceptibly into the novelists); the great scene in which the Prince de Clèves tells his wife that he has refrained from expressing his love for her because he wished to avoid conduct improper to a husband; Emma Woodhouse with Mr. Knightly at the parlor table looking at the picture album; countless other moments in early prose literature; but most of all that great forerunner, *Moll Flanders,* which is so much all of a piece in the Flaubertian canon that sometimes I think that Flaubert wrote it; or that nobody wrote either Defoe or Flaubert. For when literature reaches this stage of maturity, it is anonymous, and it matters little who writes it.

This is extravagant language. Or is it? It is no more than we are accustomed to when we talk about poetry, or music, or most of all the classical drama. The fourth-century lecture notes, to which I have already referred, some time ago licensed the most pretentious claims for the stage, and for poetry generally. I am only saying that fiction can be, has been, and *is* an art, as the various poetries are arts. Is this an extravagant claim? Only, I am convinced, in the minds of the more relaxed practitioners of this art, who excuse something less than the utmost talent and effort, and in the minds of critics who find the critical task more exacting than historical reporting, which reduces the novel to a news supplement. Was, as a matter of fact, Emma typical of young Norman womanhood? Are the Okies and Arkies just as Steinbeck represents them? What a triumph for the historians when it was found that there had actually been a young man whose end was like Julien Sorel's! And is it true what Mr. Faulkner says about Dixie? If it is, is what Mr. Stark Young says also true? This, I submit, is the temper of American criticism of fiction, with rare exceptions of little influence.

It is time now, towards the end of this *causerie,* to produce an image, an *exemplum,* something out of the art of fiction that underlies all the major problems of "picture and drama," symmetry, foreshortening, narrative pattern, pace and language—all those complexities of the novelist's art which Henry James, alone of the great fictionists, tried to explain (how much he coyly evaded!) in his famous Prefaces: problems that laid the ground for Mr. Lubbock's beautiful study. I am looking for something very simple and, in its direct impact, conclusive; a scene or an incident that achieves fullness of realization in terms of what it gives us to see and to hear. It must offer us fullness of rendition, not mere direction or statement. Don't state, says James, time and again—render! Don't tell us what is happening, let it happen! So I would translate James. For our purposes here it cannot be too great a scene, if we would see all round it: it must be a scene that will give us the most elementary instruction in that branch of the art of which the critics tell us little. What shall it be? Shall it be Prince André lying wounded under the wide heavens? Shall it be Moll Flanders peeping out of the upstairs window of the inn at her vanishing fourth (or is it fifth?) and undivorced husband, slyly avoiding him because she is in the room with her fifth or is it sixth? I could find perfect *exempla* in James himself. What could be better than Milly Theale's last soirée before she becomes too ill to appear again? Then there are James's fine "sitting-room scenes," the man and the woman talking out the destiny of one or both of them: Lambert Strether and Maria Gostrey, John Marcher and May Bartram, Merton Densher and Milly Theale. Or there is Strether looking down upon the boat in which Chad Newsome and Madame de Vionnet, unaware of Strether's scrutiny, betray that air of intimacy which discloses them for the first time to Strether as lovers.

Yet about these excellent scenes there is something outside our purpose, a clue that would sidetrack us into the terms of form and structure which I have virtually promised to neglect. Let us select an easy and perhaps even quite vulgar scene, a stock scene, in fact, that we should expect to find in a common romantic novel, or even in a Gothic story provided the setting were reduced to the bourgeois scale. Let the situation be something like this: A pretty young married woman, bored with her husband, a small-town doctor, has had an affair of sentiment with a young man, who has by this time left town. Growing more desperate, she permits herself to be seduced by a neighboring land-owner, a coarse Lothario, who soon tires of her. Our scene opens with the receipt of his letter of desertion. He is going away and will not see her again. The young woman receives the letter with agitation and runs upstairs to the attic, where having read the letter she gives way to hysteria. She looks out the window down into the street, and decides to jump and end it all. But she grows dizzy and recoils. After a moment she hears her husband's voice; the servant touches her arm; she comes to and recovers.

It is distinctly unpromising: James would not have touched it; Balzac, going the whole hog, might have let her jump, or perhaps left her poised for the jump while he resumed the adventures of Vautrin. But in any case there she stands, and as I have reported the scene you have got to take my word for it that she is there at all: you do not see her, you do not hear the rapid breathing and the beating heart, and you have, again, only my word for it that she is dizzy. What I have done here, in fact, is precisely what Mrs. Woolf accused the Georgian novelists of doing: I am trying to make you imagine for me, perhaps even covertly trying to make you write a check for the Society for the Improvement of Provincial Culture, or the Society for the Relief of Small Town Boredom, or for a subscription to the Book of the Month Club which would no doubt keep the young woman at improving her mind, and her mind off undesirable lovers. I hope that we shall do all these good things. But you must bear in mind that the Book of the Month Club would probably send her the kind of literature that I have just written for you, so that she too might take to writing checks. Is there any guarantee that they would be good checks? The question brings us up short against certain permanent disabilities of human nature, which we should do well to see as objectively as possible, in the language of a greater artist; which is just what we shall now proceed to do:

Charles was there; she saw him; he spoke to her; she heard nothing, and she went on quickly up the stairs, breathless, distraught, dumb, and ever holding this horrible piece of paper, that crackled between her fingers like a plate of sheet-iron. On the second floor she stopped before the attic-door, that was closed.

Then she tried to calm herself; she recalled the letter; she must finish it; she did not dare to. And where? How? She would be seen! "Ah, no! here," she thought, "I shall be all right."

Emma pushed open the door and went in.

The slates threw straight down a heavy heat that gripped her temples, stifled her; she dragged herself to the closed garret-window. She drew back the bolt, and the dazzling light burst in with a leap.

Opposite, beyond the roofs, stretched the open country till it was lost to sight. Down below, underneath her, the village square was empty; the stones of the pavement glittered, the weathercocks on the houses were motionless. At the corner of the street from a lower story, rose a kind of humming with strident modulations. It was Binet turning.

She leant against the embrasure of the window, and reread the letters with angry sneers. But the more she fixed her attention upon it, the more confused were her ideas. She saw him again, heard him, encircled him with her arms, and the throbs of her heart, that beat against her breast like blows of a sledge-hammer, grew faster and faster, with uneven intervals. She looked about her with the wish that the earth might crumble into pieces. Why not end it all? What restrained her? She was free. She advanced, looked at the paving-stones, saying to herself, "Come! Come!"

The luminous ray that came straight up from below drew the weight of her body towards the abyss. It seemed to her that the floor dipped on end like a tossing boat. She was right at the edge, almost hanging, surrounded by vast space. The blue of the heavens suffused her, the air was whirling in her hollow head; she had but to yield, to let herself be taken; and the humming of the lathe never ceased, like an angry voice calling her.

"Emma! Emma!" cried Charles.

She stopped.

"Wherever are you? Come!"

The thought that she had just escaped from death made her faint with terror. She closed her eyes; then she shivered at the touch of a hand on her sleeve; it was Félicité.

"Master is waiting for you, madame; the soup is on the table."

And she had to go down to sit at table.

The English translation is not good; its failure to convey the very slight elevation of tone is a fundamental failure. It is not a rhetorical elevation, but rather one of perfect formality and sobriety. We are not looking at this scene through Emma's eyes. We occupy a position slightly above and to one side, where we see her against the full setting; yet observe that at the same time we see nothing that she does not see, hear nothing that she does not hear. It is one of the amazing paradoxes of the modern novel, whose great subject is a man alone in society or even against society, almost never with society, that out of this view of man isolated we see developed to the highest possible point of virtuosity and power a technique of putting man wholly into his physical setting. The action is not stated from the point of view of the author; it is rendered in terms of situation and scene. To have made this the viable property of the art of fiction was to have virtually made the art of fiction. And that, I think, is our debt to Flaubert.

But we should linger over this scene if only to try our hands at what I shall now, for the first time, call sub-criticism, or the animal tact which permits us occasionally to see connections and correspondences which our rational powers, unaided, cannot detect. What capital feature of the scene seems (if it does) to render the actuality more than any other? The great fact, I think, is the actuality, and your sense of it is all that is necessary. Yet I like to linger over the whirring lathe of old Binet, a lay figure or "flat character" who has done little in the novel and will never do much, and whose lathe we merely noted from the beginning as a common feature of a small town like Yonville. I should like to know when Flaubert gave him the lathe, whether just to tag him for us; whether, writing the present scene, he went back and gave it to him as a "plant" for use here later; or whether, having given him the lathe, he decided it would be useful in this scene.

What is its use? James said that the work of fiction must be "a direct impression of life," a very general requirement; but in the perspective of nearly ninety years since the publication of *Madame Bovary* and the rise of the Impressionist novel through Henry James, James Joyce, and Virginia Woolf, the phrase takes on a more specific sense. Mind you the phrase is not "direct representation," which only the stage can give us. But here, using this mechanic's tool, Flaubert gives us a direct *impression* of Emma's sensation at a particular moment (which not even the drama could accomplish), and thus by rendering audible to us what Emma alone could hear he charged the entire scene with actuality. As Emma goes to the window she merely notes that Binet's lathe is turning—*C'était Binet qui tournait.* Then she looks down at the street which seems to rise towards her—*Allons! Allons!* she whispers, because she cannot find the will to jump. We have had rendered to us visually the shock of violent suicide. Now comes the subtle fusion of the reaction and of the pull toward self-destruction, which is the humming in her head: how can Flaubert *render* it for us? Shall we not have to take his word for it? Shall we not have to imagine for him? No: *l'air circulait dans sa tête creuse,* he says; and then: *le ronflement du tour ne discontinuait pas, comme une voix furieuse qui l'appelait*—"the whirring of the lathe never stopped like a voice of fury calling her." The humming vertigo that draws the street towards her is rendered audible to us by the correlative sound of the lathe.

That is all, or nearly all, there is to it; but I think it is enough to set up our image, our *exemplum.* I leave to you, as I constantly reserve for myself, the inexhaustible pleasure of tracing out the infinite strands of interconnection in this and other novels, complexities as deep as life itself but ordered, fixed, and dramatized into arrested action. If I have made too much of Flaubert, or too much of too little of Flaubert, I can only say that I have not willfully ignored men as great, or greater. It is proper to honor France, and to honor the *trouvère,* the discoverer; for it has been through Flaubert that the novel has at last caught up with poetry.

1944

Miss Emily and the Bibliographer[1]

THE SCENE is a seminar room at a large American university. It is the first meeting of the year. The eager young man asks the professor a question. "What," he says, "is the ultimate purpose of graduate research in English literature?" The professor, whose special field is English bibliography of the decade 1840–1850, does not hesitate. "To lay the foundations of literary criticism," he replies. The eager young man is pleased because secretly and discreetly he hopes that some day he may hope to be a critic. A month later the bibliographer assigns the group a paper. "Gentlemen," he says, "we must maintain in these papers the graduate point of view. There must be no impressionism. There must be no literary criticism. Anybody can write that."

I came upon this tale about a year ago but a year before that I had read one like it in an essay written by Mr. John Crowe Ransom some time before the incident that I relate occurred. I began to wonder if Mr. Ransom had made it up; then I began to hope that he had, so that the witnessed fact should stand as proof of an insight. Without the witnessed fact Mr. Ransom (I assume for my purpose that he invented the tale) would be in the position of William Faulkner after his story, *A Rose for Emily,* appeared. You will remember Mr. Faulkner's story. Miss Emily, a curious spinster, conceals the dead body of her lover in an upstairs bedroom until con-

[1] This paper was read before the English Club of Princeton University, April 10, 1940.

cealment is no longer possible. Nobody believed this tale; it was one of Mr. Faulkner's outrageous lies; it just couldn't have happened. Then it happened. This evidence of the decadence of the South emerged about three years later from a farmhouse in upstate New York. A middle-aged woman had killed her lover and kept the body.

For both Mr. Ransom and Mr. Faulkner the later facts confirmed the previous insights. Yet I must confess that for another reason altogether the analogy between the scholar and the spinster teases my fancy. Both tales are tales of horror, and I submit that the greater horror, for me, is in the scholar's insincerity. The analogy, like a good one, holds on more than one level. Must we not suspect that Miss Emily had a time of it conducting her intrigue in a provincial American community and that she probably, with the lover's last breath, breathed her sigh of relief? The need of judging him as a living man had been happily removed with the removal of his breath; the contingencies of personality were happily gone; she could have him without any of the social dangers of having him. She could now proceed without interruption to the reconstruction of the history of her love. But there was always the body, and the body wrecks the analogy. Miss Emily's historical method recognized that it was the history of something it could not ignore and had to return to. But the specialist in English bibliography of the decade 1840–1850 would doubtless bury the body at once, concealing it forever; and he would never afterwards have to be reminded what he was doing the bibliography of. Or if you will give this figure yet another turn, the analogy is wrecked again, again in favor of Miss Emily. The body has got to decompose, and its existence will become shockingly known—a crisis that the historical scholars conspire among themselves to postpone indefinitely; and if the wild discourtesy of the real world reminds them of it they say, "No, you are mistaken; we buried it long ago." But have they? Can they? And that is why Miss Emily remains a somewhat endearing horror for me. It is better to pretend with Miss Emily that something dead is living than to pretend with the bibliographer that something living is dead.[2]

The bibliographer's belief that "anybody can write that" I wish to discuss later, when I get to some of the more dialectical phases of the question. Here I should like to set off against my frivolity what many literary critics have called the insincerity of the academic mind. Between the frivolity and the insincerity, between the ignorance and the irrelevant learning, the outlook for a literary criticism in our time is dark. But as a matter of fact, whatever may be said of the party of ignorance, it would be hard to maintain that anything like personal insincerity motivates the activities of the historical scholars. Every point of view entails upon its proponents, in the act of overreaching it, its own kind of insincerity. Yet the evidence for the insincerity of our bibliographer is damaging: what, if not insincerity, lies back of his professed purpose which he, when he is pressed, shamelessly repudiates? How can he spend years laying the foundations of literary criticism when he thinks that anybody can write it? If anybody can write it does it need the collaboration of many generations of scholarship to lay its foundations?

There is insincerity here no doubt; for it is plainly an instance of a professed intention that one never expects to carry out or that one vaguely expects the future to perform for us. Does this not have an ominous and familiar sound? We hear it in the world at large and on nearly every level of our experience.

We hear it in politics, and the political voice has its counterpoint in the uneasy speculation of the journalist crit-

---

[2] The reader will suspect that I have had in mind all along the phrase "the *corpus* of English literature," widely used by scholars and their way, no doubt, of laying literature out for burial.

ics about the future of literature: some ten years ago we got from England a whole series of little books called *The Future of—;* and it is seldom that we get an essay on the present state of letters or even on a single book that does not look far beyond the occasion. We are asked as citizens to live only for the future, either in the preservation of democracy or in the creation of the classless society. Mr. T. S. Eliot has discussed this question in "Literature and the Modern World," an essay which I believe has not been reprinted in any of his books; he examines the point of view of H. G. Wells and sees in it the widespread eschatology of a secular, naturalistic philosophy. As individuals today we must subordinate our spiritual life and our material satisfactions to the single purpose of gaining superior material satisfactions in the future, which will be a naturalistic Utopia of mindless hygiene and Tom Swift's gadgets. There is no doubt that the most powerful attraction offered us by the totalitarian political philosophies is the promise of irresponsible perfection in the future, to be gained at the slight cost of our present consent to extinguish our moral natures in a group mind.

The moral nature affirms itself in judgment, and we cannot or will not judge. Because the scholars as much as other people today are involved in the naturalistic temper, they also refuse to judge. The historical scholar says that we cannot judge the literature of our time because we do not know whether the future will approve of it. Is he not obviously evading his moral responsibility? I do not say he evades it as a father or as a citizen; but he does evade it in the specific field in which he ought to exercise it, since of that field he professes knowledge.

He has reasons for the Great Refusal, and the reasons are of curious interest and at the same time of critical importance. In order to express my sense of their significance I must go a long way round. I should like to begin by citing certain critical views held by Mr. Edmund Wilson, a brilliant historian of literature, who because he puts literature above research may be expected to exhibit some of the values of the historical method when it is actually applied in criticism.

Let me first make a distinction—so broad that if it is true it will be virtually a truism. Let us assume that English critics from the late Renaissance to Coleridge had a firm sense of the differences among the *genres* of literature and that they tried constantly to state those differences critically. Whether they succeeded in this task, from our point of view, is not the question; it is rather that they tried to look upon works of literature as objective existences with respect to the different forms.

Taking up this defeated critical tradition we still from time to time consider the relation of poetry to prose fiction. Our approach to this problem was adumbrated by Coleridge in a fashion that would have been unintelligible a century before his time: in Chapter XIV of *Biographia Literaria* he remarks that a work of prose fiction will often have the imaginative qualities of poetry, no essential difference between poetry and fiction being discernible. There are concealed in this view certain metaphysical assumptions, which we still use without awareness of the metaphysics. (In the study of "English" we are forbidden to "use" philosophy—which means that we are using it badly.) We say today that there is poetry in prose fiction and, wherever you have narrative, fiction in poetry. But it ought to be easy to see that the murk enveloping the question when we try to carry it further than this arises from a certain kind of fallacy of abstraction. We are thinking in terms of substance, or essence. Those who believe that poetry and prose fiction differ in some fundamental sense assume that poetry is a distinct essence; whether prose has an essence is irrelevant since it could not have the essence of poetry; and, therefore, prose fiction being a kind of prose, it is essentially different from poetry.

Now Mr. Wilson easily disposes of this argument in a famous essay called "Is Verse a Dying Technique?" (by which I understand him to mean: Is verse becoming an unpopular technique?). He boldly denies to poetry an essence distinct from the essence of prose. In denying a difference he affirms the same essence of both: he thinks in terms of essence. He shows that *Madame Bovary* contains a great deal of "poetry" and concludes that the only interesting difference between a work like Flaubert's masterpiece and the *Aeneid* is that the one is in prose, the other in verse. That is certainly a difference; it is, according to Mr. Wilson, strictly a difference of "technique"; and he assumes the likenesses in terms of a common essence. Here we get the deepest assumption of the literary historian: the subject matter alone has objective status, the specific form of the work being external and mechanical—mere technique. This essence common to all literature is human life. Both Flaubert and Virgil were concerned with it in its largest implications.

Nobody will deny this; but it is critically irrelevant to affirm it. Within the terms of this affirmation critical thought is impossible, and we succumb to the documentary routine which "correlates" this de-formed substance with its origin, which by convention is called history.

Now the writers who see in works of literature not the specific formal properties but only the amount and range of human life brought to the reader are expressionists. Back of the many varieties of expressionist theory lies the assumption of the common or the distinct essence. If I say that the essence of *Madame Bovary* is different from the essence of the *Aeneid* and Mr. Wilson says that the essences are the same, we merely shout our opinions at each other, and the louder voice prevails. The historical method will not permit us to develop a critical instrument for dealing with works of literature as existent objects; we see them as expressive of substances beyond themselves. At the historical level the work expresses its place and time, or the author's personality, but if the scholar goes further and says anything about the work, he is expressing himself. Expressionism is here a sentiment, forbidding us to think and permitting us to feel as we please. When the bored expressionist tires of the pure artistic essence he turns into the inquisitive literary historian; or he may be both at once, as indeed he often is.

The great historical scholars of our time are notoriously deficient critics, but critics they are nevertheless. I am far from believing that the bibliographer's defense of scholarship is acceptable to all the scholars, many of whom are certain that they are already doing for criticism all that is necessary. Do you want a critic? Why, we already have one —in John Livingston Lowes. Has he not given us *Convention and Revolt?* He has; but in the course of a few pages I cannot do justice to the historical scholarship that gave us the facile seesaw picture of the history of poetry, or to the poetic learning that permitted Mr. Lowes to take seriously the late Amy Lowell. The mere literary critics took Miss Lowell seriously for a while, but the literary critics were not scholars. If you will think of *Convention and Revolt* along with *The Road to Xanadu* you will see that the literary dilettante and the historical scholar can flourish, without much communication between them, in one man.

Are we not prepared here for one of the remarkable insights of the late Irving Babbitt? His *Literature and the American College,* published in 1908, is still quoted, but there is no reason to believe that its message has ever been taken seriously by the men who most need it. At that time the late J. E. Spingarn had not imported into American criticism the term expressionism. Mr. Babbitt called the dilettantes Rousseauistic impressionists; the historical schol-

ars Baconian naturalists. Both dilettante and scholar repudiated the obligations of judgment because both alike were
victims of a naturalistic philosophy. Perhaps Mr. Babbitt did
not consider the possibility of their being the same man.
He saw on the one hand the ignorant journalist critics, "decadent romantics," for whom intensity of feeling was the sole
critical standard; and on the other hand the historical scholars, who had no critical standard at all but who amassed
irrelevant information. It was—and still is—a situation in
which it is virtually impossible for a young man to get a
critical, literary education. If he goes to a graduate school
he comes out incapacitated for criticism; if he tries to be a
critic he is not unlike the ignorant impressionist who did
not go to the graduate school. He cannot discuss the literary
object in terms of its specific form; all that he can do is to
give you its history or tell you how he feels about it. The
concrete form of the play, the poem, the novel, that gave
rise to the history or the feeling lies neglected on the hither
side of the Styx, where Virgil explains to Dante that it is
scorned alike by heaven and hell.

Mr. Babbitt saw in the aesthete and the historical scholar
the same motivation. The naturalism of the scholar lies in
his mechanical theory of history, a theory in which the literary object is dissolved into the determinism of forces surrounding it. The naturalism of the aesthete operates on the
psychological plane; he responds to the aesthetic object in
terms of sensation and if the sensation is intense the aesthetic object is good.

Mr. Babbitt scolded these erring brothers for not making
a moral judgment, and it is just here that the limitations
of his method appear. The moral obligation to judge does
not necessarily obligate us to make a moral judgment. Mr.
Babbitt's humanism contains some concealed naturalism in
its insistence upon the value of the mere substance or essence
of literature: the subject matter itself must be decorous in

order to pass the humanist examination. The specific property of a work of literary art which differentiates it from
mere historical experience he could never understand; and
it is this specific property, this particular quality of the work,
that puts upon us the moral obligation to form a judgment.
Mr. Yvor Winters remarks that Mr. Babbitt never understood "how the moral intelligence gets into poetry." It
gets in not as moral abstractions but as form, coherence of
image and metaphor, control of tone and of rhythm, the
union of these features. So the moral obligation to judge
compels us to make not a moral but a total judgment.

The question in the end comes down to this: What as literary critics are we to judge? As literary critics we must first
of all decide in what respect the literary work has a specific
objectivity. If we deny its specific objectivity then not only
is criticism impossible but literature also. We have got to
decide what it is about the whole of a work of literature
which distinguishes it from its parts—or rather the parts
we can abstract from this whole and then distribute over
the vast smudge of history, whence they presumably were
derived. It is a question of knowing before we talk what as
critics we are talking about.

From my point of view the formal qualities of a poem
are the focus of the specifically critical judgment because
they partake of an objectivity that the subject matter, ab-
stracted from the form, wholly lacks. The form of "Lycidas"
is Milton's specific achievement as a poet in the convention
of the pastoral elegy; but this convention, which is his substance, represents in itself only a subjective selection from
Milton's historical situation. Would it not be simpler to
seize at once the specific quality of "Lycidas" and try to
understand it than to grapple with that aspect which fades
into the immense perspective of history?

It would be simpler, if not easier, to discuss the form if
we had a way of discussing it; yet before we can under-

stand a literary problem we must first confess the problem exists. We no longer admit the problem because we no longer believe in the specific quality of the work of literature, the quality that distinguishes it from a work of history or even of science. As men of letters we no longer, in fact, believe in literature; we believe rather that the knowledge offered us in even the most highly developed literary forms has something factitious and illusory about it, so that before we can begin to test its validity we must translate it into an analogy derived from the sciences. The historical method is an imitation of scientific method: we entertain as interesting and valuable that portion of the literary work to which we can apply the scientific vocabularies.

Not being a literary historian I do not know when the literary profession lost confidence in literature; I suppose it was a gradual loss; we see its beginnings in the English romantics, and we do not yet see the end. The rise of the sciences, their immense practical successes, even their moral failures, intimidated the scholars and I seem to hear them say, at first secretly and late at night when black questions cannot be gainsaid: "Milton's science is false, and the scientists say that his moral and religious ideas have no empirical validity. But if I give up Milton I give up my profession, so I had better bestir myself to study scientifically Milton's unscientific science. We must get in on the wonderful scientific triumphs of the age. Nobody believes today that the arts give us a sort of cognition at least equally valid with that of scientific method; so we will just take the arts as fields of data for more scientific investigation."

The historical method is in the long run the unhistorical method. The literary historians are not first of all historians. We seldom get from them anything like Taine on English literature; no American literary scholar has produced a work of the distinction of Carl Becker's *The Heavenly City of the Eighteenth-Century Philosophers,* a book written not in the historical method but out of the historical imagination. It is a work of literature by a mind informed with a mature point of view and seasoned with exact knowledge (by knowledge I do not mean documentation) in many fields. Could Mr. Becker have written the book had he been trained in the belief that philosophy, for example, not being "English," has no place in historical writing? Could he have written it had he been compelled to suppress all the resources of his intelligence but the single one employed in the mechanical "correlation" of literature with the undigested lump of history? Is there not an instructive moral in the distinction of Mr. Becker's prose style?

I am not attacking the study or the writing of history for use in the criticism of literature. I am attacking the historical method. I trust everybody understands what this method is. It reflects at varying distances the philosophies of monism current in the nineteenth century and still prevailing today. Because the literary scholar in his monistic naturalism cannot discern the objectivity of the forms of literature, he can only apply to literature certain abstractions which he derives, two stages removed, from the naturalistic sciences; that is to say he gets these abstractions from the historians who got them from the scientists. In the period when physics was the popular science we got historical studies of influences, conceived in terms of forces, causes, and effects; then came the biological analogies that gave us organic periods where we attended to growths and developments; and today we have a broadening of the historical method which reflects the vast extension of scientific procedure in the semi-sciences— psychology, economics, and sociology.

That this method is, in a definite sense, unhistorical it would not be hard to show. Under whatever leading analogy we employ the historical method—organism, mechanism, causality—it has the immediate effect of removing the historian himself from history, so that he cannot participate as a living imagination in a great work of literature. Even those scholars, usually men interested in the eighteenth century, who are concerned with the meaning of tradition conceive of tradition itself in terms of scientific analogies, so that there is something remote and mechanical about a tradition; and the tradition that we are interested in is almost always seen as a traditional "body" of literature, not operative today—not living, as the very word body implies.

This removal of the historian from living history has curious consequences. Because it is difficult—or too easy in some respects—to get historical documents for works of the present or recent past we refuse to study them. And we also refuse to study them because their reputations are not fixed. There is here the assumption, as I think the illusion, that the reputation of any writer is ever fixed. These two illusions—the necessity of documents for the study of literature and the fixed hierarchy of the past—are not necessarily consequences of the historical method: Milton complained of similar routines of pedantry at Cambridge. Yet perhaps more today than ever we get a systematic, semi-philosophical sanction for our refusal to study literature.

I take the somewhat naïve view that the literature of the past began somewhere a few minutes ago and that the literature of the present begins, say, with Homer. While there is no doubt that we need as much knowledge of all kinds, from all sources, as we can get if we are to see the slightest lyric in all its richness of meaning, we have nevertheless an obligation, that we perilously evade, to form a judgment of the literature of our own time. It is more than an obligation; we must do it if we would keep on living. When the scholar assumes that he is judging a work of the past from a high and disinterested position, he is actually judging it from no position at all but is only abstracting from the work those qualities that his semiscientific method will permit him to see; and this is the Great Refusal.

We must judge the past and keep it alive by being alive ourselves; and that is to say that we must judge the past not with a method or an abstract hierarchy but with the present, or with as much of the present as our poets have succeeded in elevating to the objectivity of form. For it is through the formed, objective experience of our own time that we must approach the past; and then by means of a critical mastery of our own formed experience we may test the presence and the value of form in works of the past. This critical activity is reciprocal and simultaneous. The scholar who tells us that he understands Dryden but makes nothing of Hopkins or Yeats is telling us that he does not understand Dryden.

Perhaps the same scholar acknowledges the greatness of Dryden and the even more formidable greatness of Milton and Shakespeare; and if you ask him how they became great he will reply, as I have heard him reply, that History did it and that we have got to wait until History does it, or declines to do it, to writers of our own time. Who is this mysterious person named History? We are back again with our old friend, the Great Refusal, who thrives upon the naturalistic repudiation of the moral obligation to judge. If we wait for history to judge there will be no judgment; for if we are not history then history is nobody. He is nobody when he has become the historical method.

One last feature of this illusion of the fixed hierarchy I confess I cannot understand. It is the belief that the chief function of criticism is the ranking of authors rather than their use. It is the assumption that the great writers of the past occupy a fixed position. If we alter the figure slightly, admitting that History has frozen their reputations, we must assume also that the position from which we look at them is likewise fixed; for if it were not we should see them in constantly changing relations and perspectives, and we should think their positions were changing too. If you will now see this same figure as a landscape of hills, trees, plains, you will quickly become fearful for the man who from a fixed point surveys the unchanging scene; for the man, the only man, who cannot change his position is a dead man: the only man for whom the greatness of the great poets is fixed is also dead. And so, if we may look at this Homeric simile with the eyes of Bishop Berkeley, we must conclude that the great authors are dead, too, because there is nobody to look at them. I have adapted this figure from one of the Prefaces of Henry James because it seems to me to be a good way of saying that the literature of the past can be kept alive only by seeing it as the literature of the present. Or perhaps we ought to say that the literature of the past lives in the literature of the present and nowhere else; that it is all present literature.

1940

Understanding Modern Poetry

ABOUT EVERY six months I see in *The New York Times Book Review* the confident analogy between the audience of the modern poet and the audience that the English Romantics had to win in the early nineteenth century. Only wait a little while, and T. S. Eliot will be as easy for high school teachers as "The Solitary Reaper." There may be some truth in this; but I think there is very little truth in it, and my reasons for thinking so will be the substance of this essay. There is a great deal of confusion about this matter, and not a little of it comes from the comfortable habit of citing a passage in the "Preface" to *Lyrical Ballads,* in which Wordsworth says that, as soon as the objects of modern life (meaning the physical changes wrought in society by the Industrial Revolution) become as familiar to the people as the old mythologies of poetry, the difficulties of apprehension and communication will disappear. But this has not happened. It is true that no modern poet has succeeded in knowing all the physical features of modern industrial society; but neither has "society" succeeded in knowing them. It may be doubted that any poet in the past ever made a special point of studying the "techniques of production" of his time or of looking self-consciously at the objects around him as mere objects. Wordsworth himself did not.

Dante knew the science of the thirteenth century, and he was intensely aware of the physical features of his time—the ways of living, the clothing, the architecture, the implements of war, the natural landscape. But it was not a question of his becoming "familiar" with objects, though it cannot be denied that a relatively unchanging physical background, since it can be taken for granted, is an advantage to any poet. It is rather that *all* that he knew came under a philosophy which was at once dramatic myth, a body of truths, and a comprehensive view of life.

Now Wordsworth's point of view is still the point of view of the unreflecting reader, and it is a point of view appropriate and applicable to the poets of the Romantic movement who are still, to the general reader, all that poets ought to be or can be. But the modern poetry that our general reader finds baffling and obscure is a radical departure from the Romantic achievement; it contains features that his "education" has not prepared him for. Neither in perception nor in intellect is he ready for a kind of poetry that does not offer him the familiar poetical objects alongside the familiar poetical truths.

Let us say, very briefly and only for the uses of this discussion, that the Romantic movement taught the reader to look for inherently poetical objects, and to respond to them "emotionally" in certain prescribed ways, these ways being indicated by the "truths" interjected at intervals among the poetical objects.

Certain modern poets offer no inherently poetical objects, and they fail to instruct the reader in the ways he must feel about the objects. All experience, then, becomes potentially the material of poetry—not merely the pretty and the agreeable—and the modern poet makes it possible for us to "respond" to this material in all the ways in which men everywhere may feel and think. On the ground of common sense —a criterion that the reader invokes against the eccentric moderns—the modern poet has a little the better of the argument, for to him poetry is not a special package tied up in pink ribbon: it is one of the ways that we have of knowing the world. And since the world is neither wholly pretty nor wholly easy to understand, poetry becomes a very difficult affair, demanding both in its writing and in its reading all the intellectual power that we have. But it is very hard for people to apply their minds to poetry, since it is one of our assumptions that come down from the early nineteenth century that our intellects are for mathematics and science, our emotions for poetry.

Who are these modern poets? Some twenty years ago they were supposed to be Mr. Lindsay, Mr. Masters, and Mr. Carl Sandburg. When Mr. Sandburg's poetry first appeared, it was said to be both ugly and obscure; now it is easy and beautiful to high school students, and even to their teachers, whose more advanced age must have given them a prejudice in favor of the metrical, the pretty, and the "poetical" object. Doubtless the "obscure" moderns are the poets whom Mr. Max Eastman has ridiculed in *The Literary Mind,* and whom Mr. Cleanth Brooks, in *Modern Poetry and the Tradition,* distinguishes as the leaders of a poetic revolution as far reaching as the Romantic revolution brought in by *Lyrical Ballads* in 1798.

The volumes by Mr. Eastman and Mr. Brooks are of uneven value, but I recommend them to be read together; and I would suggest that it is exceedingly dangerous and misleading to read Mr. Eastman alone. Yet, although Mr. Eastman is aggressive, sensational, and personal in his attacks, he has been widely read; while Mr. Brooks, who is sober, restrained, and critical, will win one reader for Mr. Eastman's fifty. Mr. Eastman is a debater, not a critic; and he is plausible because, like the toothpaste manufacturer, he offers his product in the name of science. Reading his book some years ago, I expected on every page to see the picture of the white-coated doctor with the test tube and the goatee, and under it the caption: "Science says . . ." But why science? Simply because Mr. Eastman, being still in the Romantic movement, but not knowing that he is, insists that the poet get hold of some "truths" that will permit him to tell the reader what to think about the new poetical objects of our time: he must think scientifically or not at all. Eastman's *The Literary Mind* is an interesting document of our age; Brooks's *Modern Poetry and the Tradition* will probably survive as an epoch-making critical synthesis of the modern movement.

The poets of the new revolution range all the way from the greatest distinction to charlatanism—a feature of every revolution, literary or political. Mr. Eastman can make the best moderns sound like the worst—as no doubt he could make the great passages of "The Prelude" sound like "Peter Bell" if he set his hand to it; and he found, as he confesses with candor and chagrin, that certain passages in the later works of Shakespeare strongly resemble some of the poetry of the modern "Cult of Unintelligibility." But this hot potato, because he doesn't know what to do with it, he quickly drops. It is not my purpose to make Mr. Eastman the whipping boy of a school of critics; of his school, he is one of the best. What I wish to emphasize is the negative of his somewhat sly contention that an admirer of Eliot's *Ash Wednesday* must also be an admirer of Miss Stein's *Geography and Plays,* that there is only a great lump of modernist verse in which no distinctions are possible. By such tactics we could discredit Browning with quotations from Mrs. Hemans. I notice this palpable nonsense because Mr. Eastman has been widely read by professors of English, who are really rather glad to hear this sort of thing, since it spares them the trouble of reading a body of poetry for which there are no historical documents and of which generations of other professors have not told them what to think.

In this essay I cannot elucidate a great many modern poems—a task that at the present time would be only a slight service to the reader; for in the state of his education and mine, we should have to undertake the infinite series of elucidations. We have no critical method; we have no principles to guide us. Every poem being either a unique expression of personality or a response to an environment, we should know at the end of the tenth difficult poem only what we knew at the end of the first; we could only cite the personalities and the environments. What I wish to do here, then, is not to explain certain modern poems but rather to discuss the reasons, as I see them, why certain kinds of poetry are difficult today.

The most pervasive reason of all is the decline of the art of reading—in an age in which there is more print than the world has seen before. If you ask why this is so, the answer is that impressionistic education in all its varieties, chiefly the variety known as "progressive education," is rapidly making us a nation of illiterates: a nation of people without letters. For you do not have to attend to the letters and words on the page in order to "read" what is there. In an essay entitled "The Retreat of the Humanities" (*English Journal*, February, 1939, p. 127), Mr. Louis B. Wright quotes an interesting passage from another essay, "Supervising the Creative Teaching of Poetry," whose author Mr. Wright mercifully leaves anonymous:

The teaching of poetry divides itself naturally into two areas of enterprise, each with its essential conditioning validities. . . . Comprehending a poem need not involve any intellectual or formal concern with its technique, prose content, type, moral, diction, analysis, social implications, etc. Comprehending a poem is essentially an organic experience, essentially a response to the poetic stimulus of the author. Poetic comprehension may be verbalized or it may not.

In short, poetic comprehension does not involve anything at all, least of all the poem to be comprehended. Mr. Wright remarks that this is "equivalent to the emotion that comes from being tickled on the ear with a feather. . . . Before such ideas and such jargon, sincere advocates of learning sometimes retreat in despair." Yes; but for the sake of the good people whose "education" has doomed them to teach poetry with this monstrous jargon, I wish to examine the quotation more closely, and more in contempt than in despair. We have here, then, an offensive muddle of echoes ranging from business jargon through sociological jargon to the jargon of the Watsonian behaviorists. One must be more pleased than disappointed to find that poetry "naturally divides" itself, without any intellectual effort on our part, into "areas" having "conditioning validities" that are "essential"—an adjective that our Anonymity repeats twice adverbially in a wholly different non-sense. Now, if technique, diction, analysis, and the others are irrelevant in the reading of poetry, in what respect does poetry differ from automobiles: cannot one be conditioned to automobiles? No, that is not the answer. One is conditioned by responding to the "poetic stimulus of the author." One gets the poet's personality; and there's no use thinking about the poet's personality, since one cannot think, "verbalization" now being the substitute for thought—as indeed it is, in our Anonymity.

I am sure that thoughtful persons will have perceived, beyond this vulgar haze, an "idea" curiously resembling something that I have already alluded to in this essay: it is astonishing how regularly the pseudoscientific vocabularies are used in order to reach a poetic theory that the most ignorant "man in the street" already holds. That theory I call "decadent Romanticism," but I should like it to be plainly understood that I am not attacking the great Romantic poets. Romanticism gave us the "Ode to a Nightingale"; decadent Romanticism is now giving us the interminable ballads and local-color lyrics of Mr. Coffin and Mr. Stephen Benét—as it gave us, some twenty-five years ago, Joyce Kilmer's "Trees," the "favorite poem" of the American people, taught piously by every high school teacher, and sometimes aggressively by college professors when they want to show what poetry ought to be; surely one of the preposterously bad lyrics in any language.

What I said earlier that I should like to call attention to again is: The weakness of the Romantic sensibility is that it gave us a poetry of "poetical" (or *poetized*) objects, pre-digested perceptions; and in case there should be any mis-understanding about the poetical nature of these objects, we also got "truths" attached to them—truths that in modern jargon are instructions to the reader to "respond" in a cer-tain way to the poetical object, which is the "stimulus." And in the great body of nineteenth-century lyrical poetry—whose worst ancestor was verse like Shelley's "I arise from dreams of thee"—the poet's personal emotions became the "poetic stimulus." The poem as a formal object to be looked at, to be studied, to be construed (in more than the grammatical sense, but first of all in that sense), dissolved into biography and history, so that in the long run the poetry was only a misunderstood pretext for the "study" of the sexual life of the poet, of the history of his age, of anything else that the scholar wished to "study"; and he usually wished to study anything but poetry.

Now our Anonymity has said that prose content, morals, and social implications are irrelevant in reading poetry, and it looks as if there were a fundamental disagreement between him and the biographical and historical scholars. There is no such disagreement. Once you arrive with Anonymity at the "poetic stimulus of the author," you have reached his biog-raphy and left his poetry behind; and, on principle, Ano-nymity cannot rule out the morals and the social implica-tions (however much he may wish to rule them out), be-cause morals and social implications are what you get when you discuss personality.

At this point I ought to enter a *caveat* to those persons who are thinking that I would dispense with historical scholarship. It is, in fact, indispensable; it is pernicious only when some ham actor in an English department uses it to wring tears from the Sophomores, by describing the sad death of Percy Shelley. Let me illustrate one of its genuine uses. Here are the first two stanzas of Donne's "A Valediction: Forbidding Mourning" [1]:

> As virtuous men passe mildly away,
> And whisper to their soules, to goe,
> Whilst some of their sad friends doe say,
> The breath goes now, and some say, no:
> Soe let us melt, and make no noise,
> No teare-floods, nor sigh-tempests move,
> 'Twere prophanation of our joyes
> To tell the layetie our love.

The elaborate simile here asserts on several planes the analogy between the act of love and the moment of death. But if you happen to know that in Middle English and down through the sixteenth century the verb *die* has as a secondary meaning, "to perform the act of love," you are able to extend the analogy into a new frame of reference. The analogy contains a concealed pun. But we are detecting the pun not in order to show that a man in the late sixteenth century was still aware of the early, secondary meaning of *die;* we are simply using this piece of information to extend our knowledge of what happens in the first eight lines of the poem. It is of no interest to anybody that Donne knew how to make this pun; it is of capital interest to know what the pun does to the meaning of the poem.

I have seemed to be talking about what I consider bad poetic theory; but I have also been talking about something much larger, that cannot here be adequately discussed: I have been talking about a bad theory of education. If only briefly, I must notice it because it abets the bad poetic theory and is at the bottom of the popular complaint that modern

[1] For longer discussion of this poem, *infra*, pp. 247–252.

poetry is difficult. The complainant assumes that he understands all English poetry up to, say, about 1917—a date that I select because in that year Eliot's *Prufrock and Other Observations* was published. But, as a matter of fact, the complainant does not understand Marvell and Donne any better than he understands Eliot; and I doubt that he can read Sidney any better than he can read Pound; he could not read Raleigh at all, and he has never heard of Fulke Greville.

So it is not "modern" poetry which is difficult; it is rather a certain kind of poetry as old, in English, as the sixteenth century, and, in Italian, much older than that. It is a kind of poetry that requires of the reader the fullest cooperation of all his intellectual resources, all his knowledge of the world, and all the persistence and alertness that he now thinks only of giving to scientific studies.

This kind of poetry must have the direct and *active* participation of a reader who today, because he has been pampered by bad education, expects to lie down and be *passive* when he is reading poetry. He admits, for some obscure reason, that poetry is a part of his education; but he has been taught to believe that education is *conditioning:* something is being done to him, he is not doing anything himself. And that is why he cannot read poetry.

A conditioning theory of education may be good enough for animals in the zoo, but it is not good enough for human beings; and it is time that this symptom of decadence were known for what it is, and not as enlightenment, "science," liberalism, and democracy. I do not know whether we are living in a democracy; it is, at any rate, an anomaly of democratic theory that it should produce, in education, a theory that we are bundles of reflexes without intelligence.

The theory assumes, first of all, that education is a process of getting adjusted to an environment. Something known as "personality" is making *responses* to things known as *stimuli*. In the educational environment there are *stimuli* called "poems," to which you make responses.

Now while you are making a response, you are not doing more than a chimpanzee or a Yahoo would be doing. But should you do more than respond, you might perform an act of intelligence, of knowing, of cognition. In the conditioning theory there is no cognition because there is no intelligence. Of what use is intelligence? It does not at all help to describe the "behavior" of persons who are getting responses from the *stimuli* of poems. What the poem is in itself, what it says, is no matter. It is an irrelevant question. But if you can imagine it not to be irrelevant, if you can imagine "Lycidas" to be something more than the stimulation of "drives," "appetites," "attitudes," in certain "areas," then you have got to use your intelligence, which, after you have been progressively educated, you probably no longer have.

As I conceive this gloomy situation, it is far more complicated than the violent synopsis of it that I have just sketched. The complications would distribute the blame to many historical villains, of whom the teachers' college racketeers (some of them misguided idealists) are only a conspicuous contemporary group. The trouble goes far back, farther even than the Romantic movement, when, for the first time in Western art, we had the belief that poetry is chiefly or even wholly an emotional experience.

Does poetry give us an emotional experience? What is an "emotional experience"? And what is an "intellectual experience"?

These are difficult questions. We are proceeding today as if they were no longer questions, as if we knew the answers, and knew them as incontestable truths. If by "an emotional experience" we mean one in which we find ourselves "moved," then we mean nothing; we are only translating a Latin word into English: a tautology. If by "an intellectual experience" we mean that we are using our minds on the relations of words, the relation of words and rhythm, the relation of the abstract words to the images, all the relations together—and if, moreover, we succeed in reducing all these things to the complete determination of logic, so that there is nothing left over, then this intellectual experience is a tautology similar to that of the emotional experience: we are intellectually using our intellects, as before we were emotionally being moved. But if on the other hand, as in the great seventeenth-century poets, you find that exhaustive analysis applied to the texture of image and metaphor fails to turn up any inconsistency, and at the same time fails to get all the meaning of the poem into a logical statement, you are participating in a poetic experience. And both intellect and emotion become meaningless in discussing it.

I have had to make that statement abstract, or not at all; it needs many pages of illustration. I can cite only three examples of poetry, which I hope will somewhat illuminate it. The first example is William Browne's slight "Epitaph on the Countesse Dowager of Pembroke," a favorite anthology piece, and one that is neither in the metaphysical style of its period nor romantically modern:

> Underneath this sable Herse
> Lyes the subject of all verse:
> Sydney's sister, Pembroke's Mother:
> Death, ere thou hast slaine another
> Faire and learned and good as she,
> Time shall throw a dart at thee.

I find this poem perennially moving (exciting, interesting), and it is plain that we cannot be moved by it until we understand it; and to understand it we have got to *analyze* the meaning of the difference here asserted as existing between Time and Death, who are dramatically personified and in conflict. Since, in one of the major modes of poetry, Death is conceived as the work of Time, we must perform a dissociation of ideas, and see Time as turning against himself, so that the destruction of Death is actually the destruction of Time. However far you may take these distinctions, no inconsistency appears; nothing contradicts anything else that is said in the poem. Yet we have not reduced the poem to strict logic. Browne has offered certain particulars that are irreducible: the Sydney and Pembroke families (for the sake of whose dignity this upheaval of the order of nature will occur); and then there is the dart, a dramatic and particular image that does not contradict, yet cannot be assimilated into, a logical paraphrase of the poem. Is this poem an emotional experience? And yet it is not an "intellectual" experience.

The second quotation must be slighted, but it is so familiar that a few lines will bring the whole poem before the reader —Shelley's "When the lamp is shattered"; I quote the last stanza:

> Its [Love's] passions will rock thee,
> As the storms rock the ravens on high:
> Bright reason will mock thee,
> Like the sun from a wintry sky.
> From thy nest every rafter
> Will rot, and thine eagle home
> Leave thee naked to laughter,
> When leaves fall and cold winds come.

The general "argument" is that the passing of spiritual communion from lovers leaves them sad and, in this last stanza, the prey of lust and self-mockery, and even of the mockery of the world ("naked to laughter"). The first line sets the tone and the "response" that the reader is to maintain to the end: we are told in advance what the following lines will mean: an abstraction that will relieve us of the trouble of examining the particular instances. Indeed, when these appear, the development of their imagery is confused and vague. The ravens in the second line are eagles in the sixth; but, after all, they are only generically birds. Greater particularity in them would have compromised their poeticism as objects, or interfered with the response we are instructed to make to them. I pass over "Bright reason," the self-mockery, for the mockery of the world. Are we to suppose that other birds come by and mock the raven (eagle), or are we to shift the field of imagery and see "thee" as a woman? Now in the finest poetry we cannot have it both ways. We can have a multiple meaning through ambiguity, but we cannot have an incoherent structure of images. Shelley, in confusion, or carelessness, or haste, could not sustain the nest-bird metaphor and say all that he wished to say; so, in order to say it, he changed the figure and ruined the poem. The more we track down the implications of his imagery, the greater the confusion; the more we track down the implications of the imagery in the best verse of Donne, Marvell, Raleigh, Milton, Hopkins, Yeats, Eliot, Ransom, Stevens, the richer the meaning of the poem. Shelley's poem is confused. Are we to conclude that therefore it offers an emotional experience?

In conclusion, one more poem—this one by W. H. Auden:

> Our hunting fathers told the story
>   Of the sadness of the creatures,
> Pitied the limits and the lack
>   Set in their finished features;
> Saw in the lion's intolerant look,
>   Behind the quarry's dying glare
> Love raging for the personal glory
>   That reason's gift would add,
> The liberal appetite and power,
>   The rightness of a god.
>
> Who nurtured in that fine tradition
>   Predicted the result,
> Guessed love by nature suited to
>   The intricate ways of guilt;
> That human company could so
>   His southern gestures modify
> And make it his mature ambition
>   To think no thought but ours,
> To hunger, work illegally,
>   And be anonymous?

In this poem there is an immense complication of metaphor, but I do not propose to unravel it. I would say just this: that all the complications can be returned without confusion or contradiction to a definite, literal, and coherent field of imagery; that when the poet wishes to extend his meaning, he does it by means of this field of metaphor, not by changing the figure, which is: the hunter debases his human nature (Love) in his arrogant, predatory conquest of the world, and Love itself becomes not merely morally bad but evil. The field of imagery, to which all the implications refer, is that of the hunting squire, who by a deft ambiguity quickly becomes predatory man.

I halt the analysis here because, as I have already said, we need something more fundamental in reading poetry than the occasional analyses of poems. I would say then, in conclusion, that modern poetry is difficult because we have lost the art of reading any poetry that will not read itself to us; that thus our trouble is a fundamental problem of education, which may be more fundamental than education. We may be approaching the time when we shall no longer be able to read anything and shall be subject to passive conditioning. Until this shall happen, however, we might possibly begin to look upon language as a field of study, not as an impressionistic debauch. If we wish to understand anything, there is only the hard way; if we wish to understand Donne and Eliot, perhaps we had better begin, young, to read the classical languages, and a little later the philosophers. There is probably no other way.

1940

A Note on Critical "Autotelism"[1]

WITHOUT *The Kenyon Review* in the past ten years I doubt that we should have the New Criticism; for it was Mr. Ransom who created its myth by giving it a name. Without the myth there would not now be the decline in public favor; the decline is only a revolt against the myth. These observations ought to indicate that I do not know what the New Criticism is, that I merely acknowledge the presence of the myth. Mr. Ransom's great and actual service to us, in this period, has been his own restless exploration of the grounds of criticsm and his hospitality to other writers of various points of view who have produced evidence of being seriously *engaged*. If the New Criticism differs radically from the best Old Criticism, it differs at its own peril; nothing wholly new would seem to be critically possible at a late stage of culture, such as we find ourselves in. The new thing may be the New Literature (how new it is I do not know), and a criticism sprang up to show us how to read it. Who the authors of this criticism are everybody who reads *The Kenyon Review* already knows. Its distinguishing feature hovers round the margins of the page: a hostility to, or neglect of, the "historical method." Yet in neither Empson nor Cleanth Brooks is history left out; it ceases to appear methodologically; it no longer devours the literary text; it survives as contributory knowledge. We have *The Kenyon*

[1] From a symposium, "The Critic's Business," *The Kenyon Review*, Winter, 1949.

Review more than any other quarterly to thank for making the new "sleight" in the art of reading possible. But by concentrating the "problems" in its pages it has aroused in many of us a predictable sense of the critical limits of the several new ways of reading the new literature, or of reading the old as if it were new.

It has seemed to me that the best criticism at all times has its best function in the ordering of original insights and in passing them on, through provisional frames of reference, to other persons secondhand. Eliot may still be our best critic because his constant frames of reference are large and loose, the frame of the particular essay being improvised, tentative and variable; he does not board the juggernaut of methodology and he keeps the faith (by and large) with the work that he is presumably examining. I am suspicious of all critical generalizations, of those that I have intemperately made in the past, and of the one that I am about to make. When insights into the meanings of a work become methodology, when the picture apologizes to the frame, we get what has been called autotelic criticism. It exists; Mr. Burke is there to prove it. But I cannot think it important as literary criticism; it has almost ceased to exist for literature (though it may *be* a kind of literature) in ceasing to be dependent.

Mr. Burke's *A Grammar of Motives* is an independent work, possibly of the imagination, and if we know how to read it, it can be both entertaining and useful; it is edifying, it enlarges one's mind. But if we think of it as criticism we must see it as an example of the atomization of experience which Blackmur feels has all but undone us. Burke seems not to be concerned with literary works as wholes; he picks off the work illustrative fractions to be devoured by his Five Master Terms. (I can think of no work of the past quite comparable to the *Grammar,* except perhaps Burton's *Anatomy.*) If there are sides to take in the little controversy which Mr. Ransom's review [2] of Hyman and Blackmur seems to invite, I take the side of Blackmur, and for a good reason: he looks like a horse of another color— roughly, of my color; that is, of almost no color at all, unless one is compelled to observe the lurid shades of the Blackmurian style. There is, at any rate, no methodology.

I am the more impressed by Mr. Blackmur's almost puritanical heroism in rejecting the so-called, merely book sciences ending in *logy* (psychology, anthropology, sociology) because he has in the past, I believe, looked into them; whereas I never quite did. I must confess to having been a long time on his side, and not pretend that I ever had a side that he could be on. Should not criticism be one of the more prudently skeptical activities of the mind? When it reaches in Mr. Burke the stage of perverse skepticism at which it substitutes doubt of the value of the imaginative order for doubt of itself, is it not on the way to becoming a *logy?* I take Mr. Blackmur's "A Burden for Critics" to be a new declaration of critical skepticism; it may even be an augury of a rise in the market for the New Criticism. I see him here starting all over again, with accumulated knowledge and insight, but still with no commitment to "method." I agree with Mr. Ransom that Mr. Blackmur's position is untenable; it cannot be held. Neither can Johnson's, Coleridge's, nor Eliot's; they are all full of holes. I hope that Blackmur will not try to hold a position and that he will continue to be interested in something else; for example, how the imagination acts in a given instance.

It would be worse than folly to argue that the whole task of criticism must stop short of its philosophical implications, or of the philosophical implications of the literary work. Any criticism that increases our knowledge of litera-

[2] Stanley Hyman, *The Armed Vision* (New York, 1948), and R. P. Blackmur, "A Burden for Critics," *The Hudson Review*, Summer, 1948.

ture and its availability has its place. Only the size of the place, for those kinds that approach autotelism, is in question. The "place" of James's *Prefaces* must be larger than that of the schematization of their insights in Lubbock's *The Craft of Fiction,* even though Lubbock sharpens some of our own insights into the *Prefaces* and into James's art as a whole. There can be no end to the permutations of the critical relation to literature, philosophy, and religion. The New Criticism offers to the lingering eye as many permutations as criticism in the past has offered, and probably more. Mr. Ransom, for example, has been concerned for more than ten years with the place of the work of art in the total moral and psychic experience; and in this enquiry he has been unlike any other American critic. The New Critics look alike as Mongolians look alike to me; as Mr. Ransom might look, to the Mongolians, like the late Babe Ruth.

1949

Three Types of Poetry

I

IN THIS essay I propose to discuss three kinds of poetry that bring to focus three attitudes of the modern world. I do not say all three attitudes, because there are more than three attitudes. And there are more than three kinds of poetry.

The first attitude is motivated by the practical will: in poetry until the seventeenth century it leaned upon moral abstractions and allegory; now, under the influence of the sciences, it has appealed to physical ideas. It looks from knowledge to action. The second attitude has been developed from the second phase of the first; it is a revolt against the domination of science, and in poetry it has given us the emotion known as "romantic irony." The third attitude is nameless because it is perfect, because it is complete and whole. Criticism may isolate the imperfect and formulate that which is already abstract; but it cannot formulate the concrete whole. There is no philosophical or historical name for the kind of poetry that Shakespeare wrote. I shall call it, in this essay, the creative spirit. I use the term for convenience, and ask the reader to forget its current uses by the followers of the Expressionist school.

We happen to be dominated at the moment by the scientific spirit of the practical will. A hundred and fifty years ago rose the thin cry of romantic irony—the poet's self-pity upon the rack of science, which he mistook for reality. Most notably in the sixteenth century we had the creative spirit.

The reader is asked to keep in mind two more general statements with some brief commentary:

First, the power of seizing the inward meaning of experience, the power of poetic creation that I shall call here the vision of the whole of life, is *a quality of the imagination.* The apologists of science speak as if this were the scientific attitude, but the aim of science is to produce a dynamic whole for the service of the practical will. Our experience of nuclear energy seems to be very different from our capacity to control it. For the imaginative whole of life is the wholeness of vision at a particular moment of experience; it yields us the quality of the experience.

It may be conveyed in a poem of four or six lines or in an epic of twelve books; or the twelve books may contain less of it than the four lines. Blake's "To the Accuser" is the total vision in eight lines; Darwin's "The Loves of the Plants" is the aimlessly statistical aggregation of fact—pseudo-botany or semi-science—in a number of lines that I have not counted.

Second, there is a surer grasp of the totality of experience in Wyat's "To His Lute" than in Shelley's "Adonaïs." This is the center of my argument. We must understand that the lines

> Life like a dome of many-colored glass
> Stains the white radiance of eternity

are not poetry; they express the frustrated individual will trying to compete with science. The will asserts a rhetorical proposition about the whole of life, but the imagination has not seized upon the materials of the poem and made them into a whole. Shelley's simile is imposed upon the material from above; it does not grow out of the material. It exists as explanation external to the subject: it is an explanation of "life" that seems laden with portent and high significance, but *as explanation* it necessarily looks towards possible action, and it is there that we know that the statement is meaningless. Practical experimental knowledge can alone fit means to ends.

If the simile of the dome were an integral part of a genuine poem, the question of its specific merit as truth or falsehood would not arise. Yet Shelley's dome, as an explanation of experience, is quite as good as Edgar's reflection on his father's downfall:

> Ripeness is all.

But the figure rises from the depth of Gloucester's situation. It is a summation not only of Gloucester's tragedy but of the complex tensions of the plot before the catastrophe in the last scene. Possibly *King Lear* would be as good without Edgar's words; but it would be difficult to imagine the play without the passage ending in those words. They are implicit in the total structure, the concrete quality, of the whole experience that we have when we read *King Lear*. The specific merit of Edgar's statement as general truth or falsehood is irrelevant because it is an *experienced statement*, first from Edgar's, then from our own, point of view; and the statement remains experienced, and thus significant and comprehensible, whether it be true or false.

The truth or falsity of Shelley's figure is the only issue that it raises. This bit of Platonism must be accepted before we can accept the material of the poem "Adonaïs"; for it must be a true idea to afford to the poet a true explanation. He must have an explanation for a material that he cannot experience. The idea of the dome is asserted to strengthen a subject that the poet has not implicitly imagined.

It was this quality of modern poetry that Arnold had in mind, or doubtless should have had in mind, when he remarked that the romantics "did not know enough." We have not known enough since their time. Arnold wrote later that the Victorian critics permitted the poet "to leave poetic sense ungratified, provided that he gratifies their rhetorical sense and their curiosity." If the term rhetoric must have an invidious meaning, I think we may understand Arnold somewhat in this manner: that rhetoric is a forcing of the subject, which is abstractly conceived, not implicitly seized upon. It is external and decorative in the early romantics of the mid-eighteenth century; it is hysterical, and evasive of the material, in the great romantics—and it excites the "curiosity" of the reader, who dwells on the external details of the poem or pities the sad poet. The reader is not given an integral work of art. How could criticism since Shelly and Wordsworth be anything but personal?—strive for anything but evaluation of personality? It has been given little else to evaluate. And why should not criticism fail in evaluating Shakespeare's personality? And is this not the glory of Shakespeare?

The reader's curiosity is motivated by his will. In the lowest terms, he seeks information (even from a poet); then, more purposefully, he seeks for the information an explanation that, if it is good, is some branch of science. But like the recent neo-Humanists he tries to get explanations from the poets.

"For what is rhetoric," wrote W. B. Yeats nearly fifty years ago, "but the will trying to do the work of the imagination?" Mr. Yeats, with insight as profound as it is rare in our time, went straight to the problem. Rhetoric is the pseudo-explanation of unimagined material. The "right" explanation—the exhibit of workable relations among different parts of any material—although always provisional, is the scientific explanation. When the will tries to do the work of the imagination, it fails, and only succeeds in doing badly the work of science. When the will supplants the imagination in poetry, the task of the poet, because his instrument is not adequate to his unconscious purpose, which is that of a science, is bound to be frustrated. We get the peculiar frustration of the poet known as romantic irony.

The pure scientific spirit I shall call here without much regard for accuracy, a positive Platonism, a cheerful confidence in the limitless power of man to impose practical abstractions upon his experience. Romantic irony is a negative Platonism, a self-pitying disillusionment with the positive optimism of the other program: the romantic tries to build up a set of fictitious "explanations," by means of rhetoric, more congenial to his unscientific temper. The creative spirit occupies an aloof middle ground—it is in no sense a compromise, as the late Irving Babbitt conceived it to be—between these positions. Its function is the quality of experience, the total revelation—not explanation for the purpose of external control by the will.

I I

Dante distinguished two kinds of allegory. Religious allegory is both literally and figuratively true: we are to believe that the events of the story happened. But poetical allegory is true only in the figurative sense. The derivative meanings, called by Dante the moral and the anagogical, are legitimate, indeed they are the highest meanings; but they lean upon no basis of fact. Although fictional allegory is not popular today, it is the only sort that we can conceive. When the medieval allegorist used the Bible, it never entered his head that he was not using historical fact; and he brought the same mentality to bear upon material that even we, who are sophisticated, recognize as historical.

But a modern poet, attempting allegory, undoes the history. We accept his figures and images as amiable make-believe, knowing that historical fact and poetic figure have no real connection, simply because there is nothing true but fact. About this fact science alone can instruct us, not with a fundamentally different kind of instruction from that of the allegorist, but with the same kind, more systematic and efficient. When the author of the popular poem, "John Brown's Body," shows us the machine age growing out of Brown's body, we know that nothing of the sort happened, and we ask for the more enlightened view of the facts available in the scientific historians.

It is the kind of poetry that is primarily allegorical that seems to me to be inferior. It is inferior as science, and it is inferior as poetry. Mere allegory is a vague and futile kind of science. And because its primary direction is towards that oversimplification of life which is the mark of the scientific will, it is a one-sided poetry, ignoring the whole vision of experience. Although *The Divine Comedy* is allegorical, it would not be one of the great poems of all time if Dante had not believed its structure of action to be true. It came out of an age whose mentality held the allegorical view of experience as easily as we hold the causal and scientific; so, in Dante, allegory never rises to an insubordinate place, but consistently occupies an implicit place, from which we must derive it by analysis.

There is a general sense in which all literature may be apprehended as allegory, and that sense explains the popular level of literary appreciation. When certain moral ideas preponderate over others in any kind of literature, the crudely practical reader abstracts them, and contents himself with the illusion that they are the total meaning of the work. The naïve Roman Catholic may see only this phase of Dante, who for him might as well have written a tract. Now when the preponderance of meanings receives from the author himself the seal of his explicit approval, in face of the immense complication of our experience, then the work tends towards allegory. The work is written in the interest of social, moral, and religious ideas apart from which it has little existence or significance. It becomes aesthetic creation at a low level of intensity. If the intention is innocent, the result is didacticism. If it is deliberate and systematic, and calculated to move people into some definite course of action, we get what is called in our time propaganda.

Didactic and propagandist works frequently have great artistic merit and power. Fiction different as *The Pilgrim's Progress* and *An American Tragedy* is overwhelming evidence of this. The perception of merit in this kind of writing has become a pretext, in our age, for believing that its defects, chiefly the defect of "propaganda," are a primary motive of all literature in all times. When the deficiency or impurity of inspiration is not forthright, it is nevertheless assumed as present but concealed: this is the kind of propaganda that is supposedly written from the security of a ruling class.

Pure allegory differs from this kind of writing in that the preponderance of meaning is wholly revealed; the characters, images, symbols, ideas, are simple, and invite restatement in paraphrases that exhaust their meaning; they stand, not in themselves, but merely for something else. *The Faerie Queene* belongs to this class of allegory. The summary remarks that I shall make about that great poem by no means encompass it; for there is more to be said that would not be to my purpose.

The structural feature that first impresses the reader of the poem is the arbitrary length of each canto: there is no reason inherent in the narrative why a canto should not be longer or shorter than it is. The characters remain homogeneous throughout; that is to say, they suffer no dramatic alteration; an episode ends when they have acted out enough of the moral to please the poet. The action has no meaning apart from the preconceived abstractions, which we may call Renaissance Platonism or any other suitable name, so long as we remember that the ideas suffer no shock and receive no complication in contact with the narrative. The narrative lacks inner necessity; it is all illustration. The capacity of the poet to allegorize the "philosophy" was illimitable, and terminated only with his death, which prevented completion of the poem.

One must remember that this sort of allegory has predominated in our tradition. Anglo-American literature, with the possible exception, at his high moments, of Nathaniel Hawthorne, has not given us allegory of the Dantesque order. I allude here to Dante's ability to look into a specific experience and to recreate it in such a way that its meaning is nowhere distinct from its specific quality. The allegorical interpretation is secondary. We get a genuine creation of the imagination. We get, in the Spenserian allegory, a projection of the will.

The quality and intention of the allegorical will are the intention and quality of the will of science. With allegory the image is not a complete, qualitative whole; it is an abstraction calculated to force the situation upon which it is imposed toward a single direction. In the sixteenth century science proper had achieved none of its triumphs. The allegorist had before him no standard by which he could measure the extent of his failure to find the right abstractions for the control of nature. He could spin out his tales endlessly in serene confidence of their "truth." But by the end of the eighteenth century his optimism had waned; it had passed to the more efficient allegorist of nature, the modern scientist.

Now in a poet like Dante we may say that there is an element of "science" in so far as the allegorical interpretation is possible: *The Divine Comedy* has something to say, not only to the naïve Roman Catholic, but to the ordinary man whose prepossessions are practical, and whose literary appreciation is limited by the needs of his own will. The poem has a moral, a set of derivative ideas that seem to the reader to be relevant to practical conduct. But to say this is not to say, with most schools of modern criticism, that it is the primary significance of the work. For Dante is a poet; the didactic element is in solution with the other elements, and may be said barely to exist in itself, since it must be isolated by the violence of the reader's own will.

There is therefore a distinction to be drawn between a kind of writing in which allegorical meanings are fused with the material, and pure and explicit allegory. It is the difference between works of the creative imagination and the inferior works of the practical will. The reader will recall my first proposition: the power of creating the inner meaning of experience is a quality of the imagination. It is not a construction of the will, that perpetual modernism through which, however vast may be the physical extent of the poet's range, the poet ignores the whole of experience for some special interest. This modern literature of Platonism—a descriptive term used to set apart a kind of work in which the meanings are forced—carries with it its own critical apparatus. It is known at present as the revolutionary or social point of view. Since the rise of science it has been also the "capitalist" point of view. For our whole culture seems to be obsessed by a kind of literature that is derivative of the allegorical mentality.

By the time of Dryden allegory of the medieval variety had lost its prestige; we get the political fables of "The Hind and the Panther," of "Absalom and Achitophel," where the intention is pleasantly fictitious and local, with little pretense of universal truth. By the end of the next century the Platonic conquest of the world, the confident assertion of control over the forces of nature, had contrived a system of abstractions exact enough to assume the new name of science. So, in poetry, the allegorical mentality, which had hitherto used all the crude science available, lost confidence in its unexperimental ideas. The poetical assertion of the will took the form of revolt from its more successful counterpart, science. We find here two assertions of the same erring will, diverging for the first time: science *versus* romanticism.

I I I

With the decline then of pure allegory, we see the rise of a new systematic structure of entities called science, which makes good the primitive allegorist's futile claim to the control of nature. Between allegorist and scientist there exists the illusion of fundamental opposition. They are, however, of one origin and purpose.[1] For the apparent hostility of science to the allegorical entities is old age's preoccupation with the follies of its youth.

When this situation became fully developed, the poets, deprived of their magical fictions, and stripped of the means of affirming the will allegorically, proceeded to revolt, pitting the individual will against all forms of order, under the illusion that all order is scientific order. The order of the imagination became confused. Thus arose romanticism, not qualitatively different from the naturalism that it attacked, but identical with it, and committed in the arts to the same imperfect inspiration.

This summary will, I believe, be illuminated by a passage from Taine, who is discussing Byron:

Such are the sentiments wherewith he surveyed nature and history, not to comprehend them and forget himself before them, but to seek in them and impress upon them the image of his own passions. He does not leave the objects to speak for themselves, but forces them to answer him.

We have the endless quest of the romantic, who ranges over nature in the effort to impose his volitional ego as an absolute upon the world. Compare Taine's analysis of Byron with a sentence from Schopenhauer:

1 "Always science has grown up on religion . . . and always it signifies nothing more or less than an abstract melioration of these doctrines, considered as false because less abstract." Spengler, *The Decline of the West.*

While science, following the unresting and inconstant stream of the fourfold forms of reason and consequent, with each end attained sees further, and can never reach a final goal nor attain full satisfaction any more than by running we can reach the place where the clouds touch the horizon; art, on the contrary, is everywhere at its goal.

For the will of science and the will of the romantic poet (the frustrated allegorist) are the same will. Romanticism is science without the systematic method of asserting the will. Because it cannot participate in the infinite series of natural conquests, the romantic spirit impresses upon nature the image of its own passions:

> Make me thy lyre, even as the forest is:
> What if my leaves are falling like its own!
> The tumult of thy mighty harmonies

> Will take from both a deep autumnal tone,
> Sweet though in sadness. Be thou, Spirit fierce,
> My spirit! Be thou me, impetuous one!

It is the "will trying to do the work of the imagination." The style is inflated and emotive. The poet, instead of fixing his attention upon a single experience, instead of presenting dramatically the plight of human weakness—the subject of his poem—flies from his situation into a rhetorical escape that gives his will the illusion of power. (It may be observed that at the culmination of French romanticism in Rimbaud, the poet, still caught upon the dilemma of the will, carried this dilemma to its logical and most profound conclusion— the destruction of the will.)

The momentary illusion of individual power is a prime quality of the romantic movement. In the intervals when the illusion cannot be maintained, arise those moments of irony that create the subjective conflict of romantic poetry. In generalizing about such a quality one must take care; it differs with different poets. I have just pointed out incidentally how the individual will receives, in a late and perhaps the greatest romantic, a self-destructive motivation. Yet the dramatic effect is similar in poets as different as Rimbaud and Shelley. Throughout the nineteenth century, and in a few poets today, we get an intellectual situation like this: there is the assumption that Truth is indifferent or hostile to the desires of men; that these desires were formerly nurtured on legend, myth, all kinds of insufficient experiment; that, Truth being known at last in the form of experimental science, it is intellectually impossible to maintain illusion any longer, at the same time that it is morally impossible to assimilate the inhuman Truth.

The poet revolts from Truth; that is, he defies the cruel and naturalistic world to break him if it can; and he is broken. This moral situation, transferred to the plane of drama or the lyric, becomes romantic irony—that is, an irony of his position of which the poet himself is not aware:

> I fall upon the thorns of life! I bleed!

His will being frustrated by inhospitable Truth, Shelley is broken; falls into disillusionment; and asks the west wind to take him away and make him its lyre. In a contemporary poet, whose death two years ago was probably the climax of the romantic movement in this country, we get the same quality of irony. Invoking a symbol of primitive simplicity, Pocahontas, Crane says:

> Lie to us! Dance us back our tribal morn!

The poet confesses that he has no access to a means of satisfying his will, or to a kind of vision where the terms are not set by the demands of the practical will. He returns to a fictitious past. There he is able to maintain, for a moment, the illusion that he might realize the assertion of his will in a primitive world where scientific truth is not a fatal obstacle.

At this point we must notice a special property of the

romantic imagination. It has no insight into the total meanings of actual moral situations; it is concerned with fictitious
alternatives to them, because they invariably mean frustration of the will. This special property of escape is the Golden
Age, used in a special fashion. The romantic poet attributes
to it an historical reality. In a great poet like Shakespeare,
notably in *The Tempest,* we get the implications of the
poetic convention of the Golden Age; properly looked at, it
is more than a poetic convention, it is a moral necessity of
man. The use to which Shakespeare puts it is not involved in
the needs of his personal will; it assists in defining the quality of his insight into the permanent flaws of human character. For the Golden Age is not a moral or social possibility;
it is a way of understanding the problem of evil, being a picture of human nature with the problem removed. It is a
qualitative fiction, not a material world, that permits the
true imagination to recognize evil for what it is.

Now the romantic and allegorical poet, once he is torn
with disbelief in the adequacy of the poetic will, sees before
him two alternatives. After falling upon the thorns of life,
he may either ask the west wind to take him up, or cry for
his tribal morn in the Golden Age: this is the first alternative—disillusionment with life after defeat of the will. He
will seize this escape provided that he lacks the hardihood
of a Rimbaud, who saw that, given the satisfaction of will as
a necessity of the age, the poet must either destroy his will
or repudiate poetry for a career of action. But Rimbaud
is the exceptional, because he is the perfect, romantic poet.

The other ordinary alternative of the modern allegorist
lies in the main Spenserian tradition of ingenuous tale-tell-
ing; it is the pure Golden Age of the future, which the poet
can envisage with complacency because his will has not gone
off into the frustration of romantic irony. He enjoys something like the efficient optimism of science; he asks us to believe that a rearrangement of the external relations of man

will not alone make him a little more comfortable, but will remove the whole problem of evil, and usher in perfection. It is this type of crude, physical imagination that we find in Tennyson:

> Till the war-drums sound no longer, and the battleflags
>   are furled
> In the Parliament of Man, the Federation of the World.

The cult of the will is a specially European or Western cult; it rose after the Middle Ages, and it informs our criticism of society and the arts. For, given the assumption that poetry is only another kind of volition, less efficient than science, it is easy to believe in the superiority of the scientific method. I myself believe in it. For the physical imagination of science is, step by step, perfect, and knows no limit. The physical imagination of poetry, granting it an unlimited range, is necessarily compacted of futile and incredible fictions, which we summarily reject as inferior instruments of the will. And rightly reject, if we assume two things—and our age is convinced that it is impossible to assume anything else: (1) that the only kind of imagination is that of the will, which best realizes its purposes in external constructions or in the control of the external relations of persons and things; (2) that this sole type of imagination will be disillusioned or optimistic, according as it is either imperfectly informed, as in mere poetry, or adequately equipped by science with the "fourfold forms of reason and consequent." That is the view held by a leading school of critics in this country, the most influential of whom has been Mr. Edmund Wilson in *Axel's Castle,* a book written on the assumption that *all* poetry is only an inferior kind of social will.

The critical movement so ably represented by Mr. Wilson is the heresy that I am opposing throughout this essay. That the kind of imaginative literature demanded by this school is the third, and I think necessarily the final, stage in the history of allegory in Western culture, may not be immediately clear.

The school preoccupied with what is called the economic determinism of literature is in the direct line of descent from the crudely moralistic allegory of the Renaissance. The notion that all art is primarily an apology for institutions and classes, though it is now the weapon of the Marxists against "capitalist" literature, has been explicit in our intellectual outlook since the time of Buckle in England, and Taine and Michelet in France. It is an article of faith in the "capitalist" and utilitarian dogma that literature, like everything else, must be primarily, and thus solely, an expression of the will. From such allegory as:

> With him went Danger, clothed in ragged weeds,
>   Made of bear's skin, that him more dreadful made,
> Yet his own face was dreadful, he did need
>   Strange horror, to deform his grisly shade;
>   A net in th' one hand, and a rusty blade
> In th' other was, this Mischief, that Mishap . . .

—from this it is only a step to the sophisticated entities and abstractions of the agitation for social reform, whose vocabulary is an imitation, and an application to conduct, of the terms of physical science. Or rather, I should say, two steps; for the intermediate stage of allegory is the romantic irony of the age of Byron and Shelley. The contemporary allegorists have regained something of the easy confidence of their early forerunners; they believe as fully in the positive efficacy of the Marxian dialectic, as Spenser in the negative example of the Seven Deadly Sins.

Yet, the Seven Deadly Sins being now a little threadbare, our new allegorists are quite clear in their recognition that the arts, more especially poetry, have no specific function in society. The arts offer to society a pusillanimous instrument for the realization of its will. The better the art, one must add, the more pusillanimous. For art aims at nothing outside itself, and, in the words of Schopenhauer, "is everywhere at its goal." There is no goal for the literature of the will, whose new objective must be constantly redefined in terms of the technology, verbal or mechanical, available at the moment.

The significance of this movement in modern society is perfectly plain: by seizing exclusively those aspects of the total experience that are capable of being put to predictable and successful use, the modern spirit has committed itself to the most dangerous program in Western history. It has committed itself exclusively to this program. We should do well to consider a specimen, by Phelps Putnam, of contemporary romantic irony; the "He" in the passage is the Devil:

> He leaned his elbows on two mountain tops
> And moved his head slowly from side to side,
> Sweeping the plain with his unhurried eyes.
> He was the phoenix of familiar men,
> Of husbands I have known, the horns and all,
> But more, much more—O God, I was afraid.
> I would have hid before the eyes had come.
> Then they were there, and then
> My guts grew warm again in my despair
> And I cried "Pour la Reine" and drew my sword.
> But, Christ, I had no sword.

He had no science; the fictitious sword of the allegorical will that the hero "drew" was incompetent to deal with his desperately practical situation. Our new scientific allegorists rest their case against poetry there. What they neglect to provide for is the hero's failure in case he has a genuine sword of science. For the recognition of that other half of experience, the realm of immitigable evil—or perhaps I had better say in modern abstraction, the margin of error in social calculation—has been steadily lost. The fusion of human success and human error in a vision of the whole of life, *the vision itself being its own goal,* has almost disappeared from the modern world.

I V

I have set forth two propositions about poetry. I will now ask the reader to examine a little more narrowly the second, in the attempt to discriminate between a poetry of the will and a poetry of genuine imagination. We have seen that the poetry of the will takes two forms. There is the romantic, disillusioned irony of Shelley, or for that matter of a poet like Mr. Robinson Jeffers; there is the crude optimism of Tennyson, a moral outlook that has almost vanished from poetry, surviving today as direct political and social propaganda supported by the "social" sciences. My second proposition was a brief commentary on the lines by Shelley:

> Life like a dome of many-colored glass
> Stains the white radiance of eternity

The will asserts a general proposition about the whole of life, but there is no specific, imagined context to support the assertion. As a product of the imagination the passage is incomprehensible; as a practical, that is to say, as a scientific generalization, it is open to the just contempt of the scientific mind. What, then, is the exact purpose and function of such poetry?

In purpose it competes with science; as to function it supports the illusion of moral insight in persons who are incapable of either scientific discipline or poetic apprehension. It is an affirmation of the will in terms that are not a legitimate vehicle of the will. The proper mode of the will— proper, that is, in efficiency, but not necessarily in morals, for the question whether the will should be so expressed at all is a distinct problem—the right mode of the will is some kind of practical effort adequately informed by exact science.

Most modern schools of criticism assume that all poetry is qualitatively the same as the lines by Shelley; they assume this negatively, for the positive assumption is that poetry must of necessity be like science, a quantitative instrument for mastery of the world. This is the interesting theory of Mr. I. A. Richards: because poetry is compacted of "pseudo-statements" it cannot compete with "certified scientific statements," and must be discredited as science moves on to fresh triumphs. This point of view is doubtless inevitable in a scientific age; but it is not an inevitable point of view.

Mr. Richards's theory of the relation between poetry and our beliefs about the world appears novel to some critics. It is the latest version of the allegorical, puritan and utilitarian theory of the arts—a theory that is rendered, by Mr. Richards, the more plausible because it seems to give to the arts a very serious attention. The British utilitarians, a century ago, frankly condemned them. So, with less candor, does Mr. Richards: his desperate efforts to make poetry, after all, useful, consist in justly reducing its "explanations" to nonsense, and salvaging from the wreck a mysterious agency for "ordering our minds." Poetry is a storehouse of ordered emotional energy that properly released might reeducate the public in the principles of the good life. For brevity, I paraphrase Mr. Richards; it should be observed that the idea is set forth in terms of the will.[2]

Yet there is, even according to Mr. Richards, little hope for this kind of education. The "certified scientific statements" about the world make the metaphors, the images, the symbols, all the varieties of "pseudo-statements"—similes like the dome of many-colored glass—look extremely foolish, because in the more exact light of science, they are patently untrue. I do not intend here to discuss this theory as a whole, nor to do justice to Mr. Richards' poetic taste, which is superior. One part of the theory, I believe, may be dismissed at once. How can poetry, a tissue of lies, equip the public with "relevant responses" to an environment? Our re-

---

[2] The discussion here is based upon Mr. Richards's two principal books: *The Principles of Literary Criticism* (London, 1924), and *Practical Criticism* (London, 1929). For discussion of Mr. Richards's later views, *supra*, pp. 97–105.

sponses must work; they must be, in at least a provisional sense, scientifically true. What is this mysterious emotional function of poetry that orders our minds with falsehood?

Mr. Richards is, I believe, talking about the unstable fringe of emotion that I have called romantic irony: we have seen that this is what is left to the poet—a lugubrious residue —after he realizes that science is truth and that his own fictions are lies. This residue, alas, organizes and orders nothing whatever. Mr. Richards's underlying assumption about poetry is, like Mr. Edmund Wilson's, embedded in the humanitarian mentality of the age, where it lies too deep for examination.

If the pseudo-statement is motivated by the will (the only intention for it that Mr. Richards can conceive), it is false, and Mr. Richards is right: the poet of this sort expects potatoes to grow better when planted in the dark of the moon.

If, on the other hand, a genuine poet uses the pseudo-statement, it is neither true nor false, but is a quality of the total created object: the poem. The power to perceive this total quality has almost disappeared from modern criticism. For all the arts are assumed to be necessarily assertions of the will.

Mr. Richards, like the romantic poet of the age of Byron and Shelley, sees that science has contrived a superior instrument of the will; again like them, he tries to rescue poetry by attributing to it functions of practical volition, functions that he cannot define but which, in the true "liberal" tradition, he asserts in some realm of private hope against the "truths" of science.

Now it seems to me that the foundations of poetry, and possibly of the other creative arts, are somewhat different. We cannot understand them until we shall have eliminated from our thinking the demands of the category of will with its instrument, the practical intellect.

Let us look at Mr. Richards's famous terms: "certified

scientific statement" (science) and "pseudo-statement" (poetry). I will try to show briefly that, for poetry, the certified scientific statement is the half-statement. The pseudo-statement may be, as I have just said, neither true nor false, but a feature of the total quality of the poem. The lines

> Out, out brief candle!
> Life's but a walking shadow; a poor player
> That struts and frets his hour upon the stage,
> And then is heard no more . . .

are certainly not "true": we know that life is not a shadow, it is a vast realm of biological phenomena; nor is it a player. Neither are the lines false: they represent a stage in the dynamic unfolding of Macbeth's character, the whole created image of which is the whole play *Macbeth,* which in its turn is neither true nor false, but *exists as a created object.* None of the pseudo-statements in the play, representing the conflict of will that forms the plot, is either approved or disapproved by the poet. He neither offers us a practical formula for action nor rejects any of the volitional purposes of the characters. He creates the total object of which the pseudo-statements of the will are a single feature, and are therefore neither true nor false. What Mr. Richards's theory (and others like it) comes down to is the uneasy consciousness that such a passage as I have just quoted does not tell us how to keep out of the sort of mess that Macbeth got himself into. The ideal connection of this theory with the traditions of moralistic allegory is quite evident.

Before we may see the certified scientific statement as the half-statement, a further point of Mr. Richards's theory must be noticed. Poets, being ignorant of science and their general ideas false, ought to write poems in which appear no beliefs whatever, but in which, presumably, there is that mysterious ordering of our minds. *The Waste Land* is such a poem—supposedly. But is it? According to the poet himself and to my own simple powers of inspection, it is full of beliefs. Mr. Richards, with admirable aplomb, has seized upon a poem in which large generalizations do not appear, as an instance of his theory: that poets, to keep our respect, must order our minds without lies; that, in order to avoid saying wrong things, they must say nothing. And this "nothing" is only another species of half-statement. It leads straight to a defense of the recent school of "pure poets" in France,[3] a school that had its meeker followers in England and this country.

This half-statement may be in the pure poets an immersion in the supposedly pure sensations of experience. But in the older romantics of the nineteenth century, it is due to a sentimental escape from the abstractions of science. And indeed both fallacies are due to a misunderstanding of the exact nature of the "certified scientific statement." We saw, in the second section of this essay, how the romantics revolted from science, or one kind of half-statement, giving us romantic irony. This irony has dwindled, in our day, to the other half-statement (to the other activity of the same will) of "pure poetry." It is significant that at the present time we get, from both scientist and pure poet, a renunciation of poetry because it cannot compete with the current version of our objective world, a version that is pre-empted by the demands of the will with its certified scientific statements.

It must be remembered that this kind of statement is invariably the half-statement. It is the statement about a thing, a person, an experience, which relates it to something else, not for the purpose of giving us intensive knowledge of the thing, person, or experience, in itself and as a whole; but to give us, in varying degrees depending upon the exactness of the science under which it is viewed, the half-knowledge that limits us to the control of its extensive relations. If I feed a

[3] See Henri Bremond, *La Poésie Pure* (Paris, 1926).

horse corn every day at noon, I may expect him to do more work in the afternoon than he would do without it. I am controlling the relation between grain and horse under the general proposition: Regular feeding of grain increases an animal's capacity for work. The statement must be either true or false.

But the statements in a genuine work of art are neither "certified" nor "pseudo-"; the creative intention removes them from the domain of practicality. "In aesthetics," wrote Mr. Leo Stein a few years ago in an excellent book, "we have to do with complex wholes which are never in a rigid state of adjustment." [4] This integral character of the work of art forever resists practical formulation. The aesthetic whole invites indefinitely prolonged attention; whereas the half-statement of science arrests our attention at those features of the whole that may be put to the service of the will. In the following verses the horse cannot be *used,* but as an object arousing prolonged contemplation in its particular setting it may be *known:*

> I set her on my pacing steed,
> And nothing else saw all day long,
> For sidelong she would bend, and sing
> A faëry's song.

The stanza is neither true nor false; it is an object that exists.

I think it ought to be clear by this time that theories like Mr. Richards's, theories covertly or avowedly developed in the interest of social schemes, are not guides to the study of the immense qualitative whole of works of art; they are scientific (more or less) charts, relating the art-object to other objects at the command of the practical will. So it may be said that such theories belong to that perpetually modern impulse to *allegorize* poetry, to abstract for use those fea-

[4] Leo Stein, *The ABC of Æsthetics* (New York, 1927).

tures that are available for immediate action, and to repudiate the rest.

It ought to be clear that this is the regular course of science in the whole universe of objects; that with the arts science proceeds consistently, on principle; that society has developed an instinctive approach to the arts appropriate to the scientific temper of the age.

A man lives in a beautiful house in a beautiful place. Let him discover oil under his land. The oil has been there all the time as a feature of the total scene. But he violates the integrity of the scene by "developing" the oil. Where the house and land had previously existed as a whole of which utility was only one aspect, he abstracts one feature of it for immediate use by means of Mr. Richards's certified scientific half-statements; and destroys its wholeness. Perhaps he was a dreaming kind of man: suppose he had always meant to get out the oil, and had gone about it with an improper method. Suppose that all he could do was to write a poem, like the "Ode to the West Wind," in which he said: "O Oil, make me thy conduit, even as the earth is!" It would be a poem of the will, and Mr. Richards would have a perfect right to test the scientific efficiency of the formula urged by the poem.

It is not with this kind of poetry, but with another kind that is not a poetry of the will, that I have been concerned; and I have been offering a few commonplaces about its neglect by our advanced critics. Genuine poetry has been written in most ages—including the present—but it is a sort of poetry that was written most completely by Shakespeare. It is the sort of poetry that our "capitalist" and "communist" allegorists have forgotten how to read.

I have sketched some aspects of the poetry of the will, which in the last century and a half has taken two directions that I will summarize again. First, the optimism of science, either pure or social science, an uncritical and positive Platonism. Secondly, the negative Platonism of the romantic spirit, a pessimistic revolt of the individual against the optimism of the scientific will. The quality of volition is practical in both kinds of Platonism. But for isolated figures like Landor, Hopkins, and Dickinson in the last century, and a few today, the creative spirit has been shunted off into obscurity by the heresy of the will.

The quality of poetic vision that I have already in this essay named, with respect to the two forms of will, the middle ground of vision, and, with respect to itself, the vision of the whole, is not susceptible of logical demonstration. We may prepare our minds for its reception by the logical elimination of error. But the kind of criticism that dominates our intellectual life is that of the French mathematician who, after reading a tragedy by Racine, asked: *"Qu'est ce que cela prouve?"* It proves nothing; it creates the totality of experience in its quality; and it has no useful relation to the ordinary forms of action.

Since I have not set out to prove an argument, but to look into arguments that seem to me to be wrong, I will state a conclusion as briefly as possible: that poetry finds its true usefulness in its perfect inutility, a focus of repose for the will-driven intellect that constantly shakes the equilibrium of persons and societies with its unremitting imposition of partial formulas. When the will and its formulas are put back into an implicit relation with the whole of our experience, we get the true knowledge which is poetry. It is the "kind of knowledge which is really essential to the world, the true content of its phenomena, that which is subject to no change, and therefore is known with equal truth for all time." Let us not argue about it. It is here for those who have eyes to see.

1934

The Present Function of Criticism

Nous avons une impuissance de prouver, invincible à tout le dogmatisme. Nous avons une idée de la vérité, invincible à tout le pyrrhonisme. . . . PASCAL

I

WE ARE NOT very much concerned when we confess that communication among certain points of view is all but impossible. Let us put three persons together who soon discover that they do not agree. No matter; they quickly find a procedure, a program, an objective. So they do agree that there is something to be *done,* although they may not be certain why they are doing it, and they may not be interested in the results, the meaning of which is not very important: before they can consider the meaning they have started a new program. This state of mind is positivism. It assumes that the communication of ideas towards the formulation of truths is irrelevant to action; the program is an end in itself. But if we are interested in truth I believe that our intellectual confusion is such that we can merely write that interest upon the record of our time.

This essay represents a "point of view" which seems to have little in common with other points of view that are tolerated, and even applauded, today. It cannot be communicated at the level of the procedure and the program; it cannot, in short, be communicated to persons whose assumptions about life come out of positivism. (For positivism is not only a scientific movement; it is a moral attitude.) It has moved to contempt and rage persons whose intelligence I respect and admire.

The point of view here, then, is that historicism, scientism, psychologism, biologism, in general the confident use of the scientific vocabularies in the spiritual realm, has created or at any rate is the expression of a spiritual disorder. That disorder may be briefly described as a dilemma.

On the one hand, we assume that all experience can be ordered scientifically, an assumption that we are almost ready to confess has intensified if it has not actually created our distress; but on the other hand, this assumption has logically reduced the spiritual realm to irresponsible emotion, to what the positivists of our time see as irrelevant feeling; it is irrelevant because it cannot be reduced to the terms of positivist procedure. It is my contention here that the high forms of literature offer us the only complete, and thus the most responsible, versions of our experience. The point of view of this essay, then, is influenced by the late, neglected T. E. Hulme (and not this essay alone). It is the belief, philosophically tenable, in a radical discontinuity between the physical and the spiritual realms.

In our time the historical approach to criticism, in so far as it has attempted to be a scientific method, has undermined the significance of the material which it proposes to investigate. On principle the sociological and historical scholar must not permit himself to see in the arts meanings that his method does not assume. To illustrate some of the wide implications of this method I will try to see it as more than a method: it is the temper of our age. It has profoundly influenced our politics and our education.

What will happen to literature under the totalitarian society that is coming in the next few years—it may be, so far as critical opinion is concerned, in the next few months? The question has got to be faced by literary critics, who as men of explicit ideas must to a great extent define for imaginative literature the *milieu* in which it will flourish or decay.

The first ominous signs of this change are before us. The tradition of free ideas is as dead in the United States as it is in Germany. For at least a generation it has suffered a slow extinction, and it may receive the *coup de grâce* from the present war. The suppression of the critical spirit in this country will have sinister features that the official Nazi censorship, with all its ruthlessness, has not yet achieved, for the Nazis are, towards opinion, crude, objective, and responsible. Although it has only a harsh military responsibility, this censorship is definite, and it leaves the profession of letters in no doubt of its standing. Under this regime it has no standing at all. Increasingly since 1933 the critical intelligence under National Socialism has enjoyed the choice of extinction or frustration in exile.

Could the outlook be worse for the future of criticism? In the United States we face the censorship of the pressure group. We have a tradition of irresponsible interpretation of patriotic necessity. We are entering a period in which we shall pay dearly for having turned our public education over to the professional "educationists" and the sociologists. These men have taught the present generation that the least thing about man is his intelligence, if he have it at all; the greatest thing his adjustment to Society (not to a good society): a mechanical society in which we were to be conditioned for the realization of a *bourgeois* paradise of gadgets and of the consumption, not of the fruits of the earth, but of commodities. Happily this degraded version of the myth of reason has been discredited by the course of what the liberal mind calls "world events"; and man will at any rate be spared the indignity of achieving it. What else can he now achieve? If history had dramatic form we might be able to see ourselves going down to destruction, with a small standard flying in the all but mindless hollow of our heads; and we should have our dignity to the end.

But this vision is too bright, too optimistic; for the "democracy" of appetites, drives, and stimulus-and-response has already affected us. What we thought was to be a conditioning process in favor of a state planned by Teachers College of Columbia University will be a conditioning equally useful for Plato's tyrant state. The actuality of tyranny we shall enthusiastically greet as the development of democracy, for the ringing of the democratic bell will make our political glands flow as freely for dictatorship, as, hitherto, for monopoly capitalism.

This hypocrisy is going to have a great deal to do with literary criticism because it is going to have a very definite effect upon American thought and feeling, at every level. There is no space here to track down the intellectual pedigree of the attitude of the social scientist. As early as 1911 Hilaire Belloc published a neglected book called *The Servile State,* in which he contended that the world revolution would not come out of the Second International. Nobody paid any attention to this prophecy; the Marxists ignored it for the obvious reason, and the liberals took it to mean that the world revolution would not happen at all. Belloc meant that the revolution was inherent in our pseudo-democratic intellectual tradition, buttressed by monopoly capitalism, and that the revolution would not proceed towards social justice, but would achieve the slave state. The point of view that I am sketching here looks upon the rise of the social sciences and their influence in education, from Comtism to Deweyism, as a powerful aid to the coming of the slave society. Under the myth of reason all the vast accumulation of *data* on social behavior, social control, social dynamics, was to have been used in building a pseudo-mystical and pseudo-democratic utopia on the Wellsian plan. In this vision of mindless perfection an elementary bit of historical insight was permitted to lapse: Plato had this insight, with less knowledge of history than we have. It is simply that, if you get a society made up of persons who have surrendered their humanity to the predatory impulses, the quickest way to improve matters is to call in a dictator; for when you lose the moral and religious authority, the military authority stands ready to supervene. Professor Dewey's social integration does not supervene. Under the actuality of history our sociological knowledge is a ready-made weapon that is now being used in Europe for the control of the people, and it will doubtless soon be used here for the same purpose.

To put this point of view into another perspective it is only necessary to remember that the intellectual movement variously known as positivism, pragmatism, instrumentalism, is the expression of a middle-class culture—a culture that we have achieved in America with so little consciousness of any other culture that we often say that a class description of it is beside the point. Matthew Arnold—in spite of his vacillating hopes for the middle class—said that one of its leading traits was lack of intelligence, and that industrialism, the creation of the middle class, had "materialized the upper class, vulgarized the middle class, and brutalized the lower class."

This lack of intelligence in our middle class, this vulgarity of the utilitarian attitude, is translatable into other levels of our intellectual activity. It is, for example, but a step from the crude sociologism of the normal school to the cloistered historical scholarship of the graduate school. We are all aware, of course, of the contempt in which the scholars hold the "educationists": yet the historical scholars, once the carriers of the humane tradition, have now merely the genteel tradition; the independence of judgment, the belief in intelligence, the confidence in literature, that informed the humane tradition, have disappeared. Under the genteel tradition the scholars exhibit timidity of judgment, disbelief in intelligence, and suspicion of the value of literature. These attitudes of scholarship are the attitudes of the *haute bourgeoisie* that support it in the great universities; it is now commonplace to observe that the uncreative money culture of modern times tolerates the historical routine of the scholars. The routine is "safe," and it shares with the predatory social process at large a naturalistic basis. And this naturalism easily bridges the thin gap between the teachers' college and the graduate school, between the sociologist and the literary source-hunter, between the comptometrist of literary "reactions" and the enumerator of influences.

The naturalism of the literary scholar is too obvious to need demonstration here. His substitution of "method" for intelligence takes its definite place in the positivistic movement which, from my point of view, has been clearing the way for the slave state; and the scholar must bear his part of the responsibility for the hypocrisy that will blind us to the reality of its existence, when it arrives.

The function of criticism should have been, in our time, as in all times, to maintain and to demonstrate the special, unique, and complete knowledge which the great forms of literature afford us. And I mean quite simply *knowledge,* not historical documentation and information. But our literary critics have been obsessed by politics, and when they have been convinced of the social determinism of literature, they have been in principle indistinguishable from the academic scholars, who have demonstrated that literature does not exist, that it is merely history, which must be studied as history is studied, through certain scientific analogies. The scholars have not maintained the tradition of literature as a form of knowledge; by looking at it as merely one among many forms of social and political expression, they will have no defense against the censors of the power state, or against the hidden censors of the pressure group. Have the scholars not been saying all along that literature is only politics? Well, then, let's suppress it, since the politics of poets and novelists is notoriously unsound. And the scholars will say, yes, let's suppress it—our attempt to convert literature into science has done better than that: it has already extinguished it.

I I

What the scholars are saying, of course, is that the meaning of a work of literature is identical with their method of studying it—a method that dissolves the literature into its history. Are the scholars studying literature, or are they not? That is the question. If they are not, why then do they continue to pretend that they are? This is the scholars' contribution to the intellectual hypocrisy of the positivistic movement. But when we come to the individual critics, the word hypocrisy will not do. When we think of the powerful semi-scientific method of studying poetry associated with the name of I. A. Richards, we may say that there is a certain ambiguity of critical focus.

Mr. Richards has been many different kinds of critic, one kind being an extremely valuable kind; but the role I have in mind here is that of *The Principles of Literary Criticism,* a curious and ingenious *tour de force* of a variety very common today. The species is: literature is not really nonsense, it is in a special way a kind of science. This particular variety is: poetry is a kind of applied psychology. I am not disposing of Mr. Richards in two sentences; like everybody else of my generation I have learned a great deal from him, even from what I consider his errors and evasions; and if it is these that interest me now, it is because they get less attention than his occasional and profound insights into the art of reading poetry.

In *The Principles of Literary Criticism* there is the significant hocus-pocus of impulses, stimuli, and responses; there are even the elaborate charts of nerves and nerve systems that purport to show how the "stimuli" of poems elicit "responses" in such a way as to "organize our impulses" towards action; there is, throughout, the pretense that the study of poetry is at last a laboratory science. How many innocent young men—myself among them—thought, in 1924, that laboratory jargon meant laboratory demonstration! But for a certain uneasiness evinced by Mr. Richards in the later chapters, one could fairly see this book as a typical instance of the elaborate cheat that the positivistic movement has perpetrated upon the human spirit. For the uneasy conscience of one Richards, a thousand critics and scholars have not hesitated to write literary history, literary biography, literary criticism, with facile confidence in whatever scientific analogies came to hand.

With the candor of a generous spirit Mr. Richards has repudiated his early scientism: the critical conscience that struggled in the early work against the limitations of a positivist education won out in the end. What did Mr. Richards give up? It is not necessary to be technical about it. He had found that the picture of the world passed on to us by the poetry of the prescientific ages was scientifically false. The *things* and *processes* pointed to by the poets, even the modern poets, since they too were backward in the sciences, could not be verified by any of the known scientific procedures. As a good positivist he saw the words of a poem as *referents,* and referents have got to refer to something—which the words of even the best poem failed to do. If Mr. Richards could have read Carnap and Morris in the early twenties, he would have said that poems may *designate* but they do not *denote,* because you can designate something that does not exist, like a purple cow. Poems designate things that do not exist, and are compacted of *pseudo-statements,* Mr. Richards's most famous invention in scientese; that is, false statements, or just plain lies.

Perhaps the best way to describe Mr. Richards's uneasiness is to say that, a year or two later, in his pamphlet-size book, *Science and Poetry,* he came up short against Matthew Arnold's belief that the future of poetry was immense, that, religion being gone, poetry would have to take its place. The curious interest of Arnold's argument cannot detain us. It is enough to remember that even in *The Principles of Literary Criticism* Mr. Richards was coming round to that view. Not that poetry would bring back religion, or become a new religion! It would perform the therapeutic offices of religion, the only part of it worth keeping. In short, poetry would "order" our minds; for although science was true, it had failed to bring intellectual order—it had even broken up the older order of pseudo-statement; and although poetry was false, it would order our minds, whatever this ordering might mean.

To order our minds with lies became, for a few years, Mr. Richards's program, until at last, in *Coleridge on Imagination* (1935), the Sisyphean effort to translate Coleridge into naturalistic terms broke down; and now, I believe, Mr. Richards takes the view that poetry, far from being a desperate remedy, is an independent form of knowledge, a kind of cognition, equal to the knowledge of the sciences at least, perhaps superior. The terms in which Mr. Richards frames this insight need not concern us here: I have sketched his progress towards it in order to remind you that the repudiation of a literal positivism by its leading representative in modern criticism has not been imitated by his followers, or by other critics who, on a different road, have reached Mr. Richards's position of ten years ago. They are still there. Whether they are sociologists in criticism or practitioners of the routine of historical "correlation," they alike subscribe to a single critical doctrine. It is the Doctrine of Relevance.

I I I

The Doctrine of Relevance is very simple. It means that the subject matter of a literary work must not be isolated in terms of form; it must be tested (on an analogy to scientific techniques) by observation of the world that it "represents." Are the scene, the action, the relations of the characters in a novel, in some verifiable sense true? It is an old question. It has given rise in our time to various related sorts of criticism that frequently produce great insights. (I think here of Mr. Edmund Wilson's naturalistic interpretation of James's *The Turn of the Screw.* Mr. Wilson's view is not the whole view, but we can readily see that we had been missing the whole view until he added his partial view.)

The criterion of relevance, as we saw with Mr. Richards, has a hard time of it with an art like poetry. Of all the arts, poetry has a medium the most complex and the least reducible to any one set of correlations, be they historical, or economic, or theological, or moral. From the point of view of direct denotation of objects about all that we can say about one of Keats's odes is what I heard a child say—"It is something about a bird."

But with the novel the case is different, because the novel is very close to history—indeed, in all but the great novelists, it is not clearly set off from history. I do not intend here to get into Aristotle and to argue the difference between history and fiction. It is plain that action and character, to say nothing of place and time, point with less equivocation to observed or perhaps easily observable phenomena than even the simplest poetry ever does. The novel points with some directness towards history—or I might say with Mr. David Daiches, to the historical process.

I mention Mr. Daiches because his *The Novel and the Modern World* seems to me to be one of the few good books on contemporary fiction. Yet at bottom it is an example of what I call the Doctrine of Relevance, and I believe that he gains every advantage implicit in that doctrine, and suffers, in the range and acuteness of his perceptions, probably none of its limitations. I cannot do justice to Mr. Daiches's treatment of some of the best novelists of our time; my quotations from his final essay—which is a summary view of his critical position—will do him less than justice. His statement of his method seems to me to be narrower than his critical practice:

The critic who endeavors to see literature as a process rather than as a series of phenomena, and as a process which is bound up with an infinite series of ever wider processes, ought to realize that however wide his context, it is but a fraction of what it might be.

Admirable advice; but what concerns me in this passage is the assumption that Mr. Daiches shares with the historical scholar, that literature is to be understood chiefly as a part of the historical process. He goes on to say:

The main object is to indicate relevance and to show how understanding depends on awareness of relevance. That appreciation depends on understanding and that a theory of value can come only after appreciation, hardly need noting.

I must confess that after a brilliant performance of two hundred ten pages I feel that Mr. Daiches has let us down a little here. I am aware that he enters a shrewd list of warnings and exceptions, but I am a little disappointed to learn that he sees himself as applying to the novel a criterion of historical relevance not very different from the criterion of the graduate school. It is likely that I misunderstand Mr. Daiches. He continues:

The patterning of those events [in a novel], their relation to each other within the story, the attitude to them which emerges, the mood which surrounds them, the tone in which they are related, and the style of the writing are all equally relevant.

Yes: but relevant to what? And are they *equally* relevant? The equality of relevance points to historical documentation; or may we assume here that since the "main object is to indicate relevance," the critic must try to discover the relevance of history to the work? Or the work to history? What Mr. Daiches seems to me to be saying is that the function of criticism is to bring the work back to history, and to test its relevance to an ascertainable historical process. Does relevance, then, mean some kind of identity with an historical process? And since "understanding depends on awareness of relevance," is it understanding of history or of the novel; or is it of both at once? That I am not wholly wrong in my grasp of the terms relevance and process is borne out by this passage:

He [the critic] can neither start with a complete view of civilization and work down to the individual work of art, nor can he start with the particular work of art and work up to civilization as a whole; he must try both methods and give neither his complete trust.

Admirable advice again; but are there actually two methods here? Are they not both the historical method? When Mr. Daiches says that it is possible to start from the individual work of art and work *up* (interesting adverb, as interesting as the *down* to which you go in order to reach the work of art), he doubtless alludes to what he and many other critics today call the "formalist" method. Mr. Daiches nicely balances the claims of formalist and historian. The formalist is the critic who doesn't work up, but remains where he started, with the work of art—the "work in itself," as Mr. Daiches calls it, "an end which, though attainable, is yet unreal." Its unreality presumably consists in the critic's failure to be aware of the work's relevance to history. There may have been critics like Mr. Daiches's formalist monster, but I have never seen one, and I doubt that Mr. Daiches himself, on second thought, would believe he exists. (Or perhaps he was Aristotle, who said that the nature of tragedy is in its structure, not its reception by the audience.) I am not sure. As a critic of the novel Mr. Daiches is acutely aware of unhistorical

meanings in literature, but as a critical theorist he seems
to me to be beating his wings in the unilluminated tradition of positivism. That tradition has put the stigma of
"formalism" upon the unhistorical meaning. Critics of our
age nervously throw the balance in favor of the historical
lump. Mr. Daiches's plea for it rests upon its superior inclusiveness; the historical scholar can make formal analyses
against the background of history—he has it both ways—
while the formalist has it only one, and that one "unreal."
But here, again, Mr. Daiches's insight into the vast complexity of the critic's task prompts at least a rueful mis-
giving about the "wider context"; he admits the superiority
of the historian, "though it may be replied that inclusiveness is no necessary proof of such superiority." At this point
Mr. Daiches becomes a little confused.

I have the strong suspicion in reading Mr. Daiches (I have
it in reading the late Marxists and the sociological and historical scholars) that critics of the positivist school would
not study literature at all if it were not so handy in libraries.
They don't really like it; or they are at any rate ashamed of
it—because it is "unreal." The men of our time who have
the boldness and the logical rigor to stand by the implications of their position are the new logical positivists at Chicago—Carnap and Morris, whom I have already mentioned;
they are quite firm in their belief—with a little backsliding
on the part of Morris [1]—that poetry, and perhaps all imaginative literature, is, in Mr. Arthur Mizener's phrase, only
"amiable insanity": it designates but it does not denote anything "real."

I respect this doctrine because it is barbarism unabashed
and unashamed. But of the positivists who still hanker after
literature with yearnings that come out of the humane tradi-

---

[1] Charles W. Morris, "Science, Art and Technology," *The Kenyon Review,*
Autumn, 1939. Mr. Morris argues that, although poetry is nonsense semantically, it is the realm of "value."

tion, what can be said? The ambiguity or—since we are in our mental climate and no longer with persons—the hypocrisy of our liberal intellectual tradition appears again; or let us say the confusion. Is Mr. Daiches wrestling with a critical theory, or is he only oscillating between the extremes of a dilemma? From the strict, logical point of view he is entitled merely to the positivist horn, as the general critical outlook of our age is so entitled.

This ought to be the end of literature, if literature were logical; it is not logical but tough, and after the dark ages of our present enlightenment it will flourish again. This essay has been written from a point of view which does not admit the validity of the rival claims of formalism and history, of art-for-art's-sake and society. Literature is the complete knowledge of man's experience, and by knowledge I mean that unique and formed intelligence of the world of which man alone is capable.

1940

Modern Poetry[1]

THERE WAS a time when, to many persons on both sides of the Atlantic, 1911 seemed to have witnessed a revolution in poetry: for in that year John Masefield shocked the Anglo-American literary world with *The Everlasting Mercy,* a poem about plain people in plain language. It prompted, I believe it was Sir William Watson, to remark that the "language of Shakespeare was good enough" for him. But yet another poetic revolution had already begun. Pound's first book of verse had been published in 1908 (very quietly, in Venice); Eliot's came out almost a decade later (*Prufrock and Other Observations* appeared in 1917); Robert Frost's first book was published in 1913. This poetic revolution, which has dominated poetry in English for almost a half century, and which has sharpened our critical scrutiny of poets like Robinson and Frost, who were outside it, was brought about by two young men who were convinced that the language of Shakespeare was not merely good enough for them, but far too good.

These revolutionaries were bent upon poetic reform quite as radically as Coleridge and Wordsworth had been more than a century earlier: they vigorously set about the work of cutting down to size the post-Victorian rhetoric—to the

1 This essay first appeared in *The Sewanee Review,* Winter, 1956, and was reprinted as "Introduction to American Poetry, 1900–1950" in *Modern Verse in English 1900–1950,* edited by David Cecil and Allen Tate (London and New York, 1958).

size of what they could in that time know *as poets,* and so make actual in language. Mr. Eliot has written movingly of the plight of the young American poet before the First World War: there was literally nobody to talk to, no older living poet to take off from; there were only Moody and Woodberry, poets perhaps neither better nor worse than Watson and Sir Stephen Phillips, across the sea. That this situation shortly improved no observer of the period can doubt. The early reception in England of Robert Frost and the enormous international influence of Pound and Eliot and, later, of W. H. Auden, have at last produced an Anglo-American poetry that only by convention can be separated.

It is no part of my purpose to describe in detail the role Americans have played in the international poetic revolution; I cannot imagine a reader who might want to go over this ground again. Like a football field played on through weeks of dry weather, it has been trampled down to a flinty hardness by the historians of contemporaneity, and never a green spot, not even Whitman's spear of summer grass, remains to invite the roving eye. A modern poem becomes history for the fewer before the few, a handful of unprofessional readers, can read it, or read it long enough to dry the ink. Our critics, since Mr. Richards started them off with *The Principles of Literary Criticism* in 1924, have been perfecting an apparatus for "explicating" poems (not a bad thing to do), innocent of the permanently larger ends of criticism. They give us not only a "close reading" but the history of the sources of a new poem by Eliot or Stevens (or of an old one by Hart Crane or Dylan Thomas) before it is able to walk. Within five years of the appearance of *Four Quartets,* we knew more about the poem than Mr. Eliot knew—and quite predictably, for if a poet knew all *that,* he wouldn't have to write the poem and mankind would not need poetry. But what must strike the reader of the commentators on Eliot—on the *corpus* of Eliot, as I have seen his poetry, like Chaucer's, designated—is that they know more than anybody can know about anything. I am second to none in my admiration of the fine passages in the *Quartets;* I like to think of the speech, in "Little Gidding," of the composite shade of Mr. Eliot's teachers as the high-water mark of modern poetry. But that is not quite the point. One doubts a little more all the time, the use, to say nothing of the propriety, of writing memoirs and glosses on one's friends; and a friend is any person who is alive and whom one might conceivably meet. I know a little boy who, having asked if his grandmother was very old and would soon die, said, "Let's play like she's dead now."

In talking so much about Mr. Eliot I am poaching on the ground staked out by my collaborator; but Mr. Eliot is amphibian and, if "neither living nor dead," is likewise neither American nor English; he is both. He has borne the brunt of most of this anticipatory history; yet nobody has been safe, not even a comparatively private person like myself. The critics of our time not only have known "all about poetry": they have of late turned to fiction and examined its cannier techniques; so that one wonders why they have not considered critically the relation of their points of view to what they are looking at. In writing criticism they forget that they occupy "posts of observation," that they themselves are "trapped spectators"—these technical revelations having been delivered to us canonically two generations ago by a person lately described by Mr. Glenway Wescott as "that effete old hypocrite, Henry James." If what the novelist knows—or the Jamesian novelist, at any rate—is limited to what his characters see, hear, do, and think, why is the critic not similarly confined to place and moment? The answer is that he *is*. But the critic does not see himself, *his* point of view, as a variable in the historical situation that he undertakes to explain: as one motion of the history that he is writing.

I am not repudiating the immense, and immensely resourceful, critical activity that began in England with Hulme,
Eliot, Richards, and Read thirty to forty years ago, and, in
the United States at about the same time, with the Crocean
aesthetics of the late Joel Spingarn, and with the *Prefaces*
of Henry James. There were also the formidable books, now
languishing, of a great critic of ideas (not of literature), Irving Babbitt: nor should we forget the early literary essays of
Ezra Pound, until recently buried beneath the lyrical "economies" of his later writings, but now exhumed, with an
introduction, by T. S. Eliot. A second wave of this Anglo-
American criticism (I must ignore its French affiliations)
brought forward in America men as different as Wilson, Ransom, and Blackmur; yet they were all from the beginning
committed, in their several ways, to the aesthetic-historical
reading of literature. We have been concerned in this country with the language of the literary work at its particular
moment in time.

This glance at forty years of criticism is not, I must repeat, meant to dismiss it: I have been getting round to the
American poetry that, from this fifty-year period, and in the
fixed limits of an anthology, I could hope to include. A
glance at the criticism is by no means irrelevant to a selection of the poetry. For the poetry of our time, as I began
to see it after nearly a year of new reading and rereading—
by turns reluctant, desultory, and concentrated—is also well
within the aesthetic-historical mode. I shall do something
with this phrase presently. (Towards the end of my reading it would not be denied; and I could consider no other.)
Never have poetry and criticism in English been so close together, so mutually sensitive, the one so knowing about
the other. This has been partly but not altogether the result
of their appearing so often in the same person: many of
our best poets, Eliot, Ransom, Auden, R. P. Warren, Jarrell,
are among the most useful critics; and even that least pro-

fessional of the best American poets, the late Wallace Stevens, tried his hand at criticism in a volume of meditations and *obiter dicta* on poetry, entitled *The Necessary Angel*. In another age, would these men have been critics at all? It is an unreal question; yet that so many poets have turned critics points to an historically unique self-consciousness among men of letters, which must inevitably reflect the more elusive conditions of the individual and society.

If poetry and criticism have been conducting a dialogue, the reasons for it are not very different from those that have brought about an isolated community of critics and poets. This state of affairs is frequently reprehended by the common man, a person of our age who can be either "educated" or merely arrogant. Reflections on the last half century of American poetry ought, I think, to include some notice of this question, not because it has been the subject of literary polemics and of historical speculation, but because it has got into the poetry itself. The isolation of the literary community was known first by Poe, as one phase of the alienation of the contemplative man that we have been talking about in England and America with increasing metaphysical cunning since the publication of *Ulysses* in 1922. Alienation as a subject for poetry seems to take two directions: first, the relation of the poet to the world—and this ranges all the way from a quasi-religious sense of man's isolation in the decentralized universe, down to the crass question of the poet's "contribution to society"; and, secondly, poems about the meaning of poetry itself. I suppose never before in the history of poetry in any language have so many poems been written, as in the American English of this century, *about* poetry.

Wallace Stevens's justly admired "Sunday Morning" ties up the entire subject in one package: the passive and alienated heroine (significantly, not a hero) meditates on the interior darkness of the soul, which has a brief exterior life

in the intensity, not of passion, which would be active and
humanly committed, but of refined sense perception, which
is passive, and which at last can be aware only of its own
ultimate extinction. This poem is one of Stevens' many
parables of the poet's relation to the modern world. If our
common man (in his less arrogant phase) tends to look at
the fastidious diction of "Sunday Morning" as a sort of
Frenchified mannerism, I can only invite him to read, along
with Stevens's poem, Mr. Frost's "Birches": these worlds
are not so far apart as he may imagine. For what seems at
first sight the sentimentality, or even bathos, of asking us to
take second thought about a boy swinging on a birch sap-
ling, turns out (on second thought) to be not only a self-
contained image but an emblem of the meaning of poetry:
if we have got to be doing something, then let's do something
disinterested that has its end in itself. I should guess that
more than half of Mr. Frost's poems are little essays on the
poetic imagination. He is just as sophisticated and modern as
anybody, and his way of being sophisticated and modern is to
pretend in his diction that he is not: he is quite as self-
conscious, in his grasp of the aesthetic-historic mode of perception, as the late Hart Crane, or Stevens himself.

The anthologist will apply absolute standards at the risk
of boring the educated common reader, of confessing himself
a prig, and of ending up perhaps without an anthology.
Nor may he apportion space to the poets, the most to the
best, a little less than most to the least good (if, to these, any
at all), in the belief that his own hierarchy has been or-
dained on high. If he sets up for God he will resemble
Swift's mathematical tailor on the flying island of Laputa.

Nevertheless, pragmatical doubt is not the only consideration back of my choice of poems. My interests in the past
thirty years having been not aloof but committed, a certain
compound of philosophical bias, common loyalty, and obscure prejudice must insensibly have affected my views of

the entire half century. It was not possible that I should think Stephen Benét, an amiable and patriotic rhymester, as important as Hart Crane, an imperfect genius whose profound honesty drove him to suicide after years of debauchery had stultified his mind. I have, in short, been concerned not with a group or school, but with a certain high contemporary tradition. It is not a tradition of the grand style or of the great subject. But it has resisted the strong political pressures which ask the poet to "communicate" to passively conditioned persons what a servile society expects them to feel. The best American poets (Crane is one of a handful) have tried to discover new and precise languages by which poetry now as always must give us knowledge of the human condition—knowledge that seems to reach us partly in the delight that one gets from rhythms and insights that one has not already heard and known. What particular qualities go to make up an original poet now or at any time, I shall attempt to describe. It has seemed to me that the best American poets of our age have used a certain mode of perception, that I have named the aesthetic-historical.

What poets know and how they know it are questions that go beyond the usual scope of criticism, for what a poet of the past knows is viewed historically, not for what it is, and we take it for granted. But with a poetry which is near us in time, or contemporaneous, much of the difficulty that appears to be in the language as such, is actually in the unfamiliar focus of feeling, belief, and experience which directs the language from the concealed depths that we must try laboriously to enter. The difference between Pound's "Mauberley" and Arnold's "Obermann" is not merely a difference of diction or of subject; it is the subtle difference between two ways of trying to get out of history what Herbert or Crashaw would have expected only from God. Both Arnold and Pound are asking history to make them whole—Arnold through philosophy, Pound through art, or aesthetic sensi-

bility; and unless this difference is grasped the critic will
pull himself up short at the mere differences of "style." How
far into the past a poetry must recede before we can understand it in depth it is difficult to decide. I have used the
word aesthetic not to point to a philosophy of art, but to
indicate the way in which American poets have seemed to
me to understand their world; nor by aesthetic do I mean art
for its own sake. I mean a mode of perception, a heightened
sensitivity, that began with Poe and Baudelaire and that
produced in our generation concentrated metaphors like
Crane's:

> O thou steeled Cognizance whose leap commits
> The agile precincts of the lark's return

or Stevens's:

> The pale intrusions into blue
> Are corrupting pallors . . . ay di mi,
>
> Blue buds or pitchy blooms. Be content—
> Expansions, diffusions—contents to be
>
> The unspotted imbecile revery,
> The heraldic center of the world
>
> Of blue, blue sleek with a hundred chins,
> The amorist Adjective aflame . . .

This controlled disorder of perception has been the means of
rendering a direct impression of the poets' historical situation.

We are indebted to an English critic, the late Michael
Roberts, for a clearer understanding of the American development of the aesthetic-historical mode. In his introduction to *The Faber Book of Modern Verse* (1936), Roberts
pointed out that American poets are less firmly rooted in a
settled poetic tradition than the British; they are thus
able to size and digest traditions and influences from
many languages and periods. Roberts paradoxically de-

scribed the American poet as "European," cosmopolitan, and far-ranging into the past; the British—in the Georgian period, before the "European" influence of T. S. Eliot—as national or even insular. The English insularity of a fine poet like Ralph Hodgson, who can assume that the language of his moment in British culture needs no further development, is very different from the aggressive provincialism, which he calls American nationalism, of Mr. Carl Sandburg. This self-conscious Midwesternism posits a *new* world, with a deliberately anti-historical glance at a corrupt Europe; but even in the Middle West, Europe, like Everest, is always *there*. The sense of likeness, or of difference from Europe, and the poet's alienation from the secularized community (not uniquely but acutely American), have brought about a self-consciousness that perhaps cannot be matched by any earlier poetry of the West. Mr. Stephen Spender, in a review of Wallace Stevens's first book under an English imprint, observed that a modern American poem is frequently a "cultural act," a conscious affirmation of an international culture above the commercialized mass culture of the United States at large.

My neighbor cannot understand or even try to read my poems, but I am expressing something about him that he himself doesn't know. This is what American poets say to themselves if they are influenced by Walt Whitman. I suspect that Dr. William Carlos Williams says it every morning, and it can issue in still another version of the aesthetic-historical mode. Dr. Williams is one of its most interesting specimens: his exaltation of the common man, in the common rhythm and the common word, asserts the doctrine that all Americans are common, except T. S. Eliot, who has "betrayed his class." This rhetorical Rousseauism may be a little too sophisticated to pass indefinitely for American primitivism. One cannot think it less highbrow than Stevens's and Mr. Ransom's serene neglect of everything common. Our British friends occasionally tell us that Mr. Ransom is a very good poet who but for the unhappy agitation of 1776 would be English.

The common man in a servile society is everybody; the modern society is everywhere servile; everybody must accept the servile destruction of leisure and of the contemplative life if he would live without alienation. On this subject I suppose that there has been more complicated nonsense written by literary critics in the past thirty years than on all other matters connected with literature combined. The liberal, utopian, "totalitarian" mind assumes that one must give up alienation at any cost. High on the list of costs would be poetry; and if we would sacrifice it, in the illusion that its sacrifice alone would propitiate the powers of darkness, we should forfeit along with it the center of consciousness in which free and disinterested men must live. There are some things from which man, if he is to remain human, must remain permanently alienated. One of these is the idolatry of the means as the end. Modern American poetry exhibits, often with power and distinction, its own infection by idolatry, and by the ritual of idolatry which is the language of magic. Frost and Stevens at the beginning, Hart Crane in the middle, and Robert Lowell towards the end of our period, once more confirm the commonplace that good poets are both above and of their age. The verbal shock, the violent metaphor, as a technique of magic, forces into *linguistic existence* subjective meanings and insights that poets can no longer discover in the common world.

This is the aesthetic consciousness, aware of its isolation at a moment of time. Whether this special stance of the modern poet will shift (or merely collapse) in the second half of the century nobody can know or ought to think that he knows. One looks in vain at the work of the brilliant young poets of the fifth decade for the signs of a new poetry such as Pound, Eliot, Stevens, Miss Moore, Ransom, Cummings, and Crane gave us thirty-five years ago. The only distinguished American poet, the magnitude and precision of whose work might conceivably have attracted a younger generation, was Robinson; but his origins were in the nineteenth century; and although at his death in 1935 he had admirers, there were no first-rate poets who could be said to have derived from him, in the sense that Crane came out of Eliot and Pound. Mr. Frost is likewise an end, not a beginning. But poetry has its own way of surprising us. If we suppose that we are at the end of a period, or of a period style (I think we are), we must nevertheless be ready for something entirely new from a poet whose work may seem to be complete, or, from a new poet expect a style altogether new, which persons who have reached middle age would probably dislike. But the future of American or any other poetry we may leave to the puritans who cannot look at the world as it is; the future is at any rate no proper subject for criticism. Modern American poetry, limited in scope to the perceiving, as distinguished from the seeing eye, has given us images of the present condition of man that we cannot find elsewhere; and we ought to have them. We should be grateful that we have got them.

1955

Poetry Modern and Unmodern[1]

A Personal Recollection

AT INTERVALS in the past fifty or more years we have heard outcries both for and against certain kinds of poetry, setting them apart from other kinds as being "modern." But nobody seems to know what modern poetry is, except insofar as we know, at a second or third glance, that it is not unmodern. When we ask what a thing is we are asking for a definition, and if poetry in general cannot be defined (all definitions are general), it would seem to be a hopeless task to define *modern* poetry, which, assuming that it is poetry at all, must be the *species* of a *genus*. If Alexander Pope and Ezra Pound are both poets, is it necessary to distinguish modern from unmodern? For they could be said to represent two species of Poet, and the difference between modern and unmodern becomes irrelevant. It will be observed at this point that I do not oppose modern to ancient, as Pope and Swift did; for the point at which antiquity, for us, leaves off, and modernity begins, cannot be discerned: there are different views for the different angles of the historical vision. For the Beat poets, antiquity ends at about 1956, with a few poets foreshadowing them as far back as Hart Crane in 1926. Some academic scholars cut antiquity off at the end of the second century A.D.; but these are the Latinists and Hellenists, who

[1] This essay was originally published in *The Hudson Review*, Summer, 1968.

are more severe than even the Renaissance literary scholars. These latter historians allow modern literature to begin with the Renaissance, perceiving a few rays of light as far back as *The Divine Comedy*.

Such views of the past have an analogy to a game of contract bridge, in which there are no partners and each man is for himself, making his own "contract" as the game proceeds. There are nevertheless today two discernible factions that only for the purposes of polemics line up facing each other: the linguists on the one side, the historians of ideas on the other. Their antagonism is, from the point of view of my inquiry, frivolous; for both factions dislike poetry. The linguists study language but do not use it well; it is difficult to ascertain just what the historians of ideas are studying. For the linguists classical Latin deteriorates after Tacitus; Tibullus and Propertius are decadent, with connotations of moral decay. The case of Dante is somewhat different. His language was modern only in the sense that it was not Latin; an ambitious poem had not hitherto been written in Italian. Yet Dante is almost a Modern, in the Renaissance sense, because although his cosmos is God-centered, his characters remain stubbornly individualist, particularly in Hell, and are therefore about two centuries ahead of their time. This version of Dante is generally held by historians of ideas, or by the proponents of the Great Ideas without history which are compiled in *syntopica* written in virtually no language at all.

If we limit this inquiry to the past half-century, we may put aside for the moment the term modern, and try another one: I suggest contemporary. Should the title of this discussion have been Poetry Contemporary and Uncontemporary? Such a title would smuggle into my inquiry a popular judgment, for it is frequently said that certain poets are not "contemporary" and are thus irrelevant; one must always be contemporary. It was often said of T. S. Eliot that his poems were *very* contemporary but that his ideas (here stalks the shadow of the historian of ideas) were all frozen in the past. I think it is evident at this point that the word contemporary, used to distinguish one kind of poetry from another, confronts us with a critical muddle. For contemporary can mean almost anything involving the idea of co-existence in time. (It applies, I believe, to persons, whereas contemporaneous applies to things. Is poetry a person or a thing?) I must pursue this critical shadow-boxing a little further. If co-existence in time is the first meaning that comes to mind, what shall we make of co-existence in space? It would seem that a reasonable proximity in space is as essential to the contemporaneity of poets as co-existence in time. I co-exist in time with poets in the Gujarati and Marathi derivatives of Sanskrit, but I do not co-exist with them culturally for two reasons; first, the barrier of their languages, which I have no desire to learn, or cultural necessity to learn, as in the case of French or Italian; and, second, a vast space which separates us. In the ordinary sense of the phrase "contemporary poets," I am not contemporary with living poets in those languages. But am I contemporary with all living or recently living poets of the English language? I do not think so. I could cite a living poet considerably older and a living poet considerably younger than I: Carl Sandburg and Karl Shapiro. I am contemporary with neither. These poets, different as they seem to be, write about vitality, the immediacy of the American experience, the superiority of the instinctive man; yet I can find in their later poems (I exclude Shapiro's early fine poems) neither vitality, nor immediacy, nor instinct; for the languages in which these abstractions are praised are appropriately dead.

If in these observations I am to arrive at a critical distinction that will oppose modern to unmodern, I shall have to start over again, and risk the impropriety of alluding to my own experience. I first began to read the "Later Yeats" in the early nineteen-twenties. I remember as if it were yesterday the impact of "The Second Coming" and "In Memory of Major Robert Gregory." In retrospect it is difficult to define or even describe that impact, or explain why I thought these two poems, among others I shall cite in a moment, were entirely new, something that I had not seen in poetry before. At a glance the poems looked quite conventional. The diction was plain; the versification, iambic pentameter with no more than the usual variations and substitutions to be found in Tennyson or Arnold.

Yet the two poems by Yeats could not have been written before 1914. I felt at once that here was a poet with whom, by hard labor, I might make myself contemporary. Yet there was only a kind of arithmetical co-existence in time; he was my contemporary the second half of his life and perhaps more than the first half of mine. I saw him once, at a distance; later, in Oxford, I might have met him; but I was afraid I should not know what to say, being too callow to know that I should not have had to say anything; so I refused to let the poet, L. A. G. Strong, take me to see him. I do not regret my stupidity. I learned some years later that Yeats could be harsh, arrogant, or just plain silly. My youthful hero-worship might have felt compromised.

At about the same time I was writing some verse—I remember a single poem then entitled "Euthanasia"—which I was soon told resembled the poetry of a man of whom I had heard very little, named T. S. Eliot; and I had not read anything by him. I got his *Poems* (1920) at once and I couldn't write anything for several months. This man, though by no means famous at that time, was evidently so thoroughly my contemporary that I had been influenced by him before I had read a line of his verse. There were two great poems in that volume that seemed to do everything that I wanted to do: "Gerontion" and "The Love Song of J. Alfred Prufrock." There were the juxtaposition of contraries, progression by association, alternations of the plain, or "drab" style, with rhetorical splendor—all done with a brilliance and mastery that a Vanderbilt undergraduate could scarcely hope to emulate. I thought I had better do something else than become a writer; but there was nothing else that I was competent to do, whether or not I could ever write good poems. Some time before I began to read Eliot I had read Pound's "Hugh Selwyn Mauberley" and had got nothing out of it; but now after I was *in* Eliot's poems Pound began to make sense; for here was another man who could write what Edmund Wilson later called the "conversational ironic" style, or what I prefer to call sub-lyrical satire, not quite the same thing, yet a style that could be developed from the conversational-ironic in the direction of high rhetoric.

I did not describe my intention at that time as sub-lyrical satire; I didn't call it anything; I was in a muddle of experiment. I had tried a little of Robinson's version of the drab style, but for my purposes Robinson was a dead-end, though I thought him and still think him a great poet. I could do nothing with Frost, and likewise with my master, John Crowe Ransom, whose style was so completely his own as not to be viable; an imitator would have made a fool of himself. But who in the long run knows what influences have counted in the formation of one's mind and work? I was evidently "influenced" by Eliot before I had read him. My background and my education (such as it was) were radically different from Eliot's. What could a boy who had lived entirely in Kentucky and Tennessee have in common with the scion of New England Brahmins settled in St. Louis, whose education had been in New England and in Europe? Nothing; yet in a sense everything. For one of the mysteries of literary influence, not often understood by the historical scholars, is that influence is not linear from A to B. Perhaps the mistake of the scholars is their attempt to understand influence at all. We usually invoke the *zeitgeist* when the situation becomes complex, and causal ideas fail to explain anything. That is what I am invoking now to "explain" an

affinity with Eliot before I knew him. Back of my reading
of Pound, Eliot, and Yeats was desultory reading in a great
many English and a few French poets. I could do nothing
with the great English poets; and if one eventually does
something with Milton, or Donne, or Wordsworth, or Keats,
one gets back to them not directly but through older contemporaries, such as the poets I have mentioned. My Greek
wasn't good enough to make much of Archilochos or Ly-
cambes, but they were satirists, and they encouraged me in
the mode I am calling sub-lyrical satire. At the age of nineteen I had just recovered from Omar Khayyam and moved
on with James Thomson (B. V.) into *The City of Dreadful
Night* from which, after a football victory over the University of Virginia and the two drinking teams had collided, I
could recite this passage:

> As I came through the desert thus it was,
> As I came through the desert: Eyes of fire
> Glared at me throbbing with a starved desire;
> The hoarse and heavy and carnivorous breath
> Was hot upon me from the jaws of death. . . .

I could quote more then; but what I have quoted here is
enough. What I am getting at is that for some months I
could not see much difference between James Thomson (B.
V.) and Charles Baudelaire, whom, as my French improved
under the whip of an irascible Swiss scholar, I was trying
to read for the wrong reason; that is, I might have changed
Fleurs du Mal to *Fleurs Méchantes*—"Naughty Flowers," the
kind that were within reach of an unusually immature young
man. (But very soon I was playing with translations of about
a dozen of Baudelaire's poems, two of which later on I
thought well enough of to keep: *Une Charogne* and *Correspondances*). After reading Baudelaire I could no longer
believe that romantic Beauty was the end of poetry; for in
him the sordid and the sublime could be grasped in a single
complex of experience; for that was the lesson taught by

Baudelaire's great sonnet. The larger lesson taught by Baudelaire, the poet of the *fourmillante Cité,* was that the entire
range of sensibility from low to high was not intractable to
formal versification; for was not Baudelaire a master of the
classical French Alexandrine as well as other kinds of formal
verse? Like everybody else at that time I tried free-verse,
but it always turned out to be irregular metrical verse, and
I soon gave it up.

Formal versification is the primary structure of poetic order, the assurance to the reader and to the poet himself that
the poet is in control of the disorder both outside him and
within his own mind. Here is a theoretical difficulty that
I cannot deal with any better than I could have dealt with it
forty years ago. Yet is not much of the so-called poetry of
the past twenty or more years merely anti-poetry, a parasite
on the body of positive poetry, without significance except
that it reminds us that poetry can be written, or has been
written? What has been recently called "decreation" is another thing altogether; Mr. Spender many years ago called it
the "destructive element"; for decreation was as necessary to
Yeats and Eliot as it was to Wordsworth and Coleridge in
1798. Its watchword might well be as follows: Tear down the
old order, but in the very process of destruction build a
new one; for the destruction and the reconstruction are a
single activity. In self-incineration of the Phoenix is its rebirth.

The one-sided process of merely undoing the old order
results in what Yvor Winters called the fallacy of imitative
or expressive form; that is, chaos should be rendered in
chaotic language.[2] Winters and I have had for more than

---

[2] I wrote this essay before Yvor Winters's death. Although he thought very
little of my writings, I consider his death a great loss to the literary community. He was one of the best poets of the century; but unfortunately he
wanted everybody else to write like either T. Sturge Moore or his own
disciples.

thirty years a running argument about his poetics. (At this moment I am enjoying an agreement with him, which I shall presently qualify.) Regardless of other extensions of Mr. Winters's theory, the fallacy of imitative form gives us a way of understanding the anti-poetry of our time as no other insight does; but it also allows him a too literal application of his theory, by which he is led to reject all contemporary poetry which lacks an explicit logical structure. The motion from first line to last of a poem of imitative form is described by Mr. Winters as "qualitative progression," mere sensuous perception, mere associationism which has been undermining the traditional logical progression of English poetry since the time of John Locke and the Earl of Shaftesbury. Such historical generalizations are beyond my competence. What concerns me in Mr. Winters's critical theory is not only its value, but also its failure to see the special kind of rational (I do not say logical) form in a poem of qualitative progression.

Before I try to illustrate this failure of application, I must review briefly Winters's theory, which is less a theory than a formula. The poet has an experience; an emotion results from the experience; but the emotion must be *motivated* by a concept, a logical and moral evaluation of the experience. The poem will thus be a coherent progression of statements *about* the experience; otherwise there is no evaluation.

The first question that one must ask Winters is: Must poets be limited to their own experience? At times he seems to say yes, at others, no. In *The Function of Criticism* he says: "But it seems to me obvious that *The Iliad, Macbeth,* and 'To the Virgins to Make Much of Time' all deal with human experiences. In each work there is a content which is rationally apprehensible, and each work endeavors to communicate the emotion which is appropriate to the rational apprehension of the subject. The work is thus a judgment,

rational and emotional, of the experience. . . ." [3] The *Iliad*
and *Macbeth* are beyond my present scope; but I believe I
am right in saying that "To the Virgins" contains no experience whatever. Herrick is merely telling young women to
have a full life before old age and death overtake them;
there is an experience neither of the virgins nor of Robert
Herrick. I take pleasure in reading Herrick's poem, and I
suppose pleasure is an emotion; but I feel pleasure in one
degree or another in reading hundreds of other poems; and
I don't know that my pleasure in reading "To the Virgins"
is appropriate to a rational apprehension of the work; nor
can I see the poem as a judgment: in simple paraphrase the
poem is opinion, not judgment, derived at once from common sense and from the ancient convention of *carpo diem*,
hedged a little, one must confess, by Christian prudence; for
the virgins are not exhorted to loose conduct; they are told
to get married lest by waiting they lose their looks and remain spinsters. What concept motivates what emotion here
it is difficult to see. To this extremity of exclusion has Mr.
Winters gone in order to slay the dragon of anti-poetry. He
wants to see all the sense perceptions and feelings safely
laid out in a logical order of progression, a laudable demand, but made at the risk of losing about half of the great
poetry in the English language. It narrows the range of poetry to the personal experience of the poet, who then in the
poem evaluates his experience rationally. Mr. Winters is as
deeply committed to the short poem of rational evaluation
as Poe was committed to the short poem of sub-rational
emotion.

I must stay with Mr. Winters a little longer in order to
try to see whether there is a difference between anti-poetry
and the poetry of qualitative progression. Related to his idea
of qualitative progression there is another, which he calls

[3] Yvor Winters, *The Function of Criticism* (Denver, 1957), p. 26.

pseudo-reference; that is, reference to things, persons, events which never existed or happened. In *Primitivism and Decadence,* the section entitled "Pseudo-Reference," sub-section "Reference to a non-existing plot," Winters quotes the following lines from T. S. Eliot's "Gerontion":

> To be eaten, to be divided, to be drunk
> Among whispers; by Mr. Silvero
> With caressing hands, at Limoges
> Who walked all night in the next room;
>
> By Hakagawa, bowing among the Titians;
> By Madame de Tornquist, in the dark room
> Shifting the candles; Fräulein von Kulp
> Who turned in the hall, one hand on the door. . . .

Of these lines Mr. Winters says:

Each of the persons is denoted in the performance of an act, and each act, save possibly that of Hakagawa, implies an anterior situation, is a link in a chain of action; even that of Hakagawa implies an anterior and unexplained personality. Yet we have no hint of the nature of the history implied. A feeling is claimed by the poet, the motivation, or meaning, of which is withheld, and of which in all likelihood he has no clearer notion than his readers can have . . . But obscurity it is: discreetly modulated diffuseness. A more direct and economical convention seems to me preferable.[4]

I repeat: ". . . the motivation, or meaning, of which is withheld." It is not Eliot, it is Winters, who has withheld the meaning of the entire passage; and is there evidence that the poet is "claiming a feeling"? No; and it is Winters who is obscure. What he has withheld is the context which gives significance to the gestures (they are not *acts*) of Mr. Silvero, Hakagawa, Madame de Tornquist, and Fräulein von Kulp. It may not occur to the unwary reader to ask what it is that

---

[4] Yvor Winters, *In Defense of Reason* (Denver, 1951), pp. 46–47.

these people are to eat, to divide, and to drink among whispers. Here are the lines preceding those quoted by Winters:

> In the juvescence of the year came Christ the tiger
> In depraved May, dogwood and chestnut, flowering
> judas . . .

Then "To be eaten, to be divided, to be drunk/ Among whispers" by the strange assortment of frustrated persons whose names and gestures follows. What they eat and drink and divide is somewhat complicated, but extraordinary intelligence is not necessary to understand it: what they eat, drink, and divide is nothing less than the reason or meaning or even the "motivation" of their gestures. It is nothing less than a secularized version of the Eucharist; or perhaps one had better describe it as an anthropological version. Eliot may be glancing at the primitive Christian representation of Christ as a leopard; yet if he is, the cat in this context is merely a beast of prey. The renewal of nature in the spring, the renewal of human life through the Resurrection, are now merely naturalistic phenomena. The Host itself contains not only the Body of Christ (the white dogwood blossom) but the body of His betrayer, Judas Iscariot. This strange Eucharist, instead of uniting men in the Mystical Body, now divides them. They are grievously divided, for they or their forbears or their society have made the great betrayal; more than any other sin, treachery separates man from God and man from all other men. Mr. Silvero may be an unattractive character, but he walks all night in his spiritual isolation; Hakagawa has repudiated his religion for art, an art that has no relation to his religion; Madame de Tornquist, the fortune-teller, the prototype of Madame Sosostris, practices magic; the young fräulein is the climactic character who is etched in a moment of desperate indecision. Their significance lies in *what they have eaten;* but the moral consequences are not stated by the poet; they are "rendered" in incomplete acts which, cut off from the context in which they happen, are meaningless, as Mr. Winters makes them meaningless when he suppresses the tiger, the dogwood, and the judas-tree. What Eliot was doing in "Gerontion" was modern in a sense that I shall presently try to make explicit.

The poet does not intervene to judge these deprived persons or even to tell us in a general proposition, which Mr. Winters seems to demand, how they became deprived. I have already tried to offer a paraphrase of the implicit "concept" (Mr. Winters's word) of which the passage gives us the inductive images. The passage is definitely qualitative progression, but it is qualitative progression with an implicit rational order which would be compromised and even obscured if it were reduced to a series of versified logical statements and judgments. Insofar as the people are judged, they judge themselves in what they cannot do: Eliot does not judge them. The judgment is in the poem, not imposed from the outside. Elsewhere Mr. Winters tells us that he is bored by reading about the perceptions and sensations of a man walking along a street. I am not certain whether he alludes to Stephen Dedalus or J. Alfred Prufrock. In any case, Prufrock sufficiently judges himself: again Eliot does not move upstage to tell us what a weak fellow Prufrock is; Prufrock himself tells us this in a series of "acts" which add up to no action at all; and that is Prufrock's "meaning" because what he *is* is his meaning. Eliot might have ended the poem by versifying some such statement as this: A man named Prufrock, a man in a frock coat who is a prude, has lived so long with romantic illusions that when they fail him he is destroyed because he cannot face reality. I submit that what Prufrock says at the end is better than this; it is, in fact, one of the great passages in twentieth-century poetry:

> I have heard the mermaids singing, each to each.
> I do not think that they will sing to me.

> I have seen them riding seaward on the waves
> Combing the white hair of the waves blown back
> When the wind blows the water white and black.
>
> We have lingered in the chambers of the sea
> By sea-girls wreathed with seaweed red and brown
> Till human voices wake us and we drown.

I do not like the word "method" when it is used to describe the way a poet goes about his business, but I can think of no better word at present. So I shall ask a question: when and where did this impressionistic "method" of rendition begin to replace the affirmative statement which the poet made to the reader from his own point of view? (A scholar should investigate the historical background.) My guess is that it began in the novel as a conscious technique by means of which the novelist could render the typically modern hero—or anti-hero—in such a way as to give an implicit judgment of his anti-heroism. I suggest that the ancestors of Prufrock, of Mr. Silvero, of Fräulein von Kulp, are Roderick Usher, John Marcher, Gabriel Conroy, and on a more complex level of intelligence and sensibility, Lambert Strether. All these characters are in one degree or another incapable of positive moral action; only Strether, among them, seems able to assume a positive, affirmative stance in the paradox of renunciation. If what is wrong with these characters is their incapacity to do anything, their failure to fulfill themselves morally, it was necessary for the literary artist to discover a technique which would render them qualitatively by means of perception and sensibility, since they are incapable of action. But this does not mean, as Mr. Winters seems to think it does, that the poet or the novelist has himself succumbed to the *malaise* from which Prufrock and Fräulein von Kulp suffer. There is a stern moral judgment implicit in the way they are rendered, and this judgment extends to the entire civilization in which they live: a civilization which began to

take shape in the early nineteenth century; a civilization of
which Baudelaire was the first great poet to become fully
conscious.

It is the civilization of the *fourmillante Cité* recently
described by Sir Herbert Read as the "most vulgar civilization in the history of mankind." Baudelaire saw in the Paris
of the eighteen-fifties spectres walking in broad daylight. Am
I exceeding the limits of critical propriety if I see these spectres as other ancestors of J. Alfred Prufrock? And may we say
that neither Poe, nor Baudelaire, nor James, nor Joyce, nor
T. S. Eliot perversely invented them? They were made by
the "form and pressure of the time"; the best literary intelligences perceived them and invented techniques of rendering them. I vary a little my previous question: when did this
way of rendering the form and pressure of the time come
into poetry in English? Not all at once, certainly; there were
preparations; for example, the verse of Stephen Crane. And
of course there was another line of development, equally rec-
usant from the seething and dehumanizing world-city: W.
B. Yeats, whose traditional prosody must not be allowed to
conceal from us his profound modernism. Philosophically
more restless and ambitious than his younger contemporaries, Pound and Eliot, he invented a "system" that allowed
him to speak in his own person and in that manner, also, to
wear the disguise of a pre-modern poet.

As I bring these observations and prejudices to a close, I
must revert to myself, if only to suggest one small *exemplum*
of the infiltration of modernism in one poet who has never
been quite able to do what he wanted to do, one reason for
this perhaps being the difficulty of discovering what he
wanted to do. I have never considered myself much of a
literary critic, but rather a writer of programmatic essays
covertly eliminating kinds of poetry that I was sure I did
not want to write, and perhaps uncandidly, because unconsciously, justifying what I was attempting.

However this may be—to extend the *exemplum*—I did not discover modernism, or perhaps I had better say, the shock to the twentieth-century sensibility out of which modernism developed, through Yeats, Eliot, or Pound. Without knowing what I was seeing, I saw it first in that curious Victorian poet James Thomson (B. V.), whose inflated rhetoric and echolalia merely adumbrated the center of psychic and moral interest of later and better poets. It remained to find the right language and to establish a center from which it could be spoken; for the poet is never wholly aware of his subject until his language is able to speak it, and to render it to the entire human being, to both the sensibility and the intellect, at that focus of awareness at which he does not know whether he is thinking or feeling. This is what one has merely tried to do.

1968

II

A Note on Donne

I

DONNE'S MODERN REPUTATION has risen so suddenly that writers born since 1900 may look back to the time when he was a name in *The Oxford Book of English Verse* at the head of seven poems, two of which we now know that he did not write. *A Garland for John Donne*,[1] the collection of essays edited by Mr. Theodore Spencer for the tercentenary of the poet's death, attempts to revalue the poetry and to enquire into the causes of its present influence. The uncertainty of these critics about Donne's place is remarkable in the case of a poet three hundred years dead. The uncertainty comes of Donne's being still alive. He "ranks" possibly a little above Marvell, but Marvell's interest for us is not nearly so great. The reasons for his influence are at once more difficult to discover and more fruitful to pursue than his rank. The essayists in this volume are united in the belief that many of Donne's problems are our own.

Johnson blamed the vices of metaphysical style upon "a voluntary deviation from nature in pursuit of something new and strange." The eighteenth century on the whole regarded Donne as a prodigy of perverse learning. Although Donne's style, the bold images and learned conceits, had a distinct effect upon Cowley and Carew, and even Richard Crashaw; although the conversational tone influenced Dryden, it has

---

[1] *A Garland for John Donne, 1631–1931*, edited by Theodore Spencer (Cambridge, Mass., 1931).

remained for our own age to relate him to the main stream of English verse. It has been our task to understand the seriousness of the impulse and the integrity, which once seemed the perversity, of style; our task to see the whole intellectual structure of the poetry, along with the rough versification, in the light of the underlying problems of the age of Donne. For the first time he is being felt as a contemporary.

The eight essays are admirably distributed over the two kinds of problem that a great poet of the past inevitably creates—the historical and the critical problem. There are five historical essays. Mr. Spencer has written, in "Donne and His Age," a study of the intellectual climate in which Donne lived: although he suggests more problems than he can solve in so brief a space, his discussion of the revolutionary effect of the sixteenth-century "picture of the physical world" on moral ideas is a valuable contribution to Elizabethan criticism. Mr. John Sparrow's "The Date of Donne's Travels" reviews difficult and perhaps insoluble problems of the poet's biography; incidentally Mr. Sparrow throws some light on the origin of Donne's geographical allusions—whether they were bookish or drawn from observation. "A Note on Donne the Preacher," by Mr. John Hayward, presents a side of Donne that would have only a minor historical value had he never written his verse. Mrs. Evelyn M. Simpson's analysis of the *Paradoxes and Problems* brings out the early influence of Martial, an influence that Mr. Spencer finds general in the 1590's and not peculiar to Donne; Mrs. Simpson's paper is chiefly valuable for its emphasis on his early "interest in science."

But here, just as Mr. Eliot warns us that Donne's skepticism, being mainly an uncertainty about the right terms of faith, was not like ours, Mrs. Simpson might well have distinguished between science as we know it and Donne's "interest" in the new cosmologists, Copernicus and Kepler. This was rather an anxiety about the physical limits of consciousness and the bearing of that question on the scholastic conception of body and soul, which Donne presents in the terminology of St. Thomas. Donne knew nothing of a scientific age, or of the later, open conflict between the two world views, science and religion. Far from having a scientific attitude towards the problem of body and soul, he grapples with it, not to get any truth out of it apart from his own personality, but to use it as the dramatic framework for his individual emotion.

This is the center of Donne. Mr. Mario Praz, in "Donne's Relation to the Poetry of His Time," says: "Donne's technique stands in the same relation to the average technique of Renaissance poetry as that of baroque to that of Renaissance painting. His sole preoccupation is with the whole effect." And, involved in the whole effect, is the quality of experience known to modern criticism as "emotional tone," an implicit form that is functional to the precise rendition of the individual experience. "He was," writes Mr. Praz, "like a lawyer choosing the fittest arguments for the case in hand; not a searcher after a universally valid truth": the fittest images and tropes by which to set forth, not a truth, but a complete emotion. The terms are not the terms of objective truth, to which the individual experience is trimmed down, and all the implications rejected that the terms do not contain. They are rather occasional indications of an experience that is no longer implicit in them, to be used only when they serve the purpose. The scholastic terms in "The Extasie" are quite as illustrative, and no more "philosophical," than the merely denoted violet:

> But as all severall soules containe
> Mixture of things, they know not what,
> Love, these mixt soules, doth mixe againe,
> And makes both one, each this and that.
> A single violet transplant,
> The strength, the colour, and the size . . .

Scholastic love occupies indifferent ground, with respect to truth, quite like that of the neutral conceit of the compasses in "A Valediction: Forbidding Mourning":

> If they be two, they are two so
>   As stiffe twin compasses are two,
> Thy soule the fixt foot, makes no show
> To move, but doth, if the other doe.

The conceits in both passages are "neutral" because they may be either true or false with respect to the inherent demands of the perceptions to be set forth in the poem.

This is the modernism of Donne: it is the modernism that re-establishes our own roots in the age of Donne. Mr. Praz's essay is the link between the two problems of Donne—his place in his own time and his value for us. Here Mr. T. S. Eliot, prophesying the speedy decline of Donne's new reputation, leaves its future ominously obscure. Mr. Eliot's belief that Donne's prose—the sermons, *Biathanatos,* the *Paradoxes and Problems*—is ready for oblivion, and quickly, is not to be questioned; the sermons have been mildly popular, among people who wish to be in the Donne fashion without taking the trouble to read the verse. But that the *Songs and Sonets,* the *Elegies,* most of the *Satires* and the *Divine Poems,* will not continue to be read for an indefinite time is an opinion harder to maintain.

"His learning," says Mr. Eliot, "is just information suffused with emotion . . . rather a humorous shuffling of the pieces; and we are inclined to read our own more conscious awareness of the apparent unrelatedness of things into the mind of Donne."

How much longer this "unrelatedness of things" will continue to be the background of poetry; whether it is not by now an emotional convention out of which minor poetic heresies, like Imagism or the more recent Objectivism, will at intervals appear; whether the local excitement of sensa-

tion will indefinitely obscure the formal qualities of the
Spenserian-Miltonic kind of verse—these are questions that
Mr. Spencer's memorial volume asks, but wisely does not
answer. The answers, perhaps, would contain the immediate
future of poetry.

I I

Why we are concerned with the future of any art is a
mystery that Donne and his contemporaries could not have
understood. But the difference between Donne and our age
is not, in this respect, a radical one, and there was a definite
place in Mr. Spencer's book for an essay on the rise of the
historical consciousness.

The position of Mr. George Williamson, in his excellent
paper, "Donne and Today," falls into two parts that tend to
undermine each other. On the one hand, he suggests abstract analogies between Donne and some living poets,
which would be interesting if true, but on the other hand,
his quotations from Eliot, Read, Ransom, and the late Elinor
Wylie offer as little evidence of the influence of Donne, as Mr.
Williamson understands it, as one might derive from Tennyson. Mrs. Ramsay, in "Donne's Relation to Philosophy,"
quotes stanzas from Donne and "In Memoriam" in order to
distinguish two uses of "philosophy" in verse. But the lines of
Tennyson come within Mr. Williamson's formula for Donne:
"One may say that Donne's emotion is commonly given
'conceptual' form, but not that he is a philosophical poet."

Mr. Eliot remarks that Donne first made it possible to
think in English lyrical verse; but it does not follow that his
thinking in verse was our kind of thought. We are actually
nearer to Tennyson. What thinking there is in modern verse
has the general character of historical thinking—"And all
the wars have dwindled since Troy fell." Tennyson confidently culled the scraps from the tables of "culture"; but
our dietetics is more self-conscious. We use the past and we

think about its meaning. Our framework of idea is the cultural cycle, or the awareness of the "pastness" of the past, as in the case of Mr. Archibald MacLeish. The vulgarity of the present and the purity of the past make the framework of Mr. John Crowe Ransom's irony. Even Mr. Jeffers performs a fusion of literary psychology with a fictitious primitivism that places him in the historical consciousness. Although Mr. Ezra Pound's method is a cunning imitation of the pre-historical view that seized past and present naïvely as a whole, the *Cantos* is a monument to the historical mentality. There is none of this explicitly in Donne.

There is, so far as I know, only the slightest evidence, in seventeenth-century poetry, of a sense of historical rise and fall affecting the moral temper of individuals. Milton's Latin poem, *Naturam non pati senium,* argues that nature does not inwardly decay. Civilization apart from nature is not mentioned; and the poem ends with an allusion to the Christian myth: *Ingentique rogo flagrabit machina mundi.* The decay of nature was a frequent subject of controversy in the universities, and Milton must have felt its latent hostility to his own settled belief in the relation between a fixed human nature and a perfect divine order.

It is this perfect divine order that makes Milton's mythology possible. It is the threat to such an order from the direction of the "new philosophy" which "calls all in doubt," the new cosmology, that compelled Donne to ignore the popular pastoral convention of his time; nor could he rest secure upon the more comprehensive classical or Christian mythology. These imaginative structures (to describe them in the lowest terms) were by habit or in essence involved in the medieval system. Mr. Williamson remarks: "Although mythology is banished from his verse, medieval philosophy and Renaissance science take its place, in fact become his mythology." The distinction between abstract ideas and mythology is extremely important in the study of Donne, and

I believe Mr. Williamson misses a capital point. Dante could afford to be philosophical; the terms were a system that he acknowledged as truth. But it is different with Donne; the vocabulary is merely vocabulary, and it lacks the ultimate, symbolic character of a myth. It is only a step from his lawyerlike use of ingenious terms to the intricacy of personal sensation as the center of consciousness. And from this it is but one more step, for the philosophical egoist, to the dramatization of oneself against the background of society or history. It is a step that Donne could not take, but doubtless would take were he alive today.

There was the mythological, pastoral school, begun by Wyat and Surrey, and Nicholas Grimald, improved by Sidney and Spenser, and perfected by Milton at a single stroke. There was the dramatic, introspective school which, whether in the lyric or on the stage, centered after Chapman in the individual sensibility. In the nondramatic poets of this school, of whom Donne is the great figure before Dryden, the poet himself becomes the dramatic character: Mr. Spencer finds an analogy between Donne and Hamlet's philosophical egoism of inaction: the poet's ideas, now the framework of intense excitement, are pitted against one another like characters in a play.

Therein lies the nature of the "conceit." It is an idea not inherent in the subject, but exactly parallel to it, elaborated beyond the usual stretch of metaphor into a supporting structure for a long passage or even an entire poem. It may be torn away from its original meaning, like the Angels in Donne's "Elegie XI," and yet remain the vehicle of "poetic truth"; that is to say, of heightened emotion in the poet's dramatization of his own personality. The conceit in itself is neither true nor false. From this practice it is but a step to Dryden and the eighteenth century, to the rise of the historical consciousness, and to ourselves. It is the peculiar fascination of Donne that he presents the problem of per-

sonal poetry in its simplest terms. There is the simple awareness, complicated at the surface by his immense intellectual
resources, of frustration and bewilderment—to which, for us,
is added the frustration of historical relativity. Milton stood
for the historical absolute, which is the myth. And unless it
will again be possible for men to give themselves up to a
self-contained, objective system of truths, the principles of
Donne, whether we know him or not, will continue to be our
own.

1932

The Point of Dying: Donne's "Virtuous Men"

As virtuous men passe mildly away
  And whisper to their souls, to goe,
Whilst some of their sad friends do say,
  The breath goes now, and some say no:

So let us melt and make no noise,
  No teare-floods nor sigh tempests move;
'Twere prophanation of our joyes
  To tell the layetie our love.

I BELIEVE that none of Donne's commentators has tried to follow up the implications of the analogy: the moment of death is like the secret communion of lovers. The first thing that we see is that lovers die *out of* something *into* something else. They die in order to live. This is the particular *virtue,* the Christian entelechy or final cause of mankind, and the actualization of what it is to be human.

The logical argument of "A Valediction: Forbidding Mourning" is a Christian commonplace. Through the higher love lovers achieve a unity of being which physical love, the analogue of the divine, not only preserves but both intensifies and enlarges. The implicit symbol of this union is the Aristotelian circle of archetypal motion. Union is imagined first as a mathematical point where physical and spiritual union are the same; then as an expanding circle of which the point is the center. The analogy is complete when the two legs of the draftman's compasses become congruent in the lovers' embrace, so that the legs form a vertical line standing on the "same" point. Thus Donne "reduces" a Platonic abstraction to actual form by contracting the circumference, "absence," to the point, "reunion," on the human scale, of the lovers.

Logically the mathematical point precedes the circle of which it is the center; literally it also has priority, since the lover begins his journey from the point. But the poem as action, as trope, asserts the priority of the circle, for without it nothing in the poem would move: the lovers in order to be united, or reunited, have got first to be "separated," the woman at the center, the man at the enlarging circumference, even though the separation is further and larger union. The visual image of the expanding circle is the malleable gold, which by becoming materially thinner under the hammer expands indefinitely, but not into infinity; for this joint soul of the lovers is a "formulable essence" which abhors infinity. The material gold disappears as it becomes absolutely thin, and is replaced by pure, anagogical "light"—another Christian commonplace that needs no explanation. Donne fills his circle with a physical substance that can be touched and seen; but it is the particular substance which archetypically reflects the light of heaven. Yet all this light which is contained by the circle is only an expanded point; that is to say, whether we see the lovers as occupying the contracted circle in the figure of the compasses, or the expanded point of the gold, they always occupy the same "space," and are never separated. Space is here the "letter" of a nondimensional anagoge; and likewise the circle widening towards infinity. Thus spatial essences are the analogical rhetoric of a suprarational intuition.

But "A Valediction: Forbidding Mourning" is a poem, not a philosophical discourse. And since a poem is a movement of a certain kind in which its logical definition is only a participant, we have got to try to see this poem, like any other, as an action more or less complete. For an action, even of the simplest outline, in life or in art, is not what we can say about it; it rather is what prompts us to speak. The Christian commonplaces that I have pointed out are not Donne's poem; they are, as letter and allegory, material factors that it is the business of the poet to bring to full actualization in rhetoric; and here, as always, the rhetoric, the full linguistic body of the poem which ultimately resists our analysis, is the action, the trope, the "turning" from one thing to another: from darkness to light, from ignorance to knowledge, from sight to insight. This tropological motion is the final cause (τοῦ ἕνεκα) of the poem, that towards which it moves, on account of which its logical definition, its formulable essence, exists. And it is the business of criticism to examine this motion, not the formulable essence as such.

Donne's two opening stanzas announce the theme of indissoluble spiritual union in an analogy to what seems at first glance its opposite: dissolution of soul from body. First we have dying men (not one man, not trope but allegory) who "whisper to their souls, to goe"; then, in the second stanza, lovers who "melt *and* [my italics] make no noise." The moment of death is a *separation* which virtuous men welcome, and the lovers are about to *separate* in quiet joy ("no teare-floods nor sigh-tempests move"). For the lovers too are "virtuous"—infused with a certain power or potency to be realized. They have no more to fear from separation from each other than dying men from death, or separation from life. If the lovers foresee no loss, they may expect a gain similar to that of the dying men.

At this point we may pass to another phase of the analogy. Here the difficult word is "melt." I cannot find in the history of the word, even as a secondary meaning, the idea of human separation. The meanings range from change of physical identity to feelings of tenderness. Tenderness is no doubt felt by the lovers at parting, and by the sad friends at the deathbed. But it is difficult to imagine these virtuous men feeling tender towards themselves, or sorry that they are dying. They might feel some "tenderness" for or yearning towards something beyond life, i.e., union with God, the realization of their virtue. Here the analogy holds for both lovers and dying men, but here also melting as tenderness becomes very remote; and we must fall back upon change of physical identity as the analogue to change of spiritual identity. The figure has got to work in the first place this side of a remote "higher" meaning, a univocal abstraction not caught in the burning bush of rhetorical analogy. Donne is one of the last Catholic allegorists; to him aiming high is meaningless unless the aim is sighted from a point below. Thus the sense in which both dying men and lovers may be said to melt is restricted to loss of physical substance, of physical identity. The verb "to goe" applies then to both lovers and dying men; both go out of the body, yet through the body, to unite with the object of love. "To goe" thus means to join, to unite with; to "melt" must be equated with "to goe"; it means going into something other than itself. Melting and going are species of dying, but the underlying universal is affirmed, implicitly, not overtly. If lovers die in this analogical sense, they lose their identity in each other, and the physical separation is the letter of the great anagoge, spiritual union. The lover dies out of himself into the beloved in order to gain spiritual union; and spiritual union having been gained, the bodies are no longer there; they are absent, separated. The lover leaves not only the body of the beloved, but his own; and the movement of action, the trope, provides for both journeys. For "mourning" is forbidden for two reasons. They must not mourn because "Donne" is going off to the continent; they must not mourn, since through the letter of sexual union they pass tropologically from body to spirit, where body is left behind for another kind of journey.

The structure of the poem, *at the level of trope,* turns on the pun *to die:* orgasmic ecstasy as the literal analogue to spiritual ecstasy; physical union as the analogue to spiritual. Between these extremes of inert analogy we find the moral, or tropological, movement of the poem, the central action—the passage in actualized experience from the lower to the higher. But without this egregious pun, the whole range of the pun, at that: its witty, anecdotal, even obscene implications: without it the poem would not move; for the pun is its mover, its propeller, its efficient cause.

A grammatical peculiarity of stanza two will offer indirect support for this argument. I refer to "and" between "melt *and* make no noise." I have I believe disposed of "let us be tender" as a plausible meaning of "melt." But if that were the right meaning, the conjunction should be "but," not "and." As Donne wrote the passage (we are entitled to read only what he wrote), it evidently means: Let us pass through the body, let us "die" in both senses, *and* the loss of physical self will prevent the noisy grief of "sublunary lovers" at parting and the noisy love making of physical union. Thus if "melt" were not an extension of the pun, Donne would probably have written "but make no noise"— a prudential injunction to protect the neighbors from scandal.

Two other features of the analogy seem to me to reinforce this reading. Why are the sad friends at the deathbed incapable of detecting the exact moment of death? Affection and anxiety account for it in life. This is obviously the first and literal meaning. But here it must be considered along with the lovers' reluctance to tell their love to the "laity." For the logic of the poem contains a third Christian commonplace: death-in-life of this world, life-in-death of the next. The sad friends are a similar laity and the laity is the world, where men do not know the difference between appearance and reality, between death and life. But men at the moment of death, lovers at the moment of spiritual union (through and beyond the body), have a sacerdotal secret, access to a sacramental rite, beyond the understanding of the "laity" who have not had these ultimate experiences. The dying of the lovers into life and the dying of death into life are reciprocally analogous. Donne is not saying that death is *like* love, or that love is *like* death; there is the identity, death-love, a third something, a reality that can be found only through analogy since it has no name. This reality, whether of "dying" lovers or of "dying" men, is the ultimate experience. The reciprocal conversion of the one into the other is the moral motion of the poem, its peripety, the "action" which eventually issues in the great top-level significance that Dante understood as the anagoge. This is nothing less, as it is surely nothing more, than the entire poem, an actual linguistic object that is at once all that our discourse can make of it and nothing that at any moment of discourse we are able to make of it.

1952

A Note on Elizabethan Satire

I

As THE Oxford anthologies come off the press, the disadvantages of dividing English poetry into exact centuries become more and more conspicuous. Sir Edmund Chambers, in his preface to *The Oxford Book of Sixteenth Century Verse*, remarks that the year 1600 "still finds a continuous flood of literature in mid-career." He points out that "Drayton and Chapman, who hopelessly overlap the dividing line, must be cut asunder." Drayton, for example, suffers for the absence of his "ballads" of Agincourt and the Virginian Voyage. Donne is wholly omitted, for reasons that we shall see. Given the limited range, which, in the poetry of Donne, Sir Edmund seems to define with excessive narrowness, he has done his work well, even brilliantly.

There is a good reason for the success of this anthology. It is the editor's superior taste, a gift that historical scholars a generation ago feared to exercise. "In the present case," writes Sir Edmund, "an attempt has been made to apply a standard of absolute poetry, rather than one of merely historical interest. . . ." It is a difficult standard to uphold, and if it cannot be said that the editor applies it infallibly, one must remember that the power to perceive the best does not always carry with it the will to reject the second rate.

A debatable assumption underlies Sir Edmund's view of the whole period, and there are some minor disproportions in the representation of the poets. The disproportion between Raleigh and Sir John Davies is enormous. Raleigh wrote less than Davies but that less is immeasurably superior; yet Davies has fifty-one pages to Raleigh's thirty-seven. Here one feels that Sir Edmund in spite of himself is beguiled by the historical interest of Davies's *Orchestra,* perhaps by the interminable facility of its versification—although Davies at times is still as clumsy as the earlier Gascoigne or Grimald.

One mark of Davies's inferiority is the lack of tension in his style, a lack of concentrated purpose. This inferiority is at the center of the whole Spenserian school, in which, as Sir Edmund points out, "the slightness of invention is overhung with ornamental decoration, like some great composition of Paolo Veronese. . . ." This ornamental decoration of image in Spenser and Davies arose along with the historical improvement of English versification between 1557 and 1579—a springe to catch the woodcocks of the historical method. It was, actually, the resistance, in the first half of the century, of a fluid vocabulary to the poet's meaning, joined to his metrical uncertainty, that contributed to Wyat's success in "They flee from me that sometime did me seek." It is one of a half-dozen great meditative lyrics in English.

Nevertheless, Sir Edmund justly attacks, from his own point of view, one of the hoariest pedantries in English criticism: "A rather irritating kind of scholarship insists that Wyat was chiefly notable for the acclimatization of the Italian sonnet. . . . But in lyric, sung or based on the models of song, he is a master of the first order." . . . In spite of the perhaps too generous excerpts from Davies, Daniel, and Constable, one sees everywhere the evidence of Sir Edmund's preoccupation with the quality of the verse. He has given us all of Sackville's *Induction;* sixteen poems by Fulke Greville, including the fine long piece, "Who grace for zenith had"; thirty-one pages of Sidney, who is better represented here than in any other popular collection ever made; and the ample selections from Raleigh already noticed—although a few more of his sonnets would have furthered the rising reputation of this most neglected of Elizabethan poets. Raleigh's direct, conversational ease, his intelligence and subtlety, are qualities that deserve to be better understood: it has been the custom to see in Raleigh's verse only a sort of thin lagging after Sidney. His poetry is, on the contrary, distinct, and needs separate consideration.

I I

It is ungrateful to impute to Sir Edmund Chambers any trace of wrong insight into the quality of the age. The century as a whole falls into three periods—that of Skelton, lasting until the appearance of Wyat in Tottel's *Songes and Sonets* in 1557; the period of Wyat, the most considerable figure until Sidney and Spenser, whose *Shepherd's Calendar* brought in a new era in 1579. It was by then the English Renaissance full-blown. *The Shepherd's Calendar,* a dull but original exercise in theory, offered to Spenser's successors an example of new possibilities of poetic English, and set up a pastoral convention that was to reach perfection as late as 1637. In singling out the leading impulse of the Elizabethan age one is constantly guided by the genius and magnitude of Spenser. Yet it is Milton in the next age who puts the seal of perfection on the pastoral, mythological school, and who, to no little extent, permits us to rank as highly as we do merely competent poets like Davies and Constable.

Our comparatively low rating of Greville no less than of Raleigh—Saintsbury says that Greville is "sententious and difficult"—is due to the constant introspection, the difficult self-analysis, the cynical melancholy, that break through the courtly pastoral convention to a level of feeling deeper, and historically purer, than the facile despair of the Sidneian sonneteers. Doubtless both Greville and Raleigh, as minor masters, were too much impressed with the glittering style of Sidney, and, later, of Spenser, to understand that their own sensibilities deserved a more perfectly matured style. Their work has the diffuseness of divided purpose.

There has never been enough made of Elizabethan satire. While Raleigh and Fulke Greville cannot be called pure satirists, they were not comfortable in the courtly, pastoral abstractions. In this negative feature of their verse they resemble certain of the satirists, Hall, Marston, Tourneur. If we put Raleigh and Greville together against the background of the widespread influence of Martial,[1] they, too, form a background not only for the *Satires* of Donne (1593) but for much of that great poet's most characteristic later writing.

Yet Sir Edmund says: "Only for chronology, indeed, can Donne be an Elizabethan"—an opinion that obscures the still powerful strain of medieval thought at the end of the sixteenth century. By another kind of reasoning Donne cannot be a Jacobean. For we find in Donne, significantly enough, not only the influence of Martial, but a resurgence of scholasticism—a union of classical satire and medievalism. And it is significant that "Go, soul, the body's guest" was written by the same Raleigh who wrote "The Passionate Man's Pilgrimage," a poem that is, I believe, occasionally described as charming. I cannot believe that, in order to write it, Raleigh invoked a muse different from the muse of a poem that is sophisticated, consciously erudite, and subtle. "The Passionate Man's Pilgrimage" is medieval allegory furbished up with a new awareness of the sensuous world; "Go, soul, the body's guest" is satire; and the two strains are not quite the disharmony that we are accustomed to believe them.

---

1 See T. K. Whipple, *Martial and the English Epigram from Sir Thomas Wyat to Ben Jonson* (Berkeley, 1929); and Evelyn M. Simpson, "Donne's 'Paradoxes and Problems,'" in *A Garland for John Donne, 1631–1931, op. cit.*

Possibly the last use of extended medieval allegory in verse of great distinction is Sackville's *Induction*. There are the familiar personifications—Remorse, Dread, Revenge, Misery, Death. Spenser's task was to revive allegory with a new spirit alien to the medieval mind. Although Spenser's puritanism is manifest, his allegory has a voluptuous glitter that Sackville's more medieval spareness lacked; or if you go back to Gower's treatment of the seven deadly sins it is plain that as a medieval man he was too serious about them to dress them up.

The medieval minds left over at the end of the sixteenth century tended to see the world not in terms of a fixed moral system, but with an ingrained moral prejudice about the nature of man. I allude here to the decline of Catholic theology in England, and to the rise, conspicuously in the dramatic poets, of an unmoral and antidoctrinal point of view. Marlowe is an example. But the moral temper of a less expansive, more melancholy age, a kind of interregnum between feudalism and Tudorism when the evil of life was expressed in ideas of all-pervasive mortality—this moral temper, having lost its theological framework, remained as an almost instinctive approach to the nature of man. And the nature of man, far from enjoying the easy conquest of evil that Spenser set forth in six books that might have been twelve, was on the whole unpleasant and depraved. This depravity is the theme of Elizabethan tragedy, I think, as early as *The Jew of Malta*. There is no need to cite Webster and Ford.

It is the prevailing attitude of the satirists and of most of those nondramatic poets who stand apart from the Spenserian school. In such poets we find a quality that we have shortsightedly ascribed uniquely to modern verse—the analysis of emotion and an eye chiefly to the aesthetic effect. There is here the use of symbols that are too complex to retain, throughout a long work, or from one work to another, a fixed meaning. The allegorical symbol is constant and homogeneous, like the Red Cross Knight; the richer, poetic symbol, like Prospero, does not invite the oversimplification of certain of its qualities, but asks to be taken in all its manifold richness.

It is this stream of Elizabethan poetry that has never been properly evaluated. We tend to forget, in fixing the relation of the Shakespearean drama to its sources, and of its text to the texts of contemporaries, that Shakespeare stands outside the allegorical school. It is thus difficult for us to take a further step and to see that he was closely connected with a much less conspicuous type of poetry that had been only superficially affected by the Renaissance. This was the dormant medieval which, even after the new language of Wyat, survived in Sackville's *Induction.*

In a later poet like Greene the new courtly conventions are too weak to sustain his restless sensibility. Although Greene never mastered a style, his great vitality of image and rhythm is largely due to a naïvely skeptical grasp of the conventions of Sidney and Spenser. He uses them without ever quite believing them: as in the verse of Raleigh the convention offers just enough resistance to expression to lend to the poetry tension and depth. Though Greene is imperfect, he has none of Daniel's complacently perfect dullness.

It is this resistance of the language to full expression, the strain between images and rhythm, opposites "yoked by violence together" in varying degrees of violence, that gives to English lyrical verse its true genius. It is a genius that permitted Milton to bring to the pastoral style a richness and subtlety of effect that Spenser never achieved. It is that quality of English style which is superior to age and school. It was perfectly mastered as early as Wyat:

> It was no dream; I lay broad waking:
>   But all is turned, thorough my gentleness
> Into a strange fashion of forsaking;
>   And I have leave to go of her goodness,

And she also to use newfangleness.
But since that I so kindly am served
I would fain know what she hath deserved.

It is in the lyrics, even in the political satires, of Dryden,
but it begins to disappear in Pope, to reappear in the nineteenth century perhaps in Landor and Browning alone. It
is a quality, not of system or of doctrine, but of immediate
intelligence acting directly; a definite but unpremeditated
limitation of moral and metaphysical idea to the problem
of the work to be done. It is unmoralistic and anti-allegorical.
Out of that long and neglected stream of the English tradition comes a kind of poetry that we have named in our age
symbolism—a curious misnomer borrowed from the French;
for it has no elaborate symbolism at all in the Spenserian
mode.

When Saintsbury thirty-five years ago issued the first edition of his *Short History of English Literature,* he announced
that his chief interest throughout would be form—at that
time a revolutionary point of view. But he gave to the Elizabethan satirists only a scant paragraph: they were both
"coarse" and "insincere." This view will have to be changed
before we shall be able to understand the early Donne—not
only Donne, but a great deal of the finest work of our own
time, poets like Eliot and Yeats. The satirists of the 1590's
not only read Martial, they went back through Sackville to
Lyndsay and Dunbar. The medieval sense of mortality, of
the vanity of the world, survives in the satirists, who use it
as a weapon of critical irony upon the vaunting romanticism
of the Renaissance. And we, in this age, insofar as we maintain the traditions of English verse, are still criticizing the
Renaissance.

I I I

The poetry of our own age that we find most moving and
powerful, the poetry that is tough enough to reject the easy

solutions of the human predicament that arise in every age, has a longer and more honorable lineage than we are accustomed to suppose. Yet Mr. Edmund Wilson, in *Axel's Castle,* would have us believe that modern symbolism is a method, invented by the poets, of evading the problems of modern economics: our belief in the inferiority of our own age to the past is due to the palsied irresponsibility of the Ivory Tower. But this belief is the fundamental groundwork of all poetry at all times. It is the instinctive counterattack of the intelligence against the dogma of future perfection for persons and societies. It is in this sense, perhaps, that poetry is most profoundly the criticism of life.

It must seem to readers who have preserved, in the midst of the "historical method," a vestige of the historical sense, that social and political writers wish to exempt the world of secular policy from the criticism with which the arts are constantly threatening the latest programs of social improvement. It has always been so with the proponents of "proletarian" art; it was so with Spenser. The poets are asked to oversimplify the human predicament with morality and allegory. The first great example of proletarian—that is, allegorical—poetry in English is Spenser's *Faerie Queene:* there is no real distinction possible between an art that oversimplifies our experience in favor of princes and an art that performs that callow office for the people. There has always been a small body of men—a saving remnant very different from the Victorian notion of such a minority—headed by William Shakespeare, who warn us to make haste slowly with the best-wrought schemes for the satisfaction of our desires. Let the plans be well wrought indeed, but let the arts teach us—if we demand a moral—that the plans are not and can never be absolutes. Poetry perhaps more than any other art tests with experience the illusions that the human predicament tempts us in our weakness to believe.

1932

A Reading of Keats

I

It is proper that we celebrate the hundred and fiftieth anniversary of the birth of John Keats by testing our powers of reading him. For the perpetual task of criticism, every generation or two, is to understand again the poetry of the past. Poetry which cannot survive this renewal of understanding, and live again in the critical sensibility of posterity, must contain some radical flaw of interest; it is perhaps in this sense that time is the test of poetry. This view, commonly held today, presupposes the continuity of tradition which with occasional lapses has come down to us from the Greeks; but whether the best English poets shall survive the coming age is a question bearing less upon their value for us than upon our capacity to receive it. If Keats goes unread by the next generation, whose memory will not go back to the great historical era which now seems to be closing, I cannot think that the failure will be his. He will remain one of the great English poets for a later generation to rediscover.

This sounds like the prediction of Colvin in 1917; and I see no reason to argue generally with the Victorian estimate. Perhaps of Keats alone of the English romantics does this estimate still hold, possibly because the great claims were never made for him that were made for Wordsworth and Coleridge. If definitive criticism were possible, Bridges's *A Critical Introduction to Keats* (1894, revised 1914) and A. C.

Bradley's "The Letters of Keats" (*Oxford Lectures on Poetry,* 1909) might be said to realize it; and to these should be added the fine textual study, Professor Ridley's *Keats' Craftsmanship* (1933), and Professor C. D. Thorpe's *The Mind of John Keats* (1926).[1] So, apart from the three full-length biographies by Houghton, Colvin, and Miss Lowell, there are four excellent critical studies of Keats, two from the late Victorian age, two from our own: there is probably less useless writing about Keats than about the other great English romantics. The reasons for this are obvious if a little hard to state: the bulk of Keats's work is comparatively slight; at his best (the odes, "Lamia," "The Eve of St. Agnes," and parts of "Hyperion") he has a masterful simplicity of purpose and control. In these poems, with the single exception of "Hyperion," the influences are so well assimilated that only the most trivial academic mind could suppose Keats's relation to the "history of ideas" to have more than the value of a few monographs. In this I take it "he is with Shakespeare." It has been easier for the critics to get at the essentials of Keats than of Wordsworth, Coleridge, and Shelley, who conceal more traps to catch scholars.

This is not to say that Keats was, in the sense of the phrase common a few years ago, a "pure poet." He was the great poet of his age, in the fullest sense; and even Matthew Arnold almost let himself see that he was. Arnold's essay remains one of the best "estimates" of Keats in the Victorian style (which goes back to Johnson) of combined moral and critical judgment. Perhaps Arnold was the last great critic to use it effectively; for since its decay in the impressionism of Pater and in the dilettanteism of the "literary essay" of

---

[1] The value of Professor Thorpe's book is somewhat diminished by the instability of his critical terms; but as a rounded descriptive study it is excellent. I have not put Mr. Murry's *Keats and Shakespeare* (1926) in this list because I find its main argument incomprehensible; though the book is valuable for many brilliant insights.

the nineties and early nineteen-hundreds, we have been getting a new sort of criticism which was brought in by Eliot's *The Sacred Wood* (1920).

Arnold's essay still has a certain interest in the history of Keats's reputation, yet it must concern us now as perhaps the best evidence of Arnold's almost perverse use of critical standards. More than any other poet Keats pinned him upon the horns of his dilemma: "Natural magic" and/or "Moral interpretation." It has been said (by whom I do not remember) that the ambiguousness of Arnold's judgment of Keats was due to his humorless sense of responsibility for the poetry of his age: Keats was the greatest "natural magician" since Shakespeare; but what poetry then *needed* was moral interpretation, and Keats had been a harmful example. This is not the place to examine Arnold's critical dialectic (that has been admirably done by Mr. Trilling); yet it is not beside the point to remark Arnold's failure to see that in Keats's "principle of beauty in all things" lay a possible way out of his dilemma. Even the *Letters* (among the great letters of the world) give a clue to its significance, to say nothing of the structure of the odes. Arnold was not interested in structure unless it was a structure of action inviting moral interpretation. He saw Keats quite simply as a "sensuous" poet.

I have belabored this question more than either Arnold or it deserves (not more than they merit) because I think it is necessary, before proceeding to Keats's poetry, to refer briefly to my own disabilities as a critic of Keats. They are not unlike Arnold's. It would be ludicrous to confess that I lack Arnold's general powers, or more particularly his capacity for awareness of what he did not like (it was this awareness that raised him above the level of the conventional Victorian moralist); but it is not beside the point to warn readers of this essay that my attitude towards Keats is reverent, yet distant without disinterestedness. Whether Keats is what we *need* I do not know; yet we neither want him nor use him.

For the past fifteen years the direction of Anglo-American poetry has been rather towards Shelley than Keats, towards "Godwin-perfectibility" and social consciousness than towards a dramatic-symbolic style. I hope I shall not sound like Margaret Fuller if I say that I am not indifferent to the utmost capacity of men for social and individual perfection; I simply do not think that poetry should be limited to exhorting men to these goods. My lack of sympathy with this school nevertheless does not qualify me as a critic of Keats, in spite of my conviction (which was Arnold's unhappy conviction) that Keats was in one of the great modes of poetry. It is perhaps a mode inaccessible to us today. I shall not try, because it is too difficult, to state directly why I think this obstacle exists. My understanding of it, such as it may be, will be implied in what I am about to say of "Ode to a Nightingale," in my opinion Keats's great poem in spite of its imperfect detail, greater than "Ode to Autumn," which because of its purity of tone and style Bridges ranks first among the odes; "Ode to Autumn" is a very nearly perfect piece of style but it has little to say. Because I believe that "Ode to a Nightingale" at least tries to say everything that poetry can say I am putting it at the center of this discussion.

I I

The testimony of the criticism of Keats which I have read (I cannot pause to summarize it here) is that he was a pictorial poet in the Spenserian tradition. I would add to this very general statement the observation: his progress from "Endymion" to the revised "Hyperion" is a direct line, at the end of which he achieved under Milton's influence a new kind of blank verse; but in it he could not control the heroic action. In a letter to Reynolds (September 21st, 1819), he said: "I have given up 'Hyperion'—there were too many Miltonic inversions in it . . ."; and in a letter to George Keats, written six days later: "I have but lately stood on my guard against Milton. Life to him would be death to me." I think the second of these explanations, general as it is, comes nearer to the truth: he could not write Miltonic verse without eventual frustration because he lacked a Miltonic subject; it would be "death" to him. For the framework of "Hyperion," of the more human, revised version no less than the first version, is pictorial, with declamatory summaries of action which Keats does not present. It is a succession of plastic scenes.

If this had been the only line of development from "Endymion," we should not, of course, have got the odes; and Keats would have remained a youthful experimenter of genius, considerably above Chatterton but not so impressive as Shelley. The other line runs in the order of time, from "Endymion" to the odes; but perhaps technically, as Professor Ridley has argued, the line is from the sonnets to the odes; that is to say, his experiments with the sonnet led him to modifications of the form which gave us the great stanzas of the "Grecian Urn" and the "Nightingale." And within that narrow, lyrical, and potentially dramatic compass he had something ready to say that he could not have said in the other kinds of verse that he had tried. "The Eve of St. Agnes" is his masterpiece in the Spenserian tradition of *ut pictura, poesis,* and the originality is in the freshness of the language. Far more instructive for technical reasons (reasons which cannot be disconnected from the higher reasons) is the versification of "Lamia," based partly upon Dryden, but, as Professor Ridley shows, in no sense imitative. For example, "Lamia" has proportionately three times as many run-on lines as Dryden's "Fables" taken as a whole, thirty-three per cent being run on; there is a large number of tercets ending with alexandrines, but there are no feminine endings. The result of this adaptation of Dryden's verse is a movement of great speed and flexibility, firm yet supple; and altogether the most original contribution to narrative verse of the nineteenth century. But it should be remembered that "Lamia" is a narrative of a minor mythological incident which Keats picked up in Burton, not epic action: although Keats failed to sustain his blank verse because he could not fill it with action, he succeeded brilliantly with a new kind of verse in which the pictorial method supports the main effect, the simple action turning on a plot of recognition. For the moment we need not go into the symbolism; but it is significant that it was material which Keats found something like the perfect means to bring into form. Written in the summer of 1819 (Part I by mid-July), "Lamia" is the height of his achievement in the long poem. The important thing to remember is that Keats finished it at about the same time he abandoned "Hyperion."

I shall briefly anticipate the end that I am heading towards by setting down a few opinions which will both indicate its direction and gauge my understanding of Keats. "Lamia" is more closely related to the two great odes, the "Nightingale" and the "Grecian Urn," than to "Hyperion," and the fact that he could successfully revise "The Eve of St. Agnes" at the time he was finishing "Lamia" is as much proof as criticism needs that it is not too far from the materials and methods of a poem which some critics would put with the other narratives, "Isabella" and the fragment "The Eve of St. Mark." Moreover, we must think of "Lamia" and "The Eve of St. Agnes" along with the great odes, as follows: "Ode to a Nightingale," "Ode on a Grecian Urn," "Ode to Psyche," "To Autumn," and "Ode on Melancholy." This cluster of poems is the center of Keats's great work, and they all deal with the same imaginative dilemma—or, if we wish to be biographical, the same conflict in Keats's experience. (I cannot agree with Bridges that there is anything in the sonnets as good as the best Shakespeare; I am convinced that they would not have won their great reputation apart from the other work; and I shall not discuss them here.)

The imaginative dilemma of Keats is, I assume, implicit in the poems, which are its best statement: the most that criticism ought to attempt is perhaps a kind of circulatory description of its movements, from poem to poem. Bridges's astute remark that "Keats's art is primarily objective and pictorial, and whatever other qualities it has are as it were *added on to things as perceived*," contains critical insight of the first order. I have italicized *added on to things as perceived*, and I would double the italics of the last two words; they point directly to the imaginative limit of Keats's poetry, one horn of the dilemma out of which it does not move, in which it must, if it is to exceed the *ut pictura, poesis* formula, seek some conversion of that limit.

I should thus offer (for what it is worth) the very general analysis: Keats as a pictorial poet was necessarily presenting in a given poem a series of scenes, and even in the narratives the action does not flow from inside the characters, but is governed pictorially from the outside. He is thus a painting poet and would have earned Lessing's censure. But like every great artist he knew (in his own terms, which are none of our business) that his problem was to work within his limitations, and to transcend them. He was a poet of space whose problem was to find a way of conveying what happens in time; for it is time in which dramatic conflict takes place; and it is only by conversion into dramatic actuality that the parts of the verbal painting achieve relation and significance. "The form of thought in Keats," says Mr. Kenneth Burke, "is mystical, in terms of an eternal present" —and, I should add, in terms of the arrested action of painting.

I I I

When Keats adds to "things as perceived," what does he add? That, it seems to me, is the special problem of Keats. In the simplest language it is the problem of adding movement to a static picture, of putting into motion the "languor which lingers in the main design" (Bridges) of even the later work.

Of the eight stanzas of "Ode to a Nightingale" six are distinctly pictorial in method; a seventh, stanza three, in which Keats expresses his complaint of common life, develops as a meditation out of the second stanza, the picture of Provence. The only stanza which does not give us or in some way pertain to a definite scene is number seven; for though the method there is pictorial, the effect is allusive—the permanence of the nightingale's song is established in a rapid series of vignettes, ending with the famous "faëry lands forlorn." It is the only stanza, as some critic has remarked, which contains a statement contradictory of our sense of common reality.

> Thou wast not born for death, immortal Bird,

he says to the nightingale; and we cannot agree. The assertion is out of form in an obvious sense, for the poem is an accumulation of pictorial situations, and the claim of immortality for the bird is dramatic and lyrical.

I am raising the question whether the metonymy which attributes to the literal nightingale the asserted immortality of the song is convincing enough to carry the whole imaginative insight of the poem. I think it is, given the limits of Keats's art, but I am still nagged by a difficulty that will not down. It seems to me that the ambivalence of the nightingale symbol contains almost the whole substance of the poem: the bird, as bird, shares the mortality of the world; as symbol, it purports to transcend it. And I feel that the pictorial technique has not been quite dramatic enough to give to the transcendence of the symbol life in some visibly presented experience. The far more implausible, even far-fetched, metaphor of the draughtsman's compasses, in Donne, comes out a little better because through a series of dialectical transformations, from the dying man to the Ptolemaic spheres, and then through the malleable gold to the compasses, there is a progression of connected analogies, given us step by step; and we acknowledge the identity of compasses and lovers as imaginatively possible. Keats merely *asserts:* song equals immortality; and I feel there is some disparity between the symbol and what it is expected to convey—not an inherent disparity, for such is not imaginatively conceivable, but a disparity such as we should get in the simple equation $A = B$ if we found that the assigned values of A and B were respectively 1 and 3.

This feature of Keats's art we shall find in "Ode on a Grecian Urn" but not in "Ode to Psyche." I confess that I do not know what to do about this anomalous poem, except to admire it. There appears to me to be very little genuine *sensation* in Keats (rather what Arnold and his contemporaries mistook for sensation), but there is more of it in "Ode to Psyche" than anywhere else in the great odes. Mr. T. S. Eliot puts it first among the odes, possibly because most of its detail is genuinely experienced and because it contains no developed attitude towards life. The other odes do; and it is an attitude less mature than that which Mr. Eliot finds in the *Letters.* With this part of his view of Keats one must agree. But it is a dangerous view, since it is very remotely possible that some letters from Shakespeare may turn up some day. But Mr. Eliot's preference for "Ode to Psyche" doubtless shares at bottom the common prejudice that romantic art tends not only to be pictorial but "off center" and lacking in that appearance of logical structure which we ordinarily associate with Donne and Dryden. I do not want to get into this classical-and-romantic affair, for the usual reason, and for a reason of my own, which is that it has a way of backfiring. Mr. Eliot has said that Coleridge and Wordsworth on one side are "as eighteenth century as anybody." So is Keats. The apostrophe to the nightingale, which I have been at some pains to try to understand, is quite

"eighteenth century"; but it is not nearly so eighteenth century as the entire third stanza, which I shall now try to
understand, assuming that what it says has a close connection with that literal part of the nightingale, the physical
bird, which Keats seemed not to know what to do with (except to make it, in the last stanza, fly away). Here it is:

> Fade far away, dissolve, and quite forget
>   What thou among the leaves hast never known,
> The weariness, the fever, and the fret
>   Here where men sit and hear each other groan;
> Where palsy shakes a few, sad, last gray hairs,
>   Where youth grows pale, and spectre-thin, and dies;
>   Where but to think is to be full of sorrow
>   And leaden-eyed despairs,
>   Where beauty cannot keep her lustrous eyes,
>   Or new Love pine at them beyond tomorrow.[2]

Looked at from any point of view, this stanza is bad; the
best that one ought to say of it perhaps is that there are
worse things in Shelley and Wordsworth, and in Keats himself. (Even Colvin's habitual tone of eulogy is restrained
when he comes to it.[3]) It is bad in the same way as the
passages in Shelley's "Adonaïs" which exhibit the troops of
mourners are bad. Keats here is relapsing into weakened
eighteenth-century rhetoric; Blake could have put into the
personifications imaginative power, and Pope genuine feeling, or at any rate an elegance and vigor which would have
carried them.

There is not space enough in an essay to go into this
matter as it needs to be gone into. What I wish to indicate,
for the consideration of more thorough readers, is that stanza
three may be of the utmost significance in any attempt to
understand the structure of Keats's poetry. It gives us a

---

[2] Quotations from the poems follow Garrod, *The Poetical Works of John Keats*
(Oxford, 1939).
[3] Sidney Colvin, *John Keats* (New York, 1917), p. 419.

"picture" of common reality, in which the life of man is all mutability and frustration. But here if anywhere in the poem the necessity to dramatize time, or the pressure of actuality, is paramount. *Keats has no language of his own for this realm of experience.* That is the capital point. He either falls into the poetic language of the preceding age, or, if he writes spontaneously, he commits his notorious errors of taste; in either case the language is not adequate to the feeling; or, to put it "cognitively," he lacks an ordered symbolism through which he may *know* the common and the ideal reality in a single imaginative act. One would like to linger upon the possible reasons for this. I suspect that evidence from another source, which I shall point out later, will be more telling than anything, even this stanza, that we can find in the odes. The consciousness of change and decay, which can, and did in Keats, inform one of the great modes of poetry, is deeply involved with his special attitude towards sexual love. He never presents love directly and dramatically; it is in terms of Renaissance tapestry, as in "The Eve of St. Agnes," or in a fable of Italian violence, as in "Isabella"; or, most interesting of all, in terms of a little myth, Lamia the snake-woman, a symbol which permits Keats to objectify the mingled attraction and repulsion which his treatment of love requires. I sometimes think that for this reason "Lamia" is his best long poem: the symbol inherently contains the repulsive element, but keeps it at a distance, so that he does not have to face it in terms of common experience, his own, or as he was aware of it in his age. Is it saying too much to suppose that Keats's acceptance of the pictorial method is to a large extent connected with his unwillingness to deal with passion dramatically? (There is sensuous detail, but no sensation as direct experience, such as we find in Baudelaire.)

I need not labor a point which even the Victorian critics and biographers, almost without exception, remarked: Keats,

both before and after his fatal illness (as other poets have
been who were not ill at all) was filled with the compulsive
image of the identity of death and the act of love (for example, "You must be mine to die upon the rack if I want
you," he wrote to Fanny Brawne); and it is only an exaggeration of emphasis to say that death and love are interchangeable terms throughout his poetry. The "ecstasy" that
the nightingale pours forth contains the Elizabethan pun
on "die" with the wit omitted, and a new semimystical
intensity of feeling added. And is it too much to say that
Keats's constant tendency was to face the moment of love
only in terms of an ecstasy so intense that he should not
survive it? When Lamia vanishes Lycius "dies." And this
affirmation of life through death is the element that Keats
"adds on to things as perceived." But life-in-death is presented pictorially, in space, as an eternal moment, not as a
moment of dramatic action in time, proceeding from previous action and looking towards its consequences.

The dialectical tension underlying "Ode to a Nightingale"
seems to me to be incapable of resolution, first in terms of
Keats's mind as we know it from other sources, and, secondly, in terms of the pictorial technique which dominates
the poetic method. This method, which seems to reflect a
compulsive necessity of Keats's experience, allows him to
present the thesis of his dilemma, the ideality of the nightingale symbol, but not the antithesis, the world of common
experience, which is the substance of stanza three. The "resolution" is suspended in the intensity of the images setting
forth the love-death identity and reaching a magnificent
climax in stanza six ("Now more than ever seems it rich to
die," etc.). But the climax contains a little less than the full
situation; it reaches us a little too simplified, as if Keats were
telling us that the best way to live is to die, or the best way
to die is to live intensely so that we may die intensely. There
may be concealed here one of the oldest syntheses of Chris-

tian thought, that we die only to live; but, if so, there has been a marked shrinkage in range of that conception since Donne wrote his "A Nocturnall upon S. Lucies Day."

Messrs. Brooks and Warren, in their excellent if somewhat confident analysis [4] of the "Nightingale" ode, argue with much conviction that the dramatic frame of the poem, the painful accession to the trance in the opening lines and the return to immediate reality ("Do I wake or sleep?") at the end, provides a sufficient form. I confess that I am not sure. I am not certain of the meaning of what happens inside the frame; but at times I am not certain that it is necessary to understand it. There is no perfection in poetry. All criticism must in the end be comparative (this does not mean critical relativity); it must constantly refer to what poetry has accomplished in order to estimate what it can accomplish, not what it ought to accomplish; we must heed Mr. Ransom's warning that perfect unity or integration in a work of art is a critical delusion. "Ode to a Nightingale" is by any standard one of the great poems of the world. Our philosophical difficulties with it are not the same as Keats's imaginative difficulties, which pertain to the order of experience and not of reason. The poem is an emblem of one limit of our experience: the impossibility of synthesizing, in the order of experience, the antinomy of the ideal and the real, and, although that antinomy strikes the human mind with a different force in different ages (Donne's dualism is not Keats's), it is sufficiently common to all men in all times to be understood.

If we glance at "Ode on a Grecian Urn," we shall see Keats trying to unify his pictorial effects by means of direct philosophical statement. "Do I wake or sleep?" at the end of the Nightingale ode asks the question: Which is reality, the symbolic nightingale or the common world? The famous

---

[4] Brooks and Warren, *Understanding Poetry* (New York, 1938), pp. 409–415.

Truth-Beauty synthesis at the end of the "Grecian Urn" contains the same question, but this time it is answered. As Mr. Kenneth Burke sees it, Truth is the practical scientific world and Beauty is the ideal world above change. The "frozen" figures on the urn, being both dead and alive, constitute a scene which is at once perceptible and fixed. "This transcendent scene," says Mr. Burke, "is the level at which the earthly laws of contradiction no longer prevail." [5] The one and the many, the eternal and the passing, the sculpturesque and the dramatic, become synthesized in a higher truth. Much of the little that I know about this poem I have learned from Mr. Burke and Mr. Cleanth Brooks, who have studied it more closely than any other critics; and what I am about to say will sound ungrateful. I suspect that the dialectical solution is Mr. Burke's rather than Keats's, and that Mr. Brooks's "irony" and "dramatic propriety" are likewise largely his own. [6] Mr. Brooks rests his case for the Truth-Beauty paradox on an argument for its "dramatic propriety"; but this is just what I am not convinced of. I find myself agreeing with Mr. Middleton Murry (whom Mr. Brooks quotes), who admits that the statement is out of place "in the context of the poem itself." I would point to a particular feature, in the last six lines of stanza four, which I feel that neither Mr. Burke nor Mr. Brooks has taken into a certain important kind of consideration. Here Keats tells us that in the background of this world of eternal youth there is another, from which it came, and that this second world has thus been emptied and is indeed a dead world:

> What little town by river or sea-shore
> Or mountain-built with peaceful citadel,
> Is emptied of this folk, this pious morn?

---

[5] Kenneth Burke, "Symbolic Action in a Poem by Keats," *Accent*, Autumn, 1943, p. 42.
[6] *The Well Wrought Urn* (New York, 1947), pp. 139–152.

And, little town, thy streets for evermore
Will silent be; and not a soul to tell
Why thou art desolate, can e'er return.

Mr. Burke quite rightly sees in this passage the key to the symbolism of the entire poem. It is properly the "constatation" of the tensions of the imagery. What is the meaning of this perpetual youth on the urn? One of its meanings is that it is perpetually anti-youth and anti-life; it is in fact dead, and "can never return." Are we not faced again with the same paradox we had in the "Nightingale" ode, that the intensest life is achieved in death? Mr. Burke brings out with great skill the erotic equivalents of the life-death symbols; and for his analysis of the developing imagery throughout we owe him a great debt. Yet I feel that Mr. Burke's own dialectical skill leads him to consider the poem, when he is through with it, a philosophical discourse; but it is, if it is anything (and it is a great deal), what is ordinarily known as a work of art. Mr. Burke's elucidation of the Truth-Beauty proposition in the last stanza is the most convincing dialectically that I have seen. But Keats did not write Mr. Burke's elucidation; and I feel that the entire last stanza, except the phrase "Cold Pastoral" (which probably ought to be somewhere else in the poem) is an illicit commentary added by the poet to a "meaning" which was symbolically complete at the end of the preceding stanza, number four. Or perhaps it may be said that Keats did to some extent write Mr. Burke's elucidation; that is why I feel that the final stanza (though magnificently written) is redundant and out of form.

To the degree that I am guilty with Mr. Burke of a prepossession which may blind me to the whole value of this poem (as his seems to limit his perception of possible defects) I am not qualified to criticize it. Here, towards the end of this essay, I glance back at the confession, which I made earlier, of the distance and detachment of my warmest admiration for Keats. It is now time that I tried to state the reasons for this a little more summarily, in a brief comparison of the two fine odes that we have been considering.

Both odes are constructed pictorially in spatial blocks, for the eye to take in serially. Though to my mind this method is better suited to the subject of the "Grecian Urn," which is itself a plastic object, than to the "Nightingale" ode, I take the latter, in spite of the blemishes of detail (only some of which we have looked at), to be the finer poem. If there is not so much in it as in the "Grecian Urn" for the elucidation of verbal complexity, there is nowhere the radical violation of its set limits that one finds in the last stanza of the "Grecian Urn":

> Thou shalt remain, in midst of other woes
> Than ours, a friend to man, to whom thou say'st,
> Beauty is truth, truth beauty,—that is all
> Ye know on earth, and all ye need to know.

It is here that the poem gets out of form, that the break in "point of view" occurs; and if it is a return to Samuel Johnson's dislike of "Lycidas" (I don't think it is) to ask how an urn can say anything, I shall have to suffer the consequences of that view. It is Keats himself, of course, who says it; but Keats is here not implicit in the structure of the poem, as he is in "Ode to a Nightingale"; what he says is what the mathematicians call an extrapolation, an intrusion of matter from another field of discourse, so that even if it be "true" philosophically it is not a visible function of what the poem says. With the "dead" mountain citadel in mind, could we not phrase the message of the urn equally well as follows: Truth is *not* beauty, since even art itself cannot do more with death than preserve it, and the beauty frozen on the urn is also dead, since it cannot move. This "pessimism" may be found as easily in the poem as Keats's comforting paradox. So I should return to the "Nightingale" ode for its superior *dramatic* credibility, even though the life-death antinomy is not more satisfactorily resolved than in the "Grecian Urn." The fall of the "I" of "Ode to a Nightingale" into the trancelike meditation in the first stanza and the shocked coming to at the end *ground* the poem in imaginable action, so that the dialectics of the nightingale symbol do not press for resolution. So I confess a reserved agreement with Brooks and Warren.

The outlines of the conflicting claims of the ideal and the actual, in Keats's mind, I have touched upon; but now, with the two great odes in mind, I wish to give those hints a somewhat greater range and try, if possible, to point towards the *kind* of experience with which Keats was dealing when he came up short against the limit of his sensibility, the identity of love and death, or the compulsive image of erotic intensity realizing itself in "dying."

IV

One of Keats's annotations to Burton's *Anatomy,* in the copy given him by Brown in 1819, in the great period, is as follows:

Here is the old plague spot; the pestilence, the raw scrofula. I mean there is nothing disgraces me in my own eyes so much as being one of a race of eyes nose and mouth beings in a planet call'd the earth who all from Plato to Wesley have always mingled goatish winnyish lustful love with the abstract adoration of the deity. I don't understand Greek—is the love of God and the Love of women express'd by the same word in Greek? I hope my little mind is wrong—if not I could . . . Has Plato separated these lovers? Ha! I see how they endeavour to divide—but there appears to be a horrid relationship.[7]

---

[7] I am indebted to a note by Colvin (*op. cit.,* p. 549) for the hint which led me to this bitter confession. It appears in Forman, *The Complete Works of John Keats,* III, p. 268.

Keats had just read in Burton the chapter "Love-Melan-
choly" in which the two Aphrodites, Urania and Pandemos,[8]
appear: there is no evidence that he ever knew more about
them than this quotation indicates. Professor Thorpe valiantly tries to show us that Keats must have known from his
literary environment something of Plato's doctrine of love,
but there is no reason to believe that he ever felt the imaginative shock of reading *The Symposium,* and of experiencing
firsthand an intuition of a level of experience that the Western world, through Platonism and Christianity, had been
trying for more than two millennia to reach. He apparently
never knew that the two Aphrodites were merely the subject of Pausanias's speech, one of the preliminaries to Socrates's great dialectical synthesis. The curious thing about
Keats's education is that it was almost entirely literary; he
had presumably read very little philosophy and religion. He
used the Greek myths, not for the complete (if pagan) religious experience in them, but to find a static and sculpturesque emblem of timeless experience—his own and the
experience of his age; hence the pictorial method, and hence
the necessity for that method.

In my reading of Keats I see his mind constantly reaching
towards and recoiling from the experience, greatly extended,
which is represented by the ambivalent Aphrodite. The conclusion of the sonnet "Bright Star! . . .":

> Still, still to hear her tender-taken breath,
> And so live ever—or else swoon to death . . .

is not Keats's best poetry, but it states very simply the conflict of emotion the symbolic limit of which I have tried to
see in terms of the double goddess. The immanence of the
Uranian in the Pandemic goddess was not beyond the range
of Keats's intellect, but it was at any rate, at the time of

---

[8] Modern readers will find the passage in the edition of Dell and Jordan-Smith,
p. 620 (New York, 1927).

his death, imaginatively beyond his reach. His goddess, in so far as she is more than a decorative symbol in Keats, was all Uranian; and to say in another way what I have already said, his faulty taste (which is probably at its worst in one of the lines in "Bright Star! . . .") lies in his inability to come to terms with her Pandemic sister. His pictorial and sculpturesque effects, which arrest time into space, tend to remove from experience the dramatic agitation of Aphrodite Pandemos, whose favors are granted and whose woes are counted in the actuality of time. (There is, of course, a great deal more in Keats than this obsessive symbol through which I see him; and there is also less of the symbol, explicitly presented, than my discussion would indicate; there are only eleven references to "Venus" in all Keats's poetry—he never calls her Aphrodite—and in no instance is very much done with her symbolically. She has only a fresh Botticellian surface; and one may observe that she is not mentioned in "Ode to Psyche.")

This "horrid relationship" between the heavenly and earthly Aphrodites had been in effect the great theme of St. Augustine, and before him of Lucretius; and it was to inform dramatically *The Divine Comedy.* It was perhaps the great achievement of the seventeenth-century English poets to have explored the relations of physical and spiritual love; of this Keats seems oblivious; yet we must admit that an awareness of the imaginative and spiritual achievements of the past would not have ensured them to him, as our own excessive awareness fails to ensure them to us. In Keats's mind there was, as I have said (why it should have had, even in so young a man, an exclusive dominance I do not know) —there was, to put it in the simplest language, a strong compulsion towards the realization of physical love, but he could not reconcile it with his idealization of the beloved. So we get what has been supposed to be a characteristically romantic attitude—that to *die* at the greatest intensity of love is to achieve that intensity without diminution. If this is the romantic attitude—and there is no reason to believe that Wordsworth's domestic pieties and evasions, or Shelley's rhetorical Godwinism and watered-down Platonism, ever achieved *as experience* a higher realization of the central human problem than Keats did—if this is romanticism, then romanticism (or romantic poetry) represents a decline in insight and in imaginative and moral power. In the interval between

> So must pure lovers soules descend
> T'affections, and to faculties,
> Which sense may reach and apprehend,
> Else a great Prince in prison lies . . .

and this:

> But Love has pitched his mansion in
> The place of excrement;
> For nothing can be sole or whole
> That has not been rent . . .

—between Donne and Yeats there was evidently a shrinkage in the range and depth of Western man's experience, as that experience was expressed in works of the imagination, and not merely in the Goethean or Wordsworthian goodwill towards comprehensiveness or the inclusion of a little of everything. Keats seems to me to have been, in England at any rate, the master of the central experience of his age. His profound honesty, his dislike of system and opinion as substitutes for what the imagination is actually able to control, and his perfect artistic courage, will keep him not only among the masters of English poetry but among the few heroes of literature. To adapt to Keats a remark of Eliot's about Arnold, I should say that he did not know, because he lacked the maturity to know, the boredom; he knew a little of the horror; but he knew much of the glory, of human life.

1945

Emily Dickinson

I

GREAT POETRY needs no special features of difficulty to make it mysterious. When it has them, the reputation of the poet is likely to remain uncertain. This is still true of Donne, and it is true of Emily Dickinson, whose verse appeared in an age unfavorable to the use of intelligence in poetry. Her poetry is not like any other poetry of her time; it is not like any of the innumerable kinds of verse written today. In still another respect it is far removed from us. It is a poetry of ideas, and it demands of the reader a point of view—not an opinion of the New Deal or of the League of Nations, but an ingrained philosophy that is fundamental, a settled attitude that is almost extinct in this eclectic age. Yet it is not the sort of poetry of ideas which, like Pope's, requires a point of view only. It requires also, for the deepest understanding, which must go beneath the verbal excitement of the style, a highly developed sense of the specific quality of poetry—a quality that most persons accept as the accidental feature of something else that the poet thinks he has to say. This is one reason why Miss Dickinson's poetry has not been widely read.

There is another reason, and it is a part of the problem peculiar to a poetry that comes out of fundamental ideas. We lack a tradition of criticism. There were no points of critical reference passed on to us from a preceding generation. I am not upholding here the so-called dead hand of tradition, but rather a rational insight into the meaning of the present in terms of some imaginable past implicit in our own lives: we need a body of ideas that can bear upon the course of the spirit and yet remain coherent as a rational instrument. We ignore the present, which is momently translated into the past, and derive our standards from imaginative constructions of the future. The hard contingency of fact invariably breaks these standards down, leaving us the intellectual chaos which is the sore distress of American criticism. Marxian criticism has become the latest disguise of this heresy.

Still another difficulty stands between us and Miss Dickinson. It is the failure of the scholars to feel more than biographical curiosity about her. We have scholarship, but that is no substitute for a critical tradition. Miss Dickinson's value to the research scholar, who likes historical difficulty for its own sake, is slight; she is too near to possess the remoteness of literature. Perhaps her appropriate setting would be the age of Cowley or of Donne. Yet in her own historical setting she is, nevertheless, remarkable and special.

Although the intellectual climate into which she was born, in 1830, had, as all times have, the features of a transition, the period was also a major crisis culminating in the war between the States. After that war, in New England as well as in the South, spiritual crises were definitely minor until the First World War.

Yet, a generation before the war of 1861–65, the transformation of New England had begun. When Samuel Slater in 1790 thwarted the British embargo on mill machinery by committing to memory the whole design of a cotton spinner and bringing it to Massachusetts, he planted the seed of the "Western spirit." By 1825 its growth in the East was rank enough to begin choking out the ideas and habits of living that New England along with Virginia had kept in unconscious allegiance to Europe. To the casual observer, perhaps, the New England character of 1830 was largely an eighteenth-century character. But theocracy was on the decline, and industrialism was rising—as Emerson, in an unusually lucid moment, put it, "Things are in the saddle." The energy that had built the meetinghouse ran the factory.

Now the idea that moved the theocratic state is the most interesting historically of all American ideas. It was, of course, powerful in seventeenth-century England, but in America, where the long arm of Laud could not reach, it acquired an unchecked social and political influence. The important thing to remember about the puritan theocracy is that it permeated, as it could never have done in England, a whole society. It gave final, definite meaning to life, the life of pious and impious, of learned and vulgar alike. It gave —and this is its significance for Emily Dickinson, and in only slightly lesser degree for Melville and Hawthorne—it gave an heroic proportion and a tragic mode to the experience of the individual. The history of the New England theocracy, from Apostle Eliot to Cotton Mather, is rich in gigantic intellects that broke down—or so it must appear to an outsider —in a kind of moral decadence and depravity. Socially we may not like the New England idea. Yet it had an immense, incalculable value for literature: it dramatized the human soul.

But by 1850 the great fortunes had been made (in the rum, slave, and milling industries), and New England became a museum. The whatnots groaned under the load of knick-knacks, the fine china dogs and cats, the pieces of Oriental jade, the chips off the leaning tower at Pisa. There were the rare books and the cosmopolitan learning. It was all equally displayed as the evidence of a superior culture. The Gilded Age had already begun. But culture, in the true sense, was disappearing. Where the old order, formidable as it was, had held all this personal experience, this eclectic excitement, in a comprehensible whole, the new order tended to flatten it out in a common experience that was not quite in common;

it exalted more and more the personal and the unique in the interior sense. Where the old-fashioned puritans got together on a rigid doctrine, and could thus be individualists in manners, the nineteenth-century New Englander, lacking a genuine religious center, began to be a social conformist. The common idea of the Redemption, for example, was replaced by the conformist idea of respectability among neighbors whose spiritual disorder, not very evident at the surface, was becoming acute. A great idea was breaking up, and society was moving towards external uniformity, which is usually the measure of the spiritual sterility inside.

At this juncture Emerson came upon the scene: the Lucifer of Concord, he had better be called hereafter, for he was the light-bearer who could see nothing but light, and was fearfully blind. He looked around and saw the uniformity of life, and called it the routine of tradition, the tyranny of the theological idea. The death of Priam put an end to the hope of Troy, but it was a slight feat of arms for the doughty Pyrrhus; Priam was an old gentleman and almost dead. So was theocracy; and Emerson killed it. In this way he accelerated a tendency that he disliked. It was a great intellectual mistake. By it Emerson unwittingly became the prophet of a piratical industrialism, a consequence of his own transcendental individualism that he could not foresee. He was hoist with his own petard.

He discredited more than any other man the puritan drama of the soul. The age that followed, from 1865 on, expired in a genteel secularism, a mildly didactic order of feeling whose ornaments were Lowell, Longfellow, and Holmes. "After Emerson had done his work," says Mr. Robert Penn Warren, "any tragic possibilities in that culture were dissipated." Hawthorne alone in his time kept pure, in the primitive terms, the primitive vision; he brings the puritan tragedy to its climax. Man, measured by a great idea outside himself, is found wanting. But for Emerson man is greater than any idea and, being himself the Over-Soul, is innately perfect; there is no struggle because—I state the Emersonian doctrine, which is very slippery, in its extreme terms—because there is no possibility of error. There is no drama in human character because there is no tragic fault. It is not surprising, then, that after Emerson New England literature tastes like a sip of cambric tea. Its center of vision has disappeared. There is Hawthorne looking back, there is Emerson looking not too clearly at anything ahead: Emily Dickinson, who has in her something of both, comes in somewhere between.

With the exception of Poe there is no other American poet whose work so steadily emerges, under pressure of certain disintegrating obsessions, from the framework of moral character. There is none of whom it is truer to say that the poet *is* the poetry. Perhaps this explains the zeal of her admirers for her biography; it explains, in part at least, the gratuitous mystery that Mrs. Bianchi, a niece of the poet and her official biographer, has made of her life. The devoted controversy that Miss Josephine Pollitt and Miss Genevieve Taggard started a few years ago with their excellent books shows the extent to which the critics feel the intimate connection of her life and work. Admiration and affection are pleased to linger over the tokens of a great life; but the solution to the Dickinson enigma is peculiarly superior to fact.

The meaning of the identity—which we merely feel—of character and poetry would be exceedingly obscure, even if we could draw up a kind of Binet correlation between the two sets of "facts." Miss Dickinson was a recluse; but her poetry is rich with a profound and varied experience. Where did she get it? Now some of the biographers, nervous in the presence of this discrepancy, are eager to find her a love affair, and I think this search is due to a modern prejudice: we believe that no virgin can know enough to write poetry. We shall never learn where she got the rich quality of her mind. The moral image that we have of Miss Dickinson stands out in every poem; it is that of a dominating spinster whose very sweetness must have been formidable. Yet her poetry constantly moves within an absolute order of truths that overwhelmed her simply because to her they were unalterably fixed. It is dangerous to assume that her "life," which to the biographers means the thwarted love affair she is supposed to have had, gave to her poetry a decisive direction. It is even more dangerous to suppose that it made her a poet.

Poets are mysterious, but a poet when all is said is not much more mysterious than a banker. The critics remain spellbound by the technical license of her verse and by the puzzle of her personal life. Personality is a legitimate interest because it is an incurable interest, but legitimate as a personal interest only; it will never give up the key to anyone's verse. Used to that end, the interest is false. "It is apparent," writes Mr. Conrad Aiken, "that Miss Dickinson became a hermit by deliberate and conscious choice"—a sensible remark that we cannot repeat too often. If it were necessary to explain her seclusion with disappointment in love, there would remain the discrepancy between what the seclusion produced and the seclusion looked at as a cause. The effect, which is her poetry, would imply the whole complex of anterior fact, which was the social and religious structure of New England.

The problem to be kept in mind is thus the meaning of her "deliberate and conscious" decision to withdraw from life to her upstairs room. This simple fact is not very important. But that it must have been her sole way of acting out her part in the history of her culture, which made, with the variations of circumstance, a single demand upon all its representatives—this is of the greatest consequence. All pity for Miss Dickinson's "starved life" is misdirected. Her life was one of the richest and deepest ever lived on this continent.

When she went upstairs and closed the door, she mastered life by rejecting it. Others in their way had done it before; still others did it later. If we suppose—which is to suppose the improbable—that the love affair precipitated the seclusion, it was only a pretext; she would have found another. Mastery of the world by rejecting the world was the doctrine, even if it was not always the practice, of Jonathan Edwards and Cotton Mather. It is the meaning of fate in Hawthorne: his people are fated to withdraw from the world and to be destroyed. And it is one of the great themes of Henry James.

There is a moral emphasis that connects Hawthorne, James, and Miss Dickinson, and I think it is instructive. Between Hawthorne and James lies an epoch. The temptation to sin, in Hawthorne, is, in James, transformed into the temptation not to do the "decent thing." A whole world-scheme, a complete cosmic background, has shrunk to the dimensions of the individual conscience. This epoch between Hawthorne and James lies in Emerson. James found himself in the post-Emersonian world, and he could not, without violating the detachment proper to an artist, undo Emerson's work; he had that kind of intelligence which refuses to break its head against history. There was left to him only the value, the historic role, of rejection. He could merely escape from the physical presence of that world which, for convenience, we may call Emerson's world: he could only take his Americans to Europe upon the vain quest of something that they had lost at home. His characters, fleeing the wreckage of the puritan culture, preserved only their honor. Honor became a sort of forlorn hope struggling against the forces of "pure fact" that had got loose in the middle of the century. Honor alone is a poor weapon against nature, being too personal, finical, and proud, and James achieved a victory by refusing to engage the whole force of the enemy.

In Emily Dickinson the conflict takes place on a vaster field. The enemy to all those New Englanders was Nature, and Miss Dickinson saw into the character of this enemy more deeply than any of the others. The general symbol of Nature, for her, is Death, and her weapon against Death is the entire powerful dumb-show of the puritan theology led by Redemption and Immortality. Morally speaking, the problem for James and Miss Dickinson is similar. But her advantages were greater than his. The advantages lay in the availability to her of the puritan ideas on the theological plane.

These ideas, in her poetry, are momently assailed by the disintegrating force of Nature (appearing as Death) which, while constantly breaking them down, constantly redefines and strengthens them. The values are purified by the triumphant withdrawal from Nature, by their power to recover from Nature. The poet attains to a mastery over experience by facing its utmost implications. There is the clash of powerful opposites, and in all great poetry—for Emily Dickinson is a great poet—it issues in a tension between abstraction and sensation in which the two elements may be, of course, distinguished logically, but not really. We are shown our roots in Nature by examining our differences with Nature; we are renewed by Nature without being delivered into her hands. When it is possible for a poet to do this for us with the greatest imaginative comprehension, a possibility that the poet cannot himself create, we have the perfect literary situation. Only a few times in the history of English poetry has this situation come about, notably, the period between about 1580 and the Restoration. There was a similar age in New England from which emerged two talents of the first order —Hawthorne and Emily Dickinson.

There is an epoch between James and Miss Dickinson. But between her and Hawthorne there exists a difference of intellectual quality. She lacks almost radically the power to seize upon and understand abstractions for their own sake; she does not separate them from the sensuous illuminations that she is so marvelously adept at; like Donne, she *perceives abstraction* and *thinks sensation.* But Hawthorne was a master of ideas, within a limited range; this narrowness confined him to his own kind of life, his own society, and out of it grew his typical forms of experience, his steady, almost obsessed vision of man; it explains his depth and intensity. Yet he is always conscious of the abstract, doctrinal aspect of his mind, and when his vision of action and emotion is weak, his work becomes didactic. Now Miss Dickinson's poetry often runs into quasi-homiletic forms, but it is never didactic. Her very ignorance, her lack of formal intellectual training, preserved her from the risk that imperiled Hawthorne. She cannot reason at all. She can only *see.* It is impossible to imagine what she might have done with drama or fiction; for, not approaching the puritan temper and through it the puritan myth, through human action, she is able to grasp the terms of the myth directly and by a feat that amounts almost to anthropomorphism, to give them a luminous tension, a kind of drama, among themselves.

One of the perfect poems in English is "The Chariot," and it illustrates better than anything else she wrote the special quality of her mind. I think it will illuminate the tendency of this discussion:

> Because I could not stop for death,
> He kindly stopped for me;
> The carriage held but just ourselves
> And immortality.
>
> We slowly drove, he knew no haste,
> And I had put away
> My labor, and my leisure too,
> For his civility.
>
> We passed the school where children played,
> Their lessons scarcely done;

We passed the fields of gazing grain,
We passed the setting sun.

We paused before a house that seemed
A swelling of the ground;
The roof was scarcely visible,
The cornice but a mound.

Since then 'tis centuries; but each
Feels shorter than the day
I first surmised the horses' heads
Were toward eternity.

If the word great means anything in poetry, this poem is one of the greatest in the English language. The rhythm charges with movement the pattern of suspended action back of the poem. Every image is precise and, moreover, not merely beautiful, but fused with the central idea. Every image extends and intensifies every other. The third stanza especially shows Miss Dickinson's power to fuse, into a single order of perception, a heterogeneous series: the children, the grain, and the setting sun (time) have the same degree of credibility; the first subtly preparing for the last. The sharp *gazing* before *grain* instills into nature a cold vitality of which the qualitative richness has infinite depth. The content of death in the poem eludes explicit definition. He is a gentleman taking a lady out for a drive. But note the restraint that keeps the poet from carrying this so far that it becomes ludicrous and incredible; and note the subtly inter-fused erotic motive, which the idea of death has presented to most romantic poets, love being a symbol interchangeable with death. The terror of death is objectified through this figure of the genteel driver, who is made ironically to serve the end of Immortality. This is the heart of the poem: she has presented a typical Christian theme in its final irresolu-tion, without making any final statements about it. There is no solution to the problem; there can be only a presentation of it in the full context of intellect and feeling. A construction of the human will, elaborated with all the abstracting powers of the mind, is put to the concrete test of experience: the idea of immortality is confronted with the fact of physical disintegration. We are not told what to think; we are told to look at the situation.

The framework of the poem is, in fact, the two abstractions, mortality and eternity, which are made to associate in equality with the images: she sees the ideas, and thinks the perceptions. She did, of course, nothing of the sort; but we must use the logical distinctions, even to the extent of paradox, if we are to form any notion of this rare quality of mind. She could not in the proper sense think at all, and unless we prefer the feeble poetry of moral ideas that flourished in New England in the eighties, we must conclude that her intellectual deficiency contributed at least negatively to her great distinction. Miss Dickinson is probably the only Anglo-American poet of her century whose work exhibits the perfect literary situation—in which is possible the fusion of sensibility and thought. Unlike her contemporaries, she never succumbed to her ideas, to easy solutions, to her private desires.

Philosophers must deal with ideas, but the trouble with most nineteenth-century poets is too much philosophy; they are nearer to being philosophers than poets, without being in the true sense either. Tennyson is a good example of this; so is Arnold in his weak moments. There have been poets like Milton and Donne, who were not spoiled for their true business by leaning on a rational system of ideas, who understood the poetic use of ideas. Tennyson tried to mix a little Huxley and a little Broad Church, without understanding either Broad Church or Huxley; the result was fatal, and what is worse, it was shallow. Miss Dickinson's ideas were deeply imbedded in her character, not taken from the latest tract. A conscious cultivation of ideas in poetry is always dangerous, and even Milton escaped ruin only by having an instinct for what in the deepest sense he understood. Even at that there is a remote quality in Milton's approach to his material, in his treatment of it; in the nineteenth century, in an imperfect literary situation where literature was confused with documentation, he might have been a pseudo-philosopher-poet. It is difficult to conceive Emily Dickinson and John Donne succumbing to rumination about "problems"; they would not have written at all.

Neither the feeling nor the style of Miss Dickinson belongs to the seventeenth century; yet between her and Donne there are remarkable ties. Their religious ideas, their abstractions, are momently toppling from the rational plane to the level of perception. The ideas, in fact, are no longer the impersonal religious symbols creeted anew in the heat of emotion, that we find in poets like Herbert and Vaughan. They have become, for Donne, the terms of personality; they are mingled with the miscellany of sensation. In Miss Dickinson, as in Donne, we may detect a singularly morbid concern, not for religious truth, but for personal revelation. The modern word is self-exploitation. It is egoism grown irresponsible in religion and decadent in morals. In religion it is blasphemy; in society it means usually that culture is not self-contained and sufficient, that the spiritual community is breaking up. This is, along with some other features that do not concern us here, the perfect literary situation.

I I

Personal revelation of the kind that Donne and Miss Dickinson strove for, in the effort to understand their relation to the world, is a feature of all great poetry; it is probably the hidden motive for writing. It is the effort of the individual to live apart from a cultural tradition that no longer sustains him. But this culture, which I now wish to discuss a little, is indispensable: there is a great deal of shallow nonsense in modern criticism which holds that poetry—and this is a half-truth that is worse than false—is essentially revolutionary. It is only indirectly revolutionary: the intellectual and religious background of an age no longer contains the whole spirit, and the poet proceeds to examine that background in terms of immediate experience. But the background is necessary; otherwise all the arts (not only poetry) would have to rise in a vacuum. Poetry does not dispense with tradition; it probes the deficiencies of a tradition. But it must have a tradition to probe. It is too bad that Arnold did not explain his doctrine, that poetry is a criticism of life, from the viewpoint of its background: we should have been spared an era of academic misconception, in which criticism of life meant a diluted pragmatism, the criterion of which was respectability. The poet in the true sense "criticizes" his tradition, either as such, or indirectly by comparing it with something that is about to replace it; he does what the root-meaning of the verb implies—he *discerns* its real elements and thus establishes its value, by putting it to the test of experience.

What is the nature of a poet's culture? Or, to put the question properly, what is the meaning of culture for poetry? All the great poets become the material of what we popularly call culture; we study them to acquire it. It is clear that Addison was more cultivated than Shakespeare; nevertheless Shakespeare is a finer source of culture than Addison. What is the meaning of this? Plainly it is that learning has never had anything to do with culture except instrumentally: the poet must be exactly literate enough to write down fully and precisely what he has to say, but no more. The source of a poet's true culture lies back of the paraphernalia of culture, and not all the historical activity of an enlightened age can create it.

A culture cannot be consciously created. It is an available source of ideas that are imbedded in a complete and homogeneous society. The poet finds himself balanced upon the moment when such a world is about to fall, when it threatens to run out into looser and less self-sufficient impulses. This world order is assimilated, in Miss Dickinson, as medievalism was in Shakespeare, to the poetic vision; it is brought down from abstraction to personal sensibility.

In this connection it may be said that the prior conditions for great poetry, given a great talent, may be reduced to two: the thoroughness of the poet's discipline in an objective system of truth, and his lack of consciousness of such a discipline. For this discipline is a number of fundamental ideas, the origin of which the poet does not know. They give form and stability to his fresh perceptions of the world; and he cannot shake them off. This is his culture, and like Tennyson's God it is nearer than hands and feet. With reasonable certainty we unearth the elements of Shakespeare's culture, and yet it is equally certain—so innocent was he of his own resources—that he would not know what our discussion is about. He appeared at the collapse of the medieval system as a rigid pattern of life, but that pattern remained in Shakespeare what Shelley called a "fixed point of reference" for his sensibility. Miss Dickinson, as we have seen, was born into the equilibrium of an old and a new order. Puritanism could not be to her what it had been to the generation of Cotton Mather—a body of absolute truths; it was an unconscious discipline timed to the pulse of her life.

The perfect literary situation: it produces, because it is rare, a special and perhaps the most distinguished kind of poet. I am not trying to invent a new critical category. Such poets are never very much alike on the surface; they show us all the varieties of poetic feeling, and like other poets they resist all classification but that of temporary convenience. But, I believe, Miss Dickinson and John Donne would have this in common: their sense of the natural world is not blunted by a too rigid system of ideas; yet the ideas, the abstractions, their education or their intellectual heritage, are not so weak as to let their immersion in nature, or their purely personal quality, get out of control. The two poles of the mind are not separately visible; we infer them from the lucid tension that may be most readily illustrated by polar activity. There is no thought as such at all; nor is there feeling. There is that unique focus of experience which is at once neither and both.

Like Miss Dickinson, Shakespeare is without opinions; his peculiar merit is also deeply involved in his failure to think about anything; his meaning is not in the content of his expression; it is in the tension of the dramatic relations of his characters. This kind of poetry is at the opposite of intellectualism. (Miss Dickinson is obscure and difficult, but that is not intellectualism.) To T. W. Higginson, the editor of *The Atlantic Monthly,* who tried to advise her, she wrote that she had no education. In any sense that Higginson could understand, it was quite true. His kind of education was the conscious cultivation of abstractions. She did not reason about the world she saw; she merely saw it. The "ideas" implicit in the world within her rose up, concentrated in her immediate perception.

That kind of world at present has for us something of the fascination of a buried city. There is none like it. When such worlds exist, when such cultures flourish, they support not only the poet but all members of society. For, from these, the poet differs only in his gift for exhibiting the structure, the internal lineaments, of his culture by threatening to tear them apart: a process that concentrates the symbolic emotions of society while it seems to attack them. The poet may hate his age; he may be an outcast like Villon; but this world is always there as the background to what he has to say. It is the lens through which he brings nature to focus and control—the clarifying medium that concentrates his personal feeling. It is ready-made; he cannot make it; with it, his poetry has a spontaneity and a certainty of direction that, without it, it would lack. No poet could have invented the ideas of "The Chariot"; only a great poet could have found their imaginative equivalents. Miss Dickinson was a deep mind writing from a deep culture, and when she came to poetry, she came infallibly.

Infallibly, at her best; for no poet has ever been perfect, nor is Emily Dickinson. Her precision of statement is due to the directness with which the abstract framework of her thought acts upon its unorganized material. The two elements of her style, considered as point of view, are immortality, or the idea of permanence, and the physical process of death or decay. Her diction has two corresponding features: words of Latin or Greek origin and, sharply opposed to these, the concrete Saxon element. It is this verbal conflict that gives to her verse its high tension; it is not a device deliberately seized upon, but a feeling for language that senses out the two fundamental components of English and their metaphysical relation: the Latin for ideas and the Saxon for perceptions—the peculiar virtue of English as a poetic language.

Like most poets Miss Dickinson often writes out of habit; the style that emerged from some deep exploration of an idea is carried on as verbal habit when she has nothing to say. She indulges herself:

> There's something quieter than sleep
> Within this inner room!
> It wears a sprig upon its breast,
> And will not tell its name.
>
> Some touch it and some kiss it,
> Some chafe its idle hand;
> It has a simple gravity
> I do not understand!

> While simple hearted neighbors
> Chat of the "early dead,"
> We, prone to periphrasis,
> Remark that birds have fled!

It is only a pert remark; at best a superior kind of punning —one of the worst specimens of her occasional interest in herself. But she never had the slightest interest in the public. Were four poems or five published in her lifetime? She never felt the temptation to round off a poem for public exhibition. Higginson's kindly offer to make her verse "correct" was an invitation to throw her work into the public ring—the ring of Lowell and Longfellow. He could not see that he was tampering with one of the rarest literary integrities of all time. Here was a poet who had no use for the supports of authorship—flattery and fame; she never needed money.

She had all the elements of a culture that has broken up, a culture that on the religious side takes its place in the museum of spiritual antiquities. Puritanism, as a unified version of the world, is dead; only a remnant of it in trade may be said to survive. In the history of puritanism she comes between Hawthorne and Emerson. She has Hawthorne's matter, which a too irresponsible personality tends to dilute into a form like Emerson's; she is often betrayed by words. But she is not the poet of personal sentiment; she has more to say than she can put down in any one poem. Like Hardy and Whitman she must be read entire; like Shakespeare she never gives up her meaning in a single line.

She is therefore a perfect subject for the kind of criticism which is chiefly concerned with general ideas. She exhibits one of the permanent relations between personality and objective truth, and she deserves the special attention of our time, which lacks that kind of truth.

She has Hawthorne's intellectual toughness, a hard, definite sense of the physical world. The highest flights to God, the most extravagant metaphors of the strange and the remote, come back to a point of casuistry, to a moral dilemma of the experienced world. There is, in spite of the homiletic vein of utterance, no abstract speculation, nor is there a message to society; she speaks wholly to the individual experience. She offers to the unimaginative no riot of vicarious sensation; she has no useful maxims for men of action. Up to this point her resemblance to Emerson is slight: poetry is a sufficient form of utterance, and her devotion to it is pure. But in Emily Dickinson the puritan world is no longer self-contained; it is no longer complete; her sensibility exceeds its dimensions. She has trimmed down its supernatural proportions; it has become a morality—instead of the tragedy of the spirit, there is a commentary upon it. Her poetry is a magnificent personal confession, blasphemous and, in its self-revelation, its honesty, almost obscene. It comes out of an intellectual life towards which it feels no moral responsibility. Cotton Mather would have burnt her for a witch.

1928

Yeats's Romanticism[1]

Notes and Suggestions

I

THE PROFUNDITY of Yeats's vision of the modern world and the width of its perspective have kept me until this occasion from writing anything about the poetry of our time which I most admire. The responsibility enjoins the final effort of understanding—an effort that even now I have not been able to make. The lesser poets invite the pride of the critic to its own affirmation; the greater poets—and Yeats is among them —ask us to understand not only their minds but our own; they ask us in fact to have minds of a related caliber to theirs. And criticism must necessarily remain in the presence of the great poets a business for the ant hill: the smaller minds pooling their efforts. For the power of a Yeats will be given to the study of other poets only incidentally, for shock and technique and for the test of its own reach: this kind of power has its own task to perform.

Ours is the smaller task. The magnitude of Yeats is already visible in the failure of the partial, though frequently valuable, insights that the critics have given us in the past twenty years. There is enough in Yeats for countless studies from many points of view, yet I suspect that we shall languish far this side of the complete version of Yeats until we

[1] This paper was written for the special Yeats number of *The Southern Review*, Winter, 1942.

cease to look into him for qualities that neither Yeats nor
any other poet can give us; until we cease to censure him
for possessing "attitudes" and "beliefs" which we do not
share. Mr. Edmund Wilson's essay on Yeats in the influential
study of symbolism, *Axel's Castle,* asks the poet for a political
and economic philosophy; or if this is unfair to Mr. Wilson,
perhaps it could be fairly said that Mr. Wilson, when he was
writing the essay, was looking for a political and economic
philosophy, and inevitably saw in Yeats and the other heirs
of symbolism an evasion of the reality that he, Mr. Wilson,
was looking for. (If you are looking for pins, you do not
want needles, though both will prick you.) Mr. Louis Mac-
Neice's book-length study of Yeats says shrewd things about
the poetry, but on the whole we get the impression that
Yeats had bad luck in not belonging to the younger group
of English poets, who had a monopoly on "reality." (The
word is Mr. MacNeice's.) Those were the days when not
to be a communist was to be fascist, which is what Mr.
MacNeice makes Yeats out to be. (Yeats liked the ancient
"nobility," of which for Mr. MacNeice, Wall Street and the
City offer examples.)

I cite these two writers on Yeats because in them we get
summed up the case for Yeats's romanticism, the view that
he was an escapist retiring from problems, forces, and theories "relevant" to the modern world. While it is true that
Yeats, like every poet in English since the end of the
eighteenth century, began with a romantic use of language
in the early poems, he ended up very differently, and he is
no more to be fixed as a romantic than Shakespeare as a
Senecan because he wrote passages of Senecan rhetoric. If
one of the historic marks of romanticism is the division between sensibility and intellect, Yeats's career may be seen
as unromantic (I do not know the opposite term) because he
closed the gap. His critics would then be the romantics. I do
not think that these squabbles are profitable. It is still true

that Yeats had a more inclusive mind than any of his critics has had.

I I

Two years before Yeats died he wrote to Dorothy Wellesley:

At this moment all the specialists are about to run together in our new Alexandria, thought is about to be unified as its own free act, and the shadow in Germany and elsewhere is an attempted unity by force. In my life I have never felt so acutely the presence of a spiritual virtue and that is accompanied by intensified desire.

Scattered throughout Yeats's prose there are similar passages, but this one is only from a letter, and it lacks the imaginative reach and synthesis of the great passages towards the end of *A Vision,* where I recall particularly the fine paragraph on early Byzantium and Section III of "Dove or Swan" in which Yeats describes the annunciation to Leda which brought in the classical civilization, as the annunciation to the Virgin brought in the Christian. Of Byzantium he says:

I think that in early Byzantium, maybe never before or since in recorded history, religious, aesthetic, and practical life were one, that architect and artificers—though not, it may be, poets, for language had been the instrument of controversy and must have gone abstract—spoke to the multitude and the few alike. The painter, the mosaic worker, the worker in gold and silver, the illuminator of sacred books, were almost impersonal, almost perhaps without the consciousness of individual design, absorbed in their subject matter and that the vision of a whole people.

Mr. Cleanth Brooks has shown that the great sonnet "Leda" is no pretty picture out of mythology, that it gets its power from the powerful forces of the imagination behind it. Section III of "Dove or Swan" begins:

I imagine the annunciation which founded Greece as made to Leda, remembering that they showed in a Spartan temple, strung up to the roof as a holy relic, an unhatched egg of hers; and that from one of her eggs came Love and from the other War. But all things are from antithesis, and when in my ignorance I try to imagine what older civilization that annunciation rejected I can but see bird and woman blotting out some corner of the Babylonian mathematical starlight.

In these three passages I believe that we get the main threads of Yeats's thought expressed in language which refers to the famous "system" but which is nevertheless sufficiently clear to persons who have not mastered the system or who even know nothing of it. Study of the Great Wheel with its gyres and cones might give us extensive references for certain ideas in the passage from the letter. We should learn that we are now in the twenty-third phase of our historical cycle, in which thought is abstract and unity of life must be imposed by force, and that culture is Alexandrian. The picture of a perfect culture that he gives us in Byzantium (which in the poem of that name becomes something more than mere historical insight) where men enjoy full unity of being has too many features in common with familiar Western ideas to be seen as an eccentric piece of utopianism. Byzantium is a new pastoral symbol and will be taken as that by anybody who sees more in the pastoral tradition than ideal shepherds and abstract sheep. The annunciation to Leda offers historical and philosophical difficulties; yet in spite of Yeats's frequently expressed belief that he had found a new historical vision, the conception is not historical in any sense that we understand today. It is a symbol established in analogical terms; that is, our literal grasp of it depends upon prior knowledge of the Annunciation to the Virgin. The "Babylonian mathematical starlight" is self-evidently clear without Yeats's scattered glosses on it: it is darkness and abstraction, quantitative relations without imagination;

and I doubt that Yeats's definitions make it much clearer than that. If Leda rejected it, we only learn from Yeats's "system" that the coming of Christ brought it back in; for an entire cultural cycle can be predominantly antithetical or predominantly primary, at the same time that it goes through the twenty-eight phases from primary to antithetical back to primary again.

In the letter to Dorothy Wellesley occurs a sentence which sounds casual, even literally confessional. There is no harm done if we take it at that level; there is merely a loss of insight such as we get in Mr. MacNeice's *The Poetry of W. B. Yeats,* in which Yeats's myth is dismissed as "arid" and "unsound." In the midst of the "attempted unity by force," he writes: "In my own life I have never felt so acutely the presence of a spiritual virtue and that is accompanied by intensified desire." The literal student of *A Vision,* coming upon statements like this, may well wonder what has become of the determinism of the system, which, with an almost perverse ingenuity, seems to fix the individual in a system of coordinates from which he cannot escape. Mr. Cleanth Brooks believes that some measure of free will lies in Yeats's conception of the False Mask, which some unpredictable force in the individual may lead him to choose instead of the True Mask. I believe this is only part of the explanation.

Does not the true explanation lie in there being *no* explanation in terms of the system? Even if we see Yeats as he saw himself, a man of Phase 17 living in Phase 23 of our civilization, the discrepancy merely introduces a complication which the system can easily take account of. Mr. MacNeice at this point enlightens us almost in spite of himself: "Freedom for Yeats, as for Engels, was a recognition of necessity—but not of economic necessity, which he considered a vulgarism." Yes; and he would have considered psychological necessity, or any inner determinism no less than an outer, economic determinism, a vulgarism also. But in the phrase the "recognition of necessity" we get a clue to Yeats's own relation to his system and to what seems to me the right way to estimate its value. He only wanted what all men want, a world larger than himself to live in; for the modern world as he saw it was, in human terms, too small for the human spirit, though quantitatively large if looked at with the scientist. If we say, then, that he wanted a *dramatic* recognition of necessity, we shall have to look at the system not as arid or unsound or eccentric, which it well may be in itself, but through Yeats's eyes, which are the eyes of his poetry.

If we begin with the poetry we shall quickly see that there is some source of power or illumination which is also in us, waiting to be aroused; and that this is true of even the greater number of the fine poems in which the imagery appears upon later study to lean upon the eccentric system. I would say, then, that even the terms of the system, when they appear in the richer texture of the poems, share a certain large margin of significance, with a wider context than they have in the system itself. May we say that Yeats's *A Vision,* however private and almost childishly eclectic it may seem, has somewhat the same relation to a central tradition as the far more rigid structure of *The Divine Comedy* has to the Christian myth? I dare say that Mr. Eliot would not chide Dante for accepting a "lower mythology." Perhaps the central tradition in Dante and Yeats lies in a force that criticism cannot specifically isolate, the force that moved both poets to the dramatic recognition of necessity; yet the visible structure of the necessity itself is perhaps not the source of that power. I do not say that Yeats is comparable in stature to Dante; only that both poets strove for a visible structure of action which is indeed necessary to what they said, but which does not explain what they said. I believe that Mr. Eliot should undertake to explain why Arnold's Higher Mythology produced poetry less interesting than Yeats's

Lower Mythology, which becomes in Yeats's verse the vehicle of insights and imaginative syntheses as profound as
those which Arnold talked about but never, as a poet, fully
achieved. Myths differ in range and intensity, but not I take
it as high and low; for they are in the end what poets can
make of them.

If Yeats could feel in the midst of the Alexandrian rigidity
and disorder the "presence of a spiritual virtue," was he denying the inclusiveness of the system; or could he have seen
his senile vigor and insight in terms of the system? Possibly
the latter; but it makes little difference.

I I I

A Vision has been described by more than one critic as a
philosophy; I speak of it here as a "system"; but I doubt
that it is a system of philosophy. What kind of system is it?
Yeats frequently stated his own purpose, but even that is a
little obscure: to put myth back into philosophy. This phrase
may roughly describe the result, but it could not stand for
the process; it attributes to the early philosophers a deliber-
ation of which they would have been incapable. The language of Plotinus, whose *Enneads* Yeats read late in life, is
compounded of primitive symbolism, the esoteric fragments
of classical myth, and the terms of Greek technical metaphysics; but there is no calculated intention of instilling myth
into philosophy.

In what sense is *A Vision* a myth? There are fragments of
many myths brought in to give dramatic and sensuous body
to the framework, which attains to the limit of visualization
that a complex geometrical picture can provide.

A broad view of this picture, with its gyres and cones, to
say nothing of the Daimons and the Principles whose relation to the Faculties defies my understanding, gleans at least
two remarkable features. I merely note them:

(1) ". . . the subjective cone is called that of the *anti-*

thetical tincture because it is achieved and defended by continual conflict with its opposite; the objective cone is called that of the *primary tincture* because whereas subjectivity—in Empedocles' 'Discord' as I think—tends to separate man from man, objectivity brings us back to the mass where we began." From this simple definition—verbally simple, but very obscure—we get the first picture of the intersecting cones; and from this the whole structure is elaborated.

It is clear visually with the aid of the diagrams; but when Yeats complicates it with his Principles and Daimons, and extends the symbol of the gyres to cover historical eras, visualization breaks down. It is an extended metaphor which increasingly tends to dissolve in the particulars which it tries to bring together into unity.

When we come to the magnificent passages on history in "Dove or Swan" all the intricacies of the geometrical metaphor disappear; and the simple figure of historical cycles, which Yeats evidently supposed came out of his gyres, is sufficient to sustain his meaning. Again Yeats's "system" overlaps a body of insight common to us all.

I would suggest, then, for the study of the relation of Yeats's "system" to his vision of man, both historical and individual, this formula: As the system broadens out and merges with the traditional insights of our culture, it tends to disappear in its specific, technical aspects. What disappears is not a philosophy, but only a vast metaphorical structure. In the great elegy, "In Memory of Major Robert Gregory," we get this couplet:

> But as the outrageous stars incline
> By opposition, square, and trine—

which is the only astrological figure in the poem. Yet it must not be assumed that Yeats on this occasion turned off the system; it must be there. Why does it not overtly appear? It has been absorbed into the concrete substance of the poem; the material to be symbolized replaces the symbol, and contains its own meaning. I would select this poem out of all others of our time as the most completely expressed: it has a perfect articulation and lucidity which cannot be found in any other modern poem in English.

(2) In his early poems Yeats is concerned with the myths of ancient Ireland. We may find unreadable today a poem like "The Wanderings of Oisin" or plays like "Deirdre" or "The Land of Heart's Desire." The later poems are less dependent upon fable and fully developed mythical plots for their structures. And yet Yeats entered his later poetic phase at about the same time he began to be interested in his system, in putting myth back into philosophy. Did this mean that he was taking myth out of his poetry?

Thus the second remarkable feature of the system, as I see it, is that it is not a mythology at all, but rather an extended metaphor, as I have already pointed out, which permits him to establish relations between the tag-ends of myths eclectically gathered from all over the world. For example, there is nothing in the geometrical structure of the system which inherently provides for the annunciation to Leda; it is an arbitrary association of two fields of imagery. But once it is established, it is not hard to pass on through analogy to the Annunciation to the Virgin.

IV

Thus it is difficult for me to follow those critics who accept Yeats's various utterances that he was concerned with a certain relation of philosophy to myth. Any statement about "life" must have philosophical implications, just as any genuine philosophical statement must have, because of the nature of language, mythical implications. Yeats's doctrine of the conflict of opposites says nothing about the fundamental nature of reality; it is rather a dramatic framework through which is made visible the perpetual oscillation of man between extreme introspection and extreme loss of the self in the world of action. The intricacies of Yeats's system provide for many of the permutations of this relation; but it cannot foresee them all, and we are constantly brought back to the individual man, not as a symbolic counter, but as a personality rich and unpredictable. Yeats's preference for the nobleman, the peasant, and the craftsman does not betray, as Mr. MacNeice's somewhat provincial contention holds, the "budding fascist"; it is a "version of pastoral" which permits Yeats to see his characters acting above the ordinary dignity of men, in a concrete relation to life undiluted by calculation and abstraction. I can only repeat here that the "system" is perpetually absorbed into action. If Yeats were only an allegorist, the meaning of his poetry could be ascertained by getting hold of the right key. The poetry would serve to illustrate the "system," as the poetry of the Prophetic Books fleshes out the homemade system of Blake.

V

Mr. Eliot's view, that Yeats got off the central tradition into a "minor mythology," and Mr. Blackmur's view, that he took "magic" (as opposed to religion) as far as any poet could, seem to me to be related versions of the same fallacy. Which is: that there must be a direct and effective correlation between the previously established truth of the poet's ideas and the value of the poetry. (I am oversimplifying Blackmur's view, but not Eliot's.) In this difficulty it is always useful to ask: *Where* are the poet's ideas? Good sense in this matter ought to tell us that while the ideas doubtless exist in some form outside the poetry, as they exist for Yeats in the letters, the essays, and *A Vision,* we must nevertheless test them in the poems themselves, and not "refute" a poem in which the gyres supply certain images by showing that gyres are amateur philosophy.

Turning and turning in the widening gyre
The falcon cannot hear the falconer. . . .

—the opening lines of "The Second Coming": and they
make enough sense apart from our knowledge of the system;
the gyre here can be visualized as the circling flight of the
bird constantly widening until it has lost contact with the
point, the center, to which it ought to be able to return. As
a symbol of disunity it is no more esoteric than Eliot's "Gull
against the wind," at the end of "Gerontion," which is a
casual, not traditional or systematic, symbol of disunity. Both
Mr. Blackmur and Mr. Brooks—Mr. Brooks more than Mr.
Blackmur—show us the systematic implications of the symbols of the poem "Byzantium." The presence of the system
at its most formidable cannot be denied to this poem. I
should like to see, nevertheless, an analysis of it in which
no special knowledge is used; I should like to see it examined with the ordinary critical equipment of the educated
critic. I should be surprised if the result were very different
from Mr. Brooks's reading of the poem. The symbols are
"made good" in the poem; they are drawn into a wider convention (Mr. Blackmur calls it the "heaven of man's mind")
than they would imply if taken separately.

I conclude these notes with the remark: the study of Yeats
in the coming generation is likely to overdo the scholarly
procedure, and the result will be the occultation of a poetry
which I believe is nearer the center of our main traditions of
sensibility and thought than the poetry of Eliot or of Pound.
Yeats's special qualities will instigate special studies of great
ingenuity, but the more direct and more difficult problem of
the poetry itself will probably be delayed. This is only to
say that Yeats's romanticism will be created by his critics.

1942

Hart Crane[1]

THE CAREER of Hart Crane will be written by future critics as a chapter in the neo-symbolist movement. An historical view of his poetry at this time would be misleading and incomplete. Like most poets of his age in America, Crane discovered Rimbaud through Eliot and the Imagists; it is certain that long before he had done any of his best work he had come to believe himself the spiritual heir of the French poet. He had an instinctive mastery of the fused metaphor of symbolism, but it is not likely that he ever knew more of the symbolist poets than he had got out of Pound's *Pavannes and Divisions*. Whether Crane's style is symbolistic, or should, in many instances, like the first six or seven stanzas of "The River," be called Elizabethan, is a question that need not concern us now.

Between *The Bridge* and "Une Saison d'Enfer" there is little essential affinity. Rimbaud achieved "disorder" out of implicit order, after a deliberate cultivation of "derangement," but in our age the disintegration of our intellectual systems is accomplished. With Crane the disorder is original and fundamental. That is the special quality of his mind that belongs peculiarly to our own time. His aesthetic problem, however, was more general; it was the historic problem of romanticism.

1 This essay is composed of two papers written several years apart, the one in 1932, a few months after Crane's death, the other in 1937 as a review of Philip Horton's *Hart Crane: The Life of an American Poet.*

Harold Hart Crane, one of the great masters of the romantic movement, was born in Garrettsville, Ohio, on July 21, 1899. His birthplace is a small town near Cleveland, in the old Western Reserve, a region which, as distinguished from the lower portions of the state, where people from the Southern up-country settled, was populated largely by New England stock. He seems to have known little of his ancestry, but he frequently said that his maternal forebears had given Hartford, Connecticut, its name, and that they went "back to Stratford-on-Avon"—a fiction surely, but one that gave him distinct pleasure. His formal education was slight. After the third year at high school, when he was fifteen, it ended, and he worked in his father's candy factory in Cleveland, where the family had removed in his childhood. He repeatedly told me that money had been set aside for his education at college, but that it had been used for other purposes. With the instinct of genius he read the great poets, but he never acquired an objective mastery of any literature, or even of the history of his country—a defect of considerable interest in a poet whose most ambitious work is an American epic.

In any ordinary sense Crane was not an educated man; in many respects he was an ignorant man. There is already a Crane legend, like the Poe legend—it should be fostered because it will help to make his poetry generally known—and the scholars will decide it was a pity that so great a talent lacked early advantages. It is probable that he was incapable of the formal discipline of a classical education, and probable, too, that the eclectic education of his time would have scattered and killed his talent. His poetry not only has defects of the surface, it has a defect of vision; but its great and peculiar value cannot be separated from its limitations. Its qualities are bound up with a special focus of the intellect and sensibility, and it would be folly to wish that his mind had been better trained or differently organized.

The story of his suicide is well-known. The information that I have seems authentic, but it is incomplete and subject to excessive interpretation. Toward the end of April, 1932, he embarked on the S.S. *Orizaba* bound from Vera Cruz to New York. On the night of April 26 he got into a brawl with some sailors; he was severely beaten and robbed. At noon the next day, the ship being in the Caribbean a few hours out of Havana, he rushed from his stateroom clad in pajamas and overcoat, walked through the smoking room out onto the deck, and then the length of the ship to the stern. There without hesitation he made a perfect dive into the sea. It is said that a life preserver was thrown to him; he either did not see it or did not want it. By the time the ship had turned back he had disappeared. Whether he forced himself down —for a moment he was seen swimming—or was seized by a shark, as the captain believed, cannot be known. After a search of thirty-five minutes his body was not found, and the *Orizaba* put back into her course.

In the summer of 1930 he had written to me that he feared his most ambitious work, *The Bridge,* was not quite perfectly "realized," that probably his soundest work was in the shorter pieces of *White Buildings,* but that his mind, being once committed to the larger undertaking, could never return to the lyrical and more limited form. He had an extraordinary insight into the foundations of his work, and I think this judgment of it will not be refuted.

From 1922 to 1928—after that year I saw him and heard from him irregularly until his death—I could observe the development of his style from poem to poem; and his letters —written always in a pure and lucid prose—provide a valuable commentary on his career. This is not the place to bring all this material together for judgment. As I look back upon his work and its relation to the life he lived, a general statement about it comes to my mind that may throw some light on the dissatisfaction that he felt with his career. It will be a judgment upon the life and works of a man whom I knew affectionately for ten years as a friend.

Suicide was the sole act of will left to him short of a profound alteration of his character. I think the evidence of this is the locked-in sensibility, the insulated egoism, of his poetry—a subject that I shall return to. The background of his death was dramatically perfect: a large portion of his finest imagery was of the sea, chiefly the Caribbean:

> O minstrel galleons of Carib fire,
> Bequeath us to no earthly shore until
> Is answered in the vortex of our grave
> The seal's wide spindrift gaze towards paradise.

His verse is full of splendid images of this order, a rich symbolism for an implicit pantheism that, whatever may be its intrinsic merit, he had the courage to vindicate with death in the end.

His pantheism was not passive and contemplative; it rose out of the collision between his own locked-in sensibility and the ordinary forms of experience. Every poem is a thrust of that sensibility into the world: his defect lay in his inability to face out the moral criticism implied in the failure to impose his will upon experience.

The Bridge is presumably an epic. How early he had conceived the idea of the poem and the leading symbolism, it is difficult to know; certainly as early as February, 1923. Up to that time, with the exception of "For the Marriage of Faustus and Helen" (1922), he had written only short poems, but most of them, "Praise for an Urn," "Black Tambourine," "Paraphrase," and "Emblems of Conduct," ² are among his finest work. It is a mistake then to suppose that all of *White Buildings* is early experimental writing; a large

---

² It is now known that this poem is an elaboration of a "sonnet" entitled "Conduct" by Samuel Greenberg. See *Poems* by Samuel Greenberg, edited by Harold Holden and Jack McManis (New York, 1947).

portion of that volume, and perhaps the least successful part of it, is made up of poems written after *The Bridge* was begun. "Praise for an Urn" was written in the spring of 1922—one of the finest elegies by an American poet—and although his later development gave us a poetry that the period would be much the less rich for not having, he never again had such perfect mastery of his subject—because he never again quite knew what his subject was.

Readers familiar with "For the Marriage of Faustus and Helen" admire it by passages, but the form of the poem, in its framework of symbol, is an abstraction empty of any knowable experience. The originality of the poem is in its rhythms, but it has the conventional diction that a young poet picks up in his first reading. Crane, I believe, felt that this was so; and he became so dissatisfied, not only with the style of the poem, which is heavily influenced by Eliot and Laforgue, but with the "literary" character of the symbolism, that he set about the greater task of writing *The Bridge*. He had looked upon his "Faustus and Helen" as an answer to the pessimism of the school of Eliot, and *The Bridge* was to be an even more complete answer.

There was a fundamental mistake in Crane's diagnosis of Eliot's problem. Eliot's "pessimism" grows out of an awareness of the decay of the individual consciousness and its fixed relations to the world; but Crane thought that it was due to something like pure "orneryness," an unwillingness "to share with us the breath released," the breath being a new kind of freedom that he identified emotionally with the age of the machine. This vagueness of purpose, in spite of the apparently concrete character of the Brooklyn Bridge, which became the symbol of his epic, he never succeeded in correcting. The "bridge" stands for no well-defined experience; it differs from the Helen and Faust symbols only in its unliterary origin. I think Crane was deceived by this difference, and by the fact that Brooklyn Bridge is "modern" and a fine piece of "mechanics." His more ambitious later project permitted him no greater mastery of formal structure than the more literary symbolism of his youth.

The fifteen parts of *The Bridge* taken as one poem suffer from the lack of a coherent structure, whether symbolic or narrative: the coherence of the work consists in the personal quality of the writing—in mood, feeling, and tone. In the best passages Crane has perfect mastery over the quality of his style; but the style lacks an objective pattern of ideas elaborate enough to carry it through an epic or heroic work. The single symbolic image, in which the whole poem centers, is at one moment the actual Brooklyn Bridge; at another, it is any bridge or "connection"; at still another, it is a philosophical pun and becomes the basis of a series of analogies.

In "Cape Hatteras," the airplane and Walt Whitman are analogous "bridges" to some transcendental truth. Because the idea is variously metaphor, symbol, and analogy, it tends to make the poem static. The poet takes it up, only to be forced to put it down again *when the poetic image of the moment is exhausted.* The idea does not, in short, fill the poet's mind; it is the starting point for a series of short flights, or inventions connected only in analogy—which explains the merely personal passages, which are obscure, and the lapses into sentimentality. For poetic sentimentality is emotion undisciplined by the structure of events or ideas of which it is ostensibly a part. The idea is not objective and articulate in itself; it lags after the poet's vision; it appears and disappears; and in the intervals Crane improvises, often beautifully, as in the flight of the airplane, sometimes badly, as in the passage on Whitman in the same poem.

In the great epic and philosophical works of the past, notably *The Divine Comedy,* the intellectual groundwork is not only simple philosophically; we not only know that the subject is personal salvation, just as we know that Crane's is the greatness of America: we are given also the complete articulation of the idea down to the slightest detail, and we are given it objectively apart from anything that the poet is going to say about it. When the poet extends his perception, there is a further extension of the groundwork ready to meet it and discipline it, and to compel the sensibility of the poet to stick to the subject. It is a game of chess; neither side can move without consulting the other. Crane's difficulty is that of modern poets generally: they play the game with half of the men, the men of sensibility, and because sensibility can make any move, the significance of all moves is obscure.

If we subtract from Crane's idea its periphery of sensation, we have left only the dead abstraction, the Greatness of America, which is capable of elucidation neither on the logical plane nor in terms of a generally known idea of America.

The theme of *The Bridge* is, in fact, an emotional over-simplification of a subject matter that Crane did not, on the plane of narrative and idea, simplify at all. The poem is emotionally homogeneous and simple—it contains a single purpose; but because it is not structurally clarified it is emotionally confused. America stands for a passage into new truths. Is this the meaning of American history? The poet has every right to answer yes, and this he has done. But just what in America or about America stands for this? Which American history? The historical plot of the poem, which is the groundwork on which the symbolic bridge stands, is arbitrary and broken, where the poet would have gained an overwhelming advantage by choosing a single period or episode, a concrete event with all its dramatic causes, and by following it up minutely, and being bound to it. In short, he would have gained an advantage could he have found a subject to stick to.

Does American culture afford such a subject? It probably

does not. After the seventeenth century the sophisticated history of the scholars came into fashion; our popular, legendary chronicles come down only from the remoter European past. It was a sound impulse on Crane's part to look for an American myth, some simple version of our past that lies near the center of the American consciousness; an heroic tale with just enough symbolism to give his mind both direction and play. The soundness of his purpose is witnessed also by the kind of history in the poem: it is inaccurate, and it will not at all satisfy the sticklers for historical fact. It is the history of the motion picture, of naïve patriotism. This is sound; for it ignores the scientific ideal of historical truth-in-itself, and looks for a cultural truth which might win the spontaneous allegiance of the people. It is on such simple integers of truth, not truth of fact but of religious necessity, that men unite. The American mind was formed by the eighteenth-century Enlightenment, which broke down the European "truths" and gave us a temper deeply hostile to the making of new religious truths of our own.

The impulse in *The Bridge* is religious, but the soundness of an impulse is no warrant that it will create a sound art form. The form depends on too many factors beyond the control of the poet. The age is scientific and pseudo-scientific, and our philosophy is Dewey's instrumentalism. And it is possibly this circumstance that has driven the religious attitude into a corner where it lacks the right instruments for its defense and growth, and where it is in a vast muddle about just what these instruments are. Perhaps this disunity of the intellect is responsible for Crane's unphilosophical belief that the poet, unaided and isolated from the people, can create a myth.

If anthropology has helped to destroy the credibility of myths, it has shown us how they rise: their growth is mysterious from the people as a whole. It is probable that no one man ever put myth into history. It is still a nice problem among higher critics, whether the authors of the Gospels were deliberate myth-makers, or whether their minds were simply constructed that way; but the evidence favors the latter. Crane was a myth-maker, and in an age favorable to myths he would have written a mythical poem in the act of writing an historical one.

It is difficult to agree with those critics who find his epic a single poem and as such an artistic success. It is a collection of lyrics, the best of which are not surpassed by anything in American literature. The writing is most distinguished when Crane is least philosophical, *when he writes from sensation.* "The River" has some blemishes towards the end, but by and large it is a masterpiece of order and style; it alone is enough to place Crane in the first rank of American poets, living or dead. Equally good but less ambitious are the "Proem: To Brooklyn Bridge," and "Harbor Dawn," and "The Dance" from the section called "Powhatan's Daughter."

These poems bear only the loosest relation to the symbolic demands of the theme; they contain allusions to the historical pattern or extend the slender structure of analogy running through the poem. They are primarily lyrical, and each has its complete form. The poem "Indiana," written presumably to complete the pattern of "Powhatan's Daughter," does not stand alone, and it is one of the most astonishing failures ever made by a poet of Crane's genius. "The Dance" gives us the American background for the coming white man, and "Indiana" carries the stream of history to the pioneer West. It is a nightmare of sentimentality. Crane is at his most "philosophical" in a theme in which he feels no poetic interest whatever.

The structural defect of *The Bridge* is due to this fundamental contradiction of purpose. In one of his best earlier poems, "The Wine Menagerie," he exclaims: "New thresholds, new anatomies!"—new sensation, but he could not subdue the new sensation to a symbolic form.

His pantheism is necessarily a philosophy of sensation without point of view. An epic is a judgment of human action, an implied evaluation of a civilization, a way of life. In *The Bridge* the civilization that contains the subway hell of the section called "The Tunnel" is the same civilization of the airplane that the poet apostrophizes in "Cape Hatteras." There is no reason why the subway should be a fitter symbol of damnation than the airplane: both were produced by the same mentality on the same moral plane. There is a concealed, meaningless analogy between, on the one hand, the height of the plane and the depth of the subway, and, on the other, "higher" and "lower" in the religious sense. At one moment Crane faces his predicament of blindness to any rational order of value, and knows that he is damned; but he cannot face it long, and he tries to rest secure upon the intensity of sensation.

To the vision of the abyss in "The Tunnel," a vision that Dante passed through midway of this mortal life, Crane had no alternative: when it became too harrowing he cried to his Pocahontas, a typically romantic and sentimental symbol:

> Lie to us—dance us back our tribal morn!

It is probably the perfect word of romanticism in this century. When Crane saw that his leading symbol, the bridge, would not hold all the material of his poem, he could not sustain it ironically, in the classical manner, by probing its defects; nor in the personal sections, like "Quaker Hill," does he include himself in his Leopardian denunciation of life. He is the blameless victim of a world whose impurity violates the moment of intensity, which would otherwise be enduring and perfect. He is betrayed, not by a defect of his own nature, but by the external world; he asks of nature, perfection—requiring only of himself, intensity. The persistent, and persistently defeated, pursuit of a natural absolute places Crane at the center of his age.

Alternately he asserts the symbol of the bridge and abandons it, because fundamentally he does not understand it. The idea of bridgeship is an elaborate blur leaving the inner structure of the poem confused.

Yet some of the best poetry of our generation is in *The Bridge*. Its inner confusion is a phase of the inner cross-purposes of the time. Crane was one of those men whom every age seems to select as the spokesmen of its spiritual life; they give the age away. The accidental features of their lives, their place in life, their very heredity, seem to fit them for their role; even their vices contribute to their preparation. Crane's biographer will have to study the early influences that confirmed him in narcissism, and thus made him typical of the rootless spiritual life of our time. The character formed by those influences represents an immense concentration, and becomes almost a symbol, of American life in this age.

Crane's poetry has incalculable moral value: it reveals our defects in their extremity. I have said that he knew little of the history of his country. It was not merely a defect of education, but a defect, in the spiritual sense, of the modern mind. Crane lacked the sort of indispensable understanding of his country that a New England farmer has who has never been out of his township. *The Bridge* attempts to include all American life, but it covers the ground with seven-league boots and, like a sightseer, sees nothing. With reference to its leading symbol, it has no subject matter. The poem is the effort of a solipsistic sensibility to locate itself in the external world, to establish points of reference.

It seems to me that by testing out his capacity to construct a great objective piece of work, in which his definition of himself should have been articulated, he brought his work to an end. I think he knew that the structure of *The Bridge* was finally incoherent, and for that reason—as I have said—he could no longer believe even in his lyrical powers; he could not return to the early work and take it up where he had left off. Far from "refuting" Eliot, his whole career is a vindication of Eliot's major premise—that the integrity of the individual consciousness has broken down. Crane had, in his later work, no individual consciousness: the hard firm style of "Praise for an Urn," which is based upon a clear-cut perception of moral relations, and upon their ultimate inviolability, begins to disappear when the poet goes out into the world and finds that the simplicity of a child's world has no universal sanction. From then on, instead of the effort to define himself in the midst of almost overwhelming complications—a situation that might have produced a tragic poet—he falls back upon the intensity of consciousness, rather than the clarity, for his center of vision. And that is romanticism.

His world had no center, and the thrust into sensation is responsible for the fragmentary quality of his most ambitious work. This thrust took two directions—the blind assertion of the will, and the blind desire for self-destruction. The poet did not face his first problem, which is to define the limits of his personality and to objectify its moral implications in an appropriate symbolism. Crane could only assert a quality of will against the world, and at each successive failure of the will he turned upon himself. In the failure of understanding—and understanding, for Dante, was a way of love—the romantic modern poet of the age of science attempts to impose his will upon experience and to possess the world.

It is this impulse of the modern period that has given us the greatest romantic poetry: Crane instinctively continued the conception of the will that was the deliberate discovery of Rimbaud. A poetry of the will is a poetry of sensation, for the poet surrenders to his sensations of the object in his effort to identify himself with it, and to own it. Some of Crane's finest lyrics—those written in the period of *The Bridge*—carry the modern impulse as far as you will find it anywhere in the French romantics. "Lachrymae Christi" and "Passage," though on the surface made up of pure images without philosophical meaning of the explicit sort in *The Bridge,* are the lyrical equivalents of the epic: the same kind of sensibility is at work. The implicit grasp of his material that we find in "Praise for an Urn," the poet has exchanged for an external, random symbol of which there is no possibility of realization. *The Bridge* is an irrational symbol of the will, of conquest, of blind achievement in space; its obverse is "Passage," whose lack of external symbolism exhibits the poetry of the will on the plane of sensation; and this is the self-destructive return of the will upon itself.

Criticism may well set about isolating the principle upon which Crane's poetry is organized. Powerful verse overwhelms its admirers, and betrays them into more than technical imitation. That is one of the arguments of Platonism against literature; it is the immediate quality of an art rather than its whole significance that sets up schools and traditions. Crane not only ends the romantic era in his own person; he ends it logically and morally. Beyond Crane no future poet can go. (This does not mean that the romantic impulse may not rise and flourish again.) The finest passages in his work are single moments in the stream of sensation; beyond the moment he goes at his peril; for beyond it lies the discrepancy between the sensuous fact, the perception, and its organizing symbol—a discrepancy that plunges him into sentimentality and chaos. But the "bridge" is empty and static, it has no inherent content, and the poet's attribution to it of the qualities of his own moral predicament is arbitrary. That explains the fragmentary and often unintelligible framework of the poem. There was neither complete action nor ordered symbolism in terms of which the distinct moments of perception could be clarified.

This was partly the problem of Rimbaud. But Crane's

problem was nearer to the problem of Keats, and *The Bridge* is a failure in the sense that "Hyperion" is a failure, and with comparable magnificence. Crane's problem, being farther removed from the epic tradition, was actually more difficult than Keats's, and his treatment of it was doubtless the most satisfactory possible in our time. Beyond the quest of pure sensation and its ordering symbolism lies the total destruction of art. By attempting an extreme solution of the romantic problem Crane proved that it cannot be solved.

1932–1937

Crane: The Poet as Hero

An Encomium Twenty Years Later

ANYBODY who knew Hart Crane will come away from his letters both depressed and relieved. I confess that I hope I shall not have to follow again the melancholy course of this desperate life. I prefer to cherish, after the violence and final frustration of a great lyric poet, an image of Crane the poet as hero. What at last destroyed him one cannot quite say, even after the copious evidence that Mr. Weber's ably edited volume [1] puts before us. The clue to the mystery is not here: it seems to lie far back of the written testimony of the letters, in his boyhood, when at eleven he became the "bloody battleground" of his father's and mother's "sex lives and troubles," which ended not only in divorce but in such disorder that the boy was set adrift. The family was by no means poor, but he was not sent to college; he was turned loose in New York when he was seventeen.

What astonishes me in the early letters—and what I had not got from Crane himself or from Mr. Philip Horton's excellent biography [2]—is not only the intellectual precocity but the precocity of moral insight. He was seventeen when he wrote to his father from New York:

[1] *The Letters of Hart Crane, 1916–1932*, edited by Brom Weber (New York, 1952).
[2] *Hart Crane: The Life of an American Poet* (New York, 1937).

When I perceive one emotion overpowering to a fact, or a statement of reason, then the only manly, worthy, sensible thing to do,
is build up the logical side, and attain balance, and in art—*formal
expression.*

In 1926, nine years later, he wrote to an anonymous friend:

. . . with the sailor no faith or such is properly *expected,* and how
jolly and cordial and warm. . . . Let my lusts be my ruin, then,
since all else is fake and mockery.

The intellectual deterioration came more slowly. What
had happened to him morally between 1917 and 1926? The
letters definitely answer this question. He had been confirmed in his homosexuality and cut off finally from any
relationship, short of a religious conversion, in which the
security necessary to mutual love was possible. I was surprised, after two years of correspondence with him, when
in 1924 I met him and learned a little later that he was a
homosexual: he had none of the characteristics popularly
attributed to homosexuality. The violence of his obscenity
(particularly about women) and his intense emotional at-
tachments to women his own age (not to middle-aged
women) convinced me even then that he was an extreme
example of the *unwilling* homosexual. It is significant that
his last love affair, quite real if not wholly "committed,"
was with a woman; his letters to her are in every sense the
letters of a man to a woman down to the full implications
of physical love.

I dwell upon this part of the record because beneath it
lies the mystery of the disintegration, at the age of thirty-
two, of the most gifted poet of his generation. The "causes"
of homosexuality are no doubt as various as the causes of
other neuroses. But the effect on the lives of its victims
seems to be uniform: they are convinced that they cannot
be loved, and they become incapable of loving. This is not
to say that they are incapable of strong affection: they are

incapable of sustaining it in a sexual relationship. They may have affection *or* sex, but not both; or if both, both are diluted and remote. Crane's intensity excluded this compromise. Incidents of the "bloody battleground" that he told me and other friends about in the late twenties have never appeared in print, and this is not the occasion to recite them. Is it not reasonable to assume that the hatred and suffering that accompanied the violent sex life of his parents were the decisive force that gave him eventually the homosexual neurosis? Was it possible for an eleven-year-old boy, or for the man later, to dissociate hate from the sexual relation with a woman? Possible for most men, but not, under all the conditions of his childhood, for Crane. Almost to the end of his life he was still trying to "explain" himself to his mother and to force from a peculiarly stupid and selfish woman the recognition and love of what he was. He could still love her because he could not be her lover.

It has always seemed to me that the defection of his mother precipitated the final disaster. He had been endowed with powerful family affections that were progressively frustrated. His letters to his divorced parents are among the most considerate, tender, and moving in literary history. He turned to his friends for the totally committed love, the disinterested *caritas,* that only one's family can sustain and that alone will condone repeatedly violent and aggressive conduct. None of us was capable in the end of taking the place of his family—and that was what he demanded of us; our failure—and I speak now not only for myself but, not improperly, I think, for his entire intimate circle—also contributed to the final disaster. But there was for us no other way: we also had families and our own lives.

Out of these conflicts, which in the end became one conflict, emerged a peculiar focus of the intelligence and sensibility that represents "modernism" in its extreme development. (Towards the end he speaks of himself as the "last romantic.") He had an abnormally acute response to the physical world, an exacerbation of the nerve ends, along with an incapacity to live within the limitations of the human condition. It has become commonplace to describe this as the mentality of "alienation." But the point to be borne in mind—and it is amply confirmed by the letters— is that Crane was never *alienated*. He did not reject, he simply could not achieve, in his own life, the full human condition: he did not for a moment suppose that there was a substitute for it. This is borne out not only by his poetry —for example, *The Bridge* is not in intention a poem of "rejection," in the tradition of Rimbaud, but of "acceptance," an attempt to assimilate a central tradition; it is confirmed also by his life, reflected day by day, year after year, in the letters. His deepest friendships were not with homosexuals; they were with Malcolm Cowley, Slater Brown, Kenneth Burke, Gorham Munson, Waldo Frank, and myself; it was with these men that he lived the life of the mind and the imagination. He could not pretend that the alienated society of the committed homosexual was complete; for this unhappy person—for his epicene manners and for his irresponsibility—he felt compassion and contempt. There is a Christian commonplace which says that God does not despise conditions. Out of the desperate conditions of his life—which included almost unimaginable horrors of depravity and perversity of will—he produced in the end a shining *exemplum* of uncompromising human dignity: his poetry.

He came to New York at seventeen equipped with an hysterical and disorderly family, almost no formal education, and the cultural inheritance of a middle-western small town; his religious training had been in Christian Science. By the time he was twenty-five, before *The Bridge* had scarcely been conceived, he had written a body of lyric poetry which for originality, distinction, and power, remains the great poetic achievement of his generation. If he is not our twentieth-century poet as hero, I do not know where else to look for him.

1952

Hardy's Philosophic Metaphors

I

AFTER Thomas Hardy had become a great literary figure on the British model—that is to say, a personage to whom one makes pilgrimages—criticism of his works languished: once the battle over the obscenity of Jude and the pessimism of his "philosophy" had been won, critics had very little to say, except that they admired him. So far as I know, only two critical works on Hardy exist: Lionel Johnson's fine study of the novels, *The Art of Thomas Hardy*, which, first published in 1894, appeared before Hardy was known as a poet; and Lascelles Abercrombie's *Thomas Hardy*, a book of considerable value for the criticism of the novels but of not much use for the poetry. One must add to these works the excellent essay, "The Poetry of Thomas Hardy," by J. E. Barton, which appears as an appendix to the John Lane edition of Johnson's study (1923). The centennial biography, *Hardy of Wessex*, by C. J. Weber, no doubt adds to our store of facts about Hardy; yet Mr. Weber's critical ineptitude contributes little to our understanding of either the poetry or the novels.

For two reasons I have wished to make this comment upon the critics of Hardy's poetry: they have given us very little to start with, and their assertion of Hardy's greatness as a poet is worse than nothing to start with. I do not intend in this commentary to deny the "greatness" of Hardy's poetry, nor to deny meaning to the pious enthusiasm of two generations of devoted readers, among whom intermittently I count myself. But the enthusiasm is largely sentimental; it implies an equivocal judgment of both the poetry and the man. It is sentimental because it does not distinguish man from poet or tell us upon what terms we may talk about them together. We have here in the case of Hardy—though for no doubt quite different reasons—the figure of the poet-sage not unlike that of Mr. Robert Frost, whose admirers will not permit the critics to dissociate the poetry from the wise man who wrote it. When without the admirers' permission Mr. R. P. Blackmur assumed that his task was to discuss Mr. Frost's language, he suffered the fanatical obloquy of a popular spellbinder, Mr. Bernard DeVoto, who promptly called Mr. Blackmur a fool.

Now very much the same sort of thing went on towards the end of Thomas Hardy's life, and one must strongly suspect, from all the evidence, that he liked it, and that he liked it because, like most critically naïve minds, he could accept the personal tribute as tribute to the power of his message, which was the message of a "philosopher." Hardy was a great poet, but I arrive at that conclusion after disposing of a prejudice against the personal qualities that have led his admirers to believe him a great man. I see him as a somewhat complacent and tiresome old gentleman, mellow and wise; a man who in his youth had set about conquering a career; who married a woman his inferior but above him socially, and could never forget the social difference—a fact that forbids us to forget it; who permitted his literary reputation to lead him into the tow of society hostesses who could have seen in him only his fame and from whom, as he frequently confessed, he got nothing. Yet he continued until late in life to appear as the literary lion. Why did he do it? It is useless to pretend that Thomas Hardy's social sense was distinguished (a distinction that has nothing to do with "class") or that he was not lacking in a certain knowledge of the world that would have been valuable even to the historian of a yeoman society: insofar as historical and biographical criticism will illuminate Hardy's poetry, it is important to keep his defects steadily in mind, for he never overcame them. Shakespeare's origins were humbler than Hardy's, yet they are irrelevant in the criticism of Shakespeare, because the confusion of feeling that one finds in Hardy cannot be found in Shakespeare. Hardy's background and education, like other backgrounds and other educations for poetry, will give us a clue to the defects of the work, but not to its merits, and it is with the merits that criticism must be specifically occupied. Literature can be written from any background, and Hardy wrote literature.

Mr. Weber quotes from Hardy's famous description of Clym Yeobright the following passage, and applies it to Hardy's own young manhood:

Mentally he was in a provincial future, that is, he was in many points abreast with the central town thinkers of his date. Much of this development he may have owed to his studious life in Paris, where he had become acquainted with ethical systems popular at the time. In consequence of this relatively advanced position, Yeobright might have been called unfortunate. The rural world was not ripe for him.

From this and other passages in the novels, in which Hardy presents himself in the disguise of certain characters, we get a portrait of the young Hardy against the background from which he sprang. Like Yeobright he was a young man "educated" out of the folk culture of his region: he had read Darwin, Huxley, Hume, Gibbon—the Victorian agnostics and their naturalistic forerunners of the eighteenth century. He began to see the world through "ethical systems popular at the time"; more than that, he began to see the people of Dorset in terms of the metaphysical bias of these systems, so that when he came back to Dorset from his studies in London he must have felt that his "advanced position" had cut him off from his people.

Yet there can be no doubt that, if this situation actually confronted Hardy at the outset of his literary career, it offered him tremendous advantages. He had been possessed from birth of an immense, almost instinctive knowledge of the life of a people rooted in ancient folk traditions and fixed, also, in the objective patterns of nature and of the occupations close to nature. This knowledge of a provincial scene, where "life had bared its bones" to him, must have toughened his skepticism against the cruder aspects of Victorian thought, liberalism, optimism, and the doctrine of progress, and he could concentrate with a sort of classical purity upon the permanent human experiences.

Yet he did have a philosophical view of the significance of the human situation. As William R. Rutland indicates in his *Thomas Hardy* (the best general book on the subject), Hardy maintained with great consistency, from the beginning of his literary career, a philosophical attitude. The attitude did not change. Mr. Rutland makes an astute analysis of it:

It is an interesting paradox that Hardy should have placed so high a value upon intellectual reason, while his own mental life was almost entirely governed by emotion . . . he criticized J. H. Newman for failing to provide logical support for his beliefs. The outlook upon life of his mature manhood was almost wholly due to emotional reactions against suffering and injustice; but he sought for intellectual explanations of the universe in the writing of the philosophers. He went on reading philosophy till he was old, but he never advanced beyond what had been in the forefront of thought during his early manhood. When, in 1915, he read that no modern philosopher subscribes to Herbert Spencer's doctrine of "the Unknowable" (which had greatly influenced him) he declared himself "utterly bewildered."

How much this philosophical reading did to make the young Hardy, like Clym Yeobright, an outsider in his own region, nobody could estimate accurately; but that it did affect him in this manner I believe no one will deny. To say that he had reached an "advanced position" is only another way of saying that he had very early come to be both inside and outside his background, which was to be the material of his art: an ambivalent point of view that, in its infinite variations from any formula that we may state for it, is at the center of the ironic consciousness. While Hardy had a direct "emotional reaction" to his Wessex people, who were the human substance of the only world he really knew, he nevertheless tried to philosophize about them in the terms of Victorial materialism.

This, I think, was his intellectual situation, and Mr. Rutland has given us a clue to its meaning that ought to receive at some future time a more detailed analysis than I can give it here. In setting forth the experiences of people deeply involved in the cycle of the earth and "conditioned" in their emotional relations by close familiarity with the processes of nature, he had constantly before him a kind of "naturalism" that only an astute philosophical mind could have kept, in that period, distinct from a naturalism of a wholly different order: the philosophic naturalism of Huxley and Spencer which, according to Mr. Rutland, Hardy tended to look upon as "explanations" of the world, not as theories. When he was shocked in 1915 by the decline of Spencer's reputation, he doubtless felt that a final conclusion had been upset; his outlook was not philosophical but brooding and ruminative; and I believe that here, again, we get the image of Clym Yeobright, the young man ill-prepared to digest the learning of the great world, the provincial amateur who sees farther than his neighbors but who, if he had seen still farther, might not have accepted, *in an act of faith,* the Darwinian naturalism of his time. As late as 1922 he wrote in the "Apology" to *Late Lyrics and Earlier* that "when belief in witches of Endor is displacing the Darwinian theory and 'the truth that shall make you free,' men's minds appear, as above noted, to be moving backwards rather than on." The witches of Endor had doubtless presided over the irrational passions of the War; but the going backwards instead of forwards indicates, I believe, a somewhat greater belief in one of the leading Victorian ideas, Progress, than is usually attributed to Hardy.

Perhaps Hardy's intense awareness of the folk realism of his people modified the liberal optimism of his time, and checked his assent to the enthusiasms of his age at a particular stage, which he described as "evolutionary meliorism." Nevertheless, the reader of Hardy's novels gets a total impression in which this doctrine of "meliorism" is occasionally stated but in which it plays little part in terms of the characters and their plots. It has often been said that Hardy's two leading ideas, Necessity and Chance, Fate and "Crass Casualty," continue the Greek tradition; but it seems more likely that his Necessity is only Victorian Mechanism, and that Chance represents the occasional intercession into the mechanical routine of the universe, of Spencer's Unknowable.

It is a curious feature of Hardy's treatment of the Dorchester peasantry that they are not permitted to have religious experiences: their religious emotions are thoroughly "psychologized" and naturalistic. It would seem, then, that Hardy, like Clym, had reached an "advanced position" which forbade him to take seriously the religious life of his people. The peculiar compound of pagan superstition and Christianity which issued in a simple miraculism (as opposed to Hardy's mechanism of fate interrupted by blind chance) he tended from the first to look at from the outside, where it seemed quaint and picturesque. This, of course, is not quite the whole story of Hardy's profound insight into human

character, or of his mastery of dramatic form which he
achieved in spite of technical limitations and of a high-
falutin' prose style of which the best that can be said is that
it has an occasional descriptive grandeur and a frequent
bathos. (He once said that while poetry requires technique,
prose writes itself—perhaps a British as well as a personal
blindness.) I have offered this brief simplification of Hardy's
intellectual "position" not as an explanation of his work, but
merely as a pointer towards a certain kind of meaning that
I have seen in his poetry.

II

One of Hardy's most powerful poems is "Nature's Questioning." It is written in a four-line stanza that seems characteristically to be derived from a hymn meter in the first two
lines, but instead of completing the 4-3-4-3 stanza that the
first two lines have led us to expect, he boldly finishes it
off, 3-6, thus:

> When I look forth at dawning, pool,
> > Field, flock, and lonely tree,
> > All seem to gaze at me
> Like chastened children sitting silent in school;

> Their faces dulled, constrained, and worn,
> > As though the master's ways
> > Through the long teaching days
> Had cowed them till their early zest was overborne.

The Alexandrines in these stanzas are prosodically among
the most successful in English: the sense overlaps the caesura,
imparting to the structure a firmness that keeps the line from
breaking down into two trimeters. The poem proceeds, after
two stanzas setting forth cosmic questions from nature:

> Or come we of an Automaton
> > Unconscious of our pains? . . .
> > Or are we live remains
> Of Godhead dying downwards, brain and eye now gone?

The two last lines are often cited as Hardy's most brilliant, and I think there can be no doubt of their magnificence. The phrase *now gone* could not be better: one is reminded of Henry James's tact concerning the presentation of supernatural beings in fiction, that "weak specifications" limit their credibility. *Now gone* is just specific enough, its colloquial tone bringing the idea of God within the range of familiarity without the risks of a too concrete image: brain and eye are not images, but rather objects denoted. The rhythm of the line seems to me to be masterly. The prevailing falling rhythm is suddenly shifted, from "brain" to the end of the line, to a counter, mounting rhythm; moreover, the trimeter line latent in the hexameter becomes explicit —"Of Godhead dying downwards"—and the shock of *downwards* has the prolonged effect of the feminine ending; when the hexameter is resumed, *brain* strikes with tremendous force, with a secondary stress on *eye;* and *now gone* reads to my ear almost as a spondee. In this last feature it seems to me that the final proof of the technical mastery appears (conscious in Hardy, or not). The rhythmic conflict in the line is never quite resolved. There has been a regular alternation of stressed and unstressed syllables, so that when we reach *now* we are under a strong compulsion to pass it over lightly; yet we cannot do so; the quantity of the syllable, reinforced by its rhetoric, stops us. Could we pass it lightly, *now gone* as an iambus would restore the prevailing pattern of mounting rhythm; as a spondee it suspends the conflict, the particular effect of meaning and rhythm being a kind of kinesthetic sensation that we soon discover that we have been attributing to the agony of the dying Godhead.

I do not apologize for laboring this point. Great passages of poetry are rare; because they are exceptionally rare in Hardy we must exert ourselves to the utmost to understand their value. There is nothing else in "Nature's Questioning" to reward our close attention—if we are looking for poetry; but there is a great deal that will illuminate our understanding of Hardy's poetry. The two last stanzas:

> Or is it that some high Plan betides,
>   As yet not understood,
>   Of Evil stormed by Good,
> We the Forlorn Hope over which Achievement strides?

> Thus things around. No answerer I . . .
>   Meanwhile the winds, and rains,
>   And Earth's old glooms and pains
> Are still the same, and Life and Death are neighbors nigh.

Now this poem as a whole fairly represents a use of metaphor practiced by certain Victorian poets. The inanimate "things around" that have asked the questions appear in the first stanza as pool, field, flock, and a tree whose sole quality is its loneliness; these objects quickly become school children, before they have been sufficiently particularized to be themselves. The transformation of the natural objects into persons is initiated with some degree of tact in terms of simile—"Like chastened children"—that we can accept because not too much is claimed for it at that stage. But in the second stanza what appeared to be simile becomes completed metaphor. We have here, in the terms of Mr. I. A. Richards, an instance of metaphor in which the "vehicle" replaces the "tenor": the natural objects (tenor) are so weakly perceived that the children (vehicle), who appear as the conveyance of their significance, cancel out the natural objects altogether; so that, as the poem proceeds to the fourth stanza, we get a group of inanimate objects as school children asking this question:

> Has some vast Imbecility,
>   Mighty to build and blend,
>   But impotent to tend,
> Framed us in jest, and left us now to hazardry?

Now Hardy is saying that the children are Nature, and would like to say, since he is a nineteenth-century monist, that they are mechanically determined, as Nature is; both human and nonhuman nature suffer the neglect of the absentee God of Deism, who is

> Mighty to build and blend,
> But impotent to tend . . .

This God is the schoolmaster of line two, stanza two; here again the metaphorical vehicle replaces the tenor; and in view of the deistic character of this God, the figure of the "master," who is the personal, anthropomorphic representation of the Unknowable, contradicts his logical significance: to render this God dramatically, Hardy has made him the God of theism, a personal, if not the Christian, God, but if he is the Automaton of stanza five, he is not equipped to teach a class; he cannot even be present if he is "impotent to tend."

Throughout this poem (and I should risk the guess, in most of the "philosophical" poems of Hardy) the margin of intelligible meaning achieved by the union of the tenor and the vehicle is very narrow. Even in the magnificent image of the "Godhead dying downwards" we get a certain degree of contradiction between tenor and vehicle: in order to say that God has left the universe to chance after setting it in motion, Hardy can merely present us with the theistic God as blind and imbecile.

So generally of Hardy it may perhaps be said that his "philosophy" tends to be a little beyond the range of his feeling: his abstractions are thus somewhat irresponsible, since he rarely shows us the experience that ought to justify them, that would give them substance, visibility, and meaning. The visible embodiment of the meaning of "Nature's Questioning" ought doubtless to be "pool, field, flock, and lonely tree," which are not experienced objects of nature, but only universals of so thinly perceived quality that Hardy apparently had no trouble at all in absorbing them into the analogy of the school children; and likewise the schoolmaster is so thinly particularized that the next analogical development, master into God, is easy and unconvincing.

It is likely that other critics will from time to time examine other examples of Hardy's verse; it will probably be many years before a comprehensive study of all his poetry can appear. I have a strong impression that the ballads, songs, and occasional lyrics, as well as the versified tales and the little ironic incidents of the *Satires of Circumstance,* exhibit the greatest freedom of sensibility of which Hardy, the poet, was capable: in the vast number of these slighter pieces Hardy is at his least philosophical; he is closer to the immediate subject, he is free to observe directly and to record the direct impression. But when he begins to think, when he begins to say what the impression, the observation, the incident means, he can only bring in his ill-digested philosophy —a *mélange* of Schopenhauer, Darwin, and Spencer, against a cosmological background of eighteenth-century Deism that he could not project imaginatively into his immediate experience.

Is this not the common situation of the Victorian poets and, with some differences, our predicament today? Our chief difference seems to consist in a greater awareness of the problem—not in its solution. Hardy's philosophical limitations permitted him to accept as "truth" Spencer's *Synthetic Philosophy,* with the result that he held to the mechanistic theories of his time with greater single-mindedness than Tennyson or Browning ever achieved. This single-mindedness probably kept him immune to the eclectic miscellany of easy speculations and solutions to which his more sensitive contemporaries succumbed. There can be no doubt that the poetic language of Hardy, particularly in poems like "God's Funeral" and "The Convergence of the Twain," achieves a weight and solidity that only Arnold of the Victorians—and then only in his best moments—could rival: perhaps his lack of a university training in literature permitted him to seize the language afresh, so that even his heavily Latinized vocabulary is capable of effects that a better educated poet in his age would have missed. It is as dangerous as it is meaningless to wish that a great poet might have either corrected, or had the literary tact to avoid the exposure of, his deficiencies. Had he been "better educated" he might have been like Browning or Swinburne—both men his inferiors; had he been worse educated, it is not inconceivable that he should have been even more like James Thomson (B.V.) than he was; but fortunately he was Thomas Hardy.

1940

Edwin Arlington Robinson

EDWIN ARLINGTON ROBINSON, most famous of living American poets, was born at Head Tide, Maine, on December 22, 1869.[1] He attended Harvard from 1891 to 1893, but left college without taking a degree. In 1896 he printed privately his first book of verse, *The Torrent and the Night Before,* which was followed a year later by *The Children of the Night,* a volume little noticed at the time but one which marks the beginning of a new era in American poetry. In the next fourteen years he published two more books, *Captain Craig* (1902) and *The Town Down the River* (1910). But it was not until 1916 that he attracted wide attention and won a notable fame. For with *The Man Against the Sky* Mr. Robinson stepped quickly into the front rank of American poetry. In his early years he wrote some of the finest lyrics of modern times: these are likely to be his permanent claim to fame.

Able critics have thought otherwise. Not only, they say, are Mr. Robinson's long narrative poems his best work; they are the perfect realization of a "tragic vision." But hear Mr. Mark Van Doren, a distinguished critic whom I do not like to disagree with:

His vision is essentially tragic in that it stresses the degeneration of ideas, the dimming of the light, when these become implicated in the rough action of the world.

Passion has its victories no less than reason. The tragic picture

[1] Mr. Robinson died on April 5, 1935.

would be incomplete without either of these. It is because Mr. Robinson's picture is fairly complete that he deserves the rare title of major American poet.[2]

I should be the last person, I hope, to dispute Mr. Robinson's right to that title. Nor should I contend for a moment that Mr. Robinson lacks the "tragic vision," but I am convinced that Mr. Van Doren's qualifying word, *essentially*, is accurate. For Mr. Robinson writes, I believe, less from the tragic vision than from the tragic sentiment; and the result is the pathetic tale of obscure ambition or thwarted passion; not tragedy.

It is true that he deals with the degeneration of ideas. The question that Mr. Van Doren does not ask, it seems to me, is this: What is the exact significance of the ideas? Is their ultimate reference to a religious or philosophical background, a realm of ideas possessing at least for their time and place the compulsion of absolute truth? Or are they the private ideas of modern persons, the personal forms of some egoistic thrust of the will? In other words, is Mr. Robinson a true tragic poet, or is he a modern poet like other modern poets, whose distinguished gifts are not enough to give him more than the romantic ego with which to work?

Talifer [3] is a psychological narrative of the order of *The Man Against the Sky*. It is the eighth or ninth specimen of this kind of poem that Mr. Robinson has given us. Because the type has grown thinner with each example, the new narrative being, I believe, the least satisfactory of them all, it is the occasion of some inquiry into the causes of Mr. Robinson's preference for this particular form. It is a form that includes the three Arthurian poems, *Merlin, Lancelot,* and *Tristram,* psychological stories that are in all respects similar to the New England tales of Nightingale, Cavender, Bartho-

---

[2] Mark Van Doren, *Edwin Arlington Robinson* (New York, 1927), pp. 34, 90.
[3] Edwin Arlington Robinson, *Talifer* (New York, 1932).

low. All is the same but time and place; for the characters are the same.

In *Talifer* there are four characters, two men and two women. The woman Althea—the name is a dry piece of irony—is in love with Talifer; she is woman domestic, sensitive, but commonplace and child-bearing. Talifer himself is an ordinary person, but he talks of his "tradition," carries himself well, and expects of life more than his inner quality entitles him to: so he imagines that he is in love with the other woman, Karen, who is beautiful, treacherous, cold, and erudite, dividing her time between inscrutable moods and incredible reading in the ancients. But she is vaguely conceived by the poet, and the motivation of the hero's action remains obscure.

Talifer has been fatuous enough to say that with Karen he expects to find Peace. Life becomes, after a year or two with her, intolerable. Then, one day in his ancestral forest, he meets Althea, who still loves him, and he decides to leave Karen. Now all this time, the other man, Doctor Quick, could have been in love with either of the women; he is too skeptical to push his desires, and his place in the story is that of commentator. He explains the confusion to the other characters, and affords to the poet a device by which the real actors become articulate. The story ends with the reappearance, after a couple of years, of Quick: in the meantime Talifer has married Althea, who has by him a child. Although Quick himself has tried to participate in life by taking Karen off to a "cottage in Wales," his return witnesses his failure. But he is not much affected by it. He proceeds to analyze for Althea and Talifer the true basis of their love, which is thoroughly commonplace after a good deal of romantic pretense.

Mr. Robinson's style in the new poem is uniform with the style of its predecessors; it is neither better nor worse than the style of *The Glory of the Nightingales* or of *Cav-*

ender's House. It requires constant reviewing by Mr. Robinson's admirers to keep these poems distinct; at a distance they lose outline; blur into one another. They constitute a single complete poem that the poet has not succeeded in writing, a poem around which these indistinct narratives have been written.

We get, in them all, a character doomed to defeat, or a character who, when the tale opens, is a failure in the eyes of his town, but who wins a secret moral victory, as in *The Man Who Died Twice.* But Talifer, whose ego betrays him into an emotional life that he cannot understand, is not quite defeated. The tragic solution of his problem being thus rejected by Mr. Robinson, and replaced by a somewhat awkward bit of domestic irony, Talifer at first sight appears to be a new kind of Robinsonian character. Yet the novelty, I think, lies in the appearance. For Talifer is the standard Robinsonian character grown weary of the tragic sentiment, accepting at last the fact that his tilt at fate had less intensity than he supposed, and

> with grateful ears
> That were attuned again to pleasant music
> Heard nothing but the mellow bells of peace.

That is the Tennysonian end of the poem.

I have remarked that the character of Karen is vaguely conceived, with the result that Talifer's relation to her is incomprehensible. Those mellow bells of peace are therefore a little hollow in sound, for their ring is as inexplicable as the noisy chaos of the erudite Karen, upon whose prior significance they entirely depend. The plot, in brief, lacks internal necessity. And the domestic peace of the conclusion remains arbitrary, in spite of Mr. Robinson's efforts through his mouthpiece, Doctor Quick, to point it up with some sly irony at the end. The irony is external—as if Mr. Robinson had not been able to tell the story for what it was, and had to say: This is what life is really like, a simple wife and a child—while ring those bells of peace that would be romantically tiresome if one had tragic dignity.

Mr. Robinson's genius is primarily lyrical; that is to say, he seldom achieves a success in a poem where the idea exceeds the span of a single emotion. It is, I think, significant that in his magnificent "The Mill" the tragic reference sustains the emotion of the poem: his narrative verse yields but a few moments of drama that are swiftly dispersed by the dry casuistry of the commentary. The early "Richard Cory" is a perfect specimen of Mr. Robinson's dramatic powers— when those powers are lyrically expressed; similarly "Luke Havergal," a poem in which the hard images glow in a fierce intensity of light, is one of the great recent lyrics:

> No, there is not a dawn in eastern skies
> To rift the fiery night that's in your eyes;
> But there, where western glooms are gathering
> The dark will end the dark, if anything . . .

Mr. Van Doren is the first critic to appreciate this peculiarly Robinsonian legerdemain with figures of light.

It is probable that the explanation of the popular success of *Tristram*, and of most of Mr. Robinson's narratives, lies in our loss of the dramatic instinct. It is a loss increasingly great since the rise of middle-class comedy in the eighteenth century. Since then, in the serious play, instead of the tragic hero whose downfall is deeply involved with his suprahuman relations, we get the romantic, sentimental hero whose problem is chiefly one of adjustment to society, on the one hand, and, on the other, one of futile self-assertion in the realm of the personal ego. Mr. Robinson's Talifer exhibits both these phases of the modern sensibility: he plays with his ego in the irrational marriage with Karen, and he later sees his difficulty strictly in terms of a social institution, or of social adjustment, in the marriage with Althea, who, of course, represents "truth."

The dramatic treatment of the situation Mr. Robinson permits himself to neglect; for the dramatic approach would have demanded the possession, by the hero, of a comprehensive moral scheme. He would have rigorously applied the scheme to his total conduct, with the result that it would have broken somewhere and thrown the hero into a tragic dilemma, from which it had been impossible for him to escape. The story as it is told is hardly more than anecdotal; Mr. Robinson turns his plot, at the end, into an easy joke about the deliquescent effects of marriage upon the pretensions of human nature.

It is one of the anomalies of contemporary literature that Mr. Robinson, who has given us a score of great lyrics, should continue to produce these long narrative poems, one after another, until the reader can scarcely tell them apart. We may only guess the reason for this. Our age provides for the poet no epos or myth, no pattern of well-understood behavior, which the poet may examine in the strong light of his own experience. For it is chiefly those times that prefer one kind of conduct to another, times that offer to the poet a seasoned code, which have produced the greatest dramatic literature. Drama depends for clarity and form upon the existence of such a code. It matters little whether it is a code for the realization of good, like Antigone's; or a code for evil like Macbeth's. The important thing is that it shall tell the poet how people try to behave, and that it shall be too perfect, whether in good or in evil, for human nature. The poet seizes one set of terms within the code—for example, feudal ambition in Macbeth—and shows that the hero's faulty application of the perfect code to his own conduct is doomed to failure. By adhering strictly to the code, the poet exhibits a typical action. The tension between the code and the hero makes the action specific, unique; the code is at once broken up and affirmed, the hero's resistance at once clarified and defined by the limits thus set to his conduct. Macbeth asserts his ego in terms of the code before him, not in terms of courtly love or of the idealism of the age of Werther: he has no choice of code. The modern character has the liberty of indefinite choice, but not the good fortune to be chosen, as Macbeth and Antigone were.

Mr. Robinson has no epos, myth, or code, no suprahuman truth, to tell him what the terminal points of human conduct are, in this age; so he goes over the same ground, again and again, writing a poem that will not be written.

It has been said by T. S. Eliot that the best lyric poetry of our time is dramatic, that it is good because it is dramatic. It is at least a tenable notion that the dramatic instinct, after the Restoration and down to our own time, survived best in the lyric poets. With the disappearance of general patterns of conduct, the power to depict action that is both single and complete also disappears. The dramatic genius of the poet is held to short flights, and the dramatic lyric is a fragment of a total action which the poet lacks the means to sustain.

It is to be hoped that Mr. Robinson will again exercise his dramatic genius where it has a chance for success: in lyrics. Meanwhile it would be no less disastrous to Mr. Robinson's later fame than to our critical standards, should we admire him too abjectly to examine him. Let him then escape the indignity of Hardy's later years when such a piece of bad verse as "Any Little Old Song" won egregious applause all over the British Isles. That Mr. Robinson is unable to write badly will not excuse us to posterity.

1933

John Peale Bishop

OF THE American poets whose first books were published between 1918 and 1929 not more than six or seven are likely to keep their reputations until the end of the present decade. Eliot and Pound are prewar. Crane, Marianne Moore, Stevens, MacLeish, and Ransom are among the slightly more than half a dozen. The two or three other places may be disputed; but I take it that since 1929 there has been no new name unless it be that of a young man, James Agee, whose first volume appeared in 1934. John Peale Bishop, whose first poetry goes back to the war period but whose first book, *Now with His Love*,[1] came out in 1932, will, I believe, rank among the best poets of the last decade.

His position has been anomalous. His contemporaries made their reputations in a congenial critical atmosphere, and they have been able to carry over a certain prestige into virtually a new age. (Ages crowd upon one another in a country that has never been young.) But Bishop has lacked that advantage. The first criticism accorded him was largely of the Marxist school. Mr. Horace Gregory, shrewdly discerning the poet's technical skill, became quickly concerned about the sincerity of a man who ignored the "class struggle." Bishop was not, in fact, asked whether he was a poet but whether he expected to survive capitalism: whether given

---

[1] Bishop's first book, *Green Fruit*, a collection of undergraduate verse, appeared in 1917. See *The Collected Poems of John Peale Bishop* (New York, 1948). Bishop was born in 1892 and died in 1944.

his roots in the war generation and the prejudices of the "ruling class," he could hope to achieve the portage over to the "main stream" of American letters recently discovered by Mr. Granville Hicks.

The problems of poetry must necessarily be the same in all ages, but no two ages come to the same solutions. Happiest is that age which, like the age of Sidney and Spenser, felt no need to reduce the problems to ultimate philosophical terms: our critical apparatus is immeasurably more thorough than theirs, our poetic performance appreciably looser. But our problems are inevitably theirs. They are the problem of language and the problem of form. The Elizabethan solution was practical, not speculative. The simple didacticism of the neo-classical Renaissance was as far as the sixteenth century got philosophically. The poets wrote better than they knew. Our knowledge is better than our performance.

In ages weak in form, such as our own age, theory will concentrate upon form, but practice upon the ultimate possibilities of language. Ages that create great varieties of forms, as the Elizabethans did in every branch of poetry, talk about language but actually take it for granted, and score their greatest triumphs with form. The powers of the language were not in the long run determined by theory, but instinctively by poets whose dominating passion was form: the language was determined by the demands of the subject. The more comprehensive the subject, the broader the symbolism, and the more profoundly relevant the scheme of reference to the whole human experience, the richer the language became. The experiment with language as such is *The Shepherd's Calendar,* and it is a failure; but even there the poet attempts only to enlarge his vocabulary with archaic words for "poetical" effect. There is no trace of that forcing of language beyond its natural limits that we find in modern verse. Propriety of diction was the problem, and it was ably discussed by Puttenham in his long *Arte of English Poesie,* a work in some respects comparable to *The Principles of Literary Criticism* by Mr. I. A. Richards, who talks not about the propriety of language but about its ultimate meaning. He thus leaves behind him language as an instrument and, by going into the *kinds* of meaning, converts the discussion into the peculiarly modern problem of form. For form is meaning and nothing but meaning: scheme of reference, supporting symbolism that ceases to support as soon as it is recognized as merely that.

Metrics as a phase of the problem of form needs attention from modern critics. It is a subject poorly understood. It is usually treated as an air-tight compartment of technical speculation. Yet surely a metrical pattern is usable only so long as it is attached to some usable form. It is a curious fact that modern metrics reflects the uncertainty of modern poets in the realm of forms. So the modern poet, struggling to get hold of some kind of meaning, breaks his head against the *impasse* of form, and when he finds no usable form he finds that he has available no metrical system either. For those fixed and, to us, external properties of poetry, rhyme and metrical pattern, are, in the ages of their invention, indeed fixed but not external. It is probable that there is an intimate relation between a generally accepted "picture of the world" and the general acceptance of a metrical system and its differentiations into patterns.

This is to say that the separate arts achieve their special formalisms out of a common center of experience. And from this center of experience, this reference of meaning, any single art will make differentiations within itself: epic, lyric, tragedy, comedy, each with its appropriate pattern of development. When the center of life disappears, the arts of poetry become the art of poetry. And in an advanced stage of the evil, in the nineteenth century and today, we get the *mélange des genres,* one art living off another, which the late Irving Babbitt so valiantly combated without having understood the influences that had brought it about. Painting tries to be music; poetry leans upon painting; all the arts "strive toward the condition of music"; till at last seeing the mathematical structure of music, the arts become geometrical and abstract, and destroy themselves.

The specialization of scientific techniques supplanting a central view of life has, as Mr. John Crowe Ransom showed in a recent essay,[2] tended to destroy the formal arts: poetry has in turn become a specialization of aesthetic effects without formal limitations. And, as Mr. Edmund Wilson has argued,[3] the novel now does the work formerly done by epic and tragedy, forms too "limited" and "artificial" for modern minds. The novel is the least formal of the literary arts; it rose, in fact, upon the débris of the *genres;* and it has been able to drive the formal literary arts from the public interest because, appealing to the ordinary sense of reality fostered by information, science, and journalism, the novelist neither sets forth symbolic fictions nor asks the reader to observe formal limitations.

The poet then at this time must ask, not what limitations he will be pleased, after the manner of the young Milton, to accept, but whether there are any that he can get. I assume that a poet is a man eager to come under the bondage of limitations if he can find them. As I understand John Peale Bishop's poetry, he is that eager man. It is a moral problem, but that phase I cannot touch here. Bishop has no settled metrics; but that too is an aspect of the formal problem that cannot be discussed in the limited space of a note.

It has been said that Bishop has imitated all the chief modern poets. He has virtually conducted his poetical education in public. But the observation is double-edged. In our age of personal expression the poet gets credit for what is "his own": the art is not the thing, but rather the informa-

---

[2] "Poets Without Laurels," first published in 1935; reprinted in *The World's Body, op. cit.,* pp. 55–75.
[3] "Is Verse a Dying Technique?" *The Triple Thinkers* (New York, 1938), pp. 20–41.

tion conveyed about a unique personality. Applauding a poet only for what is uniquely his own, we lose thereby much that is good. If a poem in Yeats's manner appears in Bishop's book, and is as good as Yeats's, it is as good there as it is anywhere else.

More than most living poets Bishop has felt the lack of a central source of form. He is not the poet of personal moods and idle sensation. He constantly strives for formal structure. He has studied closely the poets of his time who, like Yeats, seem to have achieved, out of a revived or invented mythology or by means of a consciously restricted point of view, a working substitute for the supernatural myth and the concentration that myth makes possible. It is, I think, interesting to observe that in Bishop two contemporary influences, Yeats and Eliot, meet strongly, and meet only in him of all the contemporary poets whom I know anything about: Yeats for form, Eliot for the experiment in language. Only the best Yeats is better than this:

> And Mooch of the bull-red
> Hair who had so many dears
> Enjoyed to the core
> And Newlin who hadn't one
> To answer his shy desire
> Are blanketed in the mould
> Dead in the long war.
> And I who have most reason
> Remember them only when the sun
> Is at his dullest season.

It is not necessary to illustrate the early influence of Eliot, for it appears everywhere in *Now with His Love*. I will quote two poems that are harder to "place." To critics interested in poetry as private property it may be said that they are evidently his own. The poems—they must be read as carefully climaxed wholes—seem to me to be among the most successful in modern verse:

THE RETURN

Night and we heard heavy and cadenced hoofbeats
Of troops departing: the last cohorts left
By the North Gate. That night some listened late
Leaning their eyelids toward Septentrion.

Morning flared and the young tore down the trophies
And warring ornaments: arches were strong
And in the sun but stone; no longer conquests
Circled our columns; all our state was down

In fragments. In the dust, old men with tufted
Eyebrows whiter than sunbaked faces, gulped
As it fell. But they no more than we remembered
The old sea-fights, the soldiers' names and sculptors'

We did not know the end was coming: nor why
It came; only that long before the end
Were many wanted to die. Then vultures starved
And sailed more slowly in the sky.

We still had taxes. Salt was high. The soldiers
Gone. Now there was much drinking and lewd
Houses all night loud with riot. But only
For a time. Soon the taverns had no roofs.

Strangely it was the young the almost boys
Who first abandoned hope; the old still lived
A little, at last a little lived in eyes.
It was the young whose child did not survive.

Some slept beneath the simulacra, until
The gods' faces froze. Then was fear.
Some had response in dreams, but morning restored
Interrogation. Then O then, O ruins!

Temples of Neptune invaded by the sea
And dolphins streaked like streams sportive
As sunlight rode and over the rushing floors
The sea unfurled and what was blue raced silver.

The poem avoids the difficulty of form by leaning upon a
certain violence of language. The form of "The Return" is

a very general idea about the fall of Rome. The implications of the form are not wide; and it is a typical modern form in that it offers a rough parallelism with the real subject— which in this poem is modern civilization—and not a direct approach to the subject. Where shall the poet get a form that will permit him to make direct, comprehensive statements about modern civilization? Doubtless nowhere. As a feat of historical insight the "form" of "The Return" is common-place; yet the poem is distinguished. The poet has manipulated language into painting. The line "Temples of Neptune invaded by the sea" is by no means the same as its prose paraphrase: civilizations die of an excess of the quality that made them great; we, too, shall perish when we no longer have the temple of Neptune, the form, to preserve us from the limitless energy of the sea, which the form held in check. But "Rome" is here not a symbol of anything; our inferences about modern civilization are obvious, but they are not authorized by the poem. "The poem," writes Bishop, "is a simile in which one term of the comparison is omitted." It is rather that by means of a new grasp of language, very different from the "word-painting" of eighteenth-century nature poetry, the poet achieves a plastic objectivity that to some degree liberates him from the problem of finding a structural background of idea.

What I have said about "The Return" applies with even greater force to "Perspectives Are Precipices":

> *Sister Anne, Sister Anne,*
> *Do you see anybody coming?*
>
>> I see a distance of black yews
>> Long as the history of the Jews
>>
>> I see a road sunned with white sand
>> Wide plains surrounding silence. And
>>
>> Far off, a broken colonnade
>> That overthrows the sun in shade.

Sister Anne, Sister Anne,
Do you see nobody coming?

      A man
Upon that road a man who goes
Dragging a shadow by its toes.

Diminishing he goes, head bare
Of any covering even hair.

A pitcher depending from one hand
Goes mouth down. And dry is sand

Sister Anne, Sister Anne,
What do you see?

His dwindling stride. And he seems blind
Or worse to the prone man behind.

Sister Anne! Sister Anne!

I see a road. Beyond nowhere
Defined by cirrus and blue air.

I saw a man but he is gone
His shadow gone into the sun.

    This poem I would cite as the perfect example of certain
effects of painting achieved in poetry. Criticism of this kind
of poetry must necessarily be tentative. Yet I think it is plain
that this particular poem has not only the immediate effect
of a modern abstract painting; it gives the illusion of perspective, of objects-in-the-round. Take the "road sunned with
white sand"—instead of "sunlight on a sandy road," the normal word structure for this image. Even more striking is
"Wide plains surrounding silence." I leave it to the schoolmen, wherever they are, to decide whether "silence" is commonly abstract or concrete; yet it is certain that in Bishop's
phrase it acquires a spatial, indeed almost sensory, value that
would have been sacrificed had he written: "silence over the
surrounding plains."

    It is worth remarking here that the line, "Long as the history of the Jews," is the only clear example of "metaphysical wit" that I have been able to find in Bishop's verse. It is possibly a direct adaptation of a passage from Marvell:

> And you should if you please refuse
> Till the conversion of the Jews.

Bishop's line is the more striking for its isolation in his work, but I think it is clearly a violation of the plastic technique of the poem, and a minor blemish. The influence of Eliot, which could lead two ways, to the metaphysicals and to the symbolists, led Bishop almost exclusively to the latter. And he has perfected this kind of poetry in English perhaps more than any other writer.

It is an obscure subject: the Horatian formula *ut pictura poesis* bore fruit long before Hérédia and Gautier—as early, in English verse, as Milton. But the mixtures of the *genres* acquired a new significance after the late nineteenth-century French poets began to push the borders of one sense over into another. It was not merely that the poet should be allowed to paint pictures with words—that much the Horatian phrase allowed. It was rather that the new "correspondences" among the five senses multiplied the senses and extended the medium of one art into the medium of another. Rimbaud's absurd sonnet on the colors of the vowels was the extreme statement of an experiment that achieved, in other poets and in Rimbaud's own "Bateau Ivre," brilliant results. But the process cannot go on beyond our generation unless we are willing to accept the eventual destruction of the arts. There is no satisfactory substitute in poetry for the form-symbol.

It is on this dilemma of symbolic form or plastic form that Bishop is intelligent and instructive. He has recently written: "I am trying to make more and more *statements,* without giving up all that we have gained since Rimbaud." The difficulty could not be more neatly put. Two recent poems, "The

Saints" and "Holy Nativity," are the result of this effort. The statement is form, the fixed point of reference; "all that we have gained since Rimbaud" is the enrichment of language that we have gained to offset our weakness in form.

The new experiment of Bishop's is not complete. In "Holy Nativity" the attempt to use the Christian myth collapses with a final glance at anthropology:

> Eagle, swan or dove
> White bull or cloud . . .

His treatment of the supernatural, the attempt to replace our secular philosophy, in which he does not believe, with a vision of the divine, in which he tries to believe, is an instance of our modern unbelieving belief. We are so constituted as to see our experience in two says. We are not so constituted as to see it two ways indefinitely without peril. Until we can see it in one way we shall not see it as a whole, and until we see it as a whole we shall not see it as poets. Every road is long, and all roads lead to the problem of form.

1935

MacLeish's *Conquistador*

MR. MACLEISH has been up to this time a poet like most of his contemporaries, limited to the short flight. There is, in his earlier work, no premonitory sounding of the finely sustained tone of *Conquistador*.[1] For modern poetry the poem is long. It is an epic in miniature of about two thousand lines. In versification and style, and with respect to the narrational "point of view," there is no other poem in English with which as a whole it may be compared. It is evident, of course, that MacLeish has studied Ezra Pound; but this is no disparagement of Pound's pupil. The *Cantos* are full of technical instruction for the poet who knows what he needs to learn. The followers of Eliot take his "philosophy" as well as his style, and give us work of "lower intensity" than the original. Pound's disciples are either less plausible or more independent. They exercise thinly with Mr. Dudley Fitts or practice the admirable craft of *Conquistador*.

The background of the poem is the conquest of Mexico. For a complete history of the conquest one will have to go to the historians. The poem is a reconstruction of the part played by one of the lesser heroes, Bernal Diaz del Castillo, who as an old man wrote his own story in resentment against the official histories by Gomara and others—

> The quilled professors: the taught tongues of fame:
> What have they written of us: the poor soldiers . . .

[1] Archibald MacLeish, *Conquistador* (Boston, 1932).

They call the towns for the kings that bear no scars:
They keep the names of the great for time to stare at—
The bishops rich men generals cocks-at-arms . . .

Bernal tells the story in flashes of recollection that have just enough narrative progression to give to the narrator a constantly new field of imagery. But the historical pattern of the conquest is never explicit, never obtrusive enough to take the reader's attention from the personality of Bernal and the quality of his character. For the personality of Bernal is the subject of the poem.

Thus narrowing the action down to the focus of a single mind and what it saw, MacLeish disposes of two enormous difficulties of epic poetry: he eliminates the objective detail of the total scene, at once the conventional privilege and the burden of the classical poet; and he dispenses with the need of cosmic machinery. There is no external "idea"; there is no theme; there is no "typical action."

We get the peculiarly modern situation: the personality of one man is dramatized against an historical setting. "What have they written of us: the poor soldiers"—what can the private sensibility get out of history to sustain it? What can Bernal get out of his past? Nothing appears in the story that Bernal did not see; it is all enriched by memory. Although Bernal announces his subject as "That which I have myself seen and the fighting," there is little fighting; there is little action; for the dramatic tension of the poem grows out of the narrator-hero's fear of death upon the gradual disappearance of sensation. The dramatic quality of the poem—a quality that has little to do with the story as such—lies thus in the hero's anxiety to recover his sensuous early years, upon which his identity as a person, and hence his life, depends.

This is the subject of the poem. The "meaning" of the poem is an implicit quality of Bernal's mind, but only a little logical violence will isolate it. It is the futility of individual action. For unless the hero, in his old age, can recapture the sensation of action, the action itself must fade into the obscure shuffle of abstract history. We have seen that Bernal cannot accept the public versions of the conquest. (Is Bernal, then, a soldier of the sixteenth century or of the first World War?) He cannot identify the moment of action with the ostensible common purpose for which the whole series of events took place. He is confined to memories, to the mechanism of sensation.

I dwell upon this "meaning" of *Conquistador* for two reasons. It obviously, in the first place, explains the form in which MacLeish found it necessary to cast his narrative, a form that I have briefly described; the necessity of this form explains the presence, I believe, of those features of the style that MacLeish borrowed from Pound and perfected. And, secondly, the meaning of this distinguished poem, as I apprehend it, may lead some of the younger critics to reconsider, not their enthusiasm for the workmanship, which it richly deserves, but their hasty acceptance of its "philosophy." It is a mistake to suppose that MacLeish has offered a "way out" of the introspective indecision of the school of T. S. Eliot, affirming a faith in heroic action against the moral paralysis presumably suffered by the best minds of that older generation. Not only is there, in the poem, a lack of belief in any kind of action that we might imitate; the poet does not feel much interest in the action implied by the reminiscences that support the narrative.

There is not one moment of action rendered objectively in the entire poem. There is constantly and solely the pattern of sensation that surrounded the moment of action—the fringe of the physical shock and awareness that survive in memory. The technique of rendering this special quality of memory is MacLeish's contribution to poetic style:

Gold there on that shore on the evening sand—
"Colua" they said: pointing on toward the sunset:
They made a sign on the air with their solemn hands . . .

And that voyage it was we came to the Island:
Well I remember the shore and the sound of that place
And the smoke smell on the dunes and the wind dying.

Well I remember the walls and the rusty taste of the
New-spilled blood in the air: many among us
Seeing the priests with their small arrogant faces . . .

Ah how the throat of a girl and girl's arms are
Bright in the riding sun and the young sky
And the green year of our lives where the willows are!

This clarity of sensuous reminiscence that suffuses the poem
is a new quality in American verse. The images are not imbedded in metaphor; they exist spatially in the round. Pound
supplied the model:

> Eyes brown topaz,
> Brookwater over brown sand,
> The white hounds on the slope,
> Glide of water, lights on the prore,
> Silver beaks out of night,
> Stone, bough over bough, lamps fluid in water,
> Pine by the black trunk of its shadow
> The trees melted in air.

The images are impersonal, objective, and timeless, detached from Pound's moral position. The focus of MacLeish's
imagery is personal: the image exists in terms of Bernal's
recovery of memory, of his struggle for personal identity. Its
precision has been disciplined in the workshop of Ezra
Pound, whose quality of floating clarity is localized by Mac-
Leish in a Browningesque monologue, where the casuistry
gives way to a sophisticated version of the *chanson de geste.*

Poets in this age cannot set forth with security a conscious

Ezra Pound

. . . and as for text we have taken it
from that of Messire Laurentius
and from a codex once of the Lords Malatesta. . . .

I

ONE IS NOT certain who Messire Laurentius was; one is not
very certain that it makes no difference. Yet one takes comfort in the vast range of Mr. Pound's obscure learning, which
no one man could be expected to know much about. In his
great work [1] one is continually uncertain, as to space, time,
history. The codex of the Lords Malatesta is less disconcerting than Laurentius; for more than half of the first thirty
cantos contain long paraphrases or garbled quotations from
the correspondence, public and private, of the Renaissance
Italians, chiefly Florentine and Venetian. About a third of
the lines are versified documents. Another third are classical
allusions, esoteric quotations from the ancients, fragments of
the Greek poets with bits of the Romans thrown in; all magnificently written into Mr. Pound's own text. The rest is
contemporary—anecdotes, satirical pictures of vulgar Americans, obscene stories, evenings in low Meriterranean dives,
and gossip about intrigants behind the scenes of European
power. The three kinds of material in the *Cantos* are antiquity, the Renaissance, and the modern world. They are

[1] Ezra Pound, *A Draft of XXX Cantos* (New York, 1930).

364

combined on no principle that seems in the least consistent to a first glance. They appear to be mixed in an incoherent jumble, or to stand up in puzzling contrasts.

This is the poetry which, in early and incomplete editions, has had more influence on us than any other of our time; it has had an immense "underground" reputation. And deservedly. For even the early reader of Mr. Pound could not fail to detect the presence of a new poetic form in the individual cantos, though the full value and intention of this form appears for the first time in the complete work. It is not that there is any explicit feature of the whole design that is not contained in each canto; it is simply that Mr. Pound must be read in bulk. It is only then that the great variety of his style and the apparent incoherence turn into implicit order and form. There is no other poetry like the *Cantos* in English. And there is none quite so simple in form. The form is in fact so simple that almost no one has guessed it, and I suppose it will continue to puzzle, perhaps to enrage, our more academic critics for a generation to come. But this form by virtue of its simplicity remains inviolable to critical terms: even now it cannot be technically described.

I begin to talk like Mr. Pound, or rather in the way in which most readers think Mr. Pound writes. The secret of his form is this: conversation. The *Cantos* are talk, talk, talk; not by anyone in particular to anyone else in particular; they are just rambling talk. At least each canto is a cunningly devised imitation of a casual conversation in which no one presses any subject very far. The length of breath, the span of conversational energy, is the length of a canto. The conversationalist pauses; there is just enough unfinished business left hanging in the air to give him a new start; so that the transitions between the cantos are natural and easy.

Each canto has the broken flow and the somewhat elusive climax of a good monologue: because there is no single speaker, it is a many-voiced monologue. That is the method

of the poems—though there is another quality of the form
that I must postpone for a moment—*and that is what the
poems are about.*

There are, as I have said, three subjects of conversation—
ancient times, Renaissance Italy, and the present—but these
are not what the *Cantos* are about. They are not about Italy,
nor about Greece, nor are they about us. They are not about
anything. But they are distinguished verse. Mr. Pound himself tells us:

> And they want to know what we talked about? *"de litteris et
>   de armis, praestantibus ingeniis,*
> Both of ancient times and our own; books, arms,
> And men of unusual genius
> Both of ancient times and our own, in short the usual subjects
> Of conversation between intelligent men."

I I

There is nothing in the *Cantos* more difficult than that.
There is nothing inherently obscure; nothing too profound
for any reader who has enough information to get to the
background of the allusions in a learned conversation. But
there is something that no reader, short of some years of
hard textual study, will understand. This is the very heart
of the *Cantos,* the secret of Mr. Pound's poetic character,
which will only gradually emerge from a detailed analysis of
every passage. And this is no more than our friends are
constantly demanding of us. We hear them talk, and we return to hear them talk, we return to hear them again, but
we never know what they talk about; we return for the
mysterious quality of charm that has no rational meaning
that we can define. It is only after a long time that the
order, the direction, the rhythm of the talker's mind, the
logic of his character as distinguished from anything logical
he may say—it is a long time before this begins to take on
form for us. So with Mr. Pound's *Cantos.* It is doubtless

easier for us (who are trained in the more historic brands of poetry) when the poems are about God, Freedom, and Immortality, but there is no reason why poetry should not be so perplexingly simple as Mr. Pound's, and be about nothing at all.

The ostensible subjects of the *Cantos*—ancient, middle, and modern times—are only the materials round which Mr. Pound's mind plays constantly; they are the screen upon which he throws a flowing quality of poetic thought. Now in conversation the memorable quality is a sheer accident of character, and is not designed; but in the *Cantos* the effect is deliberate, and from the first canto to the thirtieth the set tone is maintained without a lapse.

It is this tone, it is this quality quite simply which is the meaning of the *Cantos,* and although, as I have said, it is simple and direct, it is just as hard to pin down, it is as hidden in its shifting details, as a running, ever-changing conversation. It cannot be taken out of the text; and yet the special way that Mr. Pound has of weaving his three materials together, of emphasizing them, of comparing and contrasting them, gives us a clue to the leading intention of the poems. I come to that quality of the form which I postponed.

The easiest interpretation of all poetry is the allegorical: there are few poems that cannot be paraphrased into a kind of symbolism, which is usually false, being by no means the chief intention of the poet. It is very probable, therefore, that I am about to falsify the true simplicity of the *Cantos* into a simplicity that is merely convenient and spurious. The reader must bear this in mind, and view the slender symbolism that I am going to read into the *Cantos* as a critical shorthand, useful perhaps, but which when used must be dropped.

One of the finest *Cantos* is properly the first. It describes a voyage:

And then went down to the ship,
Set keel to breakers, forth on the godly sea, and
We set up mast and sail on that swart ship,
Bore sheep aboard her, and our bodies also
Heavy with weeping, and winds from sternward
Bore us out onward with bellying canvas,
Circe's this craft, the trim-coifed goddess.

They land, having come "to the place aforesaid by Circe"—
whatever place it may be—and Tiresias appears, who says:

"Odysseus
Shall return through spiteful Neptune, over dark seas,
Lose all companions." And then Anticlea came.
Lie quiet Divus. I mean, that is, Andreas Divus,
In officina Wecheli, 1538, out of Homer.
And he sailed, by Sirens and thence outward and away
And unto Circe.

Mr. Pound's world is the scene of a great Odyssey, and
everywhere he lands it is the shore of Circe, where men
"lose all companions" and are turned into swine. It would
not do at all to push this hint too far, but I will risk one
further point: Mr. Pound is a typically modern, rootless,
and internationalized intelligence. In the place of the traditional supernaturalism of the older and local cultures, he has
a cosmopolitan curiosity that seeks out marvels, which are all
equally marvelous, whether it be a Greek myth or the antics
in Europe of a lady from Kansas. He has the bright, cosmopolitan *savoir faire* which refuses to be "taken in": he will
not believe, being a traditionalist at bottom, that the "per-
verts, who have set money-lust before the pleasures of the
senses," are better than swine. And ironically, being modern
and a hater of modernity, he sees all history as deformed by
the trim-coifed goddess.

The *Cantos* are a book of marvels—marvels that he has
read about, or heard of, or seen; there are Greek myths, tales

of Italian feuds, meetings with strange people, rumors of intrigues of state, memories of remarkable dead friends like T. E. Hulme, comments on philosophical problems, harangues on abuses of the age; the "usual subjects of conversation between intelligent men."

It is all fragmentary. Now nearly every canto begins with a bit of heroic antiquity, some myth, or classical quotation, or a lovely piece of lyrical description in a grand style. It invariably breaks down. It trails off into a piece of contemporary satire, or a flat narrative of the rascality of some Italian prince. This is the special quality of Mr. Pound's form, the essence of his talk, the direction of these magnificent conversations.

For not once does Mr. Pound give himself up to any single story or myth. The thin symbolism from the Circe myth is hardly more than a leading tone, an unconscious prejudice about men which he is not willing to indicate beyond the barest outline. He cannot believe in myths, much less in his own power of imagining them out to a conclusion. None of his myths is compelling enough to draw out his total intellectual resources; none goes far enough to become a belief or even a momentary fiction. They remain marvels to be looked at, but they are meaningless, the wrecks of civilization. His powerful juxtapositions of the ancient, the Renaissance, and the modern worlds reduce all three elements to an unhistorical miscellany, timeless and without origin, and no longer a force in the lives of men.

I I I

And that is the peculiarly modern quality of Mr. Pound. There is a certain likeness in this to another book of marvels, stories of antiquity known to us as *The Golden Ass*. The *Cantos* are a sort of *Golden Ass*. There is a likeness, but there is no parallel beyond the mere historical one: both books are the productions of worlds without convictions and given over to a hard pragmatism. Here the similarity ends. For Mr. Pound is a powerful reactionary, a faithful mind devoted to those ages when the myths were not merely pretty, but true. And there is a cloud of melancholy irony hanging over the *Cantos.* He is persuaded that the myths are only beautiful, and he drops them after a glimpse, but he is not reconciled to this aestheticism: he ironically puts the myths against the ugly specimens of modern life that have defeated them. But neither are the specimens of modernity worthy of the dignity of belief:

> She held that a sonnet was a sonnet
> And ought never to be destroyed
> And had taken a number of courses
> And continued with hope of degrees and
> Ended in a Baptist learnery
>   Somewhere near the Rio Grande.

I am not certain that Mr. Pound will agree with me that he is a traditionalist; nor am I convinced that Mr. Pound, for his part, is certain of anything but his genius for poetry. He is probably one of two or three living Americans who will be remembered as poets of the first order. Yet there is no reason to infer from that that Mr. Pound, outside his craft (or outside his written conversation) knows in the least what he is doing or saying. He is and always has been in a muddle of revolution; and for some appalling reason he identifies his crusade with liberty—liberty of speech, liberty of press, liberty of conduct—in short, liberty. I do not mean to say that either Mr. Pound or his critic knows what liberty is. Nevertheless, Mr. Pound identifies it with civilization and intelligence of the modern and scientific variety. And yet the ancient cultures, which he so much admires, were, from any modern viewpoint, hatched in barbarism and superstition. One is entitled to the suspicion that Mr. Pound prefers barbarism, and that by taking up the role of revolution against it he has bitten off his nose to spite his face. He is the confirmed enemy of provincialism, never suspecting that his favorite, Lorenzo the Magnificent, for example, was provincial to the roots of his hair.

The confusion runs through the *Cantos*. It makes the irony that I have spoken of partly unconscious. For as the apostle of humane culture, he constantly discredits it by crying up a rationalistic enlightenment. It would appear from this that his philosophical tact is somewhat feminine, and that, as intelligence, it does not exist. His poetic intelligence is of the finest: and if he doesn't know what liberty is, he understands poetry, and how to write it. This is enough for one man to know. And the first thirty *Cantos* are enough to occupy a loving and ceaseless study—say a canto a year for thirty years, all thirty to be read every few weeks just for the tone.

1931

Herbert Read[1]

I FIRST MET Herbert Read in the autumn of 1928 at one of the "Criterion luncheons" in London (the same day I first saw T. S. Eliot), to which I had been taken by F. V. Morley, a friend of both these men who were to become my lifelong friends. Read and I were more nearly of an age and became friends as soon as his Yorkshire shyness allowed; this took a little time; but the twelve years between Mr. Eliot and myself were like the Grand Canyon that only after some years seemed to silt up until it was no wider than the Potomac above Washington; that is to say, about the width of the Mason and Dixon Line. I am sure that Mr. Eliot would not mind my saying that thirty-five years ago I felt closer to rural Yorkshire and to Herbert's grandmother, Jane Tate, than to Cousin Nancy Ellicott and the *Boston Evening Transcript.* I confess that in those days regional symbols did not occur to me: they will do now for something I may have felt then. What I definitely felt, and felt very strongly, was the originality and power of two books by Herbert Read: *Reason and Romanticism* (London, 1926) and *Collected Poems 1913– 1925* (London, 1926). These books had a crucial effect upon me.

In the two or three years preceding 1928 I had read Herbert Read's reviews in *The Criterion;* early in 1927 I read

1 This essay was originally published as the Foreword in Herbert Read, *Se- lected Writings: Poetry and Criticism* (London, 1963; New York, 1964). It has been amplified. Both Read and Eliot were living when I wrote the essay, but I have not changed the tense of my references to them.

372

in that journal Mr. Eliot's review of *Reason and Romanticism* and of Ramon Fernandez's *Messages*. The review was a detailed comparison of Read and Fernandez, somewhat to the advantage of the latter, whose critical theory Mr. Eliot found the more "coherent." At that time I was reviewing French books for a New York trade journal, and I had read *Messages*. I soon found a copy of *Reason and Romanticism* and read it—to the advantage of Read. Here was a young man (he was scarcely more than thirty) who was struggling with a problem which one now knows would engage him the rest of his life: the synthesis of romantic intuition and intellectual order. (When the word "problem" came into literary criticism I do not know—possibly from mathematics or economics.) My own "problem" at that time—it probably still is—was Read's intuition and/or order. It is a problem the solution of which, unlike mathematical solutions, cannot go beyond the intelligence of one's awareness of it.

Read's awareness has steadily increased over more than forty years. Starting with the Coleridgean theory of "organicism," he has assimilated to the original doctrine a large number of insights from later philosophers, particularly Kierkegaard, Lipps, Worringer, and Bergson; and after these, T. E. Hulme and Jean-Paul Sartre. These writers have contributed to Read's defense of the romantic "cult of sincerity," but at the level of metaphysics. I am not prepared to judge how well this metaphysical eclecticism has been achieved; yet it must be acknowledged that no other Anglo-American critic of our time has pursued with greater devotion, learning, and profundity a single theory of the arts. A capital point about Read's criticism that has been ignored or overlooked is the consistency of his performance; one may here and there question his placing of certain writers—Hulme, for example—in the tradition of Coleridge; but there can be no doubt that he has extended the poetics of the master far beyond any horizon that the master could see. This has been due to an historical advantage; for Read knows what Coleridge knew plus what Coleridge could not have known: (1) Coleridge himself and (2) the development by Freud and Jung of certain ideas of Coleridge that foreshadowed a collective unconscious as the source of organic form. After Coleridge rejected Hartley's associationism, he had no other "psychology" as an empirical reference for his intuitive deductions. It would be Read's claim that Jung's hypothesis of the archetype has given Coleridge his empirical reference for the theory of the Primary Imagination. There is much to be said for this theory; it is an anomaly of contemporary scholarship that the academic "Coleridgeans" seem to believe it would be unsound "scholarship" to take seriously Read's synthesis of Coleridge and Jung; for the strict academic must not allow himself to know more than Coleridge knew, or more than his colleagues have said about what Coleridge knew. The great studies of Coleridge in our time are to be found in Read's *The True Voice of Feeling* (London, New York, 1953): "The Notion of Organic Form" and "Coleridge as Critic"; and along with these one must read the sequence of eight essays under the general title "The Nature of Poetry" which appears most handily in *Collected Essays in Literary Criticism* (London, 1938; revised edition 1951; New York, 1956, as *The Nature of Literature*). The first two essays, "Organic and Abstract Form" and "The Personality of the Poet," are Read's earliest attempts to ground the distinction between Imagination and Fancy in modern depth psychology. Organic form and abstract form are respectively Imagination and Fancy.[2]

Having read these essays and others which apply the central insight to an enormous variety of individual writers— for Read's knowledge of English literature is encyclopedic—

---

[2] The other great work on Coleridge, I. A. Richards's *Coleridge on Imagination* (London, 1934), is epistemological in its method, not psychological, in spite of Richards's early training in psychology.

what may his critic say about the success of his Coleridgean
stance in a world that Coleridge could not know? The first
test, I believe, is the pragmatic one: he is not the scholar of
a "field," the man who spends his life writing two books
and writing a few "learned articles"; he is a man of letters in
the grand style; and whatever one may think at last of his
philosophical and psychological inquiries, one must acknowledge the overwhelming evidence of his *literary commitment*.
He is a literary critic before he is a psychologist or philosopher. What other critic of our time could write so well of
Swift and Shelley, Hopkins and Whitman, Sterne and Henry
James? (The essay on James [3] I do not hesitate to say is the
best short analysis of James's "discoveries" by a living critic.
Who has read it?) I have cited only a handful of the hundreds of essays that would meet the pragmatic test; I have
not referred to *The Tenth Muse* (London, 1957; New York,
1958) or to *The Forms of Things Unknown* (London, New
York, 1960). Before I leave the subject of Read's criticism I
must glance briefly at three essays: "Psycho-analysis and the
Problem of Aesthetic Value," "Poetic Diction," and "American Bards and British Reviewers." [4]

Since the former essay was written (1950), Read has moved
away from Freud towards Jung, whose theory of the collective unconscious seems to suggest a dynamic relation of conscious control to patterns of sensibility recurrent throughout
the history of the arts. Jung's collective unconscious thus becomes positive and "creative," whereas Freud's personal unconscious remains either a dry well into which we drop our
frustrations, or at worst a chamber of horrors, Blue Beard's
closet, to unlock which spells our doom; or perhaps the doom

---

[3] "Henry James," in Herbert Read, *The Sense of Glory* (Cambridge, 1929;
New York, 1930).
[4] "Psycho-analysis and the Problem of Aesthetic Value" in *The Forms of
Things Unknown*, "Poetic Diction" in *Collected Essays in Literary Criticism*,
"American Bards and British Reviewers" in *Selected Writings*.

having been faced symbolically, we come out of the closet with integrated personalities, or, as poets, with integrated poems. Whichever way we throw the emphasis, whether on Freud or on Jung, there is inevitably a springe to catch the critical woodcock, and Sir Herbert is perfectly aware of it, as Jung was aware of it before him: did not Jung warn his disciples that analytical psychology was not criticism and could not provide criteria of "aesthetic value"? Read tells us that psychoanalysis has "come to the aid of the philosophy of art in two ways, which are really two stages of application." The first was to show that "the power of art *in a civilization* (my italics) was due to its expression of the deeper levels of personality"; that is to say, the primitive, or "archaic image" (Jung's term), is assimilated to the civilized conscious ego of the poet and by him projected into a language which through our own empathy allows us to share the integration of the archaic and the conscious. But the most important aid is the second: ". . . psycho-analysis has proved that the significance of the symbol may be, and indeed generally is, hidden; and that the symbol as such need not be representational. . . ." The symbol need not be mimetic; and ultimately it is not paraphrasable.

That would be my gloss on the central aesthetic doctrine of Sir Herbert; but so phrased, it is fairly commonplace. What is not commonplace is the critical mediation that he achieves between a psychologically grounded insight and what I have called the pragmatic test, the application of the insight to the critical evaluation of poetry. The poetry, with Read, always comes first. Would he be as good a critic as he is (he is a very fine one) if he had not striven towards a systematic aesthetic? I do not know how to answer this question. He would at any rate have had a different critical vocabulary.

The essay "Poetic Diction" was written before Read's studies in depth psychology were fully developed; but there is no indication in the later writings that he has changed his views. Like his first master, Coleridge, he has constructed a theory in later life which buttresses critical standards that were earlier expressed in the more conventional terms of literary criticism. In "Poetic Diction" he revives Arnold's rejection of Dryden and Pope, and though he avoids Arnold's phrase, "classics of our prose," he dismisses them with Dryden's own phrase "wit-writing." In the context of Sir Herbert's later aesthetic speculations "wit-writing" is the result of reliance upon the conscious ego which suppresses the unconscious and organic. Wit-writing is Coleridge's Fancy, a shuffling of "fixities and definites." He cites the concluding lines of *The Dunciad* as wit-writing, in contrast with some famous lines from *Macbeth*. I do not see how Shakespeare's lines imply a standard of organic form which allows us to reject the lines of Pope; I would retain both, with some awareness of their differences. What I would conclude from my over-simplified account of Read's theory, as it is grounded in psychology, is that he remains one of the best critics in English, not only now but of any age; but one must point out, without quite knowing what to say about it, that as the philosophical aesthetics has become more and more elaborate, there is an increasing divergence between the philosopher and the poet. May one say that the philosopher is devouring the poet at the banquet of Thyestes?

Not only the philosopher, but the *political* philosopher: here the critical doctrine of organicism implies the organic society. I have strong affinities with Sir Herbert's vision of the anarchic society (literally, the society without rulers); it is an old American doctrine going back in the United States to the time Wordsworth was propagating it in England; its champion with us was Thomas Jefferson; it was revived some thirty years ago by a group of Southern writers and renamed Agrarianism. Back of the different versions of the organic society lurks the myth of unity of being: the integration of the collective unconscious with the conscious ego. This integration seems to have been broken up, for Mr. Eliot, by a "dissociation of sensibility" in the seventeenth century. (I have been accused of placing the breakup in the United States at the year 1865.) The point at issue is not whether unity of being in an organic society ever existed, or whether it could exist; we must affirm its necessity, if only to explain the disunity of being which is the primary fact of the human condition. For the poet, and for the literary critic, the idea of organicism, regardless of a particular philosophical perspective, is the postulate, almost the axiom, from which they must proceed.

The third essay I want to point out, "American Bards and British Reviewers," is one of Read's most valuable essays. Here he brings together all his superior critical gifts—historical sense, knowledge of American as well as English poetry, subtle perceptions of stylistic similarities and differences, and profound insight into the alienation, and the reasons for it, of the modern poet everywhere. It should be required reading for the American chauvinists who think that "American" has ceased to be "English," and for their British counterparts who do not want English to be American. I would call attention to these points that ought to dispel forever these linguistic superstitions: The juxtaposition, in sequence, of passages from Robert Lowell and John Masefield; I thought at first sight that Lowell had written Masefield, and *vice versa*. More than fifty years and the Atlantic Ocean separate the two passages. Read cites the late W. C. Williams's dogma that, since American speech is not iambic, American poetry must not be iambic. Read disposes of this naïve jingoism with the remark that neither is British speech iambic. (It seems that Williams needed bad theories to write good poetry.)

Having done scant justice to Read's practical criticism,

and none at all to his social and his art criticism,[5] I should like to say a word about the essays on education. The philosophy of education will tell us something about Read's poetry, which though greatly distinguished is more limited in range and slighter in body than one might reasonably expect of a man who for nearly fifty years has made the prose ancillary to the verse. His argument goes somewhat as follows: The age of science and the industrial society which through technology has dehumanized man, have made for an increasing alienation of man from the soil. This is the Wordsworthian doctrine; but Read extends it to include his own insight into the Coleridgean Primary Imagination. He goes beyond Wordsworth and Coleridge. For Read, *perception* of physical nature through the archetypes, which are both subjective and objective, the forms being both in nature and in the mind, must be the basis of all education from infancy on. This doctrine has in modern criticism corrected a balance, for the intellectualism represented by men like Eliot, Ransom, and Winters has seen order exclusively as intellectual order; whereas Read sees order in an organic relation of man (perception) and nature (forms), man being both apart from and in nature. This, as I have already intimated, is a difficult doctrine to grasp, but as Read has expounded it in book after book, it is the most searching presentation of the philosophy of romanticism that I know anywhere. What this philosophy seems to leave out, and what I should like to see put in, is what Read would call the "determinate" element; that is to say, the organic relation of man and nature maintained by an order which goes beyond individual perception —in short, religious order. The autonomous local community, in a society without rulers, would appear to be held to-

---

[5] I must pass over Sir Herbert's art criticism: I am not competent to discuss it. One surmises that his defense of abstract art is based upon a deduction from the Jungian theory of the archetype: the archetypal symbol need not be naturalistic, representational, or mimetic.

gether by the right relation of individual perception to tools, materials, and of course nature itself; and Read allows for myth as a binding element. But which myth?

Sir Herbert *uses* myths: some of the finest poems, such as "The White Isles of Leuce" and the longer "Daphne," are more than classical allusion. Helen and Daphne are symbols which set the limits of perception. The poem "Daphne" is perhaps technically the most original work that Read has ever done. I do not say the *best* poem. There are six or seven that one might call best: "The End of a War," "The Analysis of Love," "To a Conscript of 1940," "Any Crucifixion," "Time and Being," "The Falcon and the Dove," "A World Within a War" which is not only a great war poem but a great poem on a great subject: the impact upon the contemplative mind of universal violence, whether the violence be natural or man-made.

For many years I have been puzzled by Read's reputation as a poet. He is slightly younger than Eliot, Pound, and Aiken, but he is one of four poets of that generation who made their first reputations in England: he is talked about but he seems not to influence anybody and there are few references to him when his peers are mentioned. I shall not undertake comparisons; yet he belongs in this company. The three others have written long poems with elaborate formal structures, and these poems try deliberately to embody the spirit of the times. One need think only of *Four Quartets,* the *Cantos,* and *Time in the Rock.* Read is as contemporary as any of them. But although he is a poet with a philosophy, he is not a philosophic poet. The difference, I believe, is plain enough. He is a contemplative poet in the Wordsworthian tradition; and one might wish that he believed enough in Wordsworth's blank verse to write his prose autobiographies if not in blank, then in some other formal measure. (The modified Spenserian stanza of "The Gold Disc" might have been useful.) But here a strict adherence to the theory of organic form may explain Read's refusal to write in sustained meter. The emotion, the image, the perception all compose an experience in a rhythm which must move according to its own laws. Here is not only Coleridge but a trace of Imagism, and perhaps the ghost of T. E. Hulme. Meanwhile Sir Herbert Read remains one of the finest poets of our time, and will continue so to remain after our time.

1963

III

III

Our Cousin, Mr. Poe[1]

WHEN I WAS about fourteen there were in our house, along with the novels of John Esten Cooke, E. P. Roe, and Augusta Evans, three small volumes of Edgar Allan Poe. That, by my reckoning, was a long time ago. Even then the books were old and worn, whether from use (I suppose not) or from neglect, it did not occur to me to enquire. I remember, or imagine I remember the binding, which was blue, and the size, which was small, and the paper, which was yellow and very thin. One volume contained the Poems, prefaced by Lowell's famous "biography." In this volume I am sure, for I read it more than the others, was the well-known, desperate, and asymmetrical photograph, which I gazed at by the hour and which I hoped that I should some day resemble. Another volume contained most, or at least the most famous, of the Tales: "Ligeia," which I liked best (I learned in due time that Poe had, too); "Morella" and "William Wilson," which I now like best; and "The Fall of the House of Usher," which was a little spoiled for me even at fourteen by the interjection of the "Mad Tryst of Sir Launcelot Canning." Perhaps it was in this volume that I admired "Marginalia," the first "criticism" I remember reading; but I did not discern either the bogus erudition or the sense of high literature which Poe was the first Amer-

1 Address delivered before the Poe Society of Baltimore on the centenary of his death, October 7, 1949; and repeated as a Bergen Lecture at Yale University, November 14, 1949.

ican to distinguish from entertainment and self-improvement through books; the merits as well as the defects went over my head. "Marginalia" could not at any rate have been in the third volume, which was given to a single long work: *Eureka—A Prose Poem*. This astrophilosophical discourse, which the late Paul Valéry took more seriously than any English or American critic ever did, fell in with my readings in popular astronomical books. In the backyard I arranged in a straight line peas, cherries, and oranges, in the proportionate sizes and distances of the sun and planets, and some hundreds of feet away (an inch perhaps to a thousand light-years) an old volley ball of my elder brothers' to represent Alpha Lyrae.

Later, on another occasion, I expect to examine *Eureka* at length, as I read it now, not as I read it at fourteen; yet before I leave it I must mention two other circumstances of my boyhood reading and the feeling that accompanied it. It lives for me as no later experience of ideas lives, because it was the first I had. The "proposition" that Poe undertook to demonstrate has come back to me at intervals in the past thirty-six years with such unpredictable force that now I face it with mingled resignation and dismay. I can write it without looking it up:

In the original unity of the first thing lies the secondary cause of all things, with the germ of their inevitable annihilation.

This is not the place to try to say what Poe meant by it. I could not, at fourteen, have guessed what it meant even after I had read the book; yet it is a fact of my boyhood (which I cannot suppose unique) that this grandiose formula for cosmic cataclysm became a part of my consciousness through no effort of my own but seemed to come to me like a dream, and came back later, like a nursery rhyme, or a tag from a popular song, unbidden.

The other circumstance I am surer of because it was a

visible fact, a signature in faded brown ink on the fly leaf
of *Eureka:* it told me years later that the three volumes
had been printed earlier than 1870, the year the man who
had owned them died. He was my great-grandfather. My
mother had said, often enough, or on some occasion that
fixed it in memory, that her grandfather had "known Mr.
Poe." (She was of the era when all eminent men, living or
recently dead, were "Mr.") I knew as a boy that my great-
grandfather had been a "poet," and in 1930 I found some
of his poems, which I forbear to discuss. He had for a
while been editor of the *Alexandria Gazette* at about the
time of Mr. Poe's death. Both were "Virginians," though
Virginians of somewhat different schools and points of view.
I can see my great-grandfather in Poe's description of a
preacher who called upon him in the summer of 1848:
"He stood smiling and bowing at the madman Poe."

I have brought together these scattered memories of my
first reading of a serious writer because in discussing any
writer, or in coming to terms with him, we must avoid the
trap of mere abstract evaluation, and try to reproduce the
actual conditions of our relation to him. It would be difficult
for me to take Poe up, "study" him, and proceed to a
critical judgment. One may give these affairs the look of
method, and thus deceive almost everybody but oneself.
In reading Poe we are not brought up against a large, articulate scheme of experience, such as we see adumbrated in
Hawthorne or Melville, which we may partly sever from
personal association, both in the writer and in ourselves.
Poe surrounds us with Eliot's "wilderness of mirrors," in
which we see a subliminal self endlessly repeated, or, turning, a new posture of the same figure. It is not too harsh,
I think, to say that it is stupid to suppose that by "evaluating" this forlorn demon in the glass, we dispose of him.
For Americans, perhaps for most modern men, he is with
us like a dejected cousin: we may "place" him but we may

not exclude him from our board. This is the recognition of a relationship, almost of the blood, which we must in honor acknowledge: what destroyed him is potentially destructive of us. Not only this; we must acknowledge another obligation, if, like most men of my generation, we were brought up in houses where the works of Poe took their easy place on the shelf with the family Shakespeare and the early novels of Ellen Glasgow. This is the obligation of loyalty to one's experience: he was in our lives and we cannot pretend that he was not. Not even Poe's great power in Europe is quite so indicative of his peculiar "place" as his unquestioned, if unexamined, acceptance among ordinary gentle people whose literary culture was not highly developed. The horrors of Poe created not a tremor in the bosoms of young ladies or a moment's anxiety in the eyes of vigilant mothers. I suppose the gentlemen of the South did not read him much after his time; in his time, they could scarcely have got the full sweep and depth of the horror. Nothing that Mr. Poe wrote, it was said soon after his death, could bring a blush to the cheek of the purest maiden.

But I doubt that maidens read very far in the Tales. If they had they would have found nothing to disconcert the image that Miss Susan Ingram recorded from a visit of Poe to her family a few weeks before his death:

Although I was only a slip of a girl and he what seemed to me then quite an old man, and a great literary one at that, we got on together beautifully. He was one of the most courteous gentlemen I have ever seen, and that gave great charm to his manner. None of his pictures that I have ever seen look like the picture of Poe that I keep in my memory . . . there was something in his face that is in none of them. Perhaps it was in the eyes.

If he was a madman he was also a gentleman. Whether or not we accept Mr. Krutch's theory,[2] we know, as this sen-

2 The theory that Poe was sexually impotent.

sible young lady knew, that she was quite safe with him.
A gentleman? Well, his manners were exemplary (when
he was not drinking) and to the casual eye at any rate his
exalted idealization of Woman (even of some very foolish
women) was only a little more humorless, because more
intense, than the standard cult of Female Purity in the
Old South.

What Mr. Poe on his own had done with the cult it was
not possible then to know. A gentleman and a Southerner,
he was not quite, perhaps, a Southern gentleman. The
lofty intellect of Ligeia, of Madeline, of Berenice, or of
Eleanora, had little utility in the social and economic structure of Virginia, which had to be perpetuated through the
issue of the female body, while the intellect, which was
public and political, remained under the supervision of the
gentlemen. Although Morella had a child (Poe's only heroine, I believe, to be so compromised), she was scarcely
better equipped than Virginia Clemm herself to sustain
more than the immaculate half of the vocation of the Southern lady. "But the fires," writes Morella's narrator-husband,
"were not of Eros." And we know, at the end of the story,
that the daughter is no real daughter but, as Morella's empty
"tomb" reveals, Morella herself come back as a vampire to
wreak upon her "lover" the vengeance due him. Why is it
due him? Because, quite plainly, the lover lacked, as he
always lacked with his other heroines, the "fires of Eros."
The soul of Morella's husband "burns with fires it had never
before known . . . and bitter and tormenting to my spirit
was the gradual conviction that I could in no manner define
their unusual meaning, or regulate their vague intensity."
Perhaps in the soul of John Randolph alone of Virginia
gentlemen strange fires burned. The fires that were not of
Eros were generally for the land and oratory, and the two
fires were predictably regulated.

Poe's strange fire is his leading visual symbol, but there

is not space in an essay to list all its appearances. You will see it in the eye of the Raven; in "an eye large, liquid, and luminous beyond comparison," of Roderick Usher; in the burning eye of the old man in "The Tell-Tale Heart"; in "Those eyes! those large, those shining, those divine orbs," of the Lady Ligeia. Poe's heroes and heroines are always burning with a hard, gemlike flame—a bodyless exaltation of spirit that Poe himself seems to have carried into the drawing room, where its limited visibility was sufficient guarantee of gentlemanly behavior. But privately, and thus, for him, publicly, in his stories, he could not "regulate its vague intensity."

I cannot go into this mystery here as fully as I should like; yet I may, I think, ask a question: Why did not Poe use explicitly the universal legend of the vampire? Perhaps some instinct for aesthetic distance made him recoil from it; perhaps the literal, businesslike way the vampire went about making its living revolted the "ideality" of Poe. At any rate D. H. Lawrence was no doubt right in describing as vampires his women characters; the men, soon to join them as "undead," have by some defect of the moral will, made them so.

The mysterious exaltation of spirit which is invariably the unique distinction of his heroes and heroines is not quite, as I have represented it, bodyless. *It inhabits a human body but that body is dead. The spirits prey upon one another with destructive fire which is at once pure of lust and infernal.* All Poe's characters represent one degree or another in a movement towards an archetypal condition: the survival of the soul in a dead body; but only in "The Facts in the Case of Monsieur Valdemar" is the obsessive subject explicit.

In none of the nineteenth-century comment on "The Fall of the House of Usher" that I have read, and in none of our own period, is there a feeling of shock, or even of surprise, that Roderick Usher is in love with his sister: the relation not being physical, it is "pure." R. H. Stoddard, the least sympathetic of the serious early biographers, disliked Poe's morbidity, but admitted his purity. The American case against Poe, until the first World War, rested upon his moral indifference, or his limited moral range. The range is limited, but there is no indifference; there is rather a compulsive, even a profound, interest in a moral problem of universal concern. His contemporaries could see in the love stories neither the incestuous theme nor what it meant, because it was not represented literally. The theme and its meaning as I see them are unmistakable: the symbolic compulsion that drives through, and beyond, physical incest moves towards the extinction of the beloved's will in complete possession, not of her body, but of her being; there is the reciprocal force, returning upon the lover, of self-destruction. Lawrence shrewdly perceived the significance of Poe's obsession with incestuous love. Two persons of the least dissimilarity offer the least physical resistance to mutual participation in the *fire* of a common being. Poe's most casual reader perceives that his lovers never do anything but contemplate each other, or pore upon the rigmarole of preposterously erudite, ancient books, most of which never existed. They are living in each other's insides, in the hollows of which burns the fire of will and intellect.

The fire is a double symbol; it lights and it burns. It is overtly the "light" of reason but as action it becomes the consuming fire of the abstract intellect, without moral significance, which invades the being of the beloved. It is the fire that, having illuminated, next destroys. Lawrence is again right in singling out for the burden of his insight the epigraph to "Ligeia," which Poe had quoted from Glanvill: "Man does not yield himself to the angels, nor unto death utterly, save through the weakness of his own feeble will." Why do these women of monstrous will and intellect turn into vampires? Because, according to Lawrence, the lovers have not subdued them through the body to the biological level, at which sanity alone is possible, and they retaliate by devouring their men. This view is perhaps only partly right. I suspect that the destruction works both ways, that the typical situation in Poe is more complex than Lawrence's version of it.

If we glance at "The Fall of the House of Usher" we shall be struck by a singular feature of the catastrophe. Bear in mind that Roderick and Madeline are brother and sister, and that the standard hyperaesthesia of the Poe hero acquires in Roderick a sharper reality than in any of the others, except perhaps William Wilson. His naked sensitivity to sound and light is not "regulated" to the forms of the human situation; it is a mechanism operating apart from the moral consciousness. We have here something like a capacity for mere sensation, as distinguished from sensibility, which in Usher is atrophied. In terms of the small distinction that I am offering here, sensibility keeps us in the world; sensation locks us into the self, feeding upon the disintegration of its objects and absorbing them into the void of the ego. The lover, circumventing the body into the secret being of the beloved, tries to convert the spiritual object into an object of sensation: the intellect which knows and the will which possesses are unnaturally turned upon that center of the beloved which should remain inviolate.

As the story of Usher opens, the Lady Madeline is suffering from a strange illness. She dies. Her brother has, of course, possessed her inner being, and killed her; or thinks he has, or at any rate wishes to think that she is dead. This is all a little vague: perhaps he has deliberately entombed her alive, so that she will die by suffocation—a symbolic action for extinction of being. Why has he committed this

monstrous crime? Sister though she is, she is nevertheless
not entirely identical with him: she has her own otherness,
of however slight degree, resisting his hypertrophied will.
He puts her alive, though "cataleptic," into the "tomb."
(Poe never uses graves, only tombs, except in "Premature
Burial." His corpses, being half dead, are thus only half
buried; they rise and walk again.) After some days Madeline breaks out of the tomb and confronts her brother in
her bloody cerements. This is the way Poe presents the
scene:

". . . Is she not hurrying to upbraid me for my haste? Have I
not heard her footsteps on the stair? Do I not distinguish the
heavy and horrible beating of her heart? Madman!"—here he
sprang furiously to his feet, and shrieked out his syllables, as if
in his effort he were giving up his soul—*"Madman! I tell you that
she now stands without the door!"*

As if in the superhuman energy of his utterance there had been
found the potency of a spell, the huge antique panels to which
the speaker pointed threw slowly back, upon the instant, their
ponderous and ebony jaws. It was the work of the rushing gust—
but then without those doors there *did* stand the lofty and en-
shrouded figure of the Lady Madeline of Usher. There was blood
upon her white robes, and the evidence of some bitter struggle
upon every portion of her emaciated frame. For a moment she
remained trembling to and fro upon the threshold—then, with
a low moaning cry, fell heavily inward upon the person of her
brother, and in her violent and now final death-agonies, bore
him to the floor a corpse, and a victim to the terrors he had
anticipated.

Madeline, back from the tomb, neither dead nor alive, is
in the middle state of the unquiet spirit of the vampire,
whose heart beats are "heavy and horrible." There is no
evidence that Poe knew any anthropology; yet in some
legends of vampirism the undead has a sluggish pulse, or
none at all. In falling prone upon her brother she takes the

position of the vampire suffocating its victim in a sexual embrace. By these observations I do not suggest that Poe was conscious of what he was doing; had he been, he might have done it even worse. I am not saying, in other words, that Poe is offering us, in the Lady Madeline, a vampire according to Bram Stoker's specifications. An imagination of any power at all will often project its deepest assumptions about life in symbols that duplicate, without the artist's knowledge, certain meanings, the origins of which are sometimes as old as the race. If a writer ambiguously exalts the "spirit" over the "body," and the spirit must live wholly upon another spirit, some version of the vampire legend is likely to issue as the symbolic situation.

Although the action is reported by a narrator, the fictional point of view is that of Usher: it is all seen through his eyes. But has Madeline herself not also been moving towards the cataclysmic end in the enveloping action outside the frame of the story? Has not her *will to know* done its reciprocal work upon the inner being of her brother? Their very birth had violated their unity of being. They must achieve spiritual identity in mutual destruction. The physical symbolism of the fissured house, of the miasmic air, and of the special order of nature surrounding the House of Usher and conforming to the laws of the spirits inhabiting it—all this supports the central dramatic situation, which moves towards spiritual unity through disintegration.

In the original unity of the first thing lies the secondary cause of all things, with the germ of their inevitable annihilation.

Repeated here, in the context of the recurrent subject of the Tales, the thesis of *Eureka* has a sufficient meaning and acquires something of the dignity that Valéry attributed to it. Professor Quinn adduces quotations from mathematical physicists to prove that Poe, in *Eureka,* was a prophet of science. It is a subject on which I am not entitled to an opinion. But even if Professor Quinn is right, the claim is irrelevant, and is only another version of the attempt today to make religion and the arts respectable by showing that they are semi-scientific. Another sort of conjecture seems to me more profitable: that in the history of the moral imagination in the nineteenth century, Poe occupies a special place. No other writer in England or the United States, or, so far as I know, in France, went so far as Poe in his vision of dehumanized man.

His characters are, in the words of William Wilson's double, "dead to the world"; they are machines of sensation and will, with correspondences, in the physical universe, to particles and energy. Poe's engrossing obsession in *Eureka* with the cosmic destiny of man issued in a quasi-cosmology, a more suitable extension of his vision than any mythology, homemade or traditional, could have offered him. The great mythologies are populous worlds, but a cosmology need have nobody in it. In Poe's, the hyperaesthetic egoist has put all other men into his void: he is alone in the world, and thus dead to it. If we place Poe against the complete Christian imagination of Dante, whom he resembles in his insistence upon a cosmic extension of the moral predicament, the limits of his range are apparent, and the extent of his insight within those limits. The quality of Poe's imagination can be located, as I see it, in only two places in Dante's entire scheme of the after-life: Cantos XIII and XXXII of the *Inferno*. In Canto XIII, the Harpies feed upon the living trees enclosing the shades of suicides—those "violent against themselves," who will not resume their bodies at the Resurrection, for "man may not have what he takes from himself." In XXXII, we are in Caïna, the ninth circle, where traitors to their kin lie half buried in ice, up to the pubic shadow—"where the doleful shades were . . . sounding with their teeth like storks." Unmotivated treachery, for the mere intent of injury, and self-violence are Poe's obsessive subjects. He has neither Purgatory nor Heaven; and only two stations in Hell.

Let me turn briefly to the question of Poe's style. He has several styles, and it is not possible to damn them all at once. The critical style, which I shall not be able to examine here, is on occasion the best; he is a lucid and dispassionate expositor, he is capable of clear and rigorous logic (even from mistaken premises, as in "The Rationale of Verse"), when he is not warped by envy or the desire to flatter. He is most judicial with his peers, least with his inferiors, whom he either overestimates or wipes out. As for the fictional style, it, too, varies; it is perhaps at its sustained best, in point of sobriety and restraint, in the tales of deduction. Exceptions to this observation are "Descent into the Maelström," "The Narrative of Arthur Gordon Pym," and perhaps one or two others in a genre which stems from the eighteenth-century "voyage." These fictions demanded a Defoe-like verisimilitude which was apparently beyond his reach when he dealt with his obsessive theme. Again I must make an exception: "William Wilson," one of the serious stories (by serious, I mean an ample treatment of the obsession), is perspicuous in diction and on the whole credible in realistic detail. I quote a paragraph:

The extensive enclosure was irregular in form, having many capacious recesses. Of these, three or four of the largest constituted the play-ground. It was level, and covered with a hard fine gravel. I well remember it had no trees, nor benches, nor anything similar within it. Of course it was in the rear of the house. In front lay a small parterre, planted with box and other shrubs, but through this sacred division we passed only upon rare occasions indeed—such as a first advent to school or a final departure hence, or perhaps, when a parent or a friend having called upon us, we joyfully took our way home for the Christmas or midsummer holidays.

It is scarcely great prose, but it has an eighteenth-century directness, and even elegance, of which Poe was seldom capable in his stories. I surmise that the playground at Dr. Bransby's school at Stoke-Newington, where, as a child, he was enrolled for five years, recalled one of the few periods of his life which he could detach from the disasters of manhood and face with equanimity. Now a part of the description of the lady Ligeia:

. . . I examined the contour of the lofty and pale forehead—it was faultless—how cold indeed that word when applied to a majesty so divine!—the skin rivalling the purest ivory, the commanding extent and repose, the gentle prominence of the regions above the temples; and the raven-black, the glossy, the luxuriant, the naturally curling tresses, setting forth the full force of the Homeric epithet, "hyacinthine." I looked at the delicate outline of the nose. . . .

But I refrain. It is easy enough to agree with Aldous Huxley and Yvor Winters, and dismiss this sort of ungrammatical rubbish as too vulgar, or even too idiotic, to reward the time it takes to point it out. But if Poe is worth understanding at all (I assume that he is), we might begin by asking why the writer of the lucid if not very distinguished passage from "William Wilson" repeatedly fell into the bathos of "Ligeia." I confess that Poe's serious style at its typical worst makes the reading of more than one story at a sitting an almost insuperable task. The Gothic glooms, the Venetian interiors, the ancient wine cellars (from which nobody ever enjoys a vintage but always drinks "deep")—all this, done up in a glutinous prose, so fatigues one's attention that with the best will in the world one gives up, unless one gets a clue to the power underlying the flummery.

I have tried in the course of these remarks to point in the direction in which the clue, as I see it, is to be found. I do not see it in the influence of the Gothic novel. This was no doubt there; but no man is going to use so much neo-Gothic, over and over again, unless he means business with it; I think that Poe meant business. If the Gothic influence had not been to hand, he would have invented it, or something equally "unreal" to serve his purpose. His purpose in laying on the thick décor was to simulate sensation. Poe's sensibility, for reasons that I cannot surmise here, was almost completely impoverished. He could feel little but the pressure of his predicament, and his perceptual powers remained undeveloped. Very rarely he gives us a real perception because he is not interested in anything that is alive. Everything in Poe is dead: the houses, the rooms, the furniture, to say nothing of nature and of human beings. He is like a child—all appetite without sensibility; but to be in manhood all appetite, all will, without sensibility, is to be a monster: to feed spiritually upon men without sharing with them a real world is spiritual vampirism. The description of Ligeia's head is that of a dead woman's.

Does it explain anything to say that this is necrophilism? I think not. Poe's prose style, as well as certain qualities of his verse,[3] expresses the kind of "reality" to which he had access: I believe I have indicated that it is a reality sufficiently terrible. In spite of an early classical education and a Christian upbringing, he wrote as if the experience of these traditions had been lost: he was well ahead of his time. He could not relate his special reality to a wider context of insights—a discipline that might have disciplined

---

[3] Poe's verse rhythms are for the metronome, not the human ear. Their real defects are so great that it is not necessary to invent others, as Mr. T. S. Eliot seems to do in *From Poe to Valéry* (New York, 1949). Thus Mr. Eliot (and I cite only one of his observations that seem to me wrong) complains that "the saintly days of yore" could not be an appropriate time for the Raven to have lived. Elijah was fed by Ravens, a bird which was almost extinct in America in the 1840's. Ravens frequently fed hermits and saints and were in fact a fairly standard feature of saintly equipment.

his prose. From the literary point of view he combined the primitive and the decadent: primitive, because he had neither history nor the historical sense; decadent, because he was the conscious artist of an intensity which lacked moral perspective.

But writers tend to be what they are; I know of no way to make one kind into another. It may have been a condition of Poe's genius that his ignorance should have been what it was. If we read him as formal critics we shall be ready to see that it was another condition of his genius that he should never produce a poem or a story without blemishes, or a critical essay that, despite its acuteness in detail, does not evince provincialism of judgment and lack of knowledge. We must bear in mind Mr. Eliot's remark that Poe must be viewed as a whole. Even the fiction and the literary journalism that seem without value add to his massive impact upon the reader.

What that impact is today upon other readers I cannot pretend to know. It has been my limited task to set forth here a little of what one reader finds in him, and to acknowledge in his works the presence of an incentive (again, for one man) to self-knowledge. I do not hesitate to say that had Poe not written *Eureka,* I should have been able, a man of this age, myself to formulate a proposition of "inevitable annihilation." I can only invite others to a similar confession. Back of the preceding remarks lies an ambitious assumption, about the period in which we live, which I shall not make explicit. It is enough to say that, if the trappings of Poe's nightmare strike us as tawdry, we had better look to our own. That particular vision in its purity (Poe was very pure) is perhaps not capable of anything better than Mr. Poe's ludicrous décor. Nor have persons eating one another up and calling it spiritual love often achieved a distinguished style either in doing it or in writing about it. It was not Ugolino, it was Dante who wrote about Ugolino with more knowledge than Ugolino had. Mr. Poe tells us in one of his simple poems that from boyhood he had "a demon in my view." Nobody then—my great-grandfather, my mother, three generations—believed him. It is time we did. I confess that his voice is so near that I recoil a little, lest he, Montressor, lead me into the cellar, address me as Fortunato, and wall me up alive. I should join his melancholy troupe of the undead, whose voices are surely as low and harsh as the grating teeth of storks. He is so close to me that I am sometimes tempted to enter the mists of pre-American genealogy to find out whether he may not actually be my cousin.

1949

The Angelic Imagination[1]

Poe as God

WITH SOME EMBARRASSMENT I assume the part of amateur theologian and turn to a little-known figure, Edgar Allan Poe, another theologian only less ignorant than myself. How seriously one must take either Poe or his present critic in this new role I prefer not to be qualified to say. Poe will remain a man of letters—I had almost said a poet—whose interest for us is in the best sense historical. He represents that part of our experience which we are least able to face up to: the Dark Night of Sense, the cloud hovering over that edge of the eye which is turned to receive the effluvia of France, whence the literary power of his influence reaches us today. In France, the literary power has been closely studied; I shall not try to estimate it here. Poe's other power, that of the melancholy, heroic life, one must likewise leave to others, those of one's own compatriots who are not interested in literature. All readers of Poe, of the work or of the life, and the rare reader of both, are peculiarly liable to the vanity of discovery. I shall be concerned in the ensuing remarks with what I think I have seen in Poe that nobody else has seen: this undetected quality, or its

[1] This essay and "The Symbolic Imagination" which follows it were given in shorter versions as the Candlemas Lectures at Boston College, February 10–11, 1951.

401

remote source in Poe's feeling and thought, I believe partly
explains an engagement with him that men on both sides
of the Atlantic have acknowledged for more than a century.

It was recently acknowledged, with reservations, by Mr.
T. S. Eliot, whose estimate must be reckoned with: Poe,
he tells us, won a great reputation in Europe because the
continental critics habitually view an author's work as a
whole; whereas English and American critics view each work
separately and, in the case of Poe, have been stopped by
its defects. Mr. Eliot's essay [2] is the first attempt by an Eng-
lish-speaking critic to bring to Poe the continental approach
and to form a general estimate. I quote from what I take
to be Mr. Eliot's summary; Poe, he says,

appears to yield himself completely to the idea of the moment:
the effect is, that all his ideas seem to be entertained rather than
believed. What is lacking is not brain-power, but that maturity
of intellect which comes only with the maturing of the man as a
whole, the development and coordination of the various emotions.

What I shall say towards the end of this essay I believe will
show that Mr. Eliot is partly wrong, but that on the whole
his estimate of Poe's immaturity is right. Does Poe merely
"entertain" *all* his ideas? Perhaps all but one; but that one
makes all the difference. Its special difference consists in
his failure to see what the idea really was, so that he had
perpetually to shift his ground—to "entertain," one after
another, shabby rhetorics and fantasies that could never
quite contain the one great idea. He was a religious man
whose Christianity, for reasons that nobody knows anything about, had got short-circuited; he lived among fragments of provincial theologies, in the midst of which "coordination," for a man of his intensity, was difficult if not
impossible. There is no evidence that Poe used the word

[2] *From Poe to Valéry* (New York, 1949).

coordination in the sense in which Mr. Eliot finds him deficient in it; but it is justly applied. I am nevertheless surprised that Mr. Eliot seems to assume that *coordination* of the "various emotions" is ever possible: the word gives the case away to Poe. It is a morally neutral term that Poe himself might have used, in his lifelong effort to impose upon experience a mechanical logic; possibly it came into modern literary psychology from analytic geometry. I take it that the word was not used, if in Mr. Eliot's sense it was known, when considerable numbers of persons were able to experience coordination. I suppose Mr. Eliot means by it a harmony of faculties among different orders of experience; and Poe's failure to harmonize himself cannot be denied.

The failure resulted in a hypertrophy of the three classical faculties: feeling, will, and intellect. The first I have discussed elsewhere.[3] It is the incapacity to represent the human condition in the central tradition of natural feeling. A nightmare of paranoia, schizophrenia, necrophilism, and vampirism supervenes, in which the natural affections are perverted by the will to destroy. Poe's heroines—Berenice, Ligeia, Madeline, Morella, with the curious exception of the abstemious Eleanora—are ill-disguised vampires; his heroes become necromancers (in the root meaning of the word) whose wills, like the heroines' wills, defy the term of life to keep them equivocally "alive." This primary failure in human feeling results in the loss of the entire natural order of experience.

The second hypertrophy is the thrust of the will beyond the human scale of action. The evidence of this is on nearly every page of Poe's serious prose fiction. Poe's readers, especially the young, like the quotation from Glanvill that appears as the epigraph to "Ligeia": "Man does not yield

[3] "Our Cousin, Mr. Poe," *supra*, pp. 385-400.

himself to the angels, nor unto Death utterly, save only through the weakness of his feeble will." It is the theme of the major stories. The hero professes an impossibly high love of the heroine that circumvents the body and moves in upon her spiritual essence. All this sounds high and noble, until we begin to look at it more narrowly, when we perceive that the ordinary carnal relationship between man and woman, however sinful, would be preferable to the mutual destruction of soul to which Poe's characters are committed. The carnal act, in which none of them seems to be interested, would witness a commitment to the order of nature, without which the higher knowledge is not possible to man. The Poe hero tries in self-love to turn the soul of the heroine into something like a physical object which he can know in direct cognition and then possess.

Thus we get the third hypertrophy of a human faculty: the intellect moving in isolation from both love and the moral will, whereby it declares itself independent of the human situation in the quest of essential knowledge.

The three perversions necessarily act together, the action of one implying a deflection of the others. But the actual emphases that Poe gives the perversions are richer in philosophical implication than his psychoanalytic critics have been prepared to see. To these ingenious persons, Poe's works have almost no intrinsic meaning; taken together they make up a *dossier* for the analyst to peruse before Mr. Poe steps into his office for an analysis. It is important at this point to observe that Poe takes for granted the old facultative psychology of intellect, will and feeling. If we do not observe this scheme, and let it point our enquiry, we shall fail to understand two crucial elements in Poe: first, that Poe's symbols refer to a known tradition of thought, an intelligible order, apart from what he was as a man, and are not merely the index to a compulsive neurosis; and, secondly, that the symbols, cast into the framework of the three faculties, point towards this larger philosophical dimension, implicit in the serious stories, but very much at the surface in certain of Poe's works that have been almost completely ignored.

I shall discuss here these neglected works: *The Conversation of Eiros and Charmion, The Colloquy of Monos and Una, The Power of Words,* and *Eureka.* The three first are dialogues between spirits in heaven, after the destruction of the earth; all four set forth a cataclysmic end of the world, modelled on the Christian eschatology. We shall see that *Eureka* goes further, and offers us a semirational vision of the final disappearance of the material world into the first spiritual Unity, or God.

It would be folly to try to see in these works the action of a first-rate philosophical mind; there is ingenuity rather than complex thinking. What concerns us is the relation of the semi-philosophical works to Poe's imaginative fiction; that is, a particular relation of the speculative intellect to the work of imagination. I shall have to show that Poe, as a critical mind, had only a distant if impressive insight into the disintegration of the modern personality; and that this insight was not available to him as an imaginative writer, when he had to confront the human situation as a whole man. He was the victim of a disintegration that he seems only intermittently to have understood. Poe is thus a man we must return to: a figure of transition, who retains a traditional insight into a disorder that has since become typical, without being able himself to control it.

Before we examine this insight it will be necessary to fix more clearly in mind than I have yet done the character of Poe as a transitional man. Madame Raïssa Maritain, in a valuable essay, "Magie, Poésie, et Mystique," [4] says:

4 Jacques and Raïssa Maritain, *Situation de la Poésie* (Paris, 1938), p. 58.

Je ne vois guère de place dans la cosmologie d'Edgar Poe pour des recherches de recettes magiques. Et moins encore dans sa poésie, qui a toujours été parfaitement libre de toute anxiété de ce genre, et dont il n'aurait jamais voulu faire un instrument de pouvoir.

[I see little place in the cosmology of Edgar Poe for the pursuit of magic recipes. And still less in his poetry, which was always perfectly free of all anxiety of this kind, and of which he never wished to make an instrument of power.]

I am not sure that Madame Maritain is entirely right about the absence of magic, but there is no doubt that Poe *as poet* accepted certain limitations of language. He accepted them in practice. The obscurity of Poe's poetic diction is rather vagueness than the obscurity of complexity; it reflects his uncertain grasp of the relation of language to feeling, and of feeling to nature. But it is never that idolatrous dissolution of language from the grammar of a possible world, which results from the belief that language itself can be reality, or by incantation can create a reality: a superstition that comes down in French from Lautréamont, Rimbaud, and Mallarmé to the Surrealists, and in English to Hart Crane, Wallace Stevens, and Dylan Thomas. (I do not wish it to be understood that I am in any sense "rejecting" these poets, least of all under the rubric "superstition." When men find themselves cut off from reality they will frequently resort to magic rites to recover it—a critical moment of history that has its own relation to reality, from which poetry of great power may emerge.)

Poe, then, accepted his genre *in practice*. If the disorganized, synaesthetic sensibility arrives in the long run at a corresponding disintegration of the forms of grammar and rhetoric, it must be admitted that Poe stopped short at the mere *doctrine* of synaesthesia. In *The Colloquy of Monos and Una*, the angel Monos describes his passage into the after-life: "The senses were unusually active, although eccentrically so—assuming each other's functions at random. The taste and the smell were inextricably confounded, and became one sentiment, abnormal and intense." [5] But this is not the experience of synaesthesia rendered to our consciousness; to put it as Poe puts it is merely to consider it as a possibility of experience. Eighty years later we find its actuality in the language of an American poet:

> How much I would have bartered! the black gorge
> And all the singular nestings in the hills
> Where beavers learn stitch and tooth.
> The pond I entered once and quickly fled—
> I remember now its singing willow rim.

Rimbaud's "derangement of the senses" is realized. Why did not Poe take the next step and realize it himself? The question is unanswerable, for every writer is who he is, and not somebody else. The discoverer of a new sensibility seldom pushes it as far as language will take it; it largely remains a premonition of something yet to come. Another phase of Poe's disproportion of language and feeling appears in the variations of his prose style, which range from the sobriety and formal elegance of much of his critical writing, to the bathos of stories like *Ligeia* and *Berenice*. When Poe is not involved directly in his own feeling he can be a master of the *ordonnance* of eighteenth-century prose; there are passages in *The Narrative of Arthur Gordon Pym* that have the lucidity and intensity of Swift. But when he approaches the full human situation the traditional rhetoric fails him. It becomes in his hands a humorless, insensitive machine whose elaborate motions conceal what it pretends to convey; for without the superimposed order of rhetoric the disorder hidden beneath would explode to the surface, where he would not be able to manage it. Poe is the tran-

---

[5] *Cf.* Baudelaire's *Correspondances:* "Les parfums, les couleurs, et les sons se répondent."

sitional figure in modern literature because he discovered our great subject, the disintegration of personality, but kept it in a language that had developed in a tradition of unity and order. Madame Maritain is right in saying that he does not *use* language as magic. But he considers its possibility, and he thinks of language as a potential source of quasi-divine power. He is at the parting of the ways; the two terms of his conflict are thus more prominent than they would appear to be in a writer, or in an age, fully committed to either extreme. "When all are bound for disorder," says Pascal, "none seems to go that way."

Of the three dialogues that I shall discuss here, the first, *The Conversation of Eiros and Charmion,* published in 1839, was the earliest written. It is Poe's first essay at a catastrophic version of the disappearance of the earth: a comet passes over the earth, extracting the nitrogen from the atmosphere and replacing it with oxygen, so that the accelerated oxidation ends in world-wide combustion. But in treating the most unpromising materials Poe means what he says, although the occasions of journalism may not allow him to say all that he means. He *means* the destruction of the world. It is not only a serious possibility, it is a moral and logical necessity of the condition to which man has perversely brought himself.

Man's destruction of his relation to nature is the subject of the next dialogue, *The Colloquy of Monos and Una* (1841). From the perversion of man's nature it follows by a kind of Manichean logic that external nature itself must be destroyed: man's surrender to evil is projected symbolically into the world.

This dialogue, the sequel to *The Conversation of Eiros and Charmion,* is a theological fantasy of the destruction of the earth by fire. I call the vision "theological" because the destruction is not, as it was in the preceding dialogue, merely the result of an interstellar collision. Monos says,

"That man, as a race, should not become extinct, I saw that he must be *'born again.'* " Rebirth into the after-life is the mystery that Monos undertakes to explain to Una; but first he makes this long digression:

One word first, my Una, in regard to man's general condition at this epoch. You will remember that one or two of the wise men among our forefathers . . . had ventured to doubt the propriety of the term "improvement" as applied to the progress of our civilization. [They uttered] principles which should have taught our race to submit to the guidance of the natural laws, rather than attempt their control. Occasionally the poetic intellect—that intellect which we now feel to have been the most exalted of all—since those truths to us were of the most enduring importance and could only be reached by that *analogy* which speaks in proof-tones to the imagination alone, and to the unaided reason bears no weight—occasionally did this poetic intellect proceed a step farther in the evolving of the vaguely philosophic, and find in the mystic parable that tells of the tree of knowledge . . . death-pro-ducing, a distinct intimation that knowledge was not meet for man in the infant condition of his soul. . . .

Yet these noble exceptions from the general misrule served but to strengthen it by opposition. The great "movement"—that was the cant term—went on: a diseased commotion, moral and physi-cal. Art—the Arts—rose supreme, and, once enthroned, cast chains upon the intellect which had elevated them to power. Even while he stalked a God in his own fancy, an infantine imbecility came over him. As might be supposed from the origin of his disorder, he grew infected with system, and with abstraction. He en-wrapped himself in generalities. Among other odd ideas, that of universal equality gained ground; and in the face of analogy and of God—in spite of the laws of graduation so visibly pervading all things . . . —wild attempts at an omnipresent Democracy were made. Yet this evil sprang necessarily from the leading evil—knowledge. . . . Meanwhile huge smoking cities arose, innumer-able. Green leaves shrank before the hot breath of furnaces . . . now it appears that we had worked out *our own destruction in*

the perversion of our taste [italics mine] or rather in the blind
neglect of its culture in the schools. For in truth it was at this
crisis that taste alone—that faculty which, *holding a middle position between the pure intellect and the moral sense* [italics mine],
could never safely have been disregarded—it was now that taste
alone could have led us gently back to Beauty, to Nature, and to
Life.

. . . it is not impossible that the sentiment of the natural, had
time permitted it, would have regained its old ascendancy over
the harsh mathematical reasoning of the schools. . . . This the
mass of mankind saw not, or, living lustily although unhappily,
affected not to see.

I have quoted the passage at great length in the hope that
a certain number of persons at a certain place and time
will have read it. Poe's critics (if he have any critics) have
not read it. When they refer to it, it is to inform us that
Poe was a reactionary Southerner who disliked democracy
and industrialism. It would not be wholly to the purpose
but it would be edifying to comment on the passage in detail, for it adumbrates a philosophy of impressive extent
and depth. When we remember that it was written in the
United States in the early 1840's, an era of the American
experiment that tolerated very little dissent, we may well
wonder whether it was the result of a flash of insight, or
of conscious reliance upon a wider European tradition. (My
guess is that Poe's idea of "mathematical reasoning" was
derived in part from Pascal's *L'esprit de géométrie,* his "taste"
from *L'esprit de finesse.* This is a scholarly question that
cannot be investigated here.)

A clue to the connection between Poe's historical and
metaphysical insight, on the one hand, and the mode of his
literary imagination, on the other, may be found in Paul
Valéry's essay, "The Position of Baudelaire," where he says:

. . . the basis of Poe's thoughts is associated with a certain personal metaphysical system. By this system, if it directs and domi-

nates and suggests the [literary] theories . . . *by no means pene-trates them* [italics mine].[6]

His metaphysics was not available to him as experience; it did not *penetrate* his imagination. If we will consider to-gether the "harsh mathematical reasoning of the schools" and the theory of the corruption of taste, we shall get a further clue to the Christian philosophical tradition in which Poe consciously or intuitively found himself. Taste is the discipline of feeling according to the laws of the natural order, a discipline of submission to a permanent limitation of man; this discipline has been abrogated by the "mathematical reasoning" whose purpose is the control of nature. Here we have the Cartesian split—taste, feeling, respect for the depth of nature, resolved into a subjectiv-ism which denies the sensible world; for nature has become geometrical, at a high level of abstraction, in which "clear and distinct ideas" only are workable. The sensibility is frustrated, since it is denied its perpetual refreshment in nature: the operative abstraction replaces the rich perspec-tives of the concrete object. Reason is thus detached from feeling, and likewise from the moral sense, the third and executive member of the psychological triad, moving through the will. Feeling in this scheme being isolated or —as Mr. Scott Buchanan might put it—"occulted," it is strictly speaking without content, and man has lost his ac-cess to material forms. We get the hypertrophy of the in-tellect and the hypertrophy of the will. When neither in-tellect nor will is bound to the human scale, their projec-tion becomes godlike, and man becomes an angel, in M. Maritain's sense of the term:

Cartesian dualism breaks man up into two complete substances, joined to one another none knows how: on the one hand, the

6 Paul Valéry, *Variety: Second Series,* trans. from the French by William Aspen-wall Bradley (New York, 1938), "The Position of Baudelaire," p. 90.

body which is only geometrical extension; on the other, the soul which is only thought—an angel inhabiting a machine and directing it by means of the pineal gland.

. . . for human intellection is living and fresh only when it is centered upon the vigilance of sense perception. The natural roots of our knowledge being cut, a general drying up in philosophy and culture resulted, a drought for which romantic tears were later to provide only an insufficient remedy. . . . Affectivity will have its revenge.[7]

One cannot fail to see here a resemblance, *up to a point,* between the insights of Poe and of Maritain; but at that point appears the profound difference between a catastrophic acceptance and a poised estimation, of the Cartesian dualism. *The Colloquy of Monos and Una* is in the end a romantic tear, and in Poe's tales of perverted nature "affectivity" takes its terrible revenge.

We may discern the precise point at which Poe betrays his surrender to what I shall call the angelic fallacy: it is the point at which his conception of the "poetic intellect" becomes contradictory and obscure. This intellect speaks to us, he says, "by analogy," in "proof tones to the imagination alone." The trap is the adverb *alone,* which contradicts the idea of analogy. He may have meant analogy to the natural world, the higher truths emerging, as they do in Dante, from a rational structure of natural analogy; but he could not have meant all this. And I suppose nobody else in the nineteenth century understood analogy as a mode of knowledge. If the poetic intellect speaks "by analogy" it addresses more than the "imagination alone"; it engages also reason and cognition; for if it alone is addressed there is perhaps a minimum of analogy; if the imagination can work alone, it does so in direct intuition. And in fact in none

7 Jacques Maritain, *The Dream of Descartes* (New York, 1944), Chap. 4, "The Cartesian Heritage," pp. 179–180. My debt to Mr. Maritain is so great that I hardly know how to acknowledge it.

of the essays and reviews does Poe even consider the idea of analogy. Its single mysterious appearance, in anything like its full historical sense, is in *The Colloquy of Monos and Una*. (It reappears in *Eureka*, where it means simple exemplification or parallelism.) In the "Poetic Principle," the poetic intellect moves independently, with only "incidental" connections with Pure Intellect and the Moral Sense; it is thus committed exclusively to Taste raised to an autonomous faculty. "Imagination is, possibly in man," says Poe in a footnote to his famous review of Halleck and Drake, "a lesser degree of the creative power of God." This is not far from the "esemplastic power" of the Primary Imagination, a Teutonic angel inhabiting a Cartesian machine named Samuel Taylor Coleridge.

Poe's exaltation of the imagination in its Cartesian vacuum foreshadows a critical dilemma of which we have been acutely aware in our own time. His extravagant claims for poetry do not in any particular exceed, except perhaps in their "period" rhetoric, the claims made by two later generations of English critics represented by Arnold and Richards. "Religion," said Arnold, "is morality touched with emotion." But religion, he said elsewhere, has attached itself to the "fact," by which he meant science; so religion has failed us. Therefore "the future of poetry is immense" because it is its own fact; that is to say, poetry is on its own, whatever its own may be—perhaps its own emotion, which now "touches" poetry instead of religion. Therefore poetry will save us, although it has no connection with the Cartesian machine running outside my window, or inside my vascular system. (Mr. Richards's early views I have discussed on several occasions over many years; I am a little embarrassed to find myself adverting to them again.) In Richards's writings, particularly in a small volume entitled *Science and Poetry* (1926), he tells us that the pseudo-statements of poetry—poetry on its own—cannot stand against the "certified scientific statement" about the facts which for Arnold had already failed both religion and poetry. Nevertheless poetry will save us because it "orders our minds"— but with what? For Mr. Richards, twenty-five years ago, the Cartesian machine was doing business as usual. Poetry would have to save us by ordering our minds with something that was not true.

Poe's flash of unsustained insight, in *The Colloquy of Monos and Una,* has, I submit, a greater dignity, a deeper philosophical perspective, and a tougher intellectual fiber, than the academic exercises of either Arnold or Mr. Richards. (I still reserve the right to admire both of these men.) Poe is not so isolated as they, in a provincialism of *time.* He still has access, however roundabout, to the great framework of the Aristotelian psychology to which the literature of Europe had been committed for more than two thousand years: this was, and still is for modern critics, an empirical fact that must be confronted if we are to approach literature with anything better than callow systems of psychological analysis, invented overnight, that put the imaginative work of the past at a distance seriously greater than that of time.

Poe with perfect tact puts his finger upon the particular function, feeling, that has been blighted by the abstraction of the pure intellect into a transcendental order of its own. He will let neither pure intellect nor the pure moral will (both having been purified of "nature") dominate poetry; he sees that poetry must be centered in the disciplined sense perception which he inadequately calls taste; and he thus quite rightly opposes the "heresy of the didactic" and the "mathematical reasoning of the schools." He opposes both, but he gives in to the latter. Poe's idolatry of reason, ranging from the cryptogram and the detective story to the panlogism of *Eureka,* is too notorious to need pointing out. The autonomy of the will is in part the theme of the greater stories; and the autonomy of poetry, rising contradictorily and mysteriously from the ruin of its source in feeling, reflects "a lesser degree of the creative power of God." It is the creative power of the Word, man's *spoken* word, an extravagant and slippery pun on the Logos.

I now come to the third dialogue, *The Power of Words*, published in 1845, a fable in which the angelic imagination [8] is pushed beyond the limits of the angelic intelligence to the point at which man considers the possibility of creative power through verbal magic. The angels in this dialogue not only know essence directly; they also have the power of physical creation by means of *words*. We may ask here why, if Poe's insight was as profound as I think it was, he succumbed to a force of disintegration that he understood? An answer to this question is difficult. Insights of the critical intelligence, however impressive, will not always correct, they may never wholly rise above, the subtle and elusive implications of the common language to which the writer is born. As Dante well understood, this is the primary fact of his culture that he has got to reckon with. The culture of the imaginative writer is, first of all, the elementary use of language that he must hear and learn in childhood, and, in the end, not much more than a conscious manipulation of what he had received from life before the age of seven. Poe understood the spiritual disunity that had resulted from the rise of the demi-religion of scientism, but by merely opposing its excesses with equally excessive claims for the "poetic intellect," he subtly perpetuated the disunity from another direction. He set up, if we may be allowed the figure, a parallelogram of forces colliding by chance from unpredicted directions, not proceeding from a central unity. Although he was capable of envisaging the

---

[8] Strictly speaking, an *angelic imagination* is not possible. Angels by definition have unmediated knowledge of essences.

unified action of the mind through the three faculties,
his own mind acted upon its materials now as intellect,
now as feeling, now as will; never as all three together.
Had he not been bred in a society committed to the rationalism of Descartes and Locke by that eminent angel
of the rationalistic Enlightenment, Thomas Jefferson? [9]
Such commitments probably lie so deep in one's sensibility
that mere intellectual conviction, Poe's "unaided reason,"
can scarcely reach them. Perhaps this discrepancy of belief
and feeling exists in all ages, and creates the inner conflicts
from which poetry comes. If this points to something in
the nature of the literary imagination, we are bound to
say that it will always lie a little beyond our understanding.

By the time Poe came to write his fable of the power of
words, the angels of omnipotent reason could claim a victory. The scene is again the after-life; the characters two
angels who meet in interstellar space after the destruction
of the earth—a disaster assumed in all three of the dialogues
and in *Eureka,* and a possible eventuality in most of Poe's
tales. (One scarcely needs to be reminded of the collapse
of the world of Roderick Usher.) The probable meaning
of this omnivorous symbol I shall try to glance at presently.
The climax of the angels' talk will reveal the long way that
Poe had come from the philosophic insight of 1841 to the
full angelic vision of 1845:

Oinos—But why, Agathos, do you weep—and why, Oh why do
your wings droop as we hover over this fair star—which is the
greenest and yet most terrible of all we have encountered in our
flight? Its brilliant flowers look like a fairy dream—but its fierce
volcanoes like the passions of a turbulent heart.

[9] In the Virginia of Poe's time the subjects of conversation and reading were
almost exclusively politics and theology. The educated Virginian was a deist
by conviction and an Anglican or a Presbyterian by habit.

Agathos—They *are*—they *are!* This wild star it is now three centuries since, with clasped hands, and with streaming eyes, at the feet of my beloved—I spoke it—with a few passionate sentences—into birth. Its brilliant flowers *are* the dearest of all unfulfilled dreams, and its raging volcanoes *are* the passions of the most turbulent and unhallowed of hearts.

How had Agathos created this beautiful but unhallowed object? By the "physical power of words," he tells Oinos. Madame Maritain is the only critic I have read who has had the perception to take seriously this dialogue; her comment is of great interest:

Eh bien, ce texte se réfère-t-il vraiment à une conception magique de la poésie et de la parole? Je ne crois pas. Nous avons affaire ici, comme dans *Eureka,* à une philosophie et une cosmologie panthéistiques, où tout mouvement et toute action participent a l'efficicacité d'une action divine.

[Does the text then really refer to a magical conception of poetry and of the word? I do not think so. We have to do here, as in *Eureka,* with a pantheistic philosophy and cosmology, where every movement and every action participates in the efficiency of a divine action.]

There can be no doubt about Poe's pantheism here and in *Eureka,* but in both works we cannot fail to detect special variations in the direction of deism. Madame Maritain quotes Léon Bloy on the eternal consequences of every action of divine grace for the human spirit, an ancient Christian doctrine connected with the belief in the Community of Saints, for which Pascal invented the great natural analogy:

The slightest movement affects the whole of nature; a stone cast into the sea changes the whole face of it. So, in the realm of Grace, the smallest act affects the whole by its results. Therefore everything has its importance.

In every action we must consider, besides the act itself, our present, past, and future conditions, and others whom it touches, and must see the connections of it all. *And so we shall keep ourselves well in check.*[10]

It almost seems as if Poe had just read this passage and had gone at once to his desk to begin *The Power of Words;* as if he had deliberately ignored the moral responsibility, the *check* upon human power, enjoined in the last sentence, and had concentrated upon Pascal's physical analogy for divine grace: "The slightest *movement* affects the whole of nature." One more step, and the "slightest movement," a spoken *word,* will act creatively. A failure of moral responsibility towards the universe would not necessarily issue in an act of physical creation; nor would action undertaken in the state of sanctifying grace produce stars that are both beautiful and hallowed, unless, of course, the *word* is a "magic recipe," incantatory magic, which I believe we undoubtedly get in *The Power of Words.* This is not the same presumption as our own timid, superstitious reverence for an order of poetic language which creates its own reality, but rather a grandiose angelic presumption on the part of man. As usual, Poe is at least partly aware of what he is doing; for Agathos explains:

This power of retrogradation [Pascal's "the smallest action affecting the whole by its results"] in its absolute fulness and perfection—this faculty of referring *all* epochs, *all* effects to *all* causes—is of course the prerogative of the Deity alone—but in every variety of degree, short of absolute perfection, is the power itself exercised by the whole host of the Angelic intelligences.

This "power," of course, is not at this stage magical; it represents angelic knowledge rather than power. But when Agathos created his green star he was not yet an angel; he

---

[10] Pascal's *Pensées,* with an English translation, brief notes and Introduction by H. F. Stewart, D.D. (New York, 1950), *Adversaria* 16; p. 377.

was still man, but man with the creative power, just short of divine perfection, of the angelic intelligences. Wasn't his power on earth actually greater than that of the angels of Christian theology? For they are not primary creators; they are the powerful but uncreative executives of the divine will. Agathos's doctrine transcends the ideal of mere angelic knowledge: it is superangelism. Man is not only an angel, he is God in his aspect of creativity. I remark almost with regret, mingled with uneasiness, that Poe proves my argument, perhaps too well. (When criticism thinks that it has proved anything, it has become angelic itself.) But this is not all: Oinos tells Agathos that he "remembers many successful experiments in what some philosophers were weak enough to denominate animalculae." And Agathos bows to the mathematicians: "Now the mathematicians . . . saw that the results of any given impulse were absolutely endless . . . these men saw, at the same time, that this species of analysis itself had within itself a capacity for indefinite progress. . . ." Mathematicians were about to achieve the omniscience of the Son, and biologists the creative power of the Father.

Are we to conclude that in these fantasies Poe "appears to yield himself completely to the idea of the moment"? I believe that Mr. Eliot's observation is inaccurate. Poe is quite capable of faking his science, and of appearing to take seriously his own wildest inventions; but the invention is the creaking vehicle of something deeper. What he really takes seriously, and what he yields to in the end, is not an *idea* of the moment. He is progressively mastered by one great idea, deeper than any level of conscious belief and developing to the end of his life at an ever increasing rate, until at last he is engulfed by it. It is his own descent into the maelstrom.

He arrives at it, or reaches the bottom of it, in *Eureka*, which he wrote in 1848, the year before his death. I shall not go so far as to connect, symbolically or prophetically, his death and the vision of the pit at the end of *Eureka.* We may only observe that the complete vision, of which the early works represent an approximation, immediately precedes his death. The proposition of which *Eureka* is to provide the "proof," he states at the beginning:

In the original unity of the first thing lies the secondary cause of all things, with the germ of their inevitable annihilation.

This "nothingness" is a dialectical conversion, not of one symbol into its opposite by analogy, as we see it in Dante, or even in Donne, but of an abstraction into its antithesis. Thesis: the omniscient intellect of man (of Poe as man) achieves a more than angelic knowledge in comprehending the structure and purpose of the created universe. Antithesis: the final purpose of the created universe is the extinction in its own unity of the omniscient intellect of man. There is no Hegelian synthesis. After the original act of divine creation, God withdraws into his deistic aloofness, leaving the separate and local acts of creation to man. This is the sphere of secondary creations which man as angelic delegate of God is empowered to perform. Thus, says Poe at the end of *Eureka,* not only is every man his own God, every man *is* God: every man the nonspatial center into which the universe, by a reverse motion of the atoms, will contract, as into its annihilation. God destroys himself in the eventual recovery of his unity. Unity equals zero. If Poe must at last "yield himself unto Death utterly," there is a lurid sublimity in the spectacle of his taking God along with him into a grave which is not smaller than the universe.

The material universe is in a state of radical disequilibrium, every atom striving to disengage itself from material forms and to return to the original center; but this is not a center in space. It is the Pascalian center which is the everywhere and nowhere, occupied by nothing. Since matter is merely the dialectical movement of attraction and repulsion, it will have ceased to exist when it rejoins the everywhere and nowhere. Space being emptied of matter, there is not even space, for space is that which is occupied by something. We are beyond the topless and bottomless abyss of Pascal.

The image of the abyss is in all of Poe's serious writings: the mirror in "William Wilson"; burial alive; the "tarn" into which the House of Usher plunges; the great white figure towards which Pym is being borne by a current of the sea; the pit over which the pendulum swings; the dead body containing the living soul of M. Valdemar; being walled up alive; the vertigo of the maelstrom.

Poe's most useful biographer, Professor Quinn, exhibits testimonials from modern physicists to bolster up with scientific authority a work in which he probably has little confidence. Let us assume, what may well be false, that *Eureka* from the scientific point of view of any age is nonsense. That would not make *Eureka* nonsense. "The glory of man," says Valéry in his essay on *Eureka*, "and something more than his glory, is to waste his powers on the void. . . . Thus it would seem that the history of thought can be summarized in these words: *It is absurd by what it seeks; great by what it finds.*" What did Poe's "absurd" essay in eschatology inadvertently find, if indeed it found anything but nothing? Valéry again (and again the French instruct us in Poe) points, in another context, to the central meaning of *Eureka,* without perhaps quite knowing that he has done so (for Paul Valéry was himself an archangel); he says: "As soon as we leave the bounds of the moment, as soon as we attempt to enlarge and extend our presence outside of itself, our forces are exhausted in our liberty." Is this always and under all conditions necessarily true? I think not; but it was particularly true of Poe.

It was true of him because in *Eureka* he circumvented the natural world and tried to put himself not in the presence of God, but in the seat of God. *The exhaustion of force as a consequence of his intellectual liberation from the sensible world*—that is my reading of Valéry as a gloss upon the angelism of Poe. The intellectual force is exhausted because in the end it has no real object. The human intellect cannot reach God as essence; only God as analogy. Analogy to what? Plainly analogy to the natural world; for there is nothing in the intellect that has not previously reached it through the senses. Had Dante arrived at the vision of God by way of sense? We must answer yes, because Dante's Triune Circle is light, which the finite intelligence can see only in what has already been seen by means of it. But Poe's center is that place—to use Dante's great figure—"where the sun is silent." Since he refuses to see nature, he is doomed to see nothing. He has overleaped and cheated the condition of man. The reach of our imaginative enlargement is perhaps no longer than the ladder of analogy, at the top of which we may see all, if we still wish to *see* anything, that we have brought up with us from the bottom, where lies the sensible world. If we take nothing with us to the top but our emptied, angelic intellects, we shall see nothing when we get there. Poe as God sits silent in darkness. Here the movement of tragedy is reversed: there is no action. Man as angel becomes a demon who cannot initiate the first motion of love, and we can feel only compassion with his suffering, for it is potentially ours.

I have not supposed it necessary to describe in detail the structure of *Eureka,* or to call attention to its great passages of expository prose, which seem to me unsurpassed in their kind in the nineteenth century. I have not discussed Poe from what is commonly known as the literary point of view. I have tried to expound one idea, the angelism of the intellect, as one aspect of one writer. I do not hesitate in conclusion to commit Poe's heresy of the didactic, and to point a moral. We shall be so exhausted in our liberty that we shall have to take our final rest, not in the cool of the evening, but in the dark, if any one of our modes decides to set up in business for itself.

1951

The Symbolic Imagination

The Mirrors of Dante

IT IS RIGHT even if it is not quite proper to observe at the beginning of a discourse on Dante, that no writer has held in mind at one time the whole of *The Divine Comedy:* not even Dante, perhaps least of all Dante himself. If Dante and his Dantisti have not been equal to the view of the whole, a view shorter than theirs must be expected of the amateur who, as a writer of verses, vainly seeks absolution from the mortal sin of using poets for what he can get out of them. I expect to look at a single image in the *Paradiso,* and to glance at some of its configurations with other images. I mean the imagery of light, but I mean chiefly its reflections. It was scarcely necessary for Dante to have read, though he did read, the *De Anima,* to learn that sight is the king of the senses and that the human body, which like other organisms lives by *touch,* may be made actual in language only through the imitation of *sight.* And sight in language is imitated not by means of "description"—*ut pictura poesis*—but by doubling the image: our confidence in its spatial reality is won quite simply by casting the image upon a glass, or otherwise by the insinuation of space between.

I cannot undertake to examine here Dante's double imagery in all its detail, for his light alone could lead us into complexities as rich as life itself. I had almost said richer than life, if by life we mean (as we must mean) what we

424

ourselves are able daily to see, or even what certain writers have seen, with the exception of Shakespeare, and possibly of Sophocles and Henry James. A secondary purpose that I shall have in view will be to consider the dramatic implications of the light imagery as they emerge at the resolution of the poem, in Canto XXXIII of the *Paradiso*. These implications suggest, to my mind, a radical change in the interpretation of *The Divine Comedy*, and impel me to ask again: What kind of poem is it? In asking this question I shall not be concerned with what we ordinarily consider to be literary criticism; I shall be only incidentally judging, for my main purpose is to describe.

In *Purgatorio* XXX Beatrice appears to Dante first as a voice (what she says need not detain us here), then as light; but not yet the purest light. She is the light of a pair of eyes in which is reflected the image of the gryphon, a symbol of the hypostatic union, of which she herself is a "type." But before Dante perceives this image in her eyes, he says: "A thousand desires hotter than flame held my eyes bound to the shining eyes. . . ."[1] I see no reason to suppose that Dante does not mean what he says. *Mille disiri più che fiamma caldi* I take to be the desires, however interfused by this time with courtly and mystical associations, of a man for a woman: the desires that the boy Dante felt for the girl Beatrice in 1274 after he had passed her in a street of Florence. She is the same Beatrice, Dante the same Dante, with differences which do not reject but rather include their sameness. Three dancing girls appear: Dante's allegory, formidable as it is, intensifies rather than impoverishes the reality of the dancers as girls. Their dance is a real dance, their song, in which they make a charming request of Beatrice, is a real song. If

---

[1] Quotations in English from *The Divine Comedy* are from the translation by Carlyle, Okey, and Wicksteed, in the Temple Classics edition. Here and there I have taken the liberty of neutralizing certain Victorian poeticisms, which were already archaic in that period.

Dante expected us to be interested in the dancers only as the Theological Virtues, I see no good reason why he made them girls at all. They are sufficiently convincing as the Three Graces, and I cannot feel in the pun a serious violation of Dante's confidence. The request of the girls is sufficiently remarkable: *Volgi, Beatrice, volgi gli occhi santi*—"Turn, Beatrice, turn those holy eyes." Let Dante see your holy eyes; look into his eyes. Is it extravagant to substitute for the image of the gryphon the image of Dante in Beatrice's eyes? I think not. *He is in her eyes*—as later, in *Paradiso* XXXIII, he will be "in" God. Then a startling second request by the dancers: "Of thy grace do us the favor that thou unveil thy mouth to him"—*disvele / a lui la bocca tua* . . . "that he may discern the second beauty which thou hidest"—*la seconda belleza che tu cele*. At this point we get one of the innumerable proofs of Dante's greatness as a poet. We are not shown *la seconda belleza,* the smiling mouth; we are shown, instead, in the first four *terzine* of the next canto, the effect on Dante. For neither Dante nor Homer *describes* his heroine. As Beatrice's mouth is revealed, all Dante's senses but the sense of sight are *tutti spenti;* and sight itself is caught in *l'antica rete*—"the ancient net"—a variation of *l'antica fiamma*—"the ancient flame"—that he had felt again when he had first seen Beatrice in the Earthly Paradise.

What the net is doing here seems now to me plain, after some ten years of obtuseness about it. The general meaning is, as Charles Williams holds, that Dante, having chosen the Way of Affirmation through the physical image, feels here in the Earthly Paradise all that he had *felt* before, along with what he now *knows*. Why did he put the worldly emotion of his youthful life into the figure of the net? It is not demanded by the moment; we should not have the sense of missing something if it were not there. If it is a simple metaphor for the obfuscation of sensuality, it is not a powerful metaphor; we must remember that Dante uses very few linguistic metaphors, as distinguished from analogical or symbolic objects; when he uses them they are simple and powerful. The net, as I see it, is not simply a metaphor for the "catching" of Dante by Beatrice in 1274, though it is partly *that* ancient net; it is also a net of even more famous antiquity, that in which Venus caught Mars; and it is thus a symbolic object. Moreover, if Beatrice's eyes are univocally divine, why do the three Theological Dancers reproach him with gazing at her "too fixedly"—*troppo fiso*—as if he or anybody else could get too much of the divine light? He is, of course, not yet ready for the full Beatific Vision. But an astonishing feature of the great scene of the divine pageant is that, as a trope, a subjective effect, the smile of Beatrice simultaneously revives his human love (Eros) and directs his will to the anticipation of the Beatific Vision (Agapé): both equally, by means of the action indicated by the blinding effect of both; he is blinded by the net and by the light, not alternately but at one instant.[2]

To bring together various meanings at a single moment of action is to exercise what I shall speak of here as the symbolic imagination; but the line of *action* must be unmistakable, we must never be in doubt about what is happening; for at a given stage of his progress the hero does one simple thing, and one only. The symbolic imagination conducts an action through analogy, of the human to the divine, of the natural to the supernatural, of the low to the high, of time to eternity. My literary generation was deeply impressed by Baudelaire's sonnet *Correspondances,* which restated the doctrines of medieval symbolism by way of Swedenborg; we were impressed because we had lost the historical perspective

---

2 It seems scarcely necessary to remind the reader that I have followed in the scene of the Earthly Paradise only one thread of an immense number in a vastly complex pattern.

leading back to the original source. But the statement of a doctrine is very different from its possession as experience in poetry. Analogical symbolism need not move towards an act of imagination. It may see in active experience the qualities necessary for static symbolism; for example, the Grave of Jesus, which for the theologian may be a symbol to be expounded in the Illuminative Way, or for the mystic may be an object of contemplation in the Unitive Way. Despite the timeless orders of both rational discourse and intuitive contemplation, it is the business of the symbolic poet to return to the order of temporal sequence—to *action*. His purpose is to show men experiencing whatever they may be capable of, with as much meaning as he may be able to see in it; but the action comes first. Shall we call this the Poetic Way? It is at any rate the way of the poet, who has got to do his work with the body of this world, whatever that body may look like to him, in his time and place—the whirling atoms, the body of a beautiful woman, or a deformed body, or the body of Christ, or even the body of this death. If the poet is able to put into this moving body, or to find in it, a coherent chain of analogies, he will inform an intuitive act with symbolism; his will be in one degree or another the symbolic imagination.

Before I try to illustrate these general reflections, I must make a digression, for my own guidance, which I am not competent to develop as searchingly as my subject demands. The symbolic imagination takes rise from a definite limitation of human rationality which was recognized in the West until the seventeenth century; in this view the intellect cannot have direct knowledge of essences. The only created mind that has this knowledge is the angelic mind.[3] If we

---

[3] The difficulties suffered by man as angel were known at least as early as Pascal; but the doctrine of angelism, as a force in the modern mind, has been fully set forth for the first time by Jacques Maritain in *The Dream of Descartes* (New York, 1944).

do not believe in angels we shall have to invent them in order to explain by parable the remarkable appearance, in Europe, at about the end of the sixteenth century, of a mentality which denied man's commitment to the physical world, and set itself up in quasi-divine independence. This mind has intellect and will without feeling; and it is through feeling alone that we witness the glory of our servitude to the natural world, to St. Thomas' accidents, or, if you will, to Locke's secondary qualities; it is our tie with the world of sense. The angelic mind suffers none of the limitations of sense; it has immediate knowledge of essences; and this knowledge moves through the perfect will to divine love, with which it is at one. Imagination in an angel is thus inconceivable, for the angelic mind transcends the mediation of both image and discourse. I call that human imagination angelic which tries to disintegrate or to circumvent the image in the illusory pursuit of essence. When human beings undertake this ambitious program, divine love becomes so rarefied that it loses its human paradigm, and is dissolved in the worship of intellectual power, the surrogate of divinity that worships itself. It professes to know nature as essence at the same time that it has become alienated from nature in the rejection of its material forms.

It was, however high the phrases, the common thing from which Dante always started, as it was certainly the greatest and most common to which he came. His images were the natural inevitable images—the girl in the street, the people he knew, the language he learned as a child. In them the great diagrams were perceived; from them the great myths open; by them he understands the final end.[4]

This is the simple secret of Dante, but it is a secret which is not necessarily available to the Christian poet today. The Catholic faith has not changed since Dante's time. But the

[4] Charles Williams, *The Figure of Beatrice* (London, 1943), p. 44.

Catholic sensibility, as we see it in modern Catholic poetry, from Thompson to Lowell, has become angelic, and is not distinguishable (doctrinal differences aside) from poetry by Anglicans, Methodists, Presbyterians, and atheists. I take it that more than doctrine, even if the doctrine be true, is necessary for a great poetry of action. Catholic poets have lost, along with their heretical friends, the power to start with the "common thing": they have lost the gift for concrete experience. The abstraction of the modern mind has obscured their way into the natural order. Nature offers to the symbolic poet clearly denotable objects in depth and in the round, which yield the analogies to the higher syntheses. The modern poet rejects the higher synthesis, or tosses it in a vacuum of abstraction.[5] If he looks at nature he spreads the clear visual image in a complex of metaphor, from one katachresis to another through Aristotle's permutations of genus and species. He cannot sustain the prolonged analogy, the second and superior kind of figure that Aristotle doubtless had in mind when he spoke of metaphor as the key to the resemblances of things, and the mark of genius.

That the gift of analogy was not Dante's alone every medievalist knows. The most striking proof of its diffusion and the most useful example for my purpose that I know, is the letter of St. Catherine of Siena to Brother Raimondo of Capua. A young Sienese, Niccolo Tuldo, had been unjustly convicted of treason and condemned to death. Catherine became his angel of mercy, giving him daily solace—the meaning of the Cross, the healing powers of the Blood; and so reconciled him to the faith that he accepted his last end. Now I have difficulty believing people who say that they live in the Blood of Christ, for I take them to mean that they have the faith and hope some day to live in it. The evidence

---

[5] Another way of putting this is to say that the modern poet, like Valéry or Crane, tries to seize directly the anagogical meaning, without going through the three preparatory stages of letter, allegory, and trope.

of the Blood is one's power to produce it, the power to show it as a "common thing" and to make it real, literally, in action. For the report of the Blood is very different from its reality. St. Catherine does not report it; she recreates it, so that its analogical meaning is confirmed again in blood that she has seen. This is how she does it:

Then [the condemned man] came, like a gentle lamb; and seeing me he began to smile, and wanted me to make the sign of the Cross. When he had received the sign, I said, "Down! To the bridal, my sweetest brother. For soon shalt thou be in the enduring life." He prostrated himself with great gentleness, and I stretched out his neck; and bowed me down, and recalled to him the Blood of the Lamb. His lips said naught save Jesus! and Catherine! And so saying, I received his head in my hands, closing my eyes in the divine goodness and saying, "I will."

When he was at rest my soul rested in peace and quiet, and in so great fragrance of blood that I could not bear to remove the blood which had fallen on me from him.

It is deeply shocking, as all proximate incarnations of the Word are shocking, whether in Christ and the Saints, or in Dostoevsky, James Joyce, or Henry James. I believe it was T. S. Eliot who made accessible again to an ignorant generation a common Christian insight, when he said that people cannot bear very much reality. I take this to mean that only persons of extraordinary courage, and perhaps even genius, can face the spiritual truth in its physical body. Flaubert said that the artist, the soldier, and the priest face death every day; so do we all; yet it is perhaps nearer to them than to other men; it is their particular responsibility. When St. Catherine "rests in so great fragrance of blood," it is no doubt the Blood of the Offertory which the celebrant offers to God *cum odore suavitatis*, but with the literal odor of the species of wine, not of blood. St. Catherine had the courage of genius which permitted her to *smell* the Blood of Christ in Niccolo Tuldo's blood clotted on her dress: she smelled the two bloods *not alternately but at one instant,* in a single act compounded of spiritual insight and physical perception.

Chekhov said that a gun hanging on the wall at the beginning of a story has got to be fired off before the story ends: everything in potency awaits its completed purpose in act. If this is a metaphysical principle, it is also the prime necessity of the creative imagination. Is not St. Catherine telling us that the Blood of Christ must be perpetually recreated as a brute fact? If the gun has got to be fired, the Blood has got to be shed, if only because that is the first condition of its appearance; it must move towards the condition of human action, where we may smell it, touch it, and taste it again.

When ecclesiastical censorship of this deep insight in the laity exceeds a just critical prudence, the result is not merely obscurantism in the arts; it is perhaps a covert rejection of the daily renewal of the religious life. Twenty-five years ago the late W. B. Yeats had a controversy with the Irish bishops about the famous medieval "Cherry Tree Carol," which the hierarchy wished to suppress as blasphemous. The Blessed Virgin is resting under a cherry tree, too tired to reach up and pluck a cherry. Since Christ lives from the foundations of the world, He is omnipotent in the womb, and He commands the tree to lower a bough for His Mother's convenience; which it obligingly does, since it cannot do otherwise. Here again the gun is fired and the Blood is shed. If the modern Church has lost the historic experience of this kind of symbolism, which is more tolerable, I believe, in the Latin countries than with us, it is at least partial evidence that the Church has lost the great culture that it created, and that at intervals has created the life of the Church.

I return from this digression to repeat that Dante was the great master of the symbolism, the meaning of which I have been trying to suggest. But the symbolic "problem" of *The Divine Comedy* we must not suppose Dante to have under-

taken analytically; it is our problem, not his. Dr. Flanders
Dunbar has stated it with great penetration:

As with his progress he perceives more and more of ultimate
reality through the symbol [Beatrice], at the same time the symbol
occupies less and less of his attention, until ultimately it takes
its place among all created things on a petal of the rose, while he
gazes beyond it into the full glory of the sun.[6]

The symbolic problem, then, is: How shall Dante move
step by step (literally and allegorically) from the Dark
Wood, the negation of light, to the "three circles, of three
colors and one magnitude," God Himself, or pure light,
where there are no sensible forms to reflect it? There can
be no symbol for God, for that which has itself informed
step by step the symbolic progress. Vision, giving us clear
visual objects, through physical sight, moving steadily up-
ward towards its anagogical transfiguration, is the first matrix
of the vast analogical structure. As Dante sees more he sees
less: as he sees more light the nearer he comes to its source,
the less he sees of what it had previously lit up. In the
Empyrean, at the climax of the Illuminative Way, Beatrice
leaves Dante and takes her place in the Rose; St. Bernard
now guides him into the Intuitive Way.

For the Illuminative Way is the way to knowledge through
the senses, by means of aided reason, but here the "distance"
between us and what we see is always the distance between a
concept and its object, between the human situation in which
the concept arises and the realization of its full meaning. Put
otherwise, with the beginning of the *Vita Nuova* in mind,
it is the distance between the knowledge of love, which resulted from the earthly love of Dante for Beatrice, and the
distant "object," or God, that had made the love in the first
place possible: the distance between Beatrice and the light

[6] H. Flanders Dunbar, *Symbolism in Mediaeval Thought and Its Consummation in The Divine Comedy* (New Haven, 1929), p. 347.

which had made it possible for him to see her. The Kantian synthetic proposition of the entire poem, as we enter it through the symbolism of light, is: Light is Beatrice. Here the eye is still on the human image; it is still on it up to the moment when she takes her place with the other saints in the Rose, where she is only one of many who turn their eyes to the "eternal fountain." Light is Beatrice; light is her *smile;* her final smile, which Dante sees as she enters the Rose, is no longer the mere predicate of a sentence, for there is now no distance between the smile and what had lit it. Although, insofar as it is a smile at all, it is still the smile at the unveiling of the mouth, it is now the smile without the mouth, the smile of light. And thus we arrive at the converse of the proposition: Beatrice is light. Now Dante's eye is on the light itself, but he cannot see it because Beatrice, through whose image he had progressively seen more light, has disappeared; and he can see nothing. There is nothing to *see.* For that which enables sight is not an object of vision. What has been seen is, in what is surely one of the greatest passages of all poetry, "the shadowy prefaces of their truth." Illumination, or intellect guided by divine grace, powerful as it is, halts at the "prefaces." But the Unitive Way leads to the Presence, where both sight and discursive thought cease.

Whether Dante should have tried to give us an image of God, of that which is without image and invisible, is an unanswerable question. Is it possible that we have here a break in the symbolic structure, which up to the end of the poem has been committed to the visible? At the end we are with Love, whose unpredicated attribute is the entire universe. Has Dante given us, in the "three circles, of three colors and one magnitude," merely the trinitarian and doctrinal equivalent of the ultimate experience, instead of an objective symbol of the experience itself? In the terms of Dante's given structure, such a symbol was perhaps not possible; and strictly speaking it is never possible. If he was going to give us anything he doubtless had to give us just what he gave; he gave it in an act of great artistic heroism. For in the center of the circles he sees the image of man. This is the risk, magnified almost beyond conception, of St. Catherine: the return of the supra-rational and supra-sensible to the "common thing." It is the courage to see again, even in its ultimate cause, the Incarnation.

If we will look closely at the last four lines of the *Paradiso*, and double back on our tracks, I believe that we will see that there is no break in the *dramatic* structure—the structure of the action.[7] For the poem is an action: a man is acting and going somewhere, and things are happening both to him and around him; otherwise the poem would be— what I may have given the impression of its being—a symbolic machine. In the space of an essay I cannot prepare properly the background of the suggestion that I am about to offer. For one thing, we should have to decide who "Dante" is, and where he is in the action that he has depicted—questions that nobody seems to know much about. For what it may be worth, I suggest that the poet has undertaken to involve a fictional character named Dante—at once the poet and not the poet of that name—in a certain action of the greatest possible magnitude, the issue of which is nothing less, perhaps something greater, than life or death. In this action the hero fails. He fails in the sense that he will have to start over again when he steps out of the "poem," as he surely must do if he is going to write it.

Thus I see *The Divine Comedy* as essentially dramatic and, in one of its modes, tragic. Are we to suppose that the hero actually attained to the Beatific Vision? No; for nobody who had would be so foolish as to write a poem about it, if

---

7 By "dramatic" I mean something like *practic*, a possible adjective from *praxis*, a general movement of action as potency which it is the purpose of the poem to actualize. In the Thomist sequence, *potentia:actio:actus*, "dramatic" would roughly correspond to the middle term.

in that spiritual perfection it could even occur to him to do
so. The poem is a vast paradigm of the possibility of the
Beatific Vision. No more than its possibility for the individual
person, for "Dante" himself, is here entertained. What
shall we make of his failure of memory, the slipping away
of the final image, which he calls *tanto oltraggio*—"so great
an outrage"? It would be a nice question to decide whether
something had slipped away, or whether it had ever been
fully there. The vision is imagined, it is *imaged;* its essence
is not possessed. I confess that it is not an argument from the
poem to say that had Dante claimed its possession, he would
have lost that "good of the intellect" which we forfeit when
we presume to angelic knowledge; and it was through the
good of the intellect that he was able to write the poem.
But it is an external argument that I believe cannot be entirely ignored.

The last *terzina* of the last canto tells us: *All' alta fantasia
qui mancò possa*—"To the high fantasy here power failed."
What power failed? The power to write the poem, or the
power to possess as experience the divine essence? Is it a
literary or a religious failure? It is obviously and honorably
both. It makes no more sense to say Dante achieved his
final vision as direct experience than to say that Sophocles
married his mother and put out his own eyes; that the experience of the *Oedipus Rex* represents the personal experience of Sophocles. What Dante achieved is an *actual* insight
into the great dilemma, eternal life or eternal death, but he
has not hedged the dilemma like a bet to warrant himself a
favorable issue. As the poem closes, he still faces it, like the
rest of us. Like Oedipus, the fictional Dante learns in humility a certain discipline of the will: we may equate up to a
point the dark-blindness of Oedipus and the final light-
blindness of Dante; both men have succeeded through suffering in blinding themselves to knowledge-through-sense,

in the submission of *hybris* to a higher will.[8] The fictional Dante at the end steps out of the frame and becomes again the historical Dante; Oedipus steps out of his frame, his fictional plot is done, he is back in the world of unformed action, blind and, like Dante, an exile. Shall Oedipus be saved? Shall Dante? We do not know, but to ask the question is to point to a primary consideration in the interpretation of *The Divine Comedy,* particularly if we are disposed, as some commentators have been, to believe that Dante the man used his poem arrogantly to predict his own salvation.

If Dante does not wholly succeed in giving us in the "three circles, of three colors and one magnitude," an image of the Godhead, I think we are ready to see that it was not necessary; it was not a part of his purpose. Such an image is not the "final cause" of the poem. The poem is an action; it is an action to the end. For the image that Dante gives us of the Godhead is not an image to be received by the reader as essential knowledge in his own "angelic" intelligence, as an absolute apart from the action. It is a dramatic image; the image is of the action and the action is Dante's. To read Canto XXXIII in any other way would be perhaps to commit the blunder that M. Gilson warns us against: the blunder of thinking that Dante was writing a super-philosophical tract, or a pious embellishment of the doctrines of Thomas Aquinas, instead of a poem. The question, then, is not what is the right anagogical symbol for God; it is rather what symbol for God will serve tropologically (that is, morally and dramatically) for the tragic insight of the poet who knows, through the stages of the Three Ways, that the Beatific Vision is possible but uncertain of realization. Dante sees himself, Man, in the Triune Circles, and he is in the Seraphic Heaven of Love. But at the end desire and will are

[8] Oedipus does not achieve this until the end of *Oedipus at Colonus.*

like a "wheel moving equally"; motion imparted to it at one point turns it as a whole, but it has to be moved, as the wheel of our own desire and will must be moved, by a force outside it. The wheel is Dante's last symbol of the great failure. Since it must be moved, it is not yet at one, not yet in unity, with the divine will; it obeys it, as those other wheels, the sun and stars, moved by love, obey.

I take it that the wheel is the final geometrical projection of the *visual* matrix of analogy; it is what the eye sees, the material form, and what in its anagoge it eventually aspires to become. We must remember that Beatrice's eyes are spheres, no less than the physical universe itself, which is composed of concentric spheres. The first circles that Dante shows us are in Canto III of the *Inferno*, Charon's—"for round his eyes were wheels of flame." The last, the Triune Circles, are the anagoge of the visual circle, and are without extension; they are pure light, the abstraction or sublimation of flame. Flame burning in a circle and light lighting up a circle, and what it encloses, are the prime sensible symbols of the poem. Only Satan, at the geometrical center of the world, occupies a point that cannot be located on any existing arc of the cosmos. This is the spherical (or circular) expression of Satan's absolute privation of light-as-love which in the Empyrean turns the will-wheel of Dante with the cosmic spheres. These are the will of God as love; and if we ignore the dramatic structure, and fail to look closely at the symbolic, we shall conclude that Dante is at one with the purpose of the universe. But, as we have seen, the symbolic structure is complicated by the action, and in the end the action prevails. That is to say, Dante is *still moving.* Everything that moves, says Dante the Thomist in his letter to Can Grande, has some imperfection in it because it is, in the inverse degree of its rate of motion, removed from the Unmoved Mover, the Triune Circles, God. By a twist of this argument, which, of course, as I shall presently indicate, is specious, Satan himself has no imperfection: he too lies immobile—except for the fanning wings that freeze the immobile damned in Giudecca—as the Still Point in the Triune Circles is immobile. If Dante's will is turning like a wheel, he is neither damned nor saved; he is morally active in the universal human predicament. His participation in the love imparted as motion to the universe draws him towards the Triune Circles and to the immobility of peace at the center, as it draws all creatures; but a defection of the will could plunge him into the other "center."

Now Dante is astonished when he sees in the Primum Mobile a reversal of the ratio of speed of the spheres as he had observed it on earth, through the senses. "But in the universe of sense," he says to Beatrice, "we may see the circlings more divine as from the center they are more removed." In the spiritual universe the circlings are more divine the nearer they are to the center. It is a matter of perspective; from the earth outward the revolutions of the spheres are increasingly rapid up to the ninth, the Primum Mobile, whose speed is just short of infinite; the Primum Mobile is trying to achieve with all points of its surface a simultaneous contact with the Still Point of the Empyrean. What he sees in the Primum Mobile is this perspective visually reversed; instead of being the outer "crust" of the universe, the Primum Mobile is actually next to the central Still Point, whirling with inconceivable speed. God, the Still Point, is a nonspatial entity which is *everywhere* and *nowhere*. The Ptolemaic cosmos, which had been Christianized by the imposition of the angelic hierarchy of Dionysius, has been, in a way not to be completely visualized, turned inside out. The spheres, which began their career as an astronomical hypothesis, are now no longer necessary; they are replaced in the ultimate reality by nine nonspatial gradations of angelic intelligence, in three triads, the last and ninth circle of "fire" being that of the simple angels, the "farthest" removed in the nonspatial continuum from the Divine Love.

Where then is the earth, with Satan at its exact center? I think we must answer: Where it has always been. But "where" that is we had better not try to say. At any rate neither Satan nor the earth is at the spiritual center. His immobility thus has no perfection. In the full spiritual reality, of which the center of the material universe becomes an outermost "rind," beyond space, Satan does not exist: he exists in the world of sense and in the human will. The darkness of hell, from the point of view of God (if I may be allowed the expression), is not an inner darkness, but an outer. So, in the progress from hell to the Empyrean, Dante has come from the inner darkness of man to the inner light of God; from the outer darkness of God to the outer light of man.

This anagogical conversion of symbol that I have been trying to follow in one of its threads is nowhere by Dante merely *asserted;* it is constantly moving, rendered moment by moment as *action.* Like most good poets, great or minor, Dante wrote better than he had meant to do; for if we took him at his word, in the letter to Can Grande, we should conclude that the *Paradiso* is a work of rhetoric calculated "to remove those living in this life from a state of misery and to guide them to a state of happiness." It seems probable that persons now enrolled among the Blessed got there without being compelled to see on the way all that Dante saw. Were we reading the poem for that kind of instruction, and knew not where else to find it, we might conclude that Dante's *luce intellectual,* with its transformations in the fourfold system of interpretation, is too great a price to pay even for salvation; or, at any rate, for most of us, the wrong price. It would perhaps be a mistake for a man to decide that he has become a Christian at the instance of Dante, unless he is prepared to see all that Dante saw—

which is one thing, but always seen in at least two ways. A clue to two of the ways is the mirror symbol. As we approach it, the kind of warning that Dante at intervals pauses to give us is not out of place. For if the way up to now has been rough, we may expect it from now on to be even rougher. The number of persons, objects, and places in *The Divine Comedy* that are reflections, replicas, or manifestations of things more remote is beyond calculation. The entire natural world is a replica *in reverse* of the supernatural world. That, I believe, we have seen so far only on the dubious authority of my own assertion. But if Dante is a poet (I agree with M. Gilson that he is) he will not be satisfied with assertion as such, even with the authority of the Church to support it. The single authority of poetry is a difficult criterion of actuality that must always remain beyond our reach. And in some sense of this actuality Dante has got to place his vast two-way analogy (heaven like the world, the world like heaven) on the scene of action, and make it move. Let us take the stance of Dante at the beginning of *Paradiso* XXVIII, and try to suggest some of the ways in which he moves it:

as in the mirror a taper's flame, kindled behind a man, is seen by him before it be in his sight or thought,
as he turns back to see whether the glass speak truth to him, and sees that it accords with it as song-words to the music;
so my memory recalls that I did turn, gazing upon the lovely eyes whence love had made the noose to capture me;
and when I turned, and my own eyes were struck by what appears in that orb whenever upon its circling the eye is well fixed,
a point I saw which rayed forth light so keen that all the vision that it flames upon must close because of its sharp point.

(One observes in passing that even in the Primum Mobile Beatrice bears the net-noose dimension of meaning.) Beatrice's eyes are a mirror in which is reflected that "sharp point," to which Dante, still at a distance from it, now turns his direct gaze. As he looks at it he sees for the first time what its reflection in Beatrice's eyes could not convey: that it is the sensible world turned inside out. For the sensible world as well as her eyes is only a reflection of the light from the sharp point. Now he is looking at the thing-in-itself. *He has at last turned away from the mirror which is the world.* What happens when we turn away from a mirror to look directly at the object which we saw reflected? I must anticipate Beatrice's famous experiment with one of my own. If you will place upon a table a box open at one end, the open end towards a mirror, and then look into the mirror, you will see the open end. Turn from the mirror and look at the box itself. You still see the open end, and thus you see the object *reversed.* If the box were reproduced, in the sense of being continued or moved *into* the mirror, the actual box would present, when we turn to it, a closed end; for the box and its reflection would show their respectively corresponding sides in congruent projection. Quantitative visualization of the cosmic reversal is not completely possible. But through the mirror analogy Dante performs a stupendous feat of the imagination that in kind has probably not been rivalled by any other poet. And it is an analogy that has been firmly grounded in action.

In conclusion I shall try to point to its literal base; for we have seen it, in *Paradiso* XXVIII, only as a simile; and if we had not had it laid down earlier as a physical fact to which we must assent, a self-contained phenomenon of the natural order, it would no doubt lack at the end that fullness of actuality which we do not wholly understand, but which we require of poetry. The self-contained fact of the natural order is established in Canto II of the *Paradiso,* where Beatrice performs a physical experiment. Some scholars have been moved by it to admire Dante for this single ray of positivistic enlightenment feebly glowing in the mind of a medieval poet. So far as I know, our critics have not considered it necessary to be sufficiently unenlightened to see that Beatrice's experiment is merely poetry.

Before I reproduce it I shall exhibit a few more examples of the mirror symbol that appear at intervals in the five last cantos. In Canto XXIX, 25–27, form permeates matter "as in glass . . . a ray so glows that from its coming to its pervading all, there is no interval." Still in XXIX, 142–145, at the end: "See now the height and breadth of the eternal worth, since it has made itself so many mirrors in which it is reflected, remaining in itself one as before." At line 37 of Canto XXX we enter the Empyrean where Dante sees the great River of Light "issuing its living sparks"; it too is a mirror, for Beatrice explains: "The river and the topaz gems that enter and go forth, and the smiling grasses are prefaces of their truth" (i.e., of what they reflect). In Canto XXX, 85–87, Dante bends down to the waves "to make mirrors of my eyes"; and again in XXX he sees the Rose of Paradise, another mirror, in one of his great similes:

And as a hillside reflects itself in water at its foot, as if to look
    upon its own adornment, when it is rich in grasses and in
    flowers,
so, mounting in the light, around, around, casting reflection in
    more than a thousand ranks I saw all that of us have won
    return up yonder.

And finally the climactic reflection, the "telic principle" and the archetype of them all, in Canto XXX, 127–132:

The circling that in thee [in the Triune God] appeared to be con-
    ceived as a reflected light, by my eyes scanned a little,
in itself, of its own color, seemed to be painted with our effigy,
    and thereat my sight was all committed to it.

Where have these mirrors, which do their poetic work, the work of making the supra-sensible visible—one of the tasks of all poetry—where have they come from? The remote frame is doubtless the circular or spherical shape of the Ptolemaic cosmos; [9] but if there is glass in the circular frame, it reflects nothing until Virgil has left Dante to Beatrice's guidance in the Earthly Paradise (*Purgatorio* XXXI); where we have already glanced at the unveiling of mouth and eyes. I suggest that Beatrice's eyes in *Purgatorio* XXXI are the first mirror. But the image is not, at this early stage of Beatrice, sufficiently developed to bear all the strain of analogical weight that Dante intends to put upon it. For that purpose the mirror must be established as a literal mirror, a plain mirror, a "common thing."

He not only begins with the common thing; he continues with it, until at the end we come by disarming stages to a scene that no man has ever looked upon before. Every detail of Paradise is a common thing; it is the cumulative combination and recombination of natural objects beyond their "natural" relations, which staggers the imagination. "Not," says Beatrice to Dante, "that such things are in themselves harsh; but on your side is the defect, in that your sight is not yet raised so high."

A mirror is an artifact of the practical intellect, and as such can be explained by natural law: but there is no natural law which explains man as a mirror reflecting the image of God. The great leap is made in the interval between Canto II and Canto XXXIII of the *Paradiso*.

Dante, in Canto II, is baffled by the spots on the moon, supposing them to be due to alternating density and rarity of matter. No, says Beatrice in effect, this would be monism, a materialistic explanation of the diffusion of the divine light. The true explanation is very different: all saved souls are equally saved, and all the heavenly spheres are equally

---

[9] The popular "visual" translation of Aristotle's primary Unmoved Mover producing, *through being loved,* the primary cosmic motion, which is circular. The philosophical source of this idea, Book XII, Chapter 7, of the *Metaphysics,* Dante of course knew.

in heaven; but the divine light reaches the remoter spheres and souls according to the spiritual gifts of which they were capable in the natural world. "This is the formal principle," Beatrice says, summing up, "which produces, in conformity to the excellence of the object, the turbid and the clear."

Meanwhile she has asked Dante to consider a physical experiment to illustrate the unequal reception of the divine substance. Take three mirrors, she says, and set two of them side by side, and a third in the middle but farther back. Place a candle behind you, and observe its image reflected in each of the three mirrors. The middle reflection will be smaller but not less bright than the two others: "smaller" stands quantitatively for unequal reception of a quality, spiritual insight; "not less bright" likewise for equality of salvation. But what concerns us is a certain value of the experiment that Dante, I surmise, with the cunning of a great poet, slyly refuses to consider: the dramatic value of the experiment.

There are *three* [10] mirrors each reflecting the *one* light. In the heart of the Empyrean, as we have seen, Dante says:

In the profound and shining being of the deep light appeared to me *three* circles, of *three* colors and one magnitude.

In the middle is the effigy of man. The physical image of Dante had necessarily been reflected in each of the three mirrors of Canto II; but he had not seen it. I suggest that he was not then ready to see it; his dramatic (i.e., tropological) development fell short of the final self-knowledge. Self-knowledge comes to him, as an Aristotelian Recognition and Reversal, when he turns the cosmos inside out by turning away from the "real" mirrors to the one light which has cast the three separate images. For the first time he sees the

[10] Only two, placed at unequal distances from the candle, are strictly necessary for the experiment; but three are necessary as pointers towards the anagoge of the Trinity in the Triune Circles.

"one magnitude," the candle itself. And it is all done with the simple apparatus and in conditions laid down in Canto II; he achieves the final anagoge and the dramatic recognition by turning around, as if he were still in Canto II, and by looking at the candle that has been burning all the time behind his back.

I have described some motions of the symbolic imagination in Dante, and tried to develop a larger motion in one of its narrower aspects. What I have left out of this discussion is very nearly the entire poem. In the long run the light imagery is not the body, it is what permits us to *see* the body, of the poem. The rash suggestion that *The Divine Comedy* has a tragic mode—among other modes—I shall no doubt be made to regret; I cannot defend it further here. Perhaps the symbolic imagination is tragic in sentiment, if not always in form, in the degree of its development. Its every gain beyond the simple realism of experience imposes so great a strain upon any actuality of form as to set the ultimate limit of the gain as a defeat. The high order of the poetic insight that the final insight must elude us, is dramatic in the sense that its fullest image is an action in the shapes of this world: it does not reject, it includes; it sees not only with but through the natural world, to what may lie beyond it. Its humility is witnessed by its modesty. It never begins at the top; it carries the bottom along with it, however high it may climb.

1951

The Unliteral Imagination; Or,
I, too, Dislike It[1]

TO SAY THAT one does not like something is not to say that one hates it; it is only to say that one is indifferent to it, or wishes it weren't there, for it may occupy the space that could be filled by something that one positively likes. I, too, dislike it—I, too, along with Miss Marianne Moore, dislike poetry; that is to say, I am indifferent to most of it; and as I get older I am able to read less and less of it. I have wondered why people have been so kind as to describe me as a literary critic, or more narrowly as a critic of poetry; for I have never been able to concentrate on any poetry that could not be useful to me. A literary critic is a person who likes to read books, and even to study them; a critic of poetry, a person who likes to read poems and books of poems. Recently, in London, V. S. Pritchett said to me that he liked to read books, almost any books. I said to myself (not to him) that given his retentive memory and agile intelligence, the sheer love of reading, of reading what one dislikes, or even detests, is the first requisite of the literary critic. I have read certain poems, some of them quite long, hundreds of times; I have never been able to finish *The Ring and the Book;* I don't think that I shall read *Paradise Lost* again. I once read Middle English fairly well, but I could not get beyond the first hundred lines of *Piers Ploughman.*

[1] This essay was given as a lecture at the University of Cincinnati, Dartmouth College, St. Peter's College, and Rice University. It was later published in *The Southern Review,* Summer, 1965.

A literary critic may, and a literary scholar *must* read everything in his "field" (dubious word) with a selfless detachment that puts historical significance above personal preference. Is a genuine scholar expected to prefer one thing to another? He is supposed to understand everything he reads as an historical document. He may prefer Dryden to Pope, but this is nobody's business but his own. I am not denigrating the literary scholars; I could ill afford to sneer at them, since I myself am a parasite dangling from a small twig of their tree of knowledge. It is difficult for me to acquire information at the source. If I wanted to know just where John Dryden was when the Dutch fleet was sailing up the Thames, I would telephone my friend Samuel H. Monk; but since I seldom need to know this sort of thing, I telephone him often for less frivolous reasons, such as the prospect of some Jack Daniel at half-past five.

I, too, dislike it; I dislike the unliteral, or roundabout imagination; for there are poems which do not say literally what they purport to talk about, just as only a few scholars ever get literally round to the text that they hold in one hand while, with the other, they thumb a political or economic "document," which may have been printed at about the same time as the text.

Having made this sweeping generalization—or this generalized sweeping out of certain poets and scholars—I had better try to decide, since I have not yet, at this point, decided, what a *literal* reading of a poem might be, or what constitutes the *literal* element in the poem itself. Here, at the beginning of this tangled difficulty, one feels a little like Moses confronting the burning bush; one is awed by it but it is too hot to jump into; for if Moses could have been like the man of our town who jumped into the bramble bush and scratched out both his eyes, he couldn't have jumped out of the burning bush and scratched them in again, because by that time the eyes along with the rest of him would have been burnt up. One must maintain a certain distance.

The first complication that one meets in confronting literalism is happily a simple one. Take that by now ancient whipping boy, *The Road to Xanadu,* by the late John Livingston Lowes, a work cited some years ago by Mr. T. S. Eliot as a scholarly masterpiece of its kind, one example of which, said Mr. Eliot, was enough. There are other examples to complicate a univocal view of the kind of scholarship that dredges up and arranges a poet's erudition and offers it as an explanation of the poem. Or was Professor Lowes really trying to "explain" "Kubla Khan"? If he was, he didn't succeed. I can bear witness that at least one reader knew no more about "Kubla Khan" after he had read *The Road to Xanadu* than he knew before. I have read Coleridge's account of the occasion, but that was not an explanation of the poem; Coleridge merely told us why the poem was not longer than it is. That man from Porlock—is it too late to find out his name?—is surely the most important anonymous nonliterary personage in the history of English poetry. Am I right in thinking that not only Coleridge but everybody else since Coleridge has taken it for granted that "Kubla Khan" would have been better if he had not been interrupted by the man from Porlock? How can we be sure that the town of Porlock should not have a bronze plaque in memory of this anonymous benefactor of literature? In other words, how can we be sure, had Coleridge been allowed to put down on paper his entire dream, that "Kubla Khan" would not have meandered off with the sacred river into dark mazes of Coleridgean abstractions, such as he afflicted many of his other poems with?

If Coleridge could explain only the shortness of the poem, what does Professor Lowes explain? Nothing, I think; certainly nothing more than "Kubla Khan" explains about itself. What Professor Lowes did in *The Road to Xanadu* was what some great scholars, who are not mere pedants, are capable of doing: he wrote a literary masterpiece that has about the same relation to its ostensible subject as a history of Denmark has to *Hamlet*.

It is time to return from this digression to some observations that may have a bearing on the title of this discourse. If *The Road to Xanadu* has little relation to "Kubla Khan," what *has* it relation to? "Relation" is a slippery word: I wish I could proceed without calling attention to it; I must try to narrow it down to something like a precise meaning. I shall have to go about this indirectly and tentatively. It is not necessary to have read "Kubla Khan" in order to understand and enjoy *The Road to Xanadu*. Professor Lowes wrote a first-rate work of the imagination which contains within it all that one needs to know in order to understand it. What *The Road to Xanadu* has "relation" to is not Coleridge's poem, but an inchoate mass (I must speak metaphorically) of reading which is obviously Coleridge's reading; and, likewise, "Kubla Khan" has "relation" to Coleridge's reading; but neither the work of Coleridge nor the work of Lowes can be said to be *about* Coleridge's reading.

So, instead of the phrase "relation to" we now have the preposition "about." What are these works about? What, in short, are their literal meanings?

Both the poem and the prose work that purports to be about the poem are products of the romantic imagination: both works are in some sense reconstructions of a past, and that sense is perhaps the neo-Gothic impulse towards the artificial ruin. I submit that Professor Lowes's book is also an artificial ruin; or perhaps the materials of an artificial ruin lying around in some disorder waiting to be assembled. Not that Professor Lowes lacked a principle to guide him in his search for the materials: this principle was simply that of historical research. He started with the images and allu-

sions in "Kubla Khan," then tracked down as many of the
books that Coleridge had read as he could find; the result
was an orderly exhibit of disordered, or fragmented, details
which to this day retain the only kind of meaning that they
could ever have. That is to say, the form of *The Road to
Xanadu* is not unlike that of an impressionist novel, in which
one *progression d'effet* follows another, creating a mounting
suspense which compels us to ask breathlessly: What next?
Thus Professor Lowes's book has its own form, which one
might describe as autotelic; at any rate, at the end of the
book we are aware that "Kubla Khan" has disappeared, and
has become completely unnecessary to our understanding of
The Road to Xanadu.

I have labored this matter unduly. I will make one more
observation and proceed to my ostensible subject. Let us
glance at four lines of "Kubla Khan":

> Five miles meandering with a mazy motion
> Through wood and dale the sacred river ran,
> Then reached the caverns measureless to man,
> And sank in tumult to a lifeless ocean.

Professor Lowes is not helpful here; and as I think I have
indicated, we should not expect him to be. To understand
these lines a somewhat less ambitious undertaking than Professor Lowes's researches might be in order. At a glance, one
doubts that any poet could use the rhyme *motion-ocean*
except in a limerick or some other sort of doggerel. It is
a cockney rhyme, and it retains an air of serious nonsense
which is exactly right in a dream-poem. And what about the
heavy assonances and alliterations throughout? I am not the
first person to notice them. But who has noticed the synaesthetic transference of image to sound, as, in a dream, color
can become sound? Although Coleridge thought of the poem
as a "psychological curiosity," one must not take his word for
it. The entire poem—not merely the four lines quoted—re-

veals the hand of a master. Yet almost all that criticism can
do is the trifling sort of observation that I have just made;
and though Samuel Purchas, along with Professor Lowes, has
his own charms, these gentlemen have little to do with
Coleridge.

The hand of a master: but of what, in this poem, was
Coleridge a master? The best answer I can give is to beg the
question: he was a master of the romantic imagination. I get
more perverse pleasure out of this imagination than out of
any other, because I, too, insofar as I am a poet, am a romantic poet. But like Pope's Umbriel, I must have been in a
former life a Prude, and I disapprove of what that makes me;
I disapprove to the extent of wishing that I could write
poems that are not gloomily difficult, or that do not offer the
shock of the *nouveau frisson* which comes of the synaesthetic
surprise or what an early French romantic called *sorcèllerie
évocatoire*. I am talking about myself, perhaps because I like
the vanity of a brief association with Coleridge, but actually
I think because I cannot be very different from other poets
of my time, or at least of my generation; and I believe we
all wish we had been able not only to write better poems, but
poems that say much more than we have been able to say,
while at the same time seeming to say less. The seeming to
say less would consist in making the effects of shock secondary, a kind of by-product of literal statements: even simple
propositions in which denoted objects are predicated of
other denoted objects, or in which philosophical commonplaces are given motion in a common experience. I shall cite
certain passages—not touchstones—that seem to approximate
the ideal of poetry that I have in mind; and I shall begin
with Dante.

> Già era, e con paura il metto in metro,
>   là dove l'ombre eran tutte coperte,
>   e trasparean come festuca in vetro.

(Already I had come [and with fear I put
it into verse] where the souls were wholly
covered, and shone through straw like glass.)

Inf. XXXIV.

The English translation is by J. A. Carlyle, and it is good;
but there was no reason to translate *ombre* (shades) as
"souls." I point this out as an example of the nineteenth
century's failure to see the importance of literal rendition,
whether in translating a foreign language or in writing its
own English poems. To render *ombre* as souls is to miss a
dimension of meaning that Dante surely would have thought
essential. In Christian theology souls—that is, dead persons—
are not "shades": Dante's word is classical and Virgilian;
and where he uses the word *ombre* he is reminding us of
the continuity of the Christian Hell with Virgil's pagan
Hades. What Carlyle's mistranslation omits is what the late
Erich Auerbach called *figura*—the symbolic dimension rooted
firmly in a literal image or statement that does not need
the symbolic significance in order to be immediately understood. Literally, Dante's shades in Giudecca *as visually apprehended* are three-dimensional bodies; we infer of them the
capacity for pain, as if they were alive; and their pain, even
though they are in solid ice and are thus immobile, has all
the intensity of fire. But *as symbolically apprehended* they
require a further implication of the literal image: if Dante
had tried to touch one of them his hand would have met
with no physical resistance. The entire *Divine Comedy* is a
vast interior vision, an ordered, cosmic dream, peopled with
visible shades that dissolve when Dante reaches out to touch
them, as Casella in the *Purgatorio* II melts into air when
Dante tries to embrace him. But why does Carlyle, in Canto
XXXII of the *Inferno* translate *ombre* correctly as "shades":
"the doleful shades were in the ice, sounding with their

teeth like storks"? Was he at liberty to be right in one passage and wrong in another? *Ombre* always means "shades"
unless we are willing to forgo Dante's *figura* which tells us
that we may *see* literally in the mind a non-existent object
that nevertheless has *essentia* as distinguished from *existen-
tia.* This is the capital significance of Dante's allegory. It is
not an allegory which like Spenser's floats in a rarefied
medium of personified abstractions; there would be no allegory at all in the *Divine Comedy* had not Dante in the
first place seen, in the progression of his own drama of the
mind (the phrase is Francis Fergusson's), *shades* which are
analogically solid human bodies; and in the link with classical mythology we are being shown, as I have said, the continuity of all the dead, both pagan and Christian. That
Dante can tell us so much in one simple word, put into a
certain historical and theological context, need not surprise
us; yet we may stand in awe of the poet who can do this
through the simple distinction between an actual solid body
and a merely visible body that does not stop the hand trying
to touch it.

I should now like to offer a passage familiar to all readers
of poetry in English, the first quatrain of Shakespeare's
Sonnet LXXIII:

> That time of year thou mayst in me behold
> When yellow leaves, or none, or few, do hang
> Upon those boughs which shake against the cold,
> Bare ruined choirs, where late the sweet birds sang.

The lines may seem a far cry from Dante. Are they not
merely an extended simile, of which the vehicle and the
tenor are jammed together into an unconvincing metaphor?
Before I try to answer the question, I could suggest that we
might do a *Road to Xanadu* on the fourth line, if only to
show once more how irrelevant historical criticism sometimes
can be. (I could not hope to write an irrelevant masterpiece

like Professor Lowes!) Shakespeare—the argument runs, according to a commentator whose name I have forgotten—Shakespeare was a crypto-Catholic, and he wanted to notify his fellow recusants that he was still with them. He wrote the sonnet for the sake of the fourth line: "Bare ruined choirs where late the sweet birds sang." The choirs are the ruined chapels of the monasteries where Compline, the last office of the day, was sung. That it was Compline there is supporting evidence in the second quatrain: "Death's second self," sleep, follows Compline, and seals the monks up in rest. Henry VIII is therefore the remote begetter of this sonnet. In another sonnet does not Shakespeare say: "And yet this time removed was summer's time"? These were the good old days before Henry, according to Philip Hughes, had made the English people his Mystical Body.

Doubtless, nonsense has a way of instructing us critically by showing what can be *uttered,* but ought not to be *said,* about poetry.

If the substitution of "soul" for "shade" by Carlyle deprives the passage from Dante of its literal base, we could easily ruin Shakespeare's sonnet by rewriting one line as Carlyle might have written it, or for that matter, as I shall indicate presently, as Shelley might have written it.

> That time of year thou mayst in me behold
> When the leaves of life in melancholy hang, etc.

Is it necessary to point out that life has no leaves? Nevertheless, my revision of the line is fairly good second-rate romantic imagery, in which the vehicle disappears into its murky tenor. The abstract meaning is plain enough, but the image is obscure because it does not exist; and this is the way of the unliteral imagination. Shakespeare, in his way, which is not the way of Dante but a way equally brilliant, is a literalist of the imagination. What is he doing in this first quatrain of Sonnet LXXIII? Let us see first what he is not doing. He is not saying anything about life or about melancholy. He is looking not at life's inexistent leaves but at leaves on a tree, where they belong; and he is not merely pointing to them. His eye roves from a tree that still has its leaves to a bare tree, and then to a tree retaining a few leaves; because all the leaves are yellow we know that the season is late autumn or winter. But the activity of the moving eye gives the image its literal base. The metaphorical meaning of the passage—I. A. Richards's tenor—is nowhere asserted; it is completely fused with the vehicle, with the medium conveying it. I daresay Samuel Johnson, a critic who liked detachable meanings independent of their metaphorical vehicle, or meanings merely suggested by the metaphor as an attention-getting device, would not have liked Sonnet LXXIII; but we cannot be sure because he admired Shakespeare in perhaps the greatest essay ever written on this poet.

Johnson at any rate did not live long enough to have an opinion of two famous lines from "Ode to the West Wind"; perhaps we ought to be glad that he was spared the onus of an opinion. These are the lines:

> Oh, lift me as a wave, a leaf, a cloud!
> I fall upon the thorns of life! I bleed!

Everybody knows the entire poem, and will agree with me that to take the lines out of their context is to make them into a sitting duck. Shelley was a great lyric poet who persuaded himself that he was a great philosophical poet whose message came first. If the message came first, what came second? The poetry itself. If I shall seem to be carping, let me remind myself that I could carp at Sonnet LXXIII till doomsday, and Sonnet LXXIII would still be there: it is an ever-fixed mark that looks on analytical tempests and is never shaken.

Shelley was looking at a tempest, or at any rate a high wind, and he tells us that he was shaken, but wanted to be shaken more, even picked up by the west wind and dropped somewhere else, but just where he doesn't quite know. When he asks to be lifted as a wave, or a leaf, or a cloud, we get a kind of constatation of the imagery which has been developed with considerable power in the three preceding stanzas. Shelley's project of becoming a wave or a leaf, or even a cloud (clouds were perhaps somewhat more within his reach), must seem philosophically untenable, perhaps slightly beneath human dignity. Be that as it may, I am puzzled by the correlation of the three phenomena, and by the omission of the seeds which in the first stanza are being carried by the wind to germinate somewhere next spring. Waves, leaves, and clouds do not contain a principle of organic reproduction. Is Shelley telling us that he would rather be dead, after the exhilaration of being borne by the wind, than to fall upon the thorns of life? I am not sure he meant this; I am not sure what he meant. I am not sure that Shelley was sure what he meant. And where did the thorns come from? I am not much of a botanist but I believe I have heard that certain trees and shrubs produce thorns, the teleology of which is to protect them from foraging animals, and even from man, who because of the thorns is slowed down in his predatory activity of plucking a rose. Is it not difficult to visualize a rose growing on life? Some people do think that life is rosy, but this is not a very distinguished epithet for the phenomena under consideration; nor is the insight offered us in the proposition, Life is thorny, more distinguished. The elementary irony to the effect that life is both rosy and thorny seems not to have been entertained by Shelley. Does he not say elsewhere that he could lie down like a tired child and weep away the life of care? About thirty years ago I wrote some animadversions on Shelley's thorns of life, and was reproached years later by a good Shelley scholar for not taking into account the fact that when Shelley wrote "Ode to the West Wind" he was worried about the health of his little boy. One never knows just when Xanadu will suddenly reappear; almost any road will get us there.

The sitting duck has not been fired at; we have only located him. It is perhaps not necessary to shoot; the charge and the size of shot are the same that we fired at my romantic revision of Shakespeare's great line. There is no vehicle for Shelley's melancholy, or for his frustration; the thorns, like rabbits, pop out of the hat, and they have no literal location. I am at a loss to see how the thorns could be reworked into a literal vehicle for Shelley's nebulous tenor. It was easy to turn Shakespeare into Shelley; but it would be impossible to turn Shelley into Shakespeare. It is easier to debase a precious metal than to convert dross into gold.

As I approach the end of this discussion I hesitate to make generalizations about modern poetry, because I am not sure where modern poetry begins. One might guess that no poet of genius comparable to Shelley's in the seventeenth century could have written lines as bad as Shelley's humanitarian zeal often allowed him to write. (If it were a purpose of this discussion to be fair, I could cite good lines by Shelley.) A possible inference from what I have said might lead to the conclusion that modern poetry begins at the moment poets lost control of the literal significance of their metaphors. Poets have always done this, even some of the best poets in moments of fatigue. Yet it seems to me that at present, and since what we call the modern movement began early in this century, it has become almost impossible for a poet to find literal images that will not merely point to a paraphrasable meaning, but will actually contain the meaning. Mr. John Crowe Ransom told us many years ago that the best metaphysical poets *meant their metaphors*. My gloss on this observation is that the paraphrase was not necessary, nor even possible; likewise with all good poetry. If we think we are paraphrasing LXXIII by saying that the poet, or lover, is getting old, or that he is pretending that he is, and is beseeching his friend or mistress not to desert him because death will soon part them, then we are deluding ourselves: this "paraphrase" could be made of some two or three thousand other poems as the common denominator reducing them all to zero.

If the generalization suggested in the foregoing remarks can be entertained as a possible hypothesis (not a theory), without support of sufficient argument or quotation, I should like to offer an even more tenuous abstraction of the metaphysical order; I should hope that it might point towards the causes of our failure to see identities in dissimilars. Aristotle mentioned the power to see *resemblances* in dissimilars as the mark of genius. By the time we get to Donne the resemblance is so close as to become an identity. When Donne says that he is of "the first nothing the elixir grown," he is not saying that he is *like* the first nothing; he is saying that he *is* more nothing than the first nothing, an elixir of the *prima materia* of the alchemists. Or if we wish to give this outrageous metaphor a more dignified historical origin, we may see in it the Platonic *Me On,* the postulated matter which does not exist until form creates it.

But what I have said about "A Nocturnall upon S. Lucie's Day" is not Donne's poem. I have dissociated Donne's sensibility into two parts, thought and feeling—thought being the tenor and feeling the vehicle. Or is this the right way to describe my own outrage committed upon Donne's? The conceit of the "first nothing" is not *feeling,* and whatever it may be it is not joined with thought; nor is it the mere vehicle of thought. Some forty years ago Mr. Eliot was the first critic to warn us that something had gone wrong with our metaphors, but his word *sensibility* must surely have misled us: from what was sensibility dissociated? Thought, doubtless; but one cannot discern, in Sonnet LXXIII, thought as distinct from feeling, or discern a thought-feeling complex. What one discerns, with our blunt tools, is poetry, which we constantly try to talk about as if it were something else.

But if we still find useful the idea of dissociation, I suggest that what was dissociated—whenever it may have been dissociated—was not thought from feeling, nor feeling from thought; what was dissociated was the external world which by analogy could become the interior world of the mind.

> Yet it creates, transcending these,
> Far other worlds, and other seas;
> Annihilating all that's made
> To a green thought in a green shade.

The doctrine of analogy, or connaturality, becomes in poetry the actuality of the identity of world and mind. Would this not indicate the kind of difficulty we encounter when we try to find a meaning in Shakespeare's sonnet apart from his metaphor?

For some implications of my modified version of Mr. Eliot's theory of dissociation I am indebted to Father William F. Lynch's brilliant and neglected book, *Christ and Apollo.* Father Lynch's theological approach to the matter of dissociation suggests the reason, at our particular moment of history, why the dissociation has taken place. Father Lynch's theory, oversimplified, is that we are alienated from nature; that we circumvent the common reality and reach for transcendental meanings; that we use this revived Manichean heresy to justify our hatred of ourselves—a hatred that may express itself evasively in impossible attempts at human perfectibility, at the expense of human reality, or in disgust with the human condition. Shelley's nebulous metaphor of life as thorns might give us a clue to the moment of dissociation in modern poetry. Bad poets have always been dissociated; but when a poet of Shelley's genius falls into dissociation, may we see a landmark in the history of poetry?

I, too, dislike it; and so I come back to Miss Moore, whose fine poem entitled "Poetry" begins with that statement. Is it not absurd to say that one loves poetry? To say that is to say that one loves all poetry—as indiscriminate a love as the love of all women. Yet it is reasonable to prefer all women to horses. I prefer all bad poems to all good sociological tracts. But that is not the question. We must distinguish great poetry from the egotistical sublime (Wordsworth's style) and from Godwin-Methodism (Shelley's style). And we must not fall into the historical trap where, immobilized, we apply a doctrine of historical determinism to poets, and pretend that after a certain date a certain kind of poetry could not be written. I fell into the trap thirty-five years ago when I said that after Emerson had done his work, the tragic vision was henceforth impossible in America. I am glad to have been proved wrong. The poetry of the older generation of T. S. Eliot (or a great part of it), or of John Crowe Ransom, would prove me wrong if I wanted to think that all had gone wrong since Shelley. Here is a passage by a poet younger than Eliot and Ransom:

> His suit was brushed and pressed too savagely;
> one sleeve was shorter than his shirt, and showed
> a glassy cufflink with a butterfly
> inside. Nothing about him seemed to match,
> and yet I saw the bouillon of his eye
> was the same color as his frayed moustache,
> too brown, too busy, lifted from an age
> when people wore moustaches. On each lash,
> a tear had snowballed. Then he shook his page,
> tore it to pieces, and began to twist
> and trample on the mangle in his rage.

The lines conclude Robert Lowell's great poem "The Severed Head." John Donne would have understood it, and so I think would Keats.

1964

T. S. Eliot's *Ash Wednesday*

EVERY AGE, as it sees itself, is peculiarly distracted: its chroniclers notoriously make too much of the variety before their own eyes. We see the variety of the past as mere turbulence within a fixed unity, and our own uniformity of the surface as the sign of a profound disunity of impulse. We have discovered that the ideas that men lived by from about the twelfth to the seventeenth century were absolute and unquestioned. The social turmoil of European history, so this argument runs, was shortsighted disagreement as to the best ways of making these deep assumptions morally good.

Although writers were judged morally, poets purveyed ready-made moralities, and no critic expected the poet to give him a brand-new system. A poem was a piece of enjoyment for minds mature enough—that is, convinced enough of a satisfactory destiny—not to demand of every scribbler a way of life.

It is beyond the scope of this discussion, and of my own competence, to attempt an appraisal of any of the more common guides to salvation, including the uncommon one of the Thirty-nine Articles, lately subscribed to by Mr. T. S. Eliot, whose six poems published under the title *Ash Wednesday* [1] are the occasion of this review. For it is my belief that, in a discussion of Eliot's poetry, his religious doctrines in themselves have little that commands interest. Yet it ap-

[1] T. S. Eliot, *Ash Wednesday* (New York, 1931).

pears that his poetry, notwithstanding the amount of space it gets in critical journals, receives less discussion each year. The moral and religious attitude implicit in it has been related to the Thirty-nine Articles, and to a general intellectual position that Eliot has defended in his essays. The poetry and the prose are taken together as evidence that the author has made an inefficient adaptation to the modern environment; or at least he doesn't say anything very helpful to the American critics in their struggles to adapt themselves. It is an astonishing fact that, near as we are to a decade obsessed by "aesthetic standards," there is less discussion of poetry in a typical modern essay on that fine art than there is in Johnson's essay on Denham. Johnson's judgment is frankly moralistic; he is revolted by unsound morals; but he seldom capitulates to a moral sentiment because it flatters his own moral sense. He requires the qualities of generality, copiousness, perspicuity. He hates Milton for a regicide; but his judgment of *Paradise Lost* is as disinterested as any judgment we should find today; certainly no more crippled by historical prejudice than Mr. Eliot's own views of Milton. Yet Eliot's critics are a little less able each year to see the poetry for Westminster Abbey; the wood is all trees.

I do not pretend to know how far our social and philosophical needs justify a prejudice which may be put somewhat summarily as follows: all forms of human action, economics, politics, even poetry, and certainly industry, are legitimate modes of salvation, but the historic religious mode is illegitimate. It is sufficient here to point out that the man who expects to find salvation in the latest lyric or a well-managed factory will not only not find it there; he is not likely to find it anywhere else. If a young mind is incapable of moral philosophy, a mind without moral philosophy is incapable of understanding poetry. For poetry, of all the arts, demands a serenity of view and a settled temper of the mind, and most of all the power to detach one's own needs from the experience set forth in the poem. A moral sense so organized sets limits to human nature, and is content to observe them. But if the reader lack this moral sense, the poem will be only a body of abstractions either useful or irrelevant to that body of abstractions already forming, but of uncertain direction, in the reader's mind. This reader will see the poem chiefly as biography, and he will proceed to deduce from it a history of the poet's case, to which he will attach himself if his own case resembles it; if it doesn't, he will look for a more useful case. Either way, the poem as a specific object is ignored.

The reasoning that is being brought to bear upon Mr. Eliot's recent verse is as follows: Anglo-Catholicism would not all satisfy me; therefore, his poetry declines under its influence. Moreover, the poetry is not "contemporary"; it doesn't solve any labor problems; it is special, personal; and it can do us no good. Now the poetry *is* special and personal in quality, which is one of its merits, but what the critics are really saying is this—that Eliot's case history is not special at all, that it is a general scheme of possible conduct that will not do for them. To accept the poetry seems to amount to accepting an invitation to join the Anglican Church. For the assumption is that the poetry and the religious position are identical.

If this were so, why should not the excellence of the poetry induce writers to join the Church, in the hope of writing as well as Eliot, since the irrelevance of the Church to their own needs makes them reject the poetry? The answer is, of course, that both parts of this fallacy are common. There is an aesthetic Catholicism, and there is a communist-economic rejection of art because it is involved with the tabooed mode of salvation.

The belief is that Eliot's poety—all other poetry—is a simple record of the responses of a personality to an environment. The belief witnesses the modern desire to judge an art scientifically, practically, industrially—according to how it works. The poetry is viewed first as a pragmatic instrument, then examined "critically" as a pragmatic result; neither stage of the approach gives us "useful" knowledge.

Now a different heredity-environment combination would give us, of mechanical necessity, a different result, a different quantity of power to do a different and perhaps better social work. Doubtless that is true. But there is something disconcerting in this simple solution to the problem when it is looked at more closely. Two vastly different records or case histories might give us, qualitatively speaking, very similar results: Baudelaire and Eliot have in common many *qualities* but *no history*. Their "results" have at least the common features of irony, humility, introspection, reverence—qualities fit only for contemplation and not for judgment according to their utility in our own conduct.

It is in this, the qualitative sense, that Eliot's recent poetry has been misunderstood. In this sense, the poetry is special, personal, of no use, and highly distinguished. But it is held to be a general formula, not distinct from the general formula that Eliot repeated when he went into the Church.

The form of the poems in *Ash Wednesday* is lyrical and solitary, and there is almost none of the elaborate natural description and allusion that gave to *The Waste Land* a partly realistic and partly symbolic character. These six poems are a brief moment of religious experience in an age that believes religion to be a kind of defeatism and puts all its hope for man in finding the right secular order. The mixed realism and symbolism of *The Waste Land* issued in irony. The direct and lyrical method of the new poems is based upon the simpler quality of humility. The latter quality comes directly out of the former, and there is an even continuity in Eliot's work.

In *The Waste Land* the prestige of our secular faith gave to the style its special character. This faith was the hard, coherent medium through which the discredited forms of the historic cultures emerged only to be stifled; the poem is at once their vindication and the recognition of their defeat. They are defeated in fact, as a politician may be defeated by the popular vote, but their vindication consists in the critical irony that their subordinate position casts upon the modern world.

The typical scene is the seduction of the stenographer by the clerk, in "The Fire Sermon." Perhaps Mr. J. W. Krutch has not discussed this scene, but a whole generation of critics has, and from a viewpoint that Mr. Krutch has recently made popular: the seduction betrays the disillusion of the poet. The mechanical, brutal scene shows what love really is—that is to say, what it is scientifically, since "science" is truth: it is only an act of practical necessity for procreation. The telling of the story by the Greek seer Tiresias, who is chosen from a past of illusion and ignorance, permits the scene to become *a satire on the unscientific values of the past*. It was all pretense to think that love was anything but a biological necessity. The values of the past were pretty, absurd, and false; the scientific truth is both true and bitter. This is the familiar romantic dilemma, and the critics have read it into the scene from their own romantic despair.

There is no despair in the scene itself. The critics, who being in the state of mind I have described are necessarily blind to an effect of irony, have mistaken the symbols of an ironic contrast for the terms of a philosophic dilemma. It is the kind of metaphorical "logic" typical of romantic criticism since Walter Pater. Mr. Eliot knows too much about classical irony to be overwhelmed by a popular dogma in literary biology. For the seduction scene shows, not what man is, but what *for a moment* he thinks he is. In other words, the clerk stands for the secularization of the religious and qualitative values in the modern world. And the meaning of the contrast between Tiresias and the clerk is not disillusion, but irony. The scene is a masterpiece, perhaps the most profound vision that we have of modern man.

The importance of this scene as a key to the intention of *Ash Wednesday* lies in the moral identity of humility and irony and in an important difference between them aesthetically. Humility is subjective, a quality of the moral character: it is thus general, invisible, and can only be inferred, not seen. *Irony is the visible, particular, and objective instance of humility.* Irony is the objective quality of an event or situation which stimulates our capacity for humility. It is that arrangement of experience, either premeditated by art or accidentally appearing in the affairs of men, which permits to the spectator an insight superior to that of the actor; it shows him that the practical program, the special ambition, of the actor at that moment is bound to fail. The humility thus derived is the self-respect proceeding from a sense of the folly of men in their desire to dominate a natural force or a situation. The seduction scene is the picture of modern and dominating man. The arrogance and the pride of conquest of the "small house agent's clerk" are the badge of science, bumptious practicality, overweening secular faith. The very success of his conquest witnesses its aimless character; it succeeds as a wheel succeeds in turning: he can only conquer again.

His own failure to understand his position is irony, and the poet's insight into it is humility. But for the grace of God, says the poet in effect, there go I. This is essentially the poetic attitude, an attitude that Eliot has been approaching with increasing purity. It is not that his recent verse is better than that of the period ending with *The Waste Land.* Actually it is less spectacular and less complex in subject matter; for Eliot less frequently objectifies his leading emotion, humility, into irony. His new form is simple, expressive, homogeneous, and direct, and without the early elements of violent contrast.

There is a single ironic passage in *Ash Wednesday,* and significantly enough it is the first stanza of the first poem. This passage presents objectively the poet *as he thinks himself for the moment to be.* It establishes that humility towards his own merit which fixes the tone of the poems that follow. And the irony has been overlooked by the critics because they take the stanza as a literal exposition of the latest phase of the Eliot *case history*—at a time when, in the words of Mr. Edmund Wilson, "his psychological plight seems most depressing." Thus, here is the vain pose of a Titan too young to be weary of strife, but weary of it nevertheless.

> Because I do not hope to turn again
> Because I do not hope
> Because I do not hope to turn
> Desiring this man's gift and that man's scope
> I no longer strive to strive towards such things
> (Why should the aged eagle stretch its wings?)
> Why should I mourn
> The vanished power of the usual reign?

If the six poems are taken together as the focus of a specific religious emotion, the opening stanza, instead of being a naïve personal "confession," appears in the less lurid light of a highly effective technical performance. This stanza has two features that are necessary to the development of the unique imagery which distinguishes the religious emotion of *Ash Wednesday* from any other religious poetry of our time. It is possibly the only kind of imagery that is valid for religious verse today.

The first feature is the regular yet halting rhythm, the smooth uncertainty of movement which may either proceed to greater regularity or fall away into improvisation. The second feature is the imagery itself. It is trite; it echoes two familiar passages from English poetry. But the quality to be observed is this: it is secular imagery. It sets forth a special ironic situation, but the emotion is not identified with any specific experience. The imagery is thus perfectly suited to the broken rhythm. The stanza is a device for getting the poem under way, starting from a known and general emotion, in a monotonous rhythm, for a direction which, to the reader, is unknown. The ease, the absence of surprise, with which Eliot proceeds to bring out the subject of his meditation is admirable. After some further and ironic deprecation of his worldly powers, he goes on:

> And pray to God to have mercy upon us
> And pray that I may forget
> These matters that with myself I too much discuss,
> Too much explain.

We are being told, of course, that there is to be some kind of discourse on God, or a meditation; yet the emotion is still general. The imagery is even flatter than before; it is "poetical" at all only in that special context; for it is the diction of prose. And yet, subtly and imperceptibly, the rhythm has changed; it is irregular and labored. We are being prepared for a new and sudden effect, and it comes in the first lines of the second poem:

> Lady, three white leopards sat under a juniper-tree
> In the cool of the day, having fed to satiety
> On my legs my heart my liver and that which had been contained
> In the hollow round of my skull. And God said
> Shall these bones live? shall these
> Bones live?

From here on, in all the poems, there is constant and sudden change of rhythm, and there is a corresponding alternation of two kinds of imagery—the visual and tactile imagery common to all poetry, without significance in itself for any kind of experience, and the traditional religious symbols. The two orders are inextricably fused.

It is evident that Eliot has hit upon the only method now

available of using the conventional religious image in poetry. He has reduced it from symbol to image, from abstraction to the plane of sensation. And corresponding to this process, there are images of his own invention which he almost pushes over the boundary of sensation into abstractions, where they have the appearance of conventional symbols.[2] The passage I have quoted above is an example of this: for the "Lady" may be a nun, or even the Virgin, or again she may be a beautiful woman; but she is presented, through the serious tone of the invocation, with all the solemnity of a religious figure. The fifth poem exhibits the reverse of the process; it begins with a series of plays on the Logos, the most rarefied of all the Christian abstractions; and it succeeds in creating the effect of immediate experience by means of a broken and distracted rhythm:

> If the lost word is lost, if the spent word is spent
> If the unheard, unspoken
> Word is unspoken, unheard;
> Still is the unspoken word, the word unheard,
> The word without a word, the Word within
> The world and for the world. . . .

1931

[2] Mr. Yvor Winters would doubtless call this feature of the poem "pseudo-reference."

Longinus and the New Criticism

To BEGIN an essay with a silent apology to the subject is commendable, but one should not expect the reader to be interested in it. I allude to the ignorance in which I had underestimated Longinus, before I reread him after twenty years, because I am convinced that it is typical. Who reads Longinus? I do not mean to say literally that he is not read. There is an excellent recent study by Mr. Elder Olson; there are the fine books by Mr. T. R. Henn and Mr. Samuel H. Monk,[1] which persons of the critical interest should know something about and doubtless do. Until these books appeared, there had been no serious consideration of Longinus since Saintsbury's *A History of Criticism* (1900). In some twenty-five years of looking at criticism in the United States and England, I have not seen, with the exceptions already noticed, a reference to the περὶ ὕψους which is of more than historical interest. One might, with misplaced antiquarian zeal, find the name, if not much more, of Aristotle in the pages of a fashionable journal like *Horizon;* one would have to go to the learned journals, which few critics see, to find even the name of Longinus. Until Mr. Henn and Mr. Monk reminded us of him, he had been dropped out of active criticism since the end of the eighteenth century. I should like to believe that these excellent scholars have brought about a

[1] T. R. Henn, *Longinus and English Criticism* (Cambridge, 1934), and Samuel H. Monk, *The Sublime: A Study of Critical Theories in XVIII-Century England* (New York, 1935).

Longinian revival. Mr. Herbert Read informs me that Coleridge in *Table Talk* spoke of him as "no very profound critic." It must seem to us today that Coleridge buried him in that remark. I am not confident that I shall succeed where Mr. Monk and Mr. Henn failed (if they did fail), that what I am about to say will exhume Longinus.

I

This is not the occasion to establish a correct English title for περὶ ὕψους. (In the New Testament ὕψος means not the physical heavens [οὐρανός] but something like "on high.") To my mind, the idea of height or elevation contained in the title, *Of the Height of Eloquence*, which was given to the work by the first English translator, John Hall, in 1652, is more exact than *On the Sublime*, which carries with it the accretions of Boileau and the English eighteenth century, and the different meanings contributed later by Burke and Kant, which are far removed from anything that I have been able to find in this third- (or is it first-?) century treatise. So far from Kant's is Longinus's conception of "sublimity" that one pauses at the marvelous semantic history of the word. In Chapter IX Longinus quotes a passage from the *Iliad*, Book XX, about the war of the gods, and comments: "Yet these things terrible as they are, if they are not taken as an allegory are altogether blasphemous and destructive of what is seemly." To allegorize infinite magnitude, quantity beyond the range of the eye, is to reduce it to the scale of what Kant called the Beautiful as distinguished from the Sublime. The "sublimity" of the passage, in the Kantian sense, Longinus could not accept. These shifts of meaning are beyond the scope of my interest and my competence. Three other brief and confusing parallels will fix in our minds the difficulties of Longinus's title. His insight, perhaps unique in antiquity, which is contained in the distinction between the "persuasion" of oratory and the "transport" of what, for want of a better phrase, one may call the literary effect, reappears in this century as neosymbolism and surrealism. Some twenty years ago the Abbé Bremond decided that "transport" meant religious mysticism, and wrote a book called *La Poésie pure.* In England, about thirty years ago, Arthur Machen, of whom few people of the generations younger than mine have heard, the author of *The Hill of Dreams* and other novels after Huysmans, wrote a small critical book called *Hieroglyphics.* Machen proposed to discern the real thing in literature with a test that he called "ecstasy," but what made Machen ecstatic left many persons cold. At any rate, the Greek word in Longinus that we translate as "transport" is ἔκστασις. Had Boileau not stuffed Longinus with neoclassical "authority," would he have been discovered by the French and English romantics, to whom he could have spoken from another if equally wrong direction? This topic may be dropped with the observation that literary history is no more orderly than any other history.

I shall, then, in the following remarks, think of the two key terms in Longinus, ὕψος and ἔκστασις, as respectively Elevation of Language and Transport; but I cannot expect to disentangle them from each other. They contain, in their interrelations, a version of a persistent ambiguity of critical reference which appeared with Aristotle, had vigorous life up to Coleridge (with whom it comes back disguised), and now eggs on an edifying controversy of the contemporary English and American critics: Ransom, Cleanth Brooks, Read, Leavis, Richards, Blackmur, and Winters. Is Elevation an objective quality of the literary work? Is Transport its subjective reference denoting the emotions of the reader—or the "hearer," as Longinus calls him—as he receives the impact of Elevation? Does either word, Elevation or Transport, point to anything sufficiently objective to be isolated for critical discussion?

This is not the moment to answer that question, if I were competent to answer it. Our first duty is to find out how Longinus asks it. After defining Elevation tautologically, in

Chapter I, as "a kind of supreme excellence of discourse" (ἐξοχή τις λόγων ἐστὶ τὰ ὕψη), he describes its effect:

For what is out of the common affects the hearer not to persuade but to entrance (οὐ γὰρ εἰς πεθὼ τοὺς ἀκροωμένους ἀλλ' εἰς ἔκστασιν ἄγει τὰ ὑπερφυᾶ). It moves to wonder and surprise, and always wins against what is merely delightful or persuasive. It is not enough in one or two passages of a work to exhibit invention schooled by experience, nor again the fine order and distribution of its parts, nor even these qualities displayed throughout. Rather, I suggest, does the sublime, fitly expressed, pierce everything like a flash of lightning. . . . [2]

Not to persuade, but to entrance, like a flash of lightning. In these words Longinus breaks with the rhetoricians who had dominated ancient criticism since Aristotle, four to six hundred years before him, and who continued to dominate it until the seventeenth century. Neither Longinus nor Dante, in *De Vulgari Eloquentia*, had any influence on critical theory after them, until the time of Boileau, when Longinus was used to justify rules that he had never made. Dante's criticism has languished in the department of biography; at best, in the history of criticism, as a document of the time.

I I

Chapter II opens with the question: "We must first discuss whether there is an art of the sublime." In the Greek, the phrase is ὕψους τις ἢ βάθους τέχνη—"an art of height or of depth"; but the word we should attend is τέχνη, "art," which

[2] With the exception of a few phrases I quote throughout from the translation by Frank Granger (London, 1935), which seems to me the most perspicuous English version. The exceptions are the result of a collation of the Granger and other versions with what is probably the definitive scholarly translation, by W. Rhys Roberts (Cambridge, 1899). All the modern translations render ὕψος as "sublime," and it has obviously been necessary to keep the word when it occurs in a quoted passage.

the Greeks used for any teachable skill, from metal-working to music and medicine. They applied the term to all the skills of making for which an objective rationale could be devised. Longinus explains the views of Caecilius, the opponent of uncertain identity whom the περὶ ὕψους was written to refute, who believed that elevation of language came through nature alone, that the great writer, born great, needs nothing but his birth. In this controversy of lively acrimony with a man who may have been dead three hundred years (such was the leisure of antiquity), Longinus at the beginning of his essay opposes, in opposing Caecilius, both the Platonic and the Aristotelian doctrines, and holds that style is a compound of natural talent and conscious method. He thus parts with Plato's "divine madness" in the *Ion,* and implicitly claims for Thought and Diction, two of the nonstructural elements in Aristotle's analysis of tragedy, a degree of objectivity that Aristotle's rhetorical view of poetic language could not include.

If literary method cannot alone produce a style, the judgment of which, says Longinus, "is the last fruit of long experience," it can "help us to speak at the right length and to the occasion." How much interpretation of a casual observation such as this, which is only common sense, the modern scholiast is entitled to develop, I do not know. Although Longinus may have in mind merely the orator and the *public* occasion, may we just see him reaching out for a criterion of objectivity for any sort of literary composition? The "right length" is the adaptation of form to subject; and is not the "occasion" the relation between the poet and the person to whom the poem is addressed? We have, foreshadowed here, I think, a principle of dramatic propriety, a sense of the "point of view" in composition, the prime literary strategy which can never be made prescriptive, but which exhibits its necessity equally in its operation and in its lapse. Later, discussing meter, Longinus tells us that Elevation cannot be achieved in the trochaic, or tripping, meter, and we may dismiss the remark as the perennial fallacy which identifies certain fixed effects with certain meters. But if we can imagine "Lycidas" written in trochees and "The Raven" in iambuses, we might suppose the one would be worse, the other considerably better. And if we look at "length" and "occasion" in somewhat different terms, we shall find ourselves again in the thick of one of our own controversies. Does not the occasion force upon the poet the objective and communicable features of his work? Are they not Mr. Winters's theory of the relation of "feeling" to "rational content" and Mr. Ransom's theory of a "texture" within a "structure"?

In exceeding the literal text of Longinus in this matter, I hope that I have not also stretched two living critics into an agreement which they have scarcely acknowledged; nor should I ask them to acknowledge Longinus as their forerunner. I suggest that Longinus's question "Is there an art of Elevation?" is the question we are asking today, somewhat as follows: can there be a criticism of convincing objectivity which approaches the literary work through the analysis of style and which arrives at its larger aspects through that aperture?

That is the question of our time. In asking it, are we not following Longinus rather than Aristotle? Aristotle began with the conspicuous "larger aspects" of a mature literary genre, Greek tragedy, and got around to the problems of poetic language only at the end, and as a rhetorician (except for one curious remark about metaphor) who offers us shrewd but merely schematic advice about the use of figures.

I I I

If there is an art of Elevation, if there is possible a coherent criticism of literature through its language, it follows that we must examine good and bad writers together, in order to arrive, not at rules, but at that "judgment of style which is the fruit of long experience"; to arrive at that sense of the length and the occasion which will permit us, as poets, to imitate not Homer's style but its excellence, in our own language. It is here that intensive literary criticism and literary tradition work together; it is here that we arrive at the idea of a literary tradition which does not enjoin the slavery of repetition, but the emulation which comes of insight. We shall have of course to deal as best we can with the ambiguity of Longinus' word τέχνη. By the "art of height or of depth" does he mean criticism? Or does he mean the "art" of the poet? He means, I take it, both; and it is proper that he should. For our sense of the achievement of the past may issue in a critical acquisition of knowledge which is not to be put away in the attic when the creative moment comes. At this point one may profitably notice two characteristic defects, defects of its quality, that proud and self-sufficient writers fall into in attempting the elevated style. "Frigidity," says Longinus, is the overelaboration of the academic writer, a violation of length due to aiming at "the curious and the artificial." The "feeling" (or the detail) is unreal in the sense that it is on a scale smaller than its intelligible form. Likewise, the opposite fault—and in describing it Longinus has written as good criticism as any I know—of Thomas Wolfe and the contemporary lyrical novel; he says:

Theodorus calls it the mock-inspired. It is emotion out of place and empty where there is no need of it, or lack of proportion where proportion is needed. Some writers fall into a maudlin mood and digress from their subject into their own tedious emotion. Thus they show bad form and leave their audience unimpressed: necessarily, for they are in a state of rapture, and the audience is not.

If this is the performance of the writer great by nature and beyond "art," Henry James gives us his dreary portrait: "The writer who cultivates his instinct rather than his awareness sits by finally in a stale and shrinking puddle." His awareness of what? I should say of the "occasion" and the "length," the sense of limiting structure and of what, within that limit, is to be objectively communicated and made known. This sense becomes operative through "art," τέχνη, technique, the controlled awareness *through* language of what can be made actual *in* language, resulting in a just, if unpredictable, proportion between what Longinus calls the "emotion" and the "subject." Doubtless, any experienced reader of literature can point to the failures of great writers in the two extremes of disproportion corresponding to two forms of pride that prevent the complete discovery of the subject: the pride of intellect and the pride of feeling, the pride of will and the pride of instinct. (Perhaps the history of the imagination is the pendulum between these extremes.) Mr. Blackmur has shown us in the past few years how the thesis in Dostoevsky distorts or even wrecks the theme, the imaginative actuality in which the form ought to have been discovered under pressure of its internal necessity. In a more recent writer, D. H. Lawrence, we get both extremes of pride: the attack on the intellect in behalf of instinct, instinct itself hardening into a core of abstraction which operates as intellectual pride, as thesis; not as realized form.

The instances of "disproportion" could be multiplied, but I pause to remark my own digression, and to ask, as the eighteenth-century critics seem not to have done, whether there is not already, in what I have said, a certain excess of gloss, commentary cut loose from the text commented upon, a self-indulgence which seems to attribute to Longinus a comprehension which one is covertly claiming for oneself? Criticism should no doubt observe the same proprieties of occasion and length that we require of the imagination; but it has seldom done so, and I think with good reason. If criticism is only secondary to literature, it is thus the dependent partner, and for the hazards that it must face in every generation it must constantly worry the past for support, and make too much of what it revives, or perhaps even make it into something different. Perhaps I have got out of the περὶ ὕψους at this stage of the discussion only a general insight available, if not always used, as common property since Coleridge. Yet we should remember that Longinus alone seems to have achieved it in the ancient world.

I have been trying to see the outlines, before I move on to some of the particular judgments in the περὶ ὕψους, of a possible framework into which to put Longinus's profound but topical dialectic. In the same chapter (II) in which the proportions of length and occasion are held to be established through "art" or method, he writes this crucial passage:

Demosthenes says somewhere that in ordinary life luck is the greatest good, and that it cannot exist without another which is not inferior to it, namely prudent conduct. Following him, we might say, in the case of style, that nature takes the place of good luck; and art, of prudent conduct. *Most important of all, we must learn from art the fact that some elements of style depend upon nature alone.*

At this point four pages of the manuscript disappear, a loss of the first importance to critical theory. If the amateur Hellenist reads from classical criticism a passage in which the word "nature" occurs, he is likely to read it with Boileau or the English eighteenth century, and get entangled in the thickets of "nature," which they opposed to "art," when they were not effecting a compromise by making art nature to advantage dressed; and so on. It seems to me that we ought to support the passage just quoted with a full sense of the special kind of judgment that Longinus brings to bear upon the actual texture of Greek literature; he produces many examples which cannot be cited here. We could then just see in it the first declaration of independence from the practical, forensic eloquence of the rhetoricians.

"Most important of all, we must learn from art the fact that some elements of style depend upon nature alone." In trying to understand this nice oxymoron, I shall take risks which are perhaps not greater than those taken by most commentators on the *Poetics*. Most important of all, I make Longinus say, we learn from the development of technique that stylistic autonomy is a delusion, because style comes into existence only as it discovers the subject; and conversely the subject exists only after it is formed by the style. No literary work is perfect, no subject perfectly formed. Style reveals that which is not style in the process of forming it. Style does not create the subject, it discovers it. The fusion of art and nature, of technique and subject, can never exceed the approximate; the margin of imperfection, of the unformed, is always there—nature intractable to art, art unequal to nature. The converse of Longinus' aphorism will further elucidate it: we must learn from nature that some elements of subject matter, in a literary work, "depend" upon art alone. There is a reciprocal relation, not an identity—not, certainly, the identity of form and content—a dynamic, shifting relation between technique and subject; and they reveal each other. This is my sense of Longinus's primary insight. It is an insight of considerable subtlety that has a special claim to the attention of our generation.

I V

I suppose we should agree that by and large the critical method of the *Poetics* is inductive. Aristotle's generalizations proceed from a scrutiny of one kind of literature, drama, chiefly from one kind of drama, tragedy, and from one kind of tragedy, Greek. Longinus repeats Aristotle's animadversions on "character," which Aristotle seems to think need not be much developed if the "plot" is good. We must constantly remind ourselves of the narrow range of literature at the command of the two great critics of antiquity; they lacked the novel, for one thing, and Aristotle evidently did not consider the works of his great predecessor and teacher worthy of the name of "poetry." The larger conception of *literature* does not appear in the *Poetics*. Although Longinus, trained as he must have been in the rhetorical schools, did not see clearly whither he was heading, it is just the awareness of *literature at large* which raises his theory of the relation of language and subject to a higher degree of useful generality than any literary theory before him had reached. He is the first, though necessarily incomplete, literary critic. His question, put again, in its wider implications, is: what distinguishes literature from practical oratory, from history? A quality, he says in effect, beyond an immediate purpose. His discussion of imagination is what we should expect: it is the classical rhetorician's view of the image as a "mental picture," which he, along with his age, seems to believe must be laid on the work discreetly from the top. Yet the distinction between two widely different purposes in the controlled use of language puts his doctrine on a high yet accessible level of empirical generalization, and makes it possible for him to look beyond specific conventions to estimate the value of a literature offering a great variety of forms and structures.

It has been supposed by many critics that Longinus is not interested in structure, that his doctrine of "transport" and the "lightning flash" anticipates the romantic *frisson,* or that Pope did it justice when he called in Longinus to help him "snatch a grace beyond the reach of art." I think I have shown that Longinus would reject that art which is beyond its own reach. And what, in fact, I now wish to show is that Longinus is quite prepared to put his finger directly upon the problem of structure, and by implication to tell us that structure is not in the formal "type" or genre, a viable body of special conventions, such as the lyric, the ode, or the epic provides, but exists in the language of the poem.

After discussing, in Chapters VIII and IX, the five sources

of Elevation in language (to which I shall return), he analyzes the effect, from the point of view of structure, of Sappho's "Ode to Anactoria," beginning: φαίνεταί μοι κῆνος ἴσος θεοῖσιν. The analysis is brief (everything in Longinus is brief but the lacunae in the text), yet it is probably the first example in criticism of structural analysis of a lyric poem. (I ought for my purpose here to know more than I do, which is virtually nothing, about the ancient theory of the Passions.) I quote the entire passage:

Let us now go on to see whether we have anything further by means of which we can raise our words to the sublime. Since, then, in the substance of everything, we find certain elements which naturally belong to it, we should of course find one cause of the sublime by always choosing the most relevant circumstances and by compounding them (ἐπισυνθέσει) to make, so to speak, one body (ἕν τι σῶμα ποιεῖν). For the audience is attracted, first by our choice of topics (ὁ μὲν γὰρ τῇ ἐκλογῇ . . . τῶν λημμάτων), and second, by the conciseness of our exposition. For example, Sappho takes from their actual setting the feelings that accompany the frenzy of love. Where then does she display her skill? In the tact with which she chooses and binds together supreme and intense feelings.

> *Peer of Gods he seemeth to me, the blissful*
> *Man who sits and gazes at thee before him,*
> *Close beside thee sits, and in silence hears thee*
>   *Silverly speaking,*
>
> *Laughing love's low laughter. Oh this, this only*
> *Stirs the troubled heart in my breast to tremble!*
> *For should I but see thee a little moment,*
>   *Straight is my voice hushed;*
>
> *Yea, my tongue is broken, and through and through me*
> *'Neath the flesh impalpable fire runs tingling;*
> *Nothing see mine eyes, and a noise of roaring*
>   *Waves in my ear sounds;*

Sweat runs down in rivers, a tremor seizes
All my limbs, and paler than grass in autumn,
Caught by pains of menacing death, I falter,
Lost in the love trance. . . .

Do you not wonder how she gives chase at once to soul and body, to words and tongue, to sight and color, all as if scattered abroad, how *uniting contradictions,*[3] she is frozen and burns, she raves and is wise? For either she is panic-stricken or at point of death; she is haunted not by a single emotion but their *whole company.*[4]

Towards the end of the περὶ ὕψους there is some scattered commentary on the rhetorical figures; but in the criticism of Sappho the language is not that of the tropes and figures. Insofar as it concerns emotion, it is "psychological," if not very exact, even in the terms of the classical psychology of the passions; yet perhaps it is not too much to claim for Longinus's perception of opposites in this poem, of the positive compulsion given tension by its negative, that it goes deeper and is more attentive to what the poem says than anything that Arnold has to say about Keats's or Milton's poetry. *He is trying to see what is happening in the poem.* If he is hampered by his affective terms, so was Mr. T. S. Eliot when, in an early essay, he was getting at a similar play of opposites (what Mr. Cleanth Brooks has since called "paradox") by proposing his theory of the "positive" and the "negative" emotion, and more especially the theory of the central "emotion" gathering up and controlling a variety of contingent "feelings." Mr. Eliot's early theory I should call advanced romantic criticism:

3 I have inserted here W. Rhys Roberts's translation of καθ' ὑπεναντιώσεις because it conveys more accurately the force of the Greek, which means *opposite feelings* rather than "at variance within," as Granger has it.
4 Roberts has it "a concourse of passions," which is more accurate. The Greek ἵνα μὴ ἕν τι περὶ αὐτὴν πάθος φαίνηται, παθῶν δὲ σύνοδος is literally a "coming together of roads," a crossroads; so better perhaps than either "their whole company" or a "concourse of passions" are the renditions "a clash of feelings," "a crossing of feelings."

it was struggling through the subjective effect towards the objective structure of the work. Longinus's criticism of Sappho is advanced romantic criticism, as advanced as Mr. Eliot's.

One hesitates to present to Longinus a theory which I hope is not implicit in his phrase ἕν τι σῶμα ποιεῖν, "to make into one body"; it looks like an organic theory of poetry, but if we suppose that he is merely using the phrase analogically, and means by it no more than he means a moment later, when he says that the poem is a result of choosing and binding together intense feelings, we shall have to acknowledge the presence of a quite modern piece of criticism. At the least, he is telling us that in this poem contradictions are united, bound together, not that Sappho was expressing herself. We are a long step on the way to that critical moment when the affective vocabulary goes over into linguistic analysis, when, instead of what the poem "feels like," we try to decide what it says. That Longinus was farther along this road than we may at a glance suspect there is evidence in the remarkable sentence that he plumps down before us without explanation: ". . . the sublime is often found where there is no emotion." There will be something to say about this when we come to the discussion of "harmony," or composition.

V

The promise at the beginning of the treatise to produce the elements of an Art of Elevation leads to a good deal of miscellaneous specification, under five heads, for its achievement; but the dialectical links among the categories are not distinct. If we think of Longinus as Pascal's man of *finesse*, man of insights, and of Aristotle as a man of *géométrie*, man of deduction, we shall have to look twice at Mr. Olson's observation that, "Unlike Edmund Burke, who finds the sources of sublimity in qualities of the subject matter of art, Longinus finds them in the faculties of the author." This is partly true; but it is misleading, if we are led to suppose that Longinus tried but failed to erect a systematic philosophy of art, comparable to Burke's *A Philosophical Enquiry into the Origins of Our Ideas of the Sublime and Beautiful,* but placing the origin of the ideas in the author. He is ambiguous at this point, but I have shown, I hope, that his considerable originality consists in shifting the center of critical interest, without rejecting it as an "interest," from the genetic and moral judgment to the aesthetic, from the subject matter and the psychology of the author to the language of the work. When he describes the first of his five sources of Elevation as the "impulse towards what is great in thought," he speaks perhaps as a casual Platonist, but primarily as a rhetorician in the great tradition reaching from Aristotle to Cicero.

In distinguishing a critical insight from the intellectual discipline from which, to an extent, it may be a departure, we tend to assume that the insight has replaced the discipline; whereas it may merely alter it. It is not certain that we need a philosophical aesthetics in order to produce a work of art; at the Renaissance, I need hardly to observe, an education in rhetoric and oratory produced poets. Sidney is not too apologetic for "straying from Poetrie to Oratorie"; for, he says, "both have such an affinity in this wordish consideration. . . ." It was the point of view of his age. Disciplining that point of view was the art of rhetoric, one member of a tripartite whole completed by ethics and politics; rhetoric was the ethics of the public man in its appropriate discipline, the art of the enthymeme, or rhetorical syllogism.

The second of Longinus's categories, "strong and inspired emotion," proceeds from the first, or from a common source; it also is "due to nature." Here we come upon a curious and, as usual, undeveloped observation. Strong and inspired emotion is one source of, but it is not the same as, style. Pity, grief, and fear, he says, are "humble [ταπεινά:

lowly, mean] and without the note of the Sublime"—as if
in "pity" and "fear" he had a critical eye to Aristotle, whose
doctrine of *katharsis* was practical and even "sociological."
The curious observation honors the critic who puts "awareness" above system, for it enters an exception to the rule:
"The masters of panegyric," Longinus says, "are seldom
given to emotion." What, then, are they given to? An English instance will be helpful. The epigraph to "Lycidas" tells
us that "The Author bewails a Learned Friend"—but the
author does nothing of the sort; [5] the strong feeling is directed at the clergy, and even this is sufficiently assimilated
into the rich pastoral texture.

I pass over sources two and three, the "framing of rhetorical
figures" and "nobility of expression," with the remark that
Longinus is prudential, like a good teacher, and on these
topics not more rewarding than the rhetoricians, Demetrius
and Dionysius. But number five, "Composition and distribution of words and phrases into a dignified and exalted unit,"
heads up the entire argument. "It is a unity of composition,"
he says, "attained through language." If it is so attained, it is
not attained, though it may originate, in the inaccessible nobility of the author's mind. Observe again the superiority of
Longinus's insight, with the specific work in mind, to his critical apparatus, which tends to the moralistic and academic.
We may see composition here as *ordonnance,* "the best words
in the best order." It is more than that. Composition is the
total work, not the superaddition of method. Its effect is not
to persuade but to entrance; it is "out of the common," not
uncommon words, but words used uncommonly well. It is
clear that Longinus, by and large, is not recommending
the "grand style"; his translators have probably done him a
disservice in rendering his characteristic adjective μέγα as
"grand"; it is, rather, great, unusual, *uncommon;* and like-

5 Mr. John Crowe Ransom made this observation in "A Poem Nearly Anonymous," *The World's Body, op. cit.,* pp. 1–28.

wise ὕψος, "height," which I understand as "excellence." ἔκστασις is our subjective acknowledgement of the presence of the uncommon, of an objective order of unpredictable distinction. He is quite explicit in this matter. By means of "an appropriate *structure,* and by this means only, as we have sufficiently shown, the best writers give the effect of stateliness and distinction which is removed from the commonplace." In illustration he quotes a line from the *Hercules Furens* of Euripides:

γέμω κακῶν δὴ κοὐκετ' ἔσθ' ὅποι τεθῇ,
I am loaded with sorrows nor can I take on more.

"The phrase is quite commonplace but it has *gained elevation* by the arrangement of the words." The fine statement that follows ought to remove any remaining misconception of the nature of "transport," if we still suppose it to be the romantic shudder; it addresses itself to the whole mind:

. . . if a work of literature fails to disclose to the reader's intelligence an outlook beyond the range of what is said, when it dwindles under a careful and continuous inspection, it cannot be truly sublime, for it has reached the ear alone. . . . For that is truly grand [μέγα] of which the contemplation bears repeating.

There must be, in short, a total quality of the work which abides its first impact; to that total quality he gives the name of composition.

It includes rhythm. Saintsbury, whose exposition of Longinus might have revived his influence had somebody else written it, misses the originality of Longinus's treatment of this subject. Longinus's location of rhythm in the total compositon, as binding and bound up with it, is perhaps the best critical insight of its kind before Coleridge. Quoting a passage from Demosthenes, he makes the experiment of adding a syllable, and observes that the "sublime phrase is loosened and undone by lengthening of the final rhythm." Likewise, if the phrase were shortened by a syllable. His

principle of prose rhythm is negatively stated, but it seems
to me to hold for every kind of writing. It is: prose rhythm
should not have "a conspicuous movement of sound." It
must seem, even if metaphysically it is not, at one with the
meaning; it must not call attention to itself, unless—as in
Tacitus, Gibbon, Doughty, or Sir Thomas Browne—the
"conspicuous movement of sound" is a tonal vehicle that
once established is not distinguishable from, but is a part
of, the subject itself. But if it is a rhythm "like that of a
dancer taking his step before the audience," which the
audience anticipates, it distracts attention from what is
being said to who is saying it. It is a disproportion in
composition similar to that of the orator or the poet who "di-
gresses from the subject into his own tedious emotions." Had
Longinus been discussing the rhythm of verse, I should have
been able to cite Swinburne and *The Age of Anxiety* by
Mr. W. H. Auden.

VI

I have postponed consideration of the third source of Elevation to this concluding section because it pertains in part
to metaphor, the *pons asinorum* of literary criticism. If on
this subject Longinus is unsatisfactory, it is only a matter
of degree; here everybody is unsatisfactory, even Mr. I. A.
Richards, whose *Philosophy of Rhetoric* offers a good deal
but promises too much. This is a field of inquiry of a difficulty equal to that of the burden of the mystery. Here
again Longinus is prudential, but he no doubt gives us as
good an account as any of the classical precept of nothing-
too-much. Don't use too many metaphors, unless you are
overwhelmed by emotions which may make them credible.
Follow Aristotle, perhaps in the *Rhetoric*; soften the metaphor up by inserting "as if" or "just as though" and making
it a simile that does not assert improbable identities.

One goes through the περὶ ὕψους, and then the *Rhetoric,*

half-heartedly and vainly, looking for something better than this, from the literary point of view, that Longinus might have overlooked, or for something as far-reaching as Aristotle's own Delphic pronouncement in Chapter XXII of the *Poetics,* where he says:

It is a great thing indeed to make a proper use of these poetical forms, as also of compounds and strange words. But the greatest thing by far is to be a master of metaphor. It is the one thing that cannot be learnt from others; and it is also a sign of genius, since a good metaphor implies an intuitive perception of the similarity in dissimilars.

That is very nearly the beginning and the end of our own inquiries into metaphor; but I am rash enough to question whether Aristotle, as a Greek, could know, as we have known since Shakespeare and Donne, how similar dissimilars can be made to seem, or (to take an extreme view which is not unknown today) how similar they can be made to *be.* Metaphor, says Aristotle, is the transference of names, through the permutations of genus and species, or by analogy. Metaphor by analogy takes the formula of arithmetical proportion, a quantitative and relational procedure. We are thus in the Greek Cosmos, an ordering of solid objects under a physics of motion, in which the formal object offers but a narrow margin of analogy to any other. If the ancient inquiry into the structure of metaphor was less resourceful than ours, it was not I daresay because Aristotle was less intelligent than the best modern critics. Our multiverse has increasingly, since the seventeenth century, consisted of unstable objects dissolving into energy; and there has been no limit to the extension of analogy. Criticism follows whatever it is given to follow. Are the famous lucidity and the restraint of the Greeks evidence that by nature they were more lucid and more restrained than we? I doubt it. For even the physical sight may be controlled by the religious selectivity, which fixes the height and the direction of the casement framing our inspection of the world. To introduce at the end of an essay so large and so undeveloped a conception is an impropriety of length and occasion; I offer it as historical relativism in defense of Longinus and of ourselves.

On no single kind of literature is Longinus as searching as Aristotle on tragedy. But I risk the guess that he came nearer to a comprehensive theory of literary form than any other ancient critic. If he did not quite make the leap to a complete theory of the language of imagination, we must remember that nobody in the ancient world did. He shared Aristotle's sense of the simple relation between word and thing; in a world of fixed forms, thing was unyielding; the word, like its object, retained a plastic visibility. With the Greeks the "transference" of "names" was limited to the surface designation, to the comparison of objects in the round, to sculpturesque analogy. Metaphor was a feature of discourse to be described, not a metaphysical problem to be investigated. We need not see as a critical limitation Longinus' failure to investigate a problem that for him did not exist. The permanent critics do not settle the question. They compel us to ask it again. They are the rotating chairmen of a debate only the rhetoric of which changes from time to time. Among these we may think of Longinus, if we will read him not in our age, but in his own.

1948

Johnson on the Metaphysical Poets

WHEN we feel disposed to dismiss Johnson's views on the Metaphysical poets as prejudice, we ought to consider whether we are not opposing one prejudice with another, of another kind, between which sensible compromise is difficult or even impossible. I see no way to refute Johnson's attack on the school of Donne short of setting up an abstract critical dialectic which would have little bearing upon how poetry is written in any age. I should like to marshal here a set of prejudices, of my own, as cogent as Johnson's, but that would be a feat beyond my capacity, as it would surely be beyond the reach of any critic less ignorant than myself. As a man of the first half of the twentieth century, I have no doubt as many prejudices as Johnson had, but I cannot be sure that I understand mine as well as he understood his. The first obstacle to our understanding of prejudice is the liberal dogma that prejudice must not be entertained; it has, with us, something of the private, the mantic, and the wilful. In this positive ignorance we would do well to remember with Mr. F. R. Leavis that Johnson lived in a "positive culture" which made it easier than it is today for a critic to undergo a "positive training" for his profession.[1] Johnson came to *The Lives of the Poets* when

---

[1] I am indebted to Mr. Leavis for several observations: F. R. Leavis, "Samuel Johnson," in *The Importance of Scrutiny*, edited by Eric Bentley (New York, 1964), pp. 57–75. W. B. C. Watkins's *Johnson and English Poetry Before 1660* (Princeton, 1936) is indispensable in any study of Johnson's views on Donne. I have not made much explicit use of W. K. Wimsatt's two excellent books, *The Prose Style of Samuel Johnson* (New Haven, 1941) and *Philosophic*

lips; systematic abstraction is the result of labor. What Johnson seems to detect here is the doubtful application of the
operations of the mind to the river; it is a one-way metaphor in which the tenor is compromised by the vehicle. I
believe it is fair to say that Johnson liked his tenors straight,
without any nonsense from the vehicles. His remark that
the "particulars of resemblance are perspicaciously collected,"
seems incomprehensible.

Johnson would doubtless agree with us in finding little
in common between Denham's lines and the fourth stanza
of Donne's "A Nocturnall upon S. Lucie's Day." Let us look
briefly at that stanza, as well as we can, with the eyes that
Johnson turned upon Denham.

> But I am by her death, (which word wrongs her)
> Of the first nothing, the Elixer grown;
>> Were I a man, that I were one,
>> I needs must show; I should preferre,
>>> If I were any beast,
> Some ends, some means; Yea plants, yea stones detest,
> And love; All, all some properties invest;
>> If I an ordinary nothing were,
> As shadow, a light, and body must be here.

I do not know how to paraphrase the tenor of these lines, because I run at once into Johnson's difficulties with Denham. There are probably no abstractions, more abstract than
Donne's own language, into which the distinction between
an "ordinary nothing" and the "Elixer" of the "first nothing" can be paraphrased. The tenor can be located only in its
vehicle, the specific metaphorical structure of the passage.
One of Johnson's counts against the Metaphysical poets
was the failure to represent the "operations of intellect" (to
say nothing of their wilful neglect of the "scenes of life"
and the "prospects of nature"), a quality that Johnson
found preeminently in Pope. Yet it must seem to us that
Donne is more nearly an *intellectual* poet than Pope (if the

designation have meaning at all), for many of Donne's poems are, at one level or another, semi-rational operations elaborately drawn out. (These misunderstandings seize upon one slippery term after another, which will never be fixed, though it is the perpetual task of criticism to misunderstand its "problems" in new terms at intervals of about fifty years.) Johnson knew Donne's poetry thoroughly, much of it by heart, and he quotes him extensively; but his scattered comment is so brief that we cannot reconstruct a coherent view. We can only surmise that he would have found it "improper" and "vicious" for a man to imagine himself less than an "ordinary nothing." He tells us that "whatever is improper or vicious is produced by a voluntary deviation from nature in pursuit of something new and strange."

No deviation from nature, in Johnson's sense, appears in Denham's lines, on the literal plane; but in being true to nature he is not able to use the river as an accurate vehicle for an "operation of intellect"; so he accepts the tenor "metaphorically" only; that is to say, he cannot really locate it, he finds it a little incredible. But in the stanza by Donne is not the vehicle so powerful that it, even more completely than in Denham, engulfs the tenor? Donne *means* his figure; it is *exactly* what he meant to say. Johnson would doubtless have seen in what Donne says of himself (the scholastic nullity of his spirit as a consequence of the death of Lucy) something highly improper, if not vicious. I anticipate a later stage of this discussion by remarking that Donne evidently did not "enquire . . . what he should have said or done." He had no predetermined tenor in search of a perspicuous vehicle.

At this point I pass beyond certain considerations suggested by the obscure commentaries on Denham (both Johnson's and my own) into more difficult speculations; here I tread cautiously. I begin to approach directly the uncertain object of this enquiry. Johnson's piety is well known;

his views on Christianity were forthright, uncompromising, and beyond controversy; I do not intend to discuss them here. I will cite two brief paragraphs from the "Life of Waller," concerning the relation of poetry and Christian worship:

Contemplative piety, or the intercourse between God and the human soul, cannot be poetical. Man, admitted to implore the mercy of his Creator, and plead the merits of his Redeemer, is already in a higher state than poetry can confer.

The essence of poetry is invention; such invention as, by producing something unexpected, surprises and delights. The topics of devotion are few, and being few are universally known; but, few as they are, they can be made no more; they receive no grace from novelty of sentiment, and very little from novelty of expression.

There is a certain common sense in these paragraphs, if we read them very freely: Poetry is not religion, or even a substitute for it. But what Johnson actually says is that religious contemplation is not a subject for poetry; and this is nonsense. The first paragraph evinces an ignorance of religious poetry, or an indifference to it, comparable to the incapacity of an American critic three generations later, whose critical style was influenced by Johnson: Edgar Allan Poe. Whether poetry can confer a state either higher or lower than that of contemplative piety becomes a meaningless question if we ask first whether it can *confer* any sort of state. Whether religious experience can be the subject of poetry is another question equally unreal. One does not ask whether a man has two arms and two legs, and expect to deduce the Laputan answer; for he obviously has both. Great devotional poetry obviously exists. (What was Johnson doing with St. John of the Cross, the poems of St. Thomas Aquinas, or even, for that matter, with the Psalms of David?) At the end of Johnson's second paragraph one finds another dubious distinction between sentiment and expression. The sentiment remains unknown without the expression, whether it be "novel" or common. (Johnson's rhetorical parallelism frequently leads him by the nose, into saying more, or something else, than he means.) Whether from novelty of sentiment or of expression it is difficult to see how the "topics" of devotion could receive "grace." No one has ever asserted that they did, unless it be the grace snatched beyond the reach of art. Is this "grace" of the "higher state than poetry" supernatural grace sacramentally conferred? No one has ever asserted that poetry could confer it. Some poems (and their apologists) have asserted that we can get along without it; but that is another problem.

No historical considerations have entered into my rough treatment of Johnson; I am reading him out of his time, in my own time, countering his explicit prejudice with prejudice, perhaps not sufficiently explored, of my own. It would be instructive but beside the point to show that Johnson's strictures upon religious poetry are neoclassical criticism at a level of insight where as literary critic he could turn out the light, and revert to private feelings at a depth untouched by his "positive training." Johnson, like most critics whose philosophical powers are in themselves not impressive (and unlike Coleridge), is at his best when he is reading or comparing texts. If we continue to think of Johnson at his best as a critic with a positive training in the English neoclassical school, we shall understand more sympathetically his insistence that the end of poetry is delight leading to instruction; its means, invention. What he finds wrong with religious poetry is probably the same thing that he finds wrong with Denham. The devotional objects, being "universally known," provide a fixed "tenor" for which no new metaphorical vehicle or invention is adequate or necessary; for only the tenor is "true." Institutional religion is the immense paraphrase, no longer, if ever, seen as resting upon a metaphorical base, of the religious experience. The imaginative act of returning the paraphrase to the hazards of new experience (new vehicles) is an impiety, even a perversity which he reproves in the Metaphysical poets.

The foregoing digression into the quotations from the lives of Denham and Waller has seemed to me necessary in order to form as clear a notion as possible of Johnson's assumptions about metaphor. Nowhere in the "Life of Cowley," which I shall now glance at, shall we find so close a scrutiny of language as his analysis of Denham's couplets, or a limitation upon the province of poetry so clearly defined in ultimate religious terms, as in the paragraphs on Waller. The "Life of Cowley" ends with a formidable string of quotations, none of which receives a thorough going over. His strictures upon Cowley and Donne take the form of generalizations from a considerable body of poetry, but like Aristotle on poetic diction he leaves the application to us. I conceive his criticism of the Metaphysicals to be grounded in certain philosophical assumptions of his time about the meaning of Reason and Nature: I have neither competence nor space to deal extensively with such questions. Doubtless the New Learning of the seventeenth century, which Mr. Wimsatt finds typically reflected in Johnson, and the philosophy of Locke, gave a rationalistic tinge to his conceptions of reason and nature, and buttressed his literary neoclassicism and thus his views on the province of poetry.

We must now make what we can of some crucial passages from the "Life of Cowley":

. . . they [the Metaphysical poets] neither copied nature nor life; neither painted the forms of matter nor represented the operations of intellect . . . they were not successful in representing or moving the affections.

They had no regard to that uniformity of sentiment which enables us to conceive and to excite the pains and pleasures of other minds; they never enquired what on any occasion they should have said or done; but wrote rather as beholders than partakers of human nature. . . . Their wish was only to say what had never been said before.

The first of these excerpts contains Johnson's general objection, which could easily take us philosophically far afield. If we roughly equate "nature" with "forms of matter," and "life" with "operations of intellect," we get the solid objects of eighteenth century physics (inorganic: no internal change), and a rationalistic epistemology which orders the objects in fixed relations. I am not able to develop this inference further, but it may be sufficient for my purpose to guess that we have here, in the "operations of intellect" upon the "forms of matter," Locke's secondary qualities in a stable relation to the primary; so that the perception of qualities and discourse about them are a single act of mind. Likewise in Johnson's representation and moving of the affections there is both a perceptual and a cognitive limit beyond which the poet exceeds the known and fixed limits of emotion. Thus the Metaphysical poets failed to enquire into the limits of what can be said; they failed to respect, in ignoring the strict conventions of imitation, the neoclassical standard of generalized emotion, scene, and character; they lacked the uniformity of sentiment which Johnson's positive culture supported. Because they wrote outside the eighteenth century canon they wrote outside, rather than within, human nature.

At this point one should pause to distinguish certain historical differences between the situation of Donne and the old age of English Baroque, when in the 1770's it had passed into Rococo. What little I know about these differences is better known by the scholars in the two fields, though perhaps few scholars know both; I should not in any case wish to rely too much upon terms taken from architecture. And we must not assume that the Rococo artist ought to understand the origins of his style in the Baroque;

there is no reason why Johnson should have understood Donne. The age of Johnson had achieved in verse a *period* style. Whatever may have been its remote origins in the age of Donne (it became something very different from its origins), it was a style that we could not write today, and was perhaps inconceivable to Donne and his contemporaries. With the exceptions of Milton (excluding "Lycidas") and Shakespeare, both of whom were so "great" that he could scarcely miss them, he lacked the critical terms and the philosophical temper for the estimation of poetry outside his period style. Perhaps a high development of period style always entails upon its critics a provincial complacency towards the styles of the past which have not directly contributed to it (one thinks of Pound and early Eliot on Milton, both men concerned about a language for a period); and we get almost inevitably a progressive view of poetry. One of the aims of Johnson's proposed, but never written, History of Criticism was to give "An Account of the Rise and Improvement of that Art." But there is no invidious inference to be drawn from his prospectus; there is no evidence that a bad poet after Dryden could win his praise.

Whether he preferred Cowley as a forerunner of his own period style, to Donne, or whether the committee of forty-three booksellers who underwrote the Lives did not consider Donne a poet of enough " reputation" to justify a new edition, is a scholar's question; yet it is not without an answer of the internal sort if we are willing to glance at Johnson's praise of Cowley's "Of Wit." Of this poem he says:

The Ode on Wit is almost without a rival. It was about the time of Cowley that *wit,* which had been till then used for *intellection,* in contra-distinction to *will,* took the meaning, whatever it be, which it now bears. . . . Of all the passages in which poets have exemplified their own precepts, none will easily be found of greater excellence than that in which Cowley condemns exuberance of wit.

He then quotes the fifth stanza, of which we may glance at these lines:

> Several lights will not be seen,
> If there be nothing else between.
> Men doubt because they stand so thick i' the skie,
> If those be stars which paint the Galaxie.

If this does not exhibit the excess of conceit against which it was written, then one has wasted one's life in the concern for poetry (a possibility that must always be kept in view); but short of facing such a crisis one must regretfully impute to Johnson a lapse of judgment at a moment when his prejudice is flattered. The passage flatters Johnson otherwise: lines three and four are a couplet that Dryden, in a fit of absent-mindedness, might have written, and that, but for the extra syllable in the fifth foot of the third line, could have been written by Pope in a moment of fatigue.

I have disclaimed any ability to estimate Johnson's specific criticism of the Metaphysical poets; but I seem to have been judging it, perhaps inevitably; exposition without incidental judgment is not possible. But I now return to the more neutral enquiry into the contrasting uses of figurative language, of which Johnson stands for one extreme and Donne for another. The instructive paragraph for this purpose, in the "Life of Cowley," has not had much attention from critics of either Johnson or Donne; I quote it entire:

Nor was the sublime more within their reach than the pathetic; for they never attempted that comprehension and expanse which at once fills the whole mind, and of which the first effect is sudden astonishment, and the second rational admiration. Sublimity is produced by aggregation, littleness by dispersion. Great thoughts are always general, and consist in positions not limited by exceptions, and in descriptions not descending to minuteness. It is with great propriety that subtility, which in its original import means exility of particles, is taken in its metaphorical meaning for nicety of distinction. Those writers who lay on the watch for novelty, could have little hope of greatness; for great things cannot have escaped former observation. *Their attempts were always analytic; they broke every image into fragments; and could no more represent, by their slender conceits and laboured particularities, the prospects of nature, or the scenes of life, than he who dissects a sunbeam with a prism can exhibit the wide effulgence of a summer noon.*

Up to the last sentence of this remarkable pronouncement, about half of the ghost of Longinus is the presiding, if somewhat equivocal authority. (Longinus did not *oppose* the "sublime" to the "little.") Great things, even in Johnson's testimony, had escaped former observation before Shakespeare, and Shakespeare left a few to Pope. But it is good neoclassical doctrine: "But when t'examine every part he came, / Nature and Homer were, he found, the same." It is the doctrine of the Grandeur of Generality given a critical formula in the phrases "positions not limited by exceptions" and "descriptions not descending to minuteness." If Mr. Leavis is right in saying that Johnson had little dramatic sense (he could still have had it and written *Irene*), it is a defect that seems general in that age, when men assumed a static relation between the mind and its object, between poet and subject. The universals that have not escaped former observation are again the big tenors which must not be limited by too many exceptions in the vehicles: invention is all very well if the poet doesn't mean it too hard; if he does it will not win rational admiration for the "minute particulars" in which Blake saw the life not only of poetry but of the spirit. We can scarcely blame Johnson if in describing what poetry ought to be he described the weak side of Pope's and his own.

But the remarkable last sentence of the paragraph might well be set down as the main text of this commentary: I hope I shall not give it an unfair reading. "Their attempts," says Johnson, "were always analytic; they broke every image into fragments." He asks us to prejudge Cowley and his fellows before we are given to understand how we should judge them: it is, generally speaking, bad to *break* things. What are the "attempts" of the Metaphysicals? Their poems, or isolated figures? I assume that he means this: they used metaphor in such a way as to produce analytic effects; they got inside the object and exhibited it as a collection, or dispersion, of "laboured particularities." I confess that I do not understand what I have just written: I can think of no poem of the Metaphysical school of which Johnson's words or my own gloss would be a just description. One could play with an irresponsible sorites, and take analytic to mean in the Kantian and, for Johnson, anachronistic sense, a predicate containing nothing that is not already in the subject. Johnson would then be censuring the Metaphysicals for having done what he should have praised them for: for giving us "images" the qualities of which were already known. His censure is for the Kantian synthetic judgment; for the Metaphysical flight beyond the predictable character of the object, or for the internal exploration of new imaginative objects not known in the neoclassical properties. Johnson I daresay did not know that he was a neoclassicist; so he boggles at the violation of what he deemed the eternal principles of style discovered by the ancients and rediscovered by his own forerunners for the improvement of English poetry. By analytic I take it that he also meant the assertion of marginal similarities as total, like the lovers-compasses simile which virtually claims an identity on the thin ground that lovers, like compasses, must lean towards each other before they can become the two congruent lines of the embrace. By analytic he means a fragmentation of objects in pursuit of "occult resemblances."

The famous phrase brings us to the even more famous "definition" of Metaphysical poetry, in which it occurs:

> But wit, abstracted from its effects upon the hearer, may be more rigorously and philosophically considered as a kind of *discordia concors;* a combination of dissimilar images, or discovery of occult resemblances in things apparently unlike.

One is constantly impressed by Johnson's consistency of point of view, over the long pull of his self-dedication to letters. There is seldom either consistency or precision in his particular judgments and definitions—a defect that perhaps accounts negatively for his greatness as a critic: the perpetual reformulation of his standards, with his eye on the poetry, has done much to keep eighteenth-century verse alive in our day. His theories (if his ideas ever reach that level of logical abstraction) are perhaps too simple for our taste and too improvised; but his reading is disciplined and acute. There is no doubt that the definition of Metaphysical wit is an improvisation of terms, but it represents the result of long and sensitive meditation on a body of verse which he could not like but the importance of which he had to acknowledge. A brief scrutiny of this definition turns up the astonishing metaphor of sound, *discordia concors,* coming after the promise to give us not a psychological but an epistemological view of wit. We were to have got what wit is, not how it affects us. I don't want to quibble about this matter; I want to emphasize the essential accuracy of one of the great critical insights. It is a new insight based upon a long critical tradition going back to the *Poetics* (Chapter 22):

> It is a great thing indeed to make a proper use of these poetical forms, as also of compounds and strange words. But the greatest

thing by far is to be a master of metaphor. It is the one thing that cannot be learned from others; and it is also a sign of genius, since a good metaphor implies an intuitive perception of the similarity in dissimilars.

It would have been helpful in the past twenty-three hundred years if Aristotle had told us what a good metaphor is, and settled the matter. How far should the perception of similarity go? The *Poetics* seems to be a fragment, and we shall not get Aristotle's wisdom (if he had it) for our folly. We have Johnson's, in the second sentence after the quotation above; and he writes what is possibly his best descriptive criticism of the Metaphysical style:

The most heterogeneous ideas are yoked by violence together. . . .

By what kind of violence? A poetry of violence may have its own validity in its own time, and even for other times. Again we confront Johnson's point of view done up in an approximate generalization, which for all its heuristic accuracy begs the question which it conceals. The question is how much violence is allowable, and at what point does the yoking of dissimilars in similarity overreach itself and collapse under the strain? [2] It would be critical folly to decide how much stretch Johnson would allow, a folly of which he was happily not guilty. The allowed stretch is the stretch of one's age (with one eye on other ages), the tensions within the religious and moral struggle that the poet must acknowledge in himself.

If we may reasonably get around this defeating relativ-

[2] Mr. Samuel H. Monk has called my attention to a passage in the "Life of Addison" which I had overlooked: "A simile may be compared to lines converging at a point, and is more excellent as the lines approach from greater distance: an exemplification may be considered as two parallel lines which run together without approximation, never far separated, and never joined." This is itself an excellent simile, but its tenor has whatever degree of obscurity one may find in "distance." It would abstractly make room for Donne's wildest figures; but Johnson could still reply that these seldom "converge."

ism, what direction shall we take? One direction is towards the chasm; to the leap into the unhistorical and timeless generalization of the late Paul Valéry; but only skeptics who believe in unicorns had better travel that road. Another road leads to the Palace of Wisdom where there aren't any poets; and criticism may want in the end to get along without poetry. Between the chasm and the feather bed (Mr. Blackmur's version of the Palace of Wisdom), somewhere between the down and the up, lies the region that most critics inhabit without quite knowing where it is. That is not too desperate an ignorance, if one remembers that Poe was Valéry's unicorn (desperate skepticism indeed) and that autotelism is usually a bed of feathers that no longer sing. I am not confident that Johnson would like this mixture of feathers, a Palace, and a unicorn; and I am not sure that he would not be right.

Nor can I be sure that his failure to understand Donne as we think we understand him was a real failure. I have concealed the questions I have put to him, as he concealed his, by begging them. One would prefer to *note down,* as dispassionately as possible, his dogmatic rejection of all religious poetry which is not pietistic or devotional; his static psychology of perception; his fixed natural order; his fixed decorum in diction. It all adds up to a denial of validity to what in our age has been called a poetry of experience. A poetry of experience is incipiently a poetry of action; hence of drama, the sense of which Johnson seems to have lacked. The minute particulars of the wrestling with God, which we find in Donne and Crashaw, bring the religious experience into the dimension of immediate time. Johnson's implied division of poetry into the meditative and the descriptive (implied also in his own verse) fixes its limits, arresting the subject within the frame of pictorial space: *ut pictura poesis,* for his typical *period* verb for the poetic effect is that the poet *paints.* The breaking up of the image, of which he accuses the Metaphysical poets, is the discovery of a dynamic relation between the mind and its objects, in a poetry which does not recognize the traditional topic; the subject becomes the metaphorical structure, it is no longer the set theme. The ideas that result from the dynamic perception of objects (language itself is thus an object) are in constant disintegration; so inferentially are the objects themselves. The "object" which poetry like "The Extasie" or "The Canonization" suggests that we locate, is not an existence in space, but an essence created by the junction of the vehicle and the tenor of the leading metaphor. It is not *in* space; it moves with experience in time.

As I come to a close I am aware of a certain provincialism of amateur metaphysics, as well as of some critical imprecision, in the foregoing remarks; and I am not sure that I have not had in mind the poetry of our age a little more fully than the poetry of the age of Donne; that my own core of prejudice has not been witlessly revealed. That prejudice, if it is more than private, would run as follows: the great tradition of modern verse unites Shakespeare and Donne, includes Milton and much of Dryden, but passes over the eighteenth century until the year 1798. This is not to say that Dryden was a greater poet than Pope, though he may have been; it is rather to say that the neoclassical age was an interlude between modernisms, that it had bypassed the Renaissance Nature of *depth* and restored the classical Nature of *surface*. But the *Prelude* brought us back: to the breakup of the solid object in the dynamic stream of time.

That the poets may have cracked the atom before the physicists gives us the dubious pride of discovery; but I daresay few persons feel any pride in some of the more practical results. The neoclassical age died because it could not move; we may be dying because we cannot stop moving. Our poetry has become process, including its own processes. It is pleasant to remember Aristotle's summary treatment of metaphor and his elaborate description of the structure of the greatest of the genres. Were not the genres so powerful, so nearly rooted in nature herself, that their languages could be taken for granted? They would last forever. Poetic diction could be brought under arithmetical rules of thumb; it was nicely settled in its relation to the wonderful collection of solid objects scattered through space; it could never be a problem in itself. Into that space time entered not as process but as myth. It is not a question which is the better view to look down at, the classical or ours; one may not choose one's view if one expects to see anything. I end these remarks on two uses of figurative language with the observation that I have not taken them further than I did in a recent essay on Longinus. But I have taken them as far as I am able; perhaps further.

1949

Ezra Pound and the Bollingen Prize

WHAT I SHALL SAY here is not in further commentary on Mr. William Barrett's article in the April 1949 issue of *Partisan Review;* nor is it the "rational, impersonal, and calm justification" of the award of the Bollingen Prize to Ezra Pound which Mr. Barrett was kind enough to expect from me. I intend rather to set down my own reasons for voting for *The Pisan Cantos.* I shall have in mind the *Partisan* symposium on the award without, I hope, being influenced by it in reconstructing my views of last November.[1]

From the time I first read Pound's verse more than thirty years ago I have considered him a mixed poet. In an essay written in 1931,[2] on the first thirty Cantos, I expressed views which the later accretions to the work have not changed: the work to which I helped to give the Bollingen Prize is formless, eccentric, and personal. The Cantos are now, as I said then, "about nothing at all." They have a voice but no subject. As one of the commentators on Mr. Barrett's article put it, they have no beginning, middle, or end. I used similar language in 1931. It is a striking fact that in talking about this work one must say "Canto

---

[1] The first award of the Bollingen Prize was made in 1949 to Ezra Pound for *The Pisan Cantos,* published in 1948; but the prize was voted to him in November, 1948 by the Fellows in American Letters of The Library of Congress, who were then the jury of award. I was a member of the jury. Since 1950 the Bollingen Prize has been given under the auspices of the Library of Yale University.

[2] "Ezra Pound," *supra,* pp. 364–371.

XX of the *Cantos"*; there is always a Canto of Cantos, not a Canto of a substantive work with a title like Canto XX of the *Purgatorio* of the *Divina Commedia*.

Mr. Pound is incapable of sustained thought in either prose or verse. His acute verbal sensibility is thus at the mercy of random flights of "angelic insight," Icarian self-indulgences of prejudice which are not checked by a total view to which they could be subordinated. Thus his anti-Semitism—which, as Mr. Auden has said, all Gentiles have felt (I have felt it, and felt humiliated by it)—his anti-Semitism is not disciplined by an awareness of its sinister implications in the real world of men. Neither Mr. Pound nor any other man is to be censured for his private feelings; but every man must answer for what he does with his feelings. It has been often observed that Pound fails to get into his verse any sort of full concrete reality. Insofar as the *Cantos* have a subject it is made up of historical materials. But if there is any poetry of our age which may be said to be totally lacking in the historical sense, the sense of how ideas move in history, it is Pound's *Cantos*. His verse is an anomaly in an age of acute historical awareness.

I do not know what reasons, motives, or prejudices prompted the other affirmative votes. There has been some public conjecture upon this subject, but I consider it a gross impropriety. I shall do well if I am able to speak honestly for myself. I have little sympathy with the view that holds that Pound's irresponsible opinions merely lie alongside the poetry, which thus remains uncontaminated. The disagreeable opinions are right in the middle of the poetry. And they have got to be seen for what they are: they are personal, wilful, and unrelated; and they are not brought together under a mature conception of life as it is now or ever was. I infer the absence of such a mature view in the man from the incoherence of the form; but it is only the latter that concerns me. Apart from specific objections to his anti-

Semitism and fascism, there is a formal principle which, if severely applied, would have been a good enough reason for voting against *The Pisan Cantos*. Not only the anti-Semitism but all the other "insights" remain unassimilated to a coherent form. The assumption of many persons, that a vote for *The Pisan Cantos* was a vote for "formalism" and a vote against "vitality" in poetry, makes no sense at all to me.

There is nothing mysterious about coherent form. It is the presence of an order in a literary work which permits us to understand one part in relation to all the other parts. What should concern us in looking *at* the *Cantos* is the formal irresponsibility; in looking *beyond* the work, the possible effects of this irresponsibility upon society. (If Pound's *Cantos* expressed *anti*-Fascist opinions, my formal objections would be the same; but I should think that the formlessness would make him a good Communist party-line poet.) But just as Pound's broadcasts over Radio Rome never influenced anybody in this country, and were chiefly an indignity perpetrated upon himself, I cannot suppose that the anti-Semitism of the *Cantos* will be taken seriously by anybody but liberal intellectuals. Anti-Semites will not "use" it. It is too innocent. I take it seriously in the sense of disliking it, and I cannot "honor the man" for it, as the Fellows of the Library were charged with doing; but I cannot think that it will strengthen anti-Semitism.

I respect differences of opinion on this question, about which I am not well informed. What I have already said is enough to indicate that my vote for *The Pisan Cantos* was not an easy step to take: I could have voted against it. But this is not all. I had, as many men of my generation might have had, personal reasons for not voting for Mr. Pound. Insofar as he has noticed my writings at all, in conversation and correspondence—which the international literary grapevine always reports—he has noticed them with contempt. Nevertheless I voted for him, for the following reason:

the health of literature depends upon the health of society, and conversely; there must be constant vigilance for both ends of the process. The specific task of the man of letters is to attend to the health of society *not at large* but through literature—that is, he must be constantly aware of the condition of language in his age. As a result of observing Pound's use of language in the past thirty years I had become convinced that he had done more than any other man to regenerate the language, if not the imaginative forms, of English verse. I had to face the disagreeable fact that he had done this even in passages of verse in which the opinions expressed ranged from the childish to the detestable.

In literature as in life nothing reaches us pure. The task of the civilized intelligence is one of perpetual salvage. We cannot decide that our daily experience must be either aesthetic or practical—art or life; it is never, as it comes to us, either/or; it is always both/and. But as persons of a particular *ethos*, of a certain habit and character, we discharge our responsibilities to society from the point of view of the labors in which we are placed. We are placed in the profession of letters. We cannot expect the business man and the politician, the men who run the state, to know that our particular responsibility exists; we cannot ask them to understand the more difficult fact that our responsibility to them is for the language which they themselves use for the general welfare. They are scarcely aware of language at all; what one is not aware of one almost inevitably abuses. But the medium cannot be extricated from the material, the how from the what: part of our responsibility is to correct the monism of the statesman who imagines that what he says is scarcely said in language at all, that it exists apart from the medium in a "purity" of action which he thinks of as "practicality." If men of letters do not look after the medium, nobody else will. We need never fear that the practical man will fail to ignore our concern for the health of language: this he has already done by indicting Pound as if Pound, like himself, were a monist of action. Pound's language remains our particular concern. If he were a convicted traitor, I should still think that, in another direction which complicates the problem ultimately beyond our comprehension, he had performed an indispensable duty to society.

1949

IV

VI

The Profession of Letters in the South[1]

THE PROFESSION of letters in France dates, I believe, from the famous manifesto of Du Bellay and the Pléiade in 1549. It is a French habit to assume that France has supported a profession of letters ever since. There is no other country where the writer is so much honored as in France, no other people in western culture who understand so well as the French the value of literature to the state. The national respect for letters begins far down in society. In a French village where I was unknown I was able to use a letter-of-credit without identification upon my word that I was a man of letters. The French have no illusions; we are not asked to believe that all French writers are respectable. The generation of Rimbaud and Verlaine was notoriously dissolute. French letters are a profession, as law, medicine, and the army are professions. Good writers starve and lead sordid lives in France as elsewhere; yet the audience for high literature is larger in France than in any other country, and a sufficient number of the best writers find a public large enough to sustain them as a class.

It goes somewhat differently with us. The American public sees the writer as a business man because it cannot see any other kind of man, and respects him according to his income. And, alas, most writers themselves respect chiefly and fear only their competitors' sales. A big sale is a "success." How could it be otherwise? Our books are sold on a competitive

1 This essay was written for the tenth anniversary of *The Virginia Quarterly Review*, April, 1935. It has been amplified.

market; it is a book market, but it is a luxury market; and luxury markets must be fiercely competitive. It is not that the natural depravity of the writer as fallen man betrays him into imitating the tone and standards of his market; actually he cannot find a public at all, even for the most lost of lost causes, the *succès d'estime*, unless he is willing to enter the competitive racket of publishing. This racket, our society being what it is, is a purely economic process, and literary opinion is necessarily manufactured for its needs. Its prime need is shoddy goods, because it must have a big, quick turnover. The overhead in the system is so high that the author gets only ten to fifteen percent of the gross. It is the smallest return that any producer gets in our whole economic system. To live even frugally, a novelist, if he does not do odd jobs on the side, must have a sale of about thirty thousand copies every two years. Not only the publisher's but his turnover, too, must be quick. He has his own self-sweat shop. One must agree with Mr. Herbert Read, in the February, 1935, London *Mercury,* that authors under modern capitalism are a sweated class.

We have heard for years, we began hearing it as early as Jeffrey's review of the first "Hyperion," that science is driving poetry to cover. I suppose it is; and we have the weight of Mr. I. A. Richards's arguments to prove it, and Mr. Max Eastman's weight, which is fairly light. Nineteenth-century science produced a race of "problem" critics and novelists. The new "social" point of view has multiplied the race. Literature needs no depth of background or experience to deal with problems; it needs chiefly the statistical survey and the conviction that society lives by formula, if not by bread alone. The nineteenth century began this *genre,* which has become the standard mode. I confess that I cannot decide whether "science" or the mass production of books, or the Spirit that made them both, has given us shoddy in literature. We were given, for example, Bennett and Wells; Millay and

Masefield. And I surmise that not pure science but shoddy has driven the poets into exile, where, according to Eastman, they are "talking to themselves."

I shall not multiply instances. The trouble ultimately goes back to the beginnings of finance-capitalism and its creature, machine-production. Under feudalism the artist was a member of an organic society. The writer's loss of professional standing, however, set in before the machine, by which I mean the machine age as we know it, appeared. It began with the rise of mercantile aristocracy in the eighteenth century. The total loss of professionalism in letters may be seen in our age—an age that remembers the extinction of aristocracy and witnesses the triumph of a more inimical plutocratic society.

If my history is not wholly incorrect, it must follow that our unlimited pioneering, the pretext of the newness of the country, and our low standards of education, do not explain the decline of the professional author. Pioneering became our way of industrial expansion, a method of production not special to us; we are a new country insofar as our industrialism gave to the latent vices of the European mind a new opportunity; and our standards of education get lower with the increasing amount of money spent upon them. For my purposes, then, it is sufficient that we should look at the history of professionalism in letters in terms of the kinds of rule that European society, which includes American society, has had.

The South once had aristocratic rule; the planter class was about one fifth of the population; but the majority followed its lead. And so, by glancing at the South, we shall see in American history an important phase of the decline of the literary profession. There was, perhaps, in and around Boston, for a brief period, a group of professional writers. But not all of them, not even most of them, made their livings by writing. Even if they had, we should still have to explain why they were second-rate, and why the greatest of the Easterners, Hawthorne, Melville, Dickinson, had nothing to do with them or with the rising plutocracy of the East. But it is a sadder story still in the South. We had no Hawthorne, no Melville, no Emily Dickinson. We had William Gilmore Simms. We made it impossible for Poe to live south of the Potomac. Aristocracy drove him out. Plutocracy, in the East, starved him to death. I prefer the procedure of the South; it knew its own mind, knew what kind of society it wanted. The East, bent upon making money, could tolerate, as it still tolerates, any kind of disorder on the fringe of society as long as the disorder does not interfere with money making. It did not know its own social mind; it was, and still is, plutocracy.

But let us look a little at the backgrounds of Southern literature. I say backgrounds, for the South is an immensely complicated region. It begins in the Northeast with southern Maryland; it ends with eastern Texas; it includes to the north a little of Missouri. But that the people in this vast expanse of country have enough in common to bind them in a single culture cannot be denied. They often deny it themselves—writers who want to have something to jabber about, or other writers who want to offset the commercial handicap of being Southern; or newly rich persons in cities that would rather be like Pittsburgh than like New Orleans. It must be confessed that the Southern tradition has left no cultural landmark so conspicuous that the people may be reminded by it constantly of what they are. We lack a tradition in the arts; more to the point, we lack a literary tradition. We lack even a literature. We have just enough literary remains from the old régime to prove to us that, had a great literature risen, it would have been unique in modern times.

The South was settled by the same European strains as originally settled the North. Yet, in spite of war, reconstruction, and industrialism, the South to this day finds its most perfect contrast in the North. In religious and social feeling

I should stake everything on the greater resemblance to France. The South clings blindly to forms of European feeling and conduct that were crushed by the French Revolution and that, in England at any rate, are barely memories. How many Englishmen have told us that we still have the eighteenth-century amiability and consideration of manners, supplanted in their country by middle-class reticence and suspicion? And where, outside the South, is there a society that believes even covertly in the Code of Honor? This is not idle talk; we are assured of it by Professor H. C. Brearley, who, I believe, is one of the most detached students of Southern life. Where else in the modern world is the patriarchal family still innocent of the rise and power of other forms of society? Possibly in France; probably in the peasant countries of the Balkans and of Central Europe. Yet the "orientation"—let us concede the word to the University of North Carolina—the rise of new Southern points of view, even now in the towns, is tied still to the image of the family on the land. Where else does so much of the reality of the ancient land society endure, along with the infatuated avowal of beliefs that are hostile to it? Where in the world today is there a more supine enthusiasm for being amiable to forces undermining the life that supports the amiability? The anomalous structure of the South is, I think, finally witnessed by its religion. Doctor Poteat of South Carolina deplores a fact which he does not question, that only in the South does one find a convinced supernaturalism: it is nearer to Aquinas than to Calvin, Wesley, or Knox. Nor do we doubt that the conflict between modernism and fundamentalism is chiefly the impact of the new middle-class civilization upon the rural society; nor, moreover, should we allow ourselves to forget that philosophers of the State, from Sir Thomas More to John C. Calhoun, were political defenders of the older religious community.

The key to unlock the Southern mind is, fortunately, like

Bluebeard's, bloody and perilous; there is not the easy sesamé to the cavern of gaping success. The South has had reverses that permit her people to imagine what they might have been. (And only thus can people discover what they *are*.) Given the one great fact of the expanding plantation system at the dawn of the last century, which voice should the South have listened to? Jefferson, or Marshall, or Calhoun? I mean, which voice had the deepest moral and spiritual implications for the permanence of Southern civilization?

There was not time to listen to any voice very long. The great Southern ideas were strangled in the cradle, either by the South herself (for example, by too much quick cotton money in the Southwest) or by the Union armies. It is plain to modern historians of culture that peoples do not make, much less buy, a culture overnight; it takes time. Which view would have given the South a unified sense of its own destiny? Our modern "standard of living" is not a point of view, and it is necessary that a people should gather its experience round some seasoned point of view before it may boast a high culture. It must be able to illuminate from a fixed position all its experience; it must bring to full realization the high forms as well as the contradictions and miseries inherent in human society.

The miseries and contradictions bemuse and alarm us now. I hope I shall not be called flint-hearted if I dare to believe that the humanitarian spirit can never remove them. So long as society is committed to a class system—and it will probably never be committed to a classless system—the hard-hearted will keep on believing that the high forms are as necessary to the whole of society as bread to the major fraction to whom it is now denied. If man does not live by bread alone, he lives thinly upon bread and sentiment; for sentiment and bread will nourish him but little unless they partake of the peculiarly elevating virtues of form. I might even quote Shelley, whom it is becoming fashionable again to quote:

"Our calculations have outrun conception; we have eaten more than we can digest." I am willing to take the sentence in full literalness, if I may read form for conception, and produced for eaten. For the concrete forms of the social and religious life are the assimilating structure of society.

Where, as in the Old South, there were high forms, but no deep realization of the spirit was achieved, we must ask questions. (The right questions: not why the South refused to believe in Progress, or why it did not experiment with "ideas.") Was the structure of society favorable to a great literature? Suppose it to have been favorable: Was there something wrong with the intellectual life for which the social order cannot be blamed?

The answer is both yes and no to the first question. It is emphatically yes and no to the second. So our answers are confused. At a glance one would expect the rich leisured class, well educated as the Southern aristocracy was—for the South of the fifties had proportionately a larger educated minority than Massachusetts—to devote a great part of its vitality to the arts, the high and conscious arts. As for the arts otherwise, even peasant societies achieve the less conscious variety— manners, ritual, charming domestic architecture.

Assuming, as I do not think I am allowed to assume very confidently, that this society was a good soil for the high arts, there was yet a grave fault in the intellectual life. It was hag-ridden with politics. We like to think that Archimago sent the nightmare down from the North. He did. But it was partly rooted in the kind of rule that the South had, which was aristocratic rule. All aristocracies are obsessed politically. (Witness *Henry IV,* Parts One and Two; *Henry V.*) The best intellectual energy goes into politics and goes of necessity; aristocracy is class rule; and the class must fight for interest and power. Under the special conditions of the nineteenth century, the South had less excess of vitality for the dis-interested arts of literature than it might have had ordinarily.

could not deepen his sense of its life through the long series
of gradations represented by his dependents, who stood between him and the earth. He instructed his factor to buy
good furniture of the Second Empire, and remained a Colonial. But the Negro, who has long been described as a responsibility, got everything from the white man. The history
of French culture, I suppose, has been quite different. The
high arts have been grafted upon the peasant stock. We
could graft no new life upon the Negro; he was too different,
too alien.

Doubtless the confirmed if genteel romanticism of the old
Southern imaginative literature (I make exception for the
political writers of South Carolina—Hammond, Harper,
Calhoun: they are classical and realistic) was in the general
stream of romanticism; yet the special qualities that it produced, the unreal union of formless revery and correct sentiment, the inflated oratory—even in private correspondence
you see it witness a feeble hold upon place and time. The
roots were not deep enough in the soil. Professor Trent was
right; but he was right for the wrong reason. It was not that
slavery was corrupt "morally." Societies can bear an amazing amount of corruption and still produce high cultures.
Black slavery could not nurture the white man in his own
image.

Although the Southern system, in spite of the Negro, was
closer to the soil than the mercantile-manufacturing system
of the middle and New England states, its deficiencies in
spiritual soil were more serious even than those of the debased feudal society of eighteenth-century rural England.
With this society the ante-bellum South had much in common.

The South came from eighteenth-century England, its
agricultural half; there were not enough large towns in the
South to complete the picture of an England reproduced. The
Virginian and the Carolinian, however, imitated the English

squire. They held their land, like their British compeer, in absolute, that is to say unfeudal, ownership, as a result of the destruction, first under Henry VIII and then under Cromwell, of the feudal system of land tenure. The landlord might be humane, but he owed no legal obligation to his land (he could wear it out) or to his labor (he could turn it off: called "enclosure" in England, "selling" under Negro slavery). A pure aristocracy, or the benevolent rule of a landed class in the interest of its own wealth and power, had superseded royalty which, in theory at any rate, and often in practice, had tried to balance class interests under protection of the Crown.

It should be borne in mind, against modern egalitarian and Marxian superstition, that royalty and aristocracy are fundamentally opposed systems of rule; that plutocracy, the offspring of democracy, and that Marxism, the child of plutocracy, are essentially of the aristocratic political mode: they all mean class rule. Virginia took the lead in the American Revolution, not to set up democracy, as Jefferson tried to believe, but to increase the power of the tobacco-exporting aristocracy. The planters wished to throw off the yoke of the British merchant and to get access to the free world market.

But the Southern man of letters cannot permit himself to look upon the old system from a purely social point of view, or from the economic view: to him it must seem better than the system that destroyed it, better, too, than any system with which the modern planners, Marxian or other color, wish to replace the present order. Yet the very merits of the Old South tend to confuse the issue: its comparative stability, its realistic limitation of the acquisitive impulse, its preference for human relations compared to relations economic, tempt the historian to defend the poor literature simply because he feels that the old society was a better place to live in than the new. It is a great temptation—if you do not read the literature.

There is, I believe, a nice object lesson to be drawn from the changed relation of the English writer to society in the eighteenth century; it is a lesson that bears directly upon the attitude of the Old South towards the profession of letters. In the seventeenth century, in the year 1634, a young, finical man, then in seclusion at Horton after taking his degrees at Cambridge, and still unknown, was invited by the Earl of Bridgewater to write a masque for certain revels to be celebrated at Ludlow Castle. The masque was *Comus,* and the revels were in the feudal tradition. The whole celebration was "at home"; it was a part of the community life, the common people were present, and the poet was a spiritual member of the society gathered there. He might not be a gentleman: had Milton become a member of Egerton's "household" he would have been a sort of upper servant. But he would have been a member of the social and spiritual community.

Now examine the affair of Johnson and the Earl of Chesterfield: it is the eighteenth century. It was conducted in the new "aristocratic" style. For the flattery of a dedication the nobleman was loftily willing to give his patronage, a certain amount of money, to an author who had already completed the work, an author who had faced starvation in isolation from society. There is no great publishing system in question here; there were only booksellers. But there was already the cash nexus between the writer and society. The Earl of Chesterfield was a capitalist, not a feudal noble as Egerton to some extent still was: Chesterfield had lost the community; he required of the arts a compliment to the power of his class.

He was the forerunner of the modern plutocrat who thinks that the arts are thriving so long as he can buy Italian paintings, or so long as he creates "foundations" for the arts, or the sales sheets of the publishers show a large volume of "business." But the plutocrat no less than the artist participates in his society through the cash nexus. I hope I do not convince the reader that this wicked fellow has undertaken a deliberate conspiracy against the artist. The artist as man invariably has the same relation to the society of his time as everybody else has: his misfortune and his great value is his superior awareness of that relation. The "message" of modern art at present is that social man is living, without religion, morality, or art (without the high form that concentrates all three in an organic whole) in a mere system of money references through which neither artist nor plutocrat can perform as an entire person.

Is there anything in common between the Earl of Chesterfield and a dour Scots merchant building a fortune and a place in the society of Richmond, Virginia, in the first third of the nineteenth century? I think that they have something in common. It was not John Allan who drove Poe out of Virginia. The foreigner, trying to better himself, always knows the practical instincts of a society more shrewdly than the society knows them. Allan was, for once, the spokesman of Virginia, of the plantation South. There was no place for Poe in the spiritual community of Virginia; there was no class of professional writers that Poe could join in dedicating their works to the aristocracy under the system of the cash nexus. The promising young men were all in politics bent upon more desperate emergencies. It was obvious, even to John Allan, I suppose, that here was no dabbler who would write pleasant, genteel poems and stories for magazines where other dabbling gentlemen printed their pleasant, genteel stories and poems. Anybody could have looked at Poe and known that he meant business.

And until the desperate men today who mean business can become an independent class, there will be no profession of letters anywhere in America. It remains only to add to the brief history adumbrated in this essay some comment on the present situation of the desperate men of the South in particular. There are too many ladies and gentlemen, too many Congreves whose coxcombry a visit from Voltaire would do a great deal of good. I trust that I do not argue the case too well. Congreve frivolously gave up the honor of his profession when Voltaire asked to see the great dramatist and got the answer that Mr. Congreve was no scribbler but a man of fashion. They were more explicit about those things in those days. I should barely hope that the Southern writer, or the Northern or Western, for that matter, may decide that his gentility, being a quality over which he has no control, may get along as it can. For the genteel tradition has never done anything for letters in the South; yet the Southern writers who are too fastidious to become conscious of their profession have not refused to write best sellers when they could, and to profit by a cash nexus with New York. I would fain believe that matters are otherwise than so: but facts are facts. If there is such a person as a Southern writer, if there could be such a profession as letters in the South, the profession would require the speaking of unpleasant words and the violation of good literary manners.

I wish this were the whole story: only cranks and talents of the quiet, first order maintain themselves against fashion and prosperity. But even these desperate persons must live, and they cannot live in the South without an "independent income." We must respect the source of our income, that is, we ought to; and if we cannot respect it we are likely to fear it. This kind of writer is not luckier than his penniless fellow. (The only man I know who devotes a large income to changing the system that produced it is a New Yorker.) Because there is no city in the South where writers may gather, write, and live, and no Southern publisher to print their books, the Southern writer, of my generation at least, went to New York. There he was influenced not only by the necessity to live but by theories and movements drifting over from Europe.

It was, possibly, a dangerous situation. Mr. John Crowe Ransom has pointed out its implications:

If modernism is regarded as nothing but a new technique, what was wrong with the old technique? Principally, perhaps, the fact that it was old; for modernism is apt to assume that tradition is not so much a prop which may be leant upon as a dead burden which must be borne. The substance of modernism is not a technique but an attitude. And a dangerous attitude . . .

The Southern artists in going modern offer us their impression of a general decay, and that is not a pleasant thing to think about.[2]

The Southern writer was perilously near to losing his identity, becoming merely a "modern" writer. He lost the Southern feeling which, in the case of Mr. Young, informs the Southern style: he might retain a Southern subject and write about it as an outsider, with some novelty of technique and in smart, superior detachment. These bad features of the last decade may be deplored, I hope, without asking the Southerner to stay at home and starve. That, it seems to me, is what Mr. Ransom asks the Southern writer to do. It was not an uprooted modern, but the classical Milton who remarked, "Wherever we do well is home": wherever we are allowed best to realize our natures—a realization that, for an artist, presupposes permission to follow his craft—is the proper place to live. The Southern writer should if possible be a Southerner in the South. The sole condition that would make that possible is a profession of letters.

But the arts everywhere spring from a mysterious union of indigenous materials and foreign influences: there is no great art or literature that does not bear the marks of this fusion. So I cannot assume, as Mr. Ransom seems to do, that exposure to the world of modernism (Petrarchism was modernism in the England of 1540) was of itself a demoraliz-

[2] "Modern With the Southern Accent," *The Virginia Quarterly Review,* April, 1935.

ing experience. Isn't it rather that the Southerner before he left home had grown weak in his native allegiance? That his political and social history, and his domestic life, had been severely adulterated no less by his fellow Southerners than by the people in the North to whom he fled? Apart from this menace abroad, who cannot bring himself to wish that Miss Glasgow had studied James and Flaubert in her apprenticeship, and spared herself and us her first three or four novels? Could Mr. Young have written his fiction, to say nothing of his plays and criticism, had he read only Cable and Page? And, lastly, what shall we say of Mr. Ransom's own distinguished and very modern poetry?

Is not Mr. Ransom really deploring the absence, as I deplore it, of a professional spirit and professional opportunities in Southern literature? There is no reason why the Southern writer should not address a large public, but if he does he will learn sooner or later that—but for happy accidents—the market, with what the market implies, dictates the style. To create a profession of literature in the South we should require first an independent machinery of publication. I fall into the mechanical terms. A Southern publishing system would not, I imagine, publish Southern books alone; nor should Southern magazines print only Southern authors. The point of the argument leads to no such comforting simplicity. The literary artist is seldom successful as a colonial; he should be able to enjoy the normal belief that he is at the center of the world. One aid to that feeling would be a congenial medium of communication with his public. Let the world in this fashion sit at his feet; let him not have to seek the world.

The exact degree of immediate satisfaction that Southern publication would bring to its authors I cannot predict. It, too, would be the system of the cash nexus; and the Southern publisher would be a capitalist plutocrat not noticeably different from his colleague in the North. Like his Northern friend he would, for a few years at least, sell the Southern article mostly north of the border. Until he could be backed by a powerful Southern press he would need the support of the New York journals for his authors, if he expected them to be read at home. I suppose the benefits of a Southern system would lie chiefly in this: that the Southern writer would not have to run the New York gauntlet, from which he emerges with a good understanding of what he can and cannot do.

We have exchanged the reasoned indifference of aristocracy for the piratical commercialism of plutocracy. Repudiating the later master, the new profession in the South would have to tell New York, where it had hitherto hawked its wares, that no more wares of the prescribed kind would be produced. For the prescribed ware is the ware that the Southerner also must produce, and it is not heartening to observe that his own Southern public waits for the New York journals to prescribe the kind, before he can get a hearing at home. Can there be a profession of letters in the South? Our best critical writing—and we have critical writing of distinction— can never constitute a Southern criticism so long as it must be trimmed and scattered in Northern magazines, or published in books that will be read as curiously as travel literature, by Northern people alone.

The considerable achievement of Southerners in modern American letters must not beguile us into too much hope for the future. The Southern novelist has left his mark upon the age; but it is of the age. From the peculiarly historical consciousness of the Southern writer has come good work of a special order; but the focus of this consciousness is quite temporary. It has made possible the curious burst of intelligence that we get at a crossing of the ways, not unlike, on an infinitesimal scale, the outburst of poetic genius at the end of the sixteenth century when commercial England had already begun to crush feudal England. The Histories and Tragedies of Shakespeare record the death of the old régime, and Doctor Faustus gives up feudal order for world power.

The prevailing economic passion of the age once more tempts, even commands, the Southern writer to go into politics. Our neo-communism is the new form in which the writer from all sections is to be dominated by capitalism, or "economic society." It is the new political mania. And there is no escape from it. The political mind always finds itself in an emergency. And the emergency, this time real enough, becomes a pretext for ignoring the arts. We live in the sort of age that Abraham Cowley complained of—a good age to write about but a hard age to write in.

1935

The New Provincialism

With an Epilogue on the Southern Novel

I

A NOTE written around a subject needs a formidable title to remind the writer where he is going and to make the elusive subject a little clearer to the reader. I confess to feelings of peculiar inadequacy on this occasion;[1] it reminds me of a similar occasion ten years ago, when I was writing an essay for the tenth anniversary number of *The Virginia Quarterly Review*. That essay[2] (as I recall it: I have not been able to bring myself to reread it as I begin to write)—that essay was possibly a little stuffy and more certain of itself than these notes can be. It was written at the height of the Southern literary renascence. That renascence is over; or at any rate that period is over; and I write, we all write, in the time of the greatest war. Will the new literature of the South, or of the United States as a whole, be different from anything that we knew before the war? Will American literature be more alike all over the country? And more like the literature of the world?

An affirmative answer to the last question would make our literary nationalists—Mr. Van Wyck Brooks, Mr. Kazin, and Mr. De Voto—look a little old-fashioned, very much as they have actually been all along as the intellectual contempo-

[1] This essay was written for the twentieth anniversary of *The Virginia Quarterly Review*, Spring, 1945.
[2] See "The Profession of Letters in the South," *supra*, pp. 517–534.

raries of Buckle and Taine. Their influence is no longer very much felt by anybody who seriously writes; and it is sufficient here merely to state the paradox that not even literary nationalism could abort a genuine national literature when it is ready to appear; when, in fact, we become a nation. But it is more likely that we may become an internation first. These reflections are set down to prepare for something that I have long wanted the occasion to say: that mere regionalism, as we have heard it talked about in recent years, is not enough. For this picturesque regionalism of local color is a by-product of nationalism. And it is not informed enough to support a mature literature. But neither is nationalism.

Yet no literature can be mature without the regional consciousness; it can only be senile, with the renewed immaturity of senility. For without regionalism, without locality in the sense of local continuity in tradition and belief, we shall get a whole literature which Mr. John Dos Passos might have written: perhaps a whole literature which, in spite of my admiration for Mr. Dos Passos's novels, I shall not even be able to read. This new literature will probably be personal, sentimentally objective, tough, and "unsocial," and will doubtless achieve its best effects in a new version of the old travel story (like most of Mr. Dos Passos's books, which are travel stories) both abroad and at home: the account of voyages to the South and West, and to the ends of the world. New Crusoes, new Captain Singletons, new Gullivers will appear, but Gullivers who see *with,* not *through* the eye. It will not be a "national" literature, or even an "international"; it may be a provincial literature with world horizons, the horizons of the geographical world, which need not be spiritually larger than Bourbon County, Kentucky: provincialism without regionalism.

I I

If regionalism is not enough, is a world provincialism enough? It has been generally supposed in our time that the limitations of the mere regional interest, which are serious, could be corrected by giving them up for a "universal" point of view, a political or social doctrine which would "relate" or "integrate" the local community with the world in the advance of a higher culture. What this higher culture is or might be nobody was ever quite clear about. It looked political, or at any rate "social," and it ranged in imaginative emphasis all the way from the Stalinist party line, upon whose front, in this country, was written the slogan, Defense of Culture (*whose culture?*), to Mr. Wallace's Common Man, whom Mr. Wallace seemed willing to let remain common.

What it never occurred to anybody to ask was this simple question: What happens if you make the entire world into one vast region? This, it seems to me, is the trouble with our world schemes today: they contemplate a large extension of the political and philosophical limitations of the regional principle. "Let's get closer to the Chinese." "Know your fellow men, and you will like them better, and cease to fight them." Are these propositions true? I doubt it. Europeans are fighting one another today not because they didn't "know" one another. It does not, of course, follow that they are fighting because they did know one another; but that proposition makes as good sense as its contrary. For the real end is not physical communication, or parochial neighborliness on a world scale. The real end, as I see it, is *what* you are communicating after you get the physical means of communication. It is possible for men to face one another and not have anything to say. In that case it may occur to them, since they cannot establish a common understanding, to try to take something away from one another; and they may temporarily establish, as they did a generation ago, certain rules of mutual plunder that look for a time like "international cooperation."

All this has a bearing on literature today, the literature of the United States, and of the South, in the recent past and in the near future. For the logical opposite, or the historic complement, of the isolated community or region is not the

world community or world region. In our time we have been
the victims of a geographical metaphor, or a figure of space:
we have tried to compensate for the limitations of the little
community by envisaging the big community, which is not
necessarily bigger spiritually or culturally than the little
community. The complement of the regional principle, the
only force which in the past has kept the region (of whatever
size) from being provincial, from being committed to the
immediate interest, is a nonpolitical or supra-political culture such as held Europe together for six hundred years and
kept war to the "limited objective." That is to say, there was
sufficient unity, somewhere at the top, to check the drive of
mere interest, and to limit war to a few massacres prompted
by religious zeal or by the desire of rulers to keep their
neighbors from getting out of hand. The small professional
army at the top never tried to use and thus to menace the
vast, stable energy of the masses, until the age of Louis XIV;
and it was not until Napoleon that it was thought possible to
make a whole nation fight.

The kind of unity prevailing in the West until the nineteenth century has been well described by Christopher Daw-
son as a peculiar balance of Greek culture and Christian
other-worldliness, both imposed by Rome upon the northern
barbarians. It was this special combination that made European civilization, and it was this that men communicated in
the act of living together. It was this force which reduced the
regional heterogeneity to a manageable unity, or even sublimated it into universal forms. Is not this civilization just
about gone? Only men who are committed to perverse illusion or to public oratory believe that we have a Christian
civilization today: we still have Christians in every real
sense, but in neither politics nor education, by and large, do
Christian motives or standards, or even references, have an
effective part. We do not ask: Is this right? We ask: Will
this work? It is the typical question for men who represent

the decadent humanism of the Greek half of our tradition. For that humanism has ended up as the half of a half: it stands for only half of the Greek spirit, the empirical or scientific half which gives us our technology. Technology without Christianity is, I think, barbarism quite simply; but barbarism refined, violent, and decadent, not the vigorous barbarism of the forest and the soil. I do not believe that we could say of our culture what Burke said of the English in 1790, that we have not "subtilized ourselves into savagery."

This is the catastrophic view. I did not originate it. And I suppose it cannot be wholly true. A few men will still somehow evade total efficiency, and live much as they did in the past; many will be bored by machines or, like the retired banker in my community, refuse to use their products by making by hand the articles of daily utility. The individual human being will probably have in the future as in the past a natural economy to which he can occasionally return, if he is not meddled with too much by power at a distance.

This natural economy cannot be an effective check upon the standardizing forces of the outside world without the protection of the regional consciousness. For regionalism is that consciousness or that habit of men in a given locality which influences them to certain patterns of thought and conduct handed to them by their ancestors. Regionalism is thus limited in space but not in time.

The provincial attitude is limited in time but not in space. When the regional man, in his ignorance, often an intensive and creative ignorance, of the world, extends his own immediate necessities into the world, and assumes that the present moment is unique, he becomes the provincial man. He cuts himself off from the past, and without benefit of the fund of traditional wisdom approaches the simplest problems of life as if nobody had ever heard of them before. A society without arts, said Plato, lives by chance. The provincial man, locked in the present, lives by chance.

I I I

It must be plain from this train of ideas whither I am leading this discussion. For the world today is perhaps more provincial in outlook than it has been at any time since the ninth century, and even that era had, in its primitive agrarian economy, a strong regional basis for individual independence. Industrial capitalism has given us provincialism without regionalism: we are committed to chance solutions of "problems" that seem unique because we have forgotten the nature of man. And having destroyed our regional societies in the West, we are fanatically trying to draw other peoples into our provincial orbit, for the purpose of "saving" them.

Our Utopian politics is provincial. It is all very well to meet at Dumbarton Oaks or on the Black Sea to arrange the world, but unless the protagonists of these dramas of journalism have secret powers the presence of which we have hitherto had no reason to suspect, the results for the world must almost necessarily be power politics, or mere *rules of plunder which look like cooperation.* The desired cooperation is for the physical welfare of man. But it is a curious fact (I have not been able to find any history which denies the fact) that the physical welfare of man, pursued as an end in itself, has seldom prospered. The nineteenth-century dream of a secular Utopia produced Marxian socialism, National Socialism, and the two greatest wars of history; and it is perhaps only another sign of our provincialism that we ignore the causation between the dream and the wars, and urge more of the same dream to prevent other wars which the dream will doubtless have its part in causing. Nobody wants to see the Oriental peoples dominated by the Japanese and to go hungry and ill clad; yet so far in the history of civilization it has been virtually impossible to feed and clothe people with food and clothing. It is my own impression that they get fed and clothed incidentally to some other impulse, a creative power which we sometimes identify with religion and the arts.

It is small game; yet are not the Four Freedoms a typical expression of our world provincialism? Here is a radio fantasy on the secular dream of the nineteenth century. We guarantee to the world freedom of thought—to think about what? (I had supposed we were opposed to freedom of thought for the Germans and the Japanese.) Is it freedom to think *our* thoughts? We guarantee to the world freedom of worship—to worship what? Unless you cut the worship off from everything else that the Javanese, the Hottentots, the Russians, and the Americans may be doing (in our own case we have almost succeeded in this), what is to keep the Javanese, the Hottentots, the Russians, and ourselves from worshiping a war-god and putting this religion to the test of action? We guarantee to the world freedom from want. We had better— or somebody had better guarantee it, even if the guarantee is no good; for nineteenth-century industrial capitalism and our own more advanced technology have made it very difficult for "backward peoples" (to say nothing of ourselves in small units and groups) to make their living independently of somebody else nine thousand miles away. In other words we have destroyed the regional economies, and we offer a provincial remedy for the resulting evils; that is to say, a Utopian remedy which ignores our past experience. We guarantee to the world freedom from fear. On this freedom I confess that I have nothing to say. Provincial arrogance could not go further; and if my own religion had not been destroyed by the same forces that destroyed Mr. Roosevelt's and Mr. Churchill's (I do not deny them or myself feelings of common piety), I should expect the wrath of God to strike them. I infer from the hedging cynicism of their repudiation of the Four Freedoms as an "official document" the casual frivolity with which they must have written it in the first place. There was a radio on the ship. The ease of modern communication compelled these gentlemen to communicate with the world, when there was nothing to communicate.

I V

I am a little embarrassed at having used so many large conceptions, with so little specification. I ought to make plainer, before I go further, certain connections between regionalism and provincialism that I have only implied. The regional society is, with respect to high civilization, the neutral society: it can be primitive or highly cultivated, or any of the steps between. In the West our peculiar civilization was based upon regional autonomy, whose eccentricities were corrected and sublimated by the classical-Christian culture which provided a form for the highest development of man's potentialities *as man*. Man belonged to his village, valley, mountain, or seacoast; but wherever he was he was a Christian whose Hebraic discipline had tempered his tribal savagery and whose classical humanism had moderated the literal imperative of his Christianity to suicidal other-worldliness.

If this peculiar culture of the West is weakening or is even gone as a creative force, we are left with our diverse regionalisms; or *were* left with them. For the myth of science which undermined this culture and created the modern economic man rooted out the regional economies, and is now creating a world regional economy. Regional economy means interdependence of the citizens of a region, whether the region be an Alpine village or the world. And the world, like the Alpine village, can be neutral with respect to high civilization. Regionalism without civilization—which means, with us, regionalism without the classical Christian culture —becomes provincialism; and world regionalism becomes world provincialism. For provincialism is that state of mind in which regional men lose their origins in the past and its continuity into the present, and begin every day as if there had been no yesterday.

We are committed to this state of mind. We are so deeply

involved in it (I make no exception of myself) that we must participate in its better purposes, however incomplete they may be; for good will, even towards the Four Freedoms, is better than ill will; and I am convinced that even the die-hard traditionalist would deny his own shrinking tradition if he refused to act for the remnant of it left because he can't have it all. For this remnant may be useful; there will be a minority with a memory which has not been dimmed by what Christian Gauss has called the Reversal of the Time Sense. We shall not all derive our standards of human nature and of the good society from an unexperienced future imagined by the late H. G. Wells or Mr. Henry Wallace.

V

The brilliant and unexpected renascence of Southern writing between the two wars is perhaps not of the first importance in the literature of the modern world; yet for the first time the South had a literature of considerable maturity which was distinctive enough to call for a special criticism which it failed to get. The provincial ideas of the critics of the North and East (there was no Southern criticism: merely a few Southern critics)—the provincial views of Southern writing of the recent renascence followed a direction somewhat as follows: The South, backward and illiberal, and controlled by white men who cherish a unique moral perversity, does not offer in itself a worthy subject to the novelist or the poet; it follows that the only acceptable literature that the South can produce must be a literature of social agitation, through which the need of reform may be publicized.

There were dozens of Southern novels written to this prescription. (I can think of only one Southern novelist of the period who ignored it and who was continuously popular: the late Elizabeth Madox Roberts.) The formula generally imposed two limitations upon the Southern writer: first, he must ignore the historical background of his subject; and second, he must judge the subject strictly in terms of the material welfare of his characters and of the "injustice" which keeps them from getting enough of it. My testimony is perhaps not wholly disinterested, yet I am convinced that not one distinguished novel was produced in or about the South from this point of view. The novel that came nearest to real distinction was probably Miss Glasgow's *Barren Ground;* but even this excellent novel is written outside the subject, with the result that the frustration of her Virginia farmers is not examined as an instance of the decay of rural culture everywhere, but rather as a simple object-lesson in the lack of standard American "advantages." (Miss Glasgow's other and later books pose other problems, chiefly the problem of the consciously "liberal" writer who draws his knowledge of human nature from a source richer than that of his ideas, and who thus writes somewhat below the level of his historical tradition.) But this is not a roster of all the sociological novels about the South from 1918 to the present. If these notes were a parlor game, I should challenge the "critics" who hailed them in the twenties and thirties to exhibit just one novel of this school which they would be willing to let compete with the best European writing of the period.

There has been some confusion in the South as well as elsewhere about the subjects accessible to Southern writers; this confusion results from the appeal to history: what *is* the structure of Southern society? What *was* it in the eighteen-forties and -fifties? It is not necessary, fortunately, to answer those questions here. To bring these notes to a close I should like to make a few elementary distinctions. If the Southern subject is the destruction by war and the later degradation of the South by carpetbaggers and scalawags, and a consequent lack of moral force and imagination in the cynical materialism of the New South, then the sociologists of fiction and the so-called traditionalists are trying to talk about the same thing. But with this difference—and it is a difference between two worlds: the provincial world of the present, which sees in material welfare and legal justice the whole solution to the human problem; and the classical-Christian world, based upon the regional consciousness, which held that honor, truth, imagination, human dignity, and limited acquisitiveness, could alone justify a social order however rich and efficient it may be; and could do much to redeem an order dilapidated and corrupt, like the South today, if a few people passionately hold those beliefs.

So, in the period of the Southern renascence, our writers, poets as well as novelists, may be put into the two broad groups which I have indicated. Among the traditionalists whose work I believe will last I should name Stark Young, Elizabeth Madox Roberts, Katherine Anne Porter, Robert Penn Warren, Caroline Gordon, Ellen Glasgow (especially in *The Sheltered Life*), and William Faulkner, who is the most powerful and original novelist in the United States and one of the best in the modern world. It ought to be plain that by traditionalist I do not mean a writer who either accepts or rejects the conventional picture of Southern life in the past. By the traditional as opposed to the provincial writer, I mean the writer who takes the South as he knows it today or can find out about it in the past, and who sees it as a region with some special characteristics, but otherwise offering as an imaginative subject the plight of human beings as it has been and will doubtless continue to be, here and in other parts of the world.

But if the provincial outlook, as I have glanced at it here, is to prevail, there is no reason to think that the South will remain immune to it. With the war of 1914–1918, the South reentered the world—but gave a backward glance as it stepped over the border: that backward glance gave us the Southern renascence, a literature conscious of the past in the present. In the essay to which I referred in the first paragraph of these notes (I have now reread it) I said: "From the peculiarly historical consciousness of the Southern writer has come good work of a special order; but the focus of this consciousness is quite temporary. It has made possible the curious burst of intelligence that we get at a crossing of the ways, not unlike, on an infinitesimal scale, the outburst of poetic genius at the end of the sixteenth century when commercial England had already begun to crush feudal England." I see no reason to change that view.

From now on we are committed to seeing *with*, not *through* the eye: we, as provincials who do not live anywhere.

1945

What Is a Traditional Society?[1]

NOT LONG AGO, I hope with no sinister purpose, I used the word *tradition* before a group of Southern men who had met to discuss the problems of the South. A gentleman from North Carolina rose; he said that tradition was meaningless, and he moved that we drop the word. I have a certain sympathy with that view. Many features of our lives that we call traditions are meaningless; we confuse with tradition external qualities which are now, in the rich American middle class, mere stage properties of a way of life that can no longer be lived. For the stage set differs from the natural scene, I take it, in offering us a conventional surface without depth, and the additional facility of allowing us to stand before it on Saturday and Sunday and to resume, on Monday, the real business of life. Tradition as we see it today has little to do with the real business of life; at best it can make that grim reality two-sevenths less grim—if indeed the pretense of our week-end traditionalists is not actually grimmer than the reality they apologetically prefer but from which they desire, part of the time, to escape.

I do not understand this romanticism, and I bring it to your attention because, here within the walls of Mr. Jefferson's University, there is a special tradition of realism in thinking about the nature of tradition. The presiding spirit of that tradition was clear in his belief that the way of life and the livelihood of men must be the same; that the way

[1] The Phi Beta Kappa Address at the University of Virginia, June, 1936.

we make our living must strongly affect the way of life; that our way of getting a living is not good enough if we are driven by it to pretend that it is something else; that we cannot pretend to be landed gentlemen two days of the week if we are middle-class capitalists the five others. You will remember Ruskin's objection to the Gothic factory-architecture of his age—the ornamentation he suggested for the cornices of a kind of building that was new in that time. Ruskin's stylized money bags set at the right rhythmic intervals around the cornices of the Bethlehem Steel Corporation might be symbolic of something going on inside, but I think the Chairman of the Board would rightly object that Ruskin was not a good satirist, but merely a sentimentalist; and the Chairman would leave his cornices bare. Yet, while the Chairman of the Board might be committed on the one hand to an economic realism, he might on the other indulge himself in softer materials in another direction; he might buy or build a Georgian mansion somewhere near Middleburg, Virginia, and add to it—if they were not already there—the correct row of columns that Mr. Jefferson adapted to Virginia after a visit to the Maison Carré at Nîmes.

Mr. Jefferson could not know Ruskin, but he knew about medieval Europe, and he disliked it. He never visited Mr. Walpole at Strawberry Hill, but I wish he had. He would have rejoiced that Walpole's weekend Gothic—if you will allow the anachronism for the sake of the moral—meant the final destruction, in England, of the Middle Ages. He would have known that to revive something is to hasten its destruction—if it is only picturesquely and not sufficiently revived. For the moment the past becomes picturesque it is dead. I do not agree with Mr. Jefferson about the Middle Ages, but I surmise that he would have considered a revival of the past very much in this light. He himself was trying to revive the small freeholder who had been dispossessed by the rising capitalist of the eighteenth century.

Now one of the curious features of our mentality since the Renaissance is the historical imagination. No other civilization, I believe, has had this gift. I use the term not in a strict sense, but in a very general sense, and perhaps in a somewhat pejorative sense. I mean that with the revival of Greek studies men in Europe began to pose as Greeks. After a couple of centuries, when the pose, too heroic to last, grew tired, they posed as Romans of the Republic. There we have a nice historical dramatization of the common sense of the eighteenth century. We on this side of the Atlantic were not unaffected by it. There is evidence that our Revolutionary fathers were the noblest Romans of them all. There is certainly not a Virginian, nor a Southerner of Virginian ancestry, whose great-great-grandfather did not write letters to his son in the style of Addison, a vehicle nicely fitted to convey the matter of Cicero. *Libidinosa enim et intemperans adulescentia effetum corpus tradit senectuti*—it is not from the orations, but the rhythm and sentiment here were the model of the *ore orotundo* style that dominated society in the South and other parts of America for three generations. Those generations, if our records of their more elegant representatives do not lie, were not much impressed with the ravages of youthful license upon the body, which, as Cicero has just told us, passes wearily into old age. The young blade of Albemarle of 1770, sitting over a punch bowl in the tavern after a day of Cicero with the learned Parson Douglas, was not, at that moment, an exemplar of Cicero's morals, but I suspect that his conversation, even after the bottom of the bowl began to be visible, retained a few qualities of the Ciceronian style.

The style is the point of a digression that I hope you will not think frivolous. I hold no brief for Cicero—he is a dull mind in any language—but I do hold that the men of the early American Republic had a profound instinct for high style, a genius for dramatizing themselves at their own par-

ticular moment of history. They were so situated economically and politically that they were able to form a definite
conception of their human role: they were not ants in an
economic ant hill, nor were they investigating statistically
the behavior of other ants. They knew what they wanted
because they knew what they, themselves, were. They lived
in a social and economic system that permitted them to
develop a human character that functioned in every level of
life, from the economic process to the county horse race.

The Virginian of the 1790's might have found a better
part in the play than that of the Roman in *toga virilis*—as
Mr. Custis, the first Southern dilettante, liked to paint him—
but it was the easiest role to lay hold upon at that time, and
it was distinctly better than no imaginative version of himself at all. A few years ago Mr. T. S. Eliot told an audience
at this University that there are two kinds of mythology, a
higher and a lower. The Roman *toga* of our early Republic
was doubtless of a sort of lower mythology, inferior to the
higher mythology of the Christian thirteenth century, and
I suppose Mr. Eliot would prefer the higher vision, as I myself should were I allowed a preference. But we must remember that the rationalism of the eighteenth century had made
myths of all ranks exceedingly scarce, as the romantic poets
were beginning to testify; yet the Virginian did remarkably
well with the minor myth that his age permitted him to
cultivate. Mr. Custis' paintings may seem to us to be afflicted
with a sort of aesthetic giantism, and his blank-verse dramas,
in which every hero is an alabaster Washington named Mar-
cus Tullius Scipio Americanus, are unreadable today. They
must have been a kind of inexquisite torture even when they
were written. But Mr. Custis built Arlington, and Arlington is something to have built. He could not have built it, of
course, if Mr. Jefferson had not first built a house upon
a place that I believe is locally called the Little Mountain;
but then Mr. Jefferson could not have built Monticello had

he not been dominated by the lower myth of the *toga virilis*.
Perhaps this lower myth, from whatever source it may
come—Rome, Greece, the age of Cellini, the naturalism of
the South Seas, or even the Old South—this little myth is
a figment of the historical imagination, that curious faculty
of Western men that I have already mentioned. The men of
our early Republic were powerfully endowed in this faculty.
It is not the same as a religion, if by religion we mean Christianity in the Middle Ages; nor is it the same as the religious
imagination under any conceivable culture, for the religious imagination is timeless and unhistoric. The minor myth
is based upon ascertainable history.

There is a chart that we might look at for a moment, but
only for a moment; I offer it not as history, but as a device
to ease the strain of the idea of traditional society that I am
trying to give in so short a space. First, there is the religious
imagination, which can mythologize indiscriminately history, legend, trees, the sea, animals, all being humanly dramatized, somehow converted to the nature of man. Secondly,
there is the historical imagination, which is the religious
imagination *manqué*—an exercise of the myth-making pro-
pensity of man within the restricted realm of historical event.
Men see themselves in the stern light of the character of
Cato, but they can no longer see themselves under the control
of a tutelary deity. Cato actually lived; Apollo was merely
far-darting.

The third stage is the complete triumph of positivism. And
with the complete triumph of positivism, in our own time,
we get, in place of so workable a makeshift as the historical
imagination, merely a truncation of that phrase in which
the adjective has declared its independence. It has set up
for a noun. Under positivism we get just plain, everyday
history. If this is an obscure conception, I must hasten to
say that although history cannot write itself, although it must
be written by men whose minds are as little immune to

prejudice as to the law of contradiction, it is true that any sort of creative imagination is, on principle, eliminated. Yet in recognition of history's impotence to bring itself into being, the historians give us a new word: method. We live in the age of the historical method. Method brings history into being.

I shall not labor the point here, but I do think it is fair to say that *history,* although it has become attached to *method,* is still a noun of agency, as the grammarians call it, trying to do its own work. I think this is true simply because on principle scientific *method* is itself not attached to anything. It is just abstract method—from which plain, abstract, inhuman history differs not by a hair. Of course, I am talking about the historian's ideal of physical law—his belief that history must conform to the ideal of a normative science, whether or not it can mean anything written that way. The historical method then may be briefly described—by one who does not believe in its use—as the way of discovering historical "truths" that are true in some other world than that inhabited by the historian and his fellow men: truths, in a word, that are true for the historical method.

Most of you have read *The Waste Land,* but I shall ask you to hear a passage from it again for the sake of those who have not read it:

> The Chair she sat in, like a burnished throne
> Glowed on the marble, where the glass
> Held up by standards wrought with fruited vines
> From which a golden Cupidon peeped out
> (Another hid his eyes behind his wing)
> Doubled the flames of seven-branched candelabra
> Reflecting light upon the table as
> The glitter of her jewels rose to meet it
> From satin cases poured in rich profusion;
> In vials of ivory and colored glass
> Unstoppered, lurked her strange synthetic perfumes.

In this handsome *décor* the lady, I imagine, is about to dress for dinner. On the walls and ceilings are scenes from an heroic past:

> Huge sea-wood fed with copper
> Burned green and orange, framed by the colored stone,
> In which sad light a carvèd dolphin swam.
> Above the antique mantel was displayed
> As though a window gave upon the sylvan scene
> The change of Philomel, by the barbarous king
> So rudely forced; yet there the nightingale
> Filled all the desert with inviolable voice. . . .

People living in such favorable influences, partaking of the best of our history and of the arts of the great tradition, command our most interested attention: they will at least exhibit the benefits of a good lower mythology. We may expect them to show us, if not the innocence of the religious imagination, a high style that expresses, or is the expression of, the walls that we have just looked at. But no; the poet warns us as follows:

> And other withered stumps of time
> Were told upon the walls; staring forms
> Leaned out, leaning, hushing the room enclosed.
> Footsteps shuffled on the stair.

I hope you will forgive me if I venture to think that the shuffling feet are about to bring into the room the historical method. For, after some desperately aimless conversation, in which both the woman and the man seem to feel little but a bored exhaustion and vacuity of purpose, the woman suddenly says:

> "What shall I do now? What shall I do?
> "I shall rush out as I am, and walk the street
> "With my hair down, so. What shall we do tomorrow?
> "What shall we ever do?"

Her companion replies—and I ask you to place what he says against the heroic background of Renaissance art on the ceiling and walls: what he says does reduce it, I think, to withered stumps of time:

> The hot water at ten.
> And if it rains, a closed car at four.
> And we shall play a game of chess,
> Pressing lidless eyes, and waiting for a knock upon
>   the door.

Now fortunately upon this occasion I am neither poet nor literary critic. Here I am a moralist, and if I find more to my use in Mr. Eliot's poem than he would willingly allow, you will remember that moralists these days are desperate persons, and must in their weaker moments squeeze a moral even out of modern poetry. If the chess game seems trivial as a symbol of aimless intellectuality, its intention is nevertheless just. The rich experience from the great tradition depicted in the room receives a violent shock in contrast with a game that symbolizes the inhuman abstraction of the modern mind. In proposing the game of chess the man is proposing an exercise in a kind of truth that has no meaning for either of them. The woman in this remarkable scene has just said that she can think of nothing to do—the moralist would gloss that as lack of purpose—and she intends to rush out into the street with her hair down.

What does this mean? It means that in ages which suffer the decay of manners, religion, morals, codes, our indestructible vitality demands expression in violence and chaos; it means that men who have lost both the higher myth of religion and the lower myth of historical dramatization have lost the forms of human action; it means that they are no longer capable of defining a human objective, of forming a dramatic conception of human nature; it means that they capitulate from their human role to a series of pragmatic conquests which, taken alone, are true only in some other world than that inhabited by men.

The woman in Mr. Eliot's poem is, I believe, the symbol of man at the present time. He is surrounded by the grandeurs of the past, but he does not participate in them; they do not sustain him. To complete the allegory, the man represents a kind of truth that I have described in very general terms as the historical method: he offers us the exercise of intellect to no purpose, a game that we cannot relate to our conduct, an instrument of power over both past and present which we can neither control nor properly use.

Man in this plight lives in an untraditional society. For an untraditional society does not permit its members to pass to the next generation what it received from its immediate past. Why is this so? I have tried to describe in moral terms some of the defects of life in an untraditional society—and I expect merely to ask, and not to answer, whether there is not some kind of analysis that we may subject our situation to, that will show us one way of understanding the fundamental difference between tradition and non-tradition?

I shall return to a question that I asked in the beginning. Why do many modern people live one kind of life five days a week and another the two other days? Why is it that a middle-class capitalist from Pittsburgh or Birmingham desires an ante-bellum Georgian house near Lexington, Kentucky, or Middleburg, Virginia? And why was it that the men who built those houses desired only those houses, and made serious objections in the eighteen-sixties to being forcibly removed from them? There are many answers to these questions, but I have space for only one. The middle-class capitalist does not believe in the dignity of the material basis of his life; his human nature demands a homogeneous pattern of behavior that his economic life will not give him. He doubtless sees in the remains of the Old South a symbol of the homogeneous life. But the ante-bellum man saw no difference between the Georgian house and the economic basis that supported it. It was all of one piece.

I am exaggerating, but permit me the exaggeration so that I may make this matter as clear as I can. Man has never achieved a perfect unity of his moral nature and his economics; yet he has never failed quite so dismally in that greatest of all human tasks as he is failing now. Ante-bellum man, insofar as he achieved a unity between his moral nature and his livelihood, was a traditional man. He dominated the means of life; he was not dominated by it. I think that the distinguishing feature of a traditional society is simply that. In order to make a livelihood men do not have to put aside their moral natures. Traditional men are never quite making their living, and they never quite cease to make it. Or put otherwise: they are making their living all the time, and affirming their humanity all the time. The whole economic basis of life is closely bound up with moral behavior, and it is possible to behave morally all the time. It is this principle that is the center of the philosophy of Jefferson.

Yet what is there traditional about this? The answer is that if such a society could come into being now, and had no past whatever, it would be traditional because it could hand something on. That something would be a moral conception of man in relation to the material of life. The material basis of life, in such a society, is not hostile to the perpetuation of a moral code, as our finance-capitalist economics unquestionably is. It is an old story by this time that our modern economic system can be operated efficiently regardless of the moral stature of the men who operate it.

The kind of property that sustains the traditional society is not only *not* hostile to a unified moral code; it is positively the basis of it. Moreover it is the medium, just as canvas is the medium of the painter, through which that code is passed to the next generation. For traditional property in land was the primary medium through which man expressed his moral nature; and our task is to restore it or to get its equivalent today. Finance-capitalism, a system that has removed men from the responsible control of the means of a livelihood, is necessarily hostile to the development of a moral nature. Morality is responsibility to a given set of conditions. The further the modern system develops in the direction that it has taken for two generations, the more antitraditional our society will become, and the more difficult it will be to pass on the fragments of the traditions that we inherit.

The higher myth of religion, the lower myth of history, even ordinary codes of conduct, cannot preserve themselves; indeed they do not exist apart from our experience. Since the most significant feature of our experience is the way we make our living, the economic basis of life is the soil out of which all the forms, good or bad, of our experience must come.

1936

Religion and the Old South

AT A TIME not inconceivably long ago the ordinary layman, or even the extraordinary one who took up the mysteries as a gentlemanly pursuit, had an impressive respect for the professional man of religion, who for some reason not clear to us had authority to speak of the Higher Things. We have none of that respect now. The present writer, who is a layman of the more ordinary kind, is deficient in it. There are priests here and there, a Protestant clergyman or two, who as individuals seem to speak from the tripod. But they scarcely represent their class; they are only laymen of the more extraordinary kind. So I begin an essay on religion with almost no humility at all; that is to say, I begin it in a spirit of irreligion. One must think for oneself—a responsibility intolerable to the religious mind, whose proper business is to prepare the mysteries for others.

Religion is not properly a discussion of anything. A discussion of religion is an act of violence, a betrayal of the religious essence undertaken for its own good, or for the good of those who live by it. This is the sole justification of an amateur treatment of religion; my betrayal of religion betrays only my own, and instead of a public scandal it is an instance of personal indecorum that can injure no one but myself.

But there is also a certain pretension in this incivility. It is to the effect that my private fable was once more public, and that men have fallen away from it into evil days. I must therefore proceed at once to dress my fable in First Principles—which are indeed the only dress it will receive in this essay. I can hardly make a fiction convincing by leaving it in the simple condition that it enjoys in my own mind—that is, the condition of fairy story and myth. For a myth should be in conviction immediate, direct, overwhelming, and I take it that the appreciation of this kind of imagery is an art lost to the modern mind.

The reader must be entreated to follow a few pages of abstraction about religion that partakes of religion not at all. For abstraction is the death of religion no less than the death of everything else.

Religion, when it directs its attention to the horse cropping the blue grass on the lawn, is concerned with the whole horse, and not with that part of him which he has in common with other horses, or that more general part which he shares with other quadrupeds or with the more general vertebrates; and not with the abstract horse in his capacity of horse-power in general, power that he shares with other machines of making objects move. Religion admits the existence of this horse, but says that he is only half of the horse. Religion undertakes to place before us the whole horse as he is in himself.

Since this essay is not religion, but a discussion of it, it does not pretend to put before you the complete horse. It does hope to do the following: to show that the complete horse may be there in spite of the impotence of this discussion to produce him. In other words, there is a complete and self-contained horse despite the now prevailing faith that there is none simply because the abstract and scientific mind cannot see him.

This modern mind sees only half of the horse—that half which may become a dynamo, or an automobile, or any other horsepowered machine. If this mind had had much respect for the full-bodied, grass-eating horse, it would never have invented the engine which represents only half of him. The religious mind, on the other hand, has this respect; it wants the whole horse; and it will be satisfied with nothing less.

It wants the whole horse if it is a religious mind that requires more than a half-religion. A religion of the half-horse is preeminently a religion concerning how things work, and this is a modern religion. By leaving half of the horse out of account, it can easily show that abstract horsepower, ideally, everywhere, infallibly, under other abstract and *half* conditions, works. Now the half of the animal that this religion leaves out won't work at all; it isn't workable; it is a vast body of concrete qualities constantly conflicting with the workable half; today the horse saddled admirably, but yesterday he ran away—he would not work.

From this it is clear that there is another possible half-religion. It is very common at present. It asserts that nothing works—a poor if desperate refutation of the other half-religion. It says that no horse is workable; the horse is just a locus of unpredictable and immeasurable qualities, and the more you contemplate him the more you see how futile it is to pretend that there is anything regular about him. He is unique beyond cure, and you can't predict the performance of Man-o'-War tomorrow from the performance of Man-o'-War yesterday. This is as bad as saying that you can predict everything. It is another half-religion: it is the religion of the symbolist poets and of M. Henri Bergson.

But how do we know that the religion of the completely workable is a religion? It has no altars—that is, no altars that befit it entirely, for it has only usurped the altars traditionally surviving; it has no formal ritual, and no priesthood wearing anything like a cassock or telling anything like beads. We know that the cult of infallible working is a kind of religion because it sets up an irrational value: the value is irrational (a false absolute) because the whole nature of man is not to be subsumed under a concept of logical necessity; the value would still be irrational even if "reason," or science, could reach absolute natural truth. T. E. Hulme would have said that it is contrary to the full content of our experience to assume that man is continuous with nature. It is, then, irrational to believe in omnipotent human rationality. Nothing, in short, infallibly works. The new half-religionists are simply worshiping a principle, and with true half-religious fanaticism they ignore what they do not want to see—which is the breakdown of the principle in numerous instances of practice. It is a bad religion, for that very reason; it can predict only success.

The religion, then, of the whole horse predicts both success and failure. It says that the horse will work within limits, but that it is folly to tempt the horse providence too far. It takes account of the failures—that is, it is realistic, for it calls to witness the traditional experience of evil which is the common lot of the race. It is a mature religion, and it is not likely to suffer disillusion and collapse. Here it is very unlike the half-religion of work which has a short memory of failure; the half-religion can ignore its failures to a certain saturation point, beyond which they will be overwhelming, and the society living under it is riding for a crushing fall. It will be totally unprepared for collapse; it will have gone too far. It will have forgotten the symbol of itself in the career of the vaunting Oedipus, who, blind at last, cautioned us not to pronounce a man happy till we saw the end of his life. The half-religion of work has accomplished the murder of Laius and married Jocasta; it has applied its pragmatism of values with astonishing success *up to now;* but the end is yet to come. Tiresias is yet to come.

It is apparent that the image of the horse will "work" only in a limited number of illustrations; so I propose to try another image.

I I

Take the far more complex image of history, if it may be called an image at all. For as an image its content is mixed and incoherent, and reduces to a vast clutter of particular images. We are able each of us to take our choice; we may reconstruct this scene or that period. We have those people who prefer the Renaissance, and those who like better the Periclean age, or perhaps they concentrate their loyalty to a special kind of life in a particular document of an age or a people: there are Platonists and Aristotelians, Stoics, and Hedonists, and there are the Christians, or at least there were the Christians who stood by the two Testaments, both of which we are now convinced are of ancient and obscure origin and of muddled contents.

These sad, more concrete minds may be said to look at their history in a definite and now quite unfashionable way. They look at it as a concrete series that has taken place in a very real time—by which I mean, without too much definition, a time as sensible, as full of sensation, and as replete with accident and uncertainty as the time they themselves are living in, moment by moment.

But if you do not take history as an image or many images, you have got to take it as idea, abstraction, concept. You need not feel any great interest in the rival merits of the Greek and Roman cultures; they were both "ideas" comprehensible after some study under a single concept which their chief business is now to illustrate. Consider Hegel: it is thesis-antithesis-synthesis—a process that includes not only Greece, Iraq, and Rome, but (as the author warns us about his rights of translation) the Scandinavian as well. It is not that the scientific historian refuses to see that Pericles dressed, ate, and loved differently from Cincinnatus; it is rather that the particular instance fades away into a realm of phenomena related as cause and effect. The historical ideal is

the physicist's concept of natural law. There is then ideally
no accident or contingency; for accident and contingency
are names for our insufficient information. The illusion of
contingency that harassed the past (when it was still the
present) is dissolved by the Long View—which means that
the ancient versions of nature and society were so limited
that the ancients were not able to see their pluralism in
the true light of all-embracing principle. For this Long View
history becomes an abstract series, opposed to the concrete
series of the Short View.

There are several questions here that need to be asked
of the Long View: Is it not the religion of the half-horse?
Does the law of cause and effect which joins up the Greek
and Roman cultures make them identical in any other respect than law? Is it, in short, the Greek and Roman cultures
themselves? Is it these cultures in any other sense than that
the merely working horse is the actual horse?

I have said that this view makes the past an abstract series;
let it be called a logical series, and there is nothing to do
but to resort to the customary *A, B, C* of the textbooks. These
letters may follow one another at all places at all times, without sensation, accident, or contingency. But did Greek culture live and have its being without sensation? The Short
View maintains that it did not, for the Short View holds that
the proper series for history to be placed in is the temporal
or concrete series.

At this point I must do some violence to the reaches of
the argument, and say briefly: for the Short View, history is
the specific account of the doings of specific men who acted
their parts in a rich and contemporaneous setting which bewildered them. In their bewilderment they invented, or
preserved even older, simple stories with a moral. In the
times of natural bewilderment—when contingency was called
religious awe—men like Hesiod and Cynewulf pondered what
they did not understand and gave us simple stories and

charms with a moral that we find obvious. But, for the moment, I must leave the moral in a very general state, and close this part of the argument with another difference between the Long and the Short View.

It is apparent that a solvent which reduces the Greek and the Roman cultures to identity of natural law gives to us the privilege of choosing between them; for assuming even that we are the offshoot of one of them, there is yet no reason why we cannot take up the other. The Long View becomes, in brief, the cosmopolitan destroyer of tradition. Or, put otherwise, since the Christian myth is a vegetation rite, varying only in some details from countless other vegetation myths, there is no reason to prefer Christ to Adonis. Varying only in some details: this assumes that there is nothing but a quantitative difference between a horse and a dog, both being vertebrates, mammals, quadrupeds. But the Short View holds that the whole Christ and the whole Adonis are sufficiently differentiated in their respective qualities (details), and that our tradition compels us to choose more than that half of Christ which is Adonis and to take the whole, separate, and unique Christ.

There is a nice and somewhat slippery paradox here: Why should our tradition compel us to choose anything? Particularly in view of the all but accomplished fact that tradition is destroyed? If the agency is shut up, the business cannot be transacted. And we have to confess that merely living in a certain stream of civilized influence does not compel us to be loyal to it. Indeed, the act of loyalty, even the fact of loyalty, must be spontaneous to count at all. Tradition must, in other words, be automatically operative before it can be called tradition. For in its true function it is powerfully selective, and the moment it admits that Adonis is able to compete with Christ, though it regret the rivalry, it has gone over to the Long View; its faith has weakened; and we are on the verge of committing ourselves to the half religions that are no religions at all, but quite simply decisions passed on the utility, the workableness, of the religious objects with respect to the practical aims of society. The utility of the religious object is not impressive.

So this is the paradox: Is it tradition or the Long View itself which prompts the present defense of the religious attitude? It is probably a little of both; though this conception is wholly irrational. It is irrational to defend religion with the weapon that invariably discredits it, and yet this is what seems to be happening. I am trying to discover the place that religion holds, with abstract instruments, which of course tend to put religion into some logical system or series, where it vanishes.

III

But this is due to our nature, which is a very different nature from that of the Russian or eastern European mind, whose religion is quite simply supernaturalism or the naïve religion of the entire horse. It never suspects the existence of those halves that render our sanity so precarious and compel us to vacillate between a self-destroying naturalism and practicality, on the one hand, and a self-destroying mysticism, on the other. For it seems that we are not able to contemplate those qualities of the horse that are specifically religious without forgetting his merely spatial and practicable half: we cannot let the entire horse fill our minds all at once. And thus we have a special notion of tradition— a notion that tradition is not simply a fact, but a fact that must be constantly defended.

This defense is dogma. The strictly qualitative half of the horse, his special uniqueness as a sensible fact, in a word, his image, must be defended against pure practicality, or his abstraction. His defense with us is abstraction itself. For the only defense we know is rational and scientific, and it is thus evident that dogma is not a personal property of religion, but is a mere instrument. And it is an act of sheer generosity when this instrument sets about the defense of its natural enemy, the qualitative view of experience. But, in the Middle Ages, it was so enamored of this enemy that it could not be brought to destroy him, even if dogma as rationality is a half-religion and is on the way to becoming science or practicality.

It was both a great discovery and a great calamity when the Europeans found that reason could be used in another way than the defense of something alien to it. It must always seem to us a scandal that Scholasticism should have tried to make rational all those unique qualities of the horse which are spirits and myths and symbols. The men of the Renaissance effectively hushed the scandal up; they said: *Entia non sunt multiplicanda praeter necessitatem.* This razor of William of Occam's at first went only after the superfluous entities of scholastic science. Don't, it says in effect, explain reason in terms of faculties when sub-laryngeal agitation accounts adequately for the phenomena of thought. But it was only a step up from natural phenomena to supernatural noumena, once the razor had become a standard feature of the *Zeitgeist* of the Renaissance. Throw over the spirits and symbols, which are mystical anyhow, not empirically necessary, and find those quantities in nature that will explain, not *what* nature is, but *how* nature works, the quantities that are barely necessary to the working.

This was always the peril of the European mind and the medieval Church knew it. By making reason, science, or nature, an instrument of defense for the protection of the other than reasonable, the other than scientific, the other than natural, it performed a tremendous feat of spiritual unity. It was the only kind of unity that the Western mind is capable of. Its special feature is the implied belief, which of course became often explicit—I simply mean that the belief, beginning unconsciously in experience, became later necessary as a reasoned part of the system—its special feature is an ineradicable belief in the fundamental evil of nature. Western Reason has always played the ostrich by sticking its head in the Supernatural. Woe betide when it took its head out and got so used to the natural setting that it found it good. And this is what happened. For the Church had known that the only way to restrain the practical impulses of her constituency was to put into the mouth of nature the words *Noli me tangere*. The Eastern Church never had to do this, nor did it ever have to construct a plausible rationality round the supernatural to make it acceptable; it has never had a philosophy, nor a dogma in our sense; it never needed one.

The Western Church established a system of quantity for the protection of quality, but there was always the danger that quantity would revolt from servitude and suppress its master; the danger that it would apply its genius to a field more favorable to spectacular success. Once reason ceased to be the instrument through which the purely qualitative features of nature could be contemplated and enjoyed, without being corrupted by too much use, it began to see the natural setting as so many instances of quantity; that is, nature began to see the practical possibilities of knowing herself. For reason and nature are one, and that is the meaning of naturalism. The symbol and the myth meant that the external world was largely an inviolable whole; once the symbol and the myth were proved to be not natural facts, but unnatural fictions that fitted into no logical series tolerable to the rational mind, nature became simply a workable half. The votaries of this nature now think that it is a Whole of limitless practicability.

I V

This being true, how can tradition, which is always embarrassing to practicality on a large scale, be defended?

Has it not disappeared? And was it not always on the brink of compromise in the fact that it needed the support of its enemy? The answer doubtless is: It can always be defended, but a recovery and restoration is a more difficult performance.

Moreover, where can an American take hold of tradition? His country is supposed to have preserved none from Europe, and if we take the prototype of the European tradition to be medieval society, we must confess that America has performed wonders, considering her youth, in breaking it down.

Yet the very idea "America" must give us pause, for it is almost anything that a determined apologist may wish to make it. In a brief three hundred years she has recapitulated practically every form of European polity, if these separate polities may be seen as devoid of their religious background. She has repeated all the chief economic and political forms. But she has not repeated the religious forms. The religious history of America is perfectly continuous with that of Europe.

This anomaly gave us that remarkable society of the old South, which was a feudal society, without a feudal religion; hence only a semi-feudal society. The reason for this is by no means obscure. It is just possible to see the Jamestown project as the symbol of what later happened to America: it was a capitalistic enterprise undertaken by Europeans who were already convinced adherents of large-scale exploitation of nature, not to support a stable religious order, but to advance the interests of *trade as an end in itself*. They stood thus for a certain stage in the disintegration of the European religion, and their descendants stuck to their guns, which theoretically at least were Protestant, aggressive, and materialistic guns.

At the same time certain conditions of economy supported a society which was, again theoretically, Protestant, but which was not aggressive and materialistic. It was a throwback, a case of atavism. A distinguished Southern writer has argued that the Southern population was originally less rebellious against European stability than was the Northern. It is doubtful if history will support this, though I should personally like to do so, for the belief implies the myth-making tendency of the mind in one of its most valuable forms. The enemy, abstraction, or the view of history as the logical series, gives us, alas, another story. It is that soil and climate made the agrarian life generally more attractive than a barrener soil and a colder climate could have ever done, and that the propitious soil and climate made it possible for a semi-feudal system of labor to take root and thrive. A people may, in short, return to an older economy, under certain local conditions; but international conditions, certainly since the sixteenth century, have made it impossible for any community of European origin to remain spiritually isolated and to develop its genius, unless that genius is in harmony with the religious and economic drift of the civilization at large.

The South could temporarily return to an older secular polity, but the world was too much with it, and it could not create its appropriate religion.

There were two results of this anomalous position that may be stated without too much historical argument. The South, as a political atmosphere charged with eighteenth-century ideas, did not realize her genius in time. She consistently defended herself with the political terms of eighteenth-century liberalism, a doctrine better suited to the middle-class economics of the North, into whose hands she neatly played. So, waiting too long, she let her more powerful rival gain the ascendancy. The South did not achieve that inward conviction of destiny that empowers societies no less than individuals to understand their position and to act from inner necessity: we do nothing without symbols and we cannot do the right thing with the wrong symbol. There was no unity of purpose between the Southern Protestant religion and the Southern Protestant semi-feudalism. The South's religious mind was inarticulate, dissenting, and schismatical. She had a non-agrarian and trading religion that had been invented in the sixteenth century by a young finance-capitalist economy: hardly a religion at all but rather a disguised secular ambition. The Southern politicians quoted scripture to defend slavery, yet they defended their society as a whole with the catchwords of eighteenth-century politics. And this is why the South separated from the North too late, and so lost her cause.

The second result of the anomalous structure of the Southern mind is a near and contemporary one. Because the South never created a fitting religion, the social structure of the South began grievously to break down two generations after the Civil War. For the social structure depends on the economic structure, and economic conviction is still, in spite of the beliefs of economists from Adam Smith to Marx, the secular image of religion. No nation is ever simply and unequivocally beaten in war; nor was the South. Is it possible that the South shows signs of defeat? If she does, it is due to her lack of a religion which would make her special way of life the inevitable and permanently valuable one. We have been inferior to the Irish in this virtue, though much less than the Irish have we ever been beaten in war.

It appears that the question put at the beginning of this section, How can the American, or the Southern man, take hold of tradition? is further from being answered than ever.

V

Let us return to the two ways of looking at horses and history. Which are we permitted to say was the way of the Old South? The answer to this question is not necessarily disconcerting, even if we must admit both ways. And it is bound to be both because the South was a Western community, and a Western community is one that does not live in sackcloth and ashes and erect all its temples to the gods. The Southerners were capable of using their horses, as they did one day at Brandy Station, but they could also contemplate them as absolute and inviolable objects; they were virtually incapable of abstracting from the horse his horsepower, or from history its historicity. For the horse fact and the historical fact, by remaining concrete, retained a certain status as *images*, and images are only to be contemplated, and perhaps the act of contemplation after long exercise initiates a habit of restraint, and the setting up of absolute standards which are less formulas for action than an interior discipline of the mind. There is doubtless from the viewpoint of abstract history not much difference between a centaur, since we speak of horses, and a Christ, since we speak of historicity. Both are mythical figments reducible in one set of properties to the abstraction man-ness. But the Short View, as we have seen, is incorrigibly selective, and has been known to prefer Christ to the man horse.

After about 1820, in America, the Southern communities alone stood for that preference with anything like a single mind. The heresy of New England is beautifully recorded in the correspondence of John Adams and Thomas Jefferson, where the two sages discuss the possibility of morals. Jefferson calls his judgment "taste"—reliance on custom, breeding, ingrained moral decision. But Adams needs a "process of moral reasoning," which forces the individual to think out from abstract principle his role at a critical moment of action. The view of John Adams tells us how far New England had gone from Europe, how deeply she had broken with the past.

While the South in the nineteenth century trafficked with Europe in cotton, she took in exchange very little of manners, literature, or the arts. The Southerners were another community on the complete European plan, and they had no need, being independent, of importing foreign art and noblemen, commodities that New England became frantic about after 1830. For New England was one of those abstract-minded, sharp-witted, trading societies that must be parasites in two ways: they must live economically on some agrarian class or country, and they must live spiritually likewise. New England lived economically on the South, culturally on England. And this was doubtless a disguised and involved nostalgia for the land—the New England "land" being old England. The houses and the universities of New England became a European museum, stuffed with the dead symbols of what the New Englander could not create because provision for it had been left out of his original foundation.

In the nineteenth century New England confessed her loss of the past by being too much interested in Europe. If you take the Adams family at its best, you find a token of the whole New England mind: there is the tragedy of the *Education of Henry Adams*, who never quite understood what he was looking for. He spent much of his youth, like Henry James, learning the amenities of the English agrarians, without being by right of soil entitled to them, and never suspecting that the best he might hope to do was to learn them by rote. More significantly he passed his last days in Washington despising the "ignorant" and "simple" minds south of the Potomac, again never suspecting that his efforts in behalf of defeating this simplicity and ignorance in a recent war did something towards undermining the base of the civilized values that he coveted most.

If New England's break with Europe made her excessively interested in the European surface, the ignorance and the simplicity of the South's independence of Europe, in the cultural sense, witness a fact of great significance. The South could be ignorant of Europe because she *was* Europe; that is to say, the South was trying to take root in a native soil. And the South could remain simple-minded because she had no use for the intellectual agility required to define its position. Her position, alas, seemed to be self-sufficient and self-evident; it was European where the New England position was self-conscious and colonial. The Southern mind was simple, not top-heavy with learning it had no need of, unintellectual, and composed; it was personal and dramatic, rather than abstract and metaphysical; and it was sensuous because it lived close to a natural scene of great variety and interest.

Because she lived by images not highly organized, it is true, as dogma, but rather more loosely gathered from the past, the South was a traditional European community. The Southerners were incurable in their preference for Cato over the social conditions in which he historically lived. They looked at history as the concrete and temporal series—a series at all only because they required a straight metaphorical line back into the past, for the series, such as it was, was very capricious, and could hardly boast of a natural logic. They could add to the classics a lively medievalism from the novels of Sir Walter Scott. They saw themselves as human beings living by a human principle, from which they were unwilling to subtract the human so as to set the principle free to operate on an unlimited program of inhuman practicality. For that is what a principle is—the way things will work. But the Southerner, or more generally the die-hard agrarian, was not willing to let the principle proceed alone, uncontrolled; for what he valued most in the working of principle was the capacity that he retained of enjoying the fruits of the work. The old Southerners were highly critical of the kinds of work to be done. They planted no corn, they grew no cotton that did not directly contribute to the upkeep of a rich private life; and they knew little history for the sake of knowing it, but simply for the sake of contemplating it and seeing in it an image of themselves. It is probable that they liked Plutarch better than Suetonius,

and both better than Thucydides. Like all unscientific societies they cared little for natural knowledge, and cared
more for that unnaturalism which is morals. They liked very
simple stories with a moral in which again they could see
an image of themselves.

We have already considered some of the possible reasons
why they broke down.

V I

They had a religious life, but it was not enough organized
with a right mythology. In fact, their rational life was not
powerfully united to the religious experience, as it was in
medieval society, and they are a fine specimen of the tragic
pitfall upon which the Western mind has always hovered.
Not having a rational system for the defense of their religious
attitude and its base in a feudal society, they elaborated no
rational system whatever, no full-grown philosophy; so that,
when the post-bellum temptations of the devil, who, according to Milton and Aeschylus, is the exploiter of nature, confronted them, they had no defense. Since there is, in the
Western mind, a radical divison between the religious, the
contemplative, the qualitative, on the one hand, and the
scientific, the natural, the practical, on the other, the scientific mind always plays havoc with the spiritual life when
it is not powerfully enlisted in its cause; it cannot be permitted to operate alone.

It operated separately (yet along with other ideas that
ignored it and one another) in Thomas Jefferson, and the
form that it took in his mind may be reduced to a formula:
*The ends of man are sufficiently contained in his political
destiny.* Now the political destiny of men is the way they
work, toward ends they hope to achieve in community by
the operation of secular laws. It is not necessary to labor the
point, or to draw out the enormous varieties that such a
theory may exhibit. It is sufficient to point out that the

ante-bellum Southerners never profoundly believed it. It is highly illuminating to reflect that, as I have said, *they acted as if they did.* There was, of course, a good deal of dissent: the Virginia Constitutional Convention repudiated Jefferson in 1832. It was a first step; but the last step was so far off that it could not possibly have preceded 1861.

The modern Southerner inherits the Jeffersonian formula. This is only to say that he inherits a concrete and very unsatisfactory history. He can almost wish for his ease the Northern contempt for his kind of history; he would like to believe that history is not a vast body of concrete fact to which he must be loyal, but only a source of mechanical formulas; for then he might hope to do what the Northern industrialist has just about succeeded in doing—making a society out of abstractions. The Southerner would conjure up some magic abstraction to spirit back to him his very concrete way of life. He would, in short, in his plight, apply the formula, because he has no other, of his inheritance—that the ends of man may be fully achieved by political means.

The South would not have been defeated had she possessed a sufficient faith in her own kind of God. She would not have been defeated, in other words, had she been able to bring out a body of doctrine setting forth her true conviction that the ends of man require more for their realization than politics. The setback of the war was of itself a very trivial one.

We are very near an answer to our question: How may the Southerner take hold of his tradition?

The answer is: by violence.

For this answer, if we want an answer, is inevitable. He cannot fall back upon his religion, simply because it was never articulated and organized for him. If he could do this, he would constitute himself a "borer from within," and might hope to effect gradually a secular revolution in his favor. As we have said, economy is the secular image of religious conviction. His religious conviction is inchoate and unorganized; it never had the opportunity to be anything else.

Since he cannot bore from within, he has left the sole alternative of boring from without. This method is political, active, and, in the nature of the case, violent and revolutionary. Reaction is the most radical of programs; it aims at cutting away the overgrowth and getting back to the roots. A forward-looking radicalism is a contradiction; it aims at rearranging the foliage.

The Southerner is faced with this paradox: He must use an instrument, which is political, and so unrealistic and pretentious that he cannot believe in it, to re-establish a private, self-contained, and essentially spiritual life. I say that he must do this; but that remains to be seen.

1930

A Southern Mode of the Imagination

I

WHAT I AM about to say will be composed of obscure speculation, mere opinion, and reminiscence verging upon auto-
biography. But having issued this warning, and given notice
to the scholars of American literature that the entire affair
will be somewhat unreliable, I must allude to some of the
things that I shall not try to say. I shall not discuss or "place"
any of the Southern writers of the period now somewhat
misleadingly called the Southern Renaissance. It was more
precisely a birth, not a rebirth. The eyes of the world are on
William Faulkner; for that reason I shall not talk about
him. I take it to be a commonplace of literary history that
no writer of Mr. Faulkner's power could emerge from a literary and social vacuum. It is a part of Mr. Faulkner's legend about himself that he did appear, like the sons of Cad-
mus, full grown, out of the unlettered soil of his native
state, Mississippi. But we are under no obligation to take
his word for it. Two other modern writers of prose-fiction,
Mr. Stark Young and Miss Eudora Welty, quite as gifted as
Mr. Faulkner, if somewhat below him in magnitude and
power, are also natives of that backward state, where fewer
people can read than in any other state in the Union. I shall
not pause to explain my paradoxical conviction, shared I
believe by Mr. Donald Davidson, that the very backward-
ness of Mississippi, and of the South as a whole, might
partially explain the rise of a new literature which has won

the attention not only of Americans but of the Western world.

If the Elizabethan age would still be the glory of English literature without Shakespeare, the new literature of the Southern states would still be formidable without Faulkner. I have promised not to discuss any one writer in detail, but I shall invoke certain names: Elizabeth Madox Roberts, Robert Penn Warren, Eudora Welty, Stark Young, Dubose Heyward, Ellen Glasgow, James Branch Cabell, Katherine Anne Porter, Carson McCullers, Tennessee Williams, Thomas Wolfe, Paul Green, Caroline Gordon, Flannery O'Connor, Truman Capote, Ralph Ellison, John Crowe Ransom, Donald Davidson, Peter Taylor, Andrew Lytle. It is scarcely chauvinism on my part to point out that, with the exception of Fitzgerald and Hemingway, the region north of the Potomac and Ohio Rivers has become the stepsister of American fiction. And it has been said, so often that I almost believe it, that the American branch of the New Criticism is of Southern origin—a distinction about which my own feelings are neutral.

Before I turn to the more speculative part of this discussion, I should like to quote a paragraph written in the Reconstruction period—that is, around 1870—by a New England novelist who had come to the South as a benign carpetbagger to observe and to improve what he observed. He was John William De Forest, of Connecticut, whose works were almost completely forgotten until about ten years ago. He was not only one of the best nineteenth-century American novelists; he was a shrewd social commentator, whose dislike of Southerners did not prevent him from seeing them more objectively than any other Northerner of his time. I quote:

Not until Southerners get rid of some of their social vanity, not until they cease talking of themselves in a spirit of self-adulation, not until they drop the idea that they are Romans and must write in the style of Cicero, will they be able to so paint life that the world shall crowd to see the picture. Meanwhile let us pray that a true Southern novelist will soon arise, for he will be able to furnish us vast amusement and some instruction. His day is passing; in another generation his material will be gone; the chivalrous Southron will be as dead as the slavery that created him.

It was not until fifty years later that De Forest's demands upon the Southern novelist were fulfilled, when the writers whose names I have listed began to appear. My own contemporaries called the nineteenth-century Ciceronian Southern style "Confederate prose," and we avoided it more assiduously than sin. Of a Southern woman novelist of the 1860's, Augusta Evans, author of *St. Elmo,* it was said that her heroines had swallowed an unabridged dictionary.

My reason for adopting the *causerie* instead of the formal discourse has a quite simple explanation. I have no talent for research; or at any rate I am like the man who, upon being asked whether he could play the violin, answered that he didn't know because he had never tried. Apart from inadequate scholarship, it would be improper of me to pretend to an objectivity, which I do not feel, in the recital of certain events, in which I have been told that I played a small part. None of us—and by us I mean not only the group of poets who with unintentional prophecy styled themselves the "Fugitives," but also our contemporaries in other Southern states—none of us, thirty-five years ago, was conscious of playing any part at all. I ought not to speak for my contemporaries, most of whom are still living and able to talk. The essays and books about us that have begun to appear give me a little less than the shock of recognition. If one does not recognize oneself, one may not unreasonably expect to recognize one's friends. One writer, Mr. John Bradbury, in a formidable book of some three hundred pages entitled *The Fugitives,* says that John Crowe Ransom taught his students, of whom I had the honor to be one, the "knowledge of good and evil." I don't recognize in this role my old friend and early master; I surmise that he has found it no less disconcerting than I do. Our initiation into the knowledge of good and evil, like everybody else's, must have been at birth; our later improvement in this field of knowledge, haphazard and extra-curricular. John Ransom taught us—Robert Penn Warren, Cleanth Brooks, Andrew Lytle and myself—Kantian aesthetics and a philosophical dualism, tinged with Christian theology, but ultimately derived from the Nicomachian ethics. I allude to my own education not because it was unique, but because it was the education of my generation in the South. But we said at that time very little about the South; an anomalous reticence in a group of men who later became notoriously sectional in point of view.

We knew we were Southerners, but this was a matter of plain denotation; just as we knew that some people were Yankees; or we knew that there were people whom—if we saw them—we would think of as Yankees; we might even have said, but only among ourselves, you understand: "He's a Yankee." Brainard Cheney told me years ago that when he was a small boy in Southern Georgia, down near the Okefenokee Swamp, the rumor spread that some Yankees were coming to town. All the little boys gathered in the courthouse square to see what Yankees looked like. This was about 1910. My boyhood, in the border state of Kentucky, was evidently more cosmopolitan. There were a few Northerners, no doubt; there were a few elderly gentlemen who had been Southern Unionists, or homemade Yankees, as they were discourteously described, who had fought in the Federal Army. One of these, old Mr. Crabb, white-haired, beaknosed, and distinguished, frequently passed our house on his morning walk. He had an empty sleeve, and my mother said he had got his arm shot off at the Battle of Gettysburg. I knew that my grandfather had been in Pickett's charge, and I wondered idly whether he had shot it off. I do not remember whether I wished that he had.

This was our long moment of innocence, which I tried to recover in a poem many years later. And for men of my age, who missed the first World War by a few months, it was a new Era of Good Feeling between the sections. Some time before 1914 the North had temporarily stopped trying to improve us, or had at least paused to think about something else. Having just missed being sent to France in the A. E. F., I came to Vanderbilt University from a rural small-town society that had only a superficial Victorian veneer pasted over what was still an eighteenth-century way of living. It has been said that Kentucky seceded in 1865. In my boyhood, and even much later, Kentucky was more backward and Southern, socially and economically, than Tennessee or North Carolina. This preindustrial society meant, for people living in it, that one's identity had everything to do with land and material property, at a definite place, and very little to do with money. It was better for a person, however impoverished, of my name, to be identified with Tate's Creek Pike, in Fayette County, than to be the richest man in town without the identification of place. This was simple and innocent; it had little to do with what the English call *class*. Yet from whatever point of view one may look at it, it will in the end lead us towards the secret of what was rather grandiosely called, by the late W. J. Cash, the Southern Mind.

If I may bring to bear upon it an up-to-date and un-Southern adjective, it was an extroverted mind not much given to introspection. (I do not say meditation, which is something quite different.) Such irony as this mind was capable of was distinctly romantic; it came out of the sense of dislocated external relations: because people were not *where* they ought to be they could not be *who* they ought to be; for men had missed their proper role, which was to be attached to a place. Mr. Faulkner's lawyer Benbow and the Compson family, in *The Sound and the Fury*, are people of this sort; I know of no better examples than Mr. Andrew Lytle's Jack Cropleigh, in his novel *The Velvet Horn*, or the narrator of his powerful short story, "Mister McGregor." It is the irony of time and place out of joint. It was provincial or, if you will, ignorant of the world. It was the irony of social discrepancies, not the tragic irony of the peripety, or of interior change. It is premodern; it can be found in the early books of Ellen Glasgow and James Branch Cabell, as different at the surface as their books may appear to be.

But with the end of the first World War a change came about that literary historians have not yet explained; whether we shall ever understand it one cannot say. Southern literature in the second half of this century may cease to engage the scholarly imagination; the subject may eventually become academic, and buried with the last dissertation. Back in the nineteen-thirties, I believe it was precisely 1935, I wrote for the tenth anniversary issue of *The Virginia Quarterly Review* an essay entitled "The Profession of Letters in the South," [1] which glanced at a possible explanation by analogy to another literary period. I refer to it here in order to qualify, or at any rate to extend its agreement, not, I hope, to call attention to myself. So far as that old essay is concerned, other persons have already done this for me. When I look at the index of a work of contemporary criticism (I always look there first), and see my name, I get a little nervous because the following passage has a two-to-one chance over anything else I have written, to be quoted; I quote it again:

The considerable achievement of Southerners in modern American letters must not beguile us into too much hope for the future. The Southern novelist has left his mark upon the age; but it is

[1] *Supra*, pp. 517–534.

of the age. From the peculiarly historical consciousness of the Southern writer has come good work of a special order; but the focus of this consciousness is quite temporary. It has made possible the curious burst of intelligence that we get at a crossing of the ways, not unlike, on an infinitesimal scale, the outburst of poetic genius at the end of the sixteenth century when commercial England had already begun to crush feudal England. The Histories and Tragedies of Shakespeare record the death of the old regime, and Doctor Faustus gives up feudal order for world power.

My purpose in quoting the passage—I marvel that prose so badly written could have been quoted so much—is not to approve of the approbation it has received, but to point out that whatever rightness it may have is not right enough. It says nothing about the particular quality of the Southern writers of our time.

The quality that I have in mind, none too clearly, makes its direct impact upon the reader, even if he be the foreign reader: he knows that he is reading a Southern book. But this explains nothing, for a quality can only be pointed to or shared, not defined. Let me substitute for the word quality the phrase *mode of discourse.*

The traditional Southern mode of discourse presupposes somebody at the other end silently listening: it is the rhetorical mode. Its historical rival is the dialectical mode, or the give and take between two minds, even if one mind, like the mind of Socrates, prevail at the end. The Southerner has never been a dialectician. The ante-bellum Southerner quoted Aristotle in defense of slavery, but Plato, the dialectician, was not opposed to the "peculiar institution," and he could have been cited with equal effect in support of the South Carolinian daydream of a Greek democracy. Aristotle was chosen by the South for good reason: although the Stagirite (as the Southerners called him) was a metaphysician, the South liked the deductive method, if its application were not too abstruse, and nobody could quarrel with the arrangement, in the order of importance, of the three great Aristotelian treatises on man in society: the *Nicomachian Ethics,* the *Politics,* and the *Rhetoric.* Aristotle assumed first principles from which he—and the old Southerners after him— could make appropriate deductions about the inequalities of men. Plato reached first principles by means of dialogue, which can easily become subjective: the mind talking to itself. The Southerner always talks to somebody else, and this somebody else, after varying intervals, is given his turn; but the conversation is always among rhetoricians; that is to say, the typical Southern conversation is not going anywhere; it is not about anything. *It is about the people who are talking,* even if they never refer to themselves, which they usually don't, since conversation is only an expression of manners, the purpose of which is to make everybody happy. This may be the reason why Northerners and other uninitiated persons find the alternating, or contrapuntal, conversation of Southerners fatiguing. Educated Northerners like their conversation to be about ideas.

I I

The foregoing, rather too broad distinction between dialectic and rhetoric is not meant to convey the impression that no Southerner of the past or the present was ever given to thought; nor do I wish to imply that New Englanders were so busy thinking that they wholly neglected that form of rhetoric which may be described as the manners of men talking in society. Emerson said that the "scholar is man thinking." Had Southerners of that era taken seriously the famous lecture entitled "The American Scholar," they might have replied by saying that the gentleman is man talking. The accomplished Christian gentleman of the old South was the shadow, attenuated by evangelical Calvinism, of his Renaissance spiritual ancestor, who had been the creation of the rhetorical tradition, out of Aristotle through Cicero, distilled finally by Castiglione. By contrast, the New England sage, embodied in Ralph Waldo Emerson, took seriously what has come to be known since the Industrial Revolution as the life of the mind: an activity a little apart from life, and perhaps leading to the fashionable alienation of the "intellectual" of our time. The protective withdrawal of the New England sage into dialectical truth lurks back of Emerson's famous definition of manners as the "invention of a wise man to keep a fool at a distance." (There is little doubt of the part Emerson conceived himself as playing.) The notorious lack of self-consciousness of the ante-bellum Southerner made it almost impossible for him to define anything; least of all could he imagine the impropriety of a definition of manners. Yet had a Southern contemporary of Emerson decided to argue the question, he might have retorted that manners are not *inventions*, but *conventions* tacitly agreed upon to protect the fool from consciousness of his folly. I do not wholly subscribe to this Southern view; there is to be brought against it Henry Adams's unkind portrait of Rooney Lee, a son of Robert E. Lee, who soon became a Confederate officer. The younger Lee, said Adams, when they were fellow students at Harvard, seemed to have only the habit of command, and no brains. (Adams didn't say it quite so rudely, but that is what it came to.) Rooney Lee, like his famous father, was a man of action, action through the habit of command being a form of rhetoric: he acted upon the assumptions of identification by place. The Lee identification, the whole Virginian myth of the rooted man, was the model of the more homely mystique of Tate's Creek Pike in the frontier state of Kentucky, whose citizens the Virginians thought were all Davy Crocketts—a frontiersman who described himself as "half-horse and half-alligator." Virginia was the model for the entire Upper South.

Northern historians were for years puzzled that Lee and the Southern yeoman farmer fought for the South, since neither had any interest in slavery. The question was usually put in this form: Why did Lee, who never owned a slave and detested slavery, become the leader of the slavocracy? Because he was a rhetorican who would have flunked Henry Adams's examination as miserably as his son. A Southern dialectician, could he be imagined in Lee's predicament, would have tossed his loyalties back and forth and come out with an abstraction called Justice, and he would have fought in the Federal Army or not at all. The record seems to indicate that the one dialectical abstraction that Lee entertained came to him after the war: the idea of constitutional government, for which in retrospect he considered that he had fought. Perhaps he did fight for it; yet I have the temerity to doubt his word. He fought for the local community which he could not abstract into fragments. He was in the position of the man who is urged by an outsider to repudiate his family because a cousin is an embezzler, or of the man who tries to rectify his ill-use of his brother by pretending that his entire family is a bad lot. I trust that in this analogy it is clear that the brother is the Negro slave.

What Robert E. Lee has to do with Southern literature is a question that might at this point quite properly be asked. Lee has a good deal to do with it, if we are going to look at Southern literature as the rhetorical expression of a Southern Mind. But even to be conscious of the possibility of a Southern Mind could lead us into a mode of discourse radically different from that of the rhetorician. We are well on the way towards dialectics. If we say that the old Southern Mind was rhetorical we must add that our access to it must be through its public phase, which was almost exclusively political. I do not believe that the ante-bellum Southerners, being wholly committed to the rhetorical mode, were capable of the elementary detachment that has permitted modern Southerners to discern the significance of that commitment, and to relate it to other modes of discourse. For the rhetorical mode is related to the myth-making faculty, and the mythopoeic mind assumes that certain great typical actions embody human truth. The critical detachment which permits me to apply this commonplace to the Southern Mind would not, I believe, have been within the grasp of better intellects than mine in the South up to the first World War. It has been said that the failure of the old Southern leaders to understand the Northern mind (which was then almost entirely the New England mind) was a failure of intelligence. In view of the task which the South had set for itself —that is, the preservation of local self-government within a framework of republican federalism—the charge is no doubt true. The old Southerners, being wholly committed to the rhetoric of politics, could not come to grips with the dynamic forces in the North that were rapidly making the exclusively political solution of their problem obsolete: they did not understand economics. The Southern public *persona* was supported by what W. J. Cash called, in a neo-Spenglerian phrase, the "proto-Dorian" myth. This *persona* was that of the agrarian patriot, a composite image of Cincinnatus dropping the plough for the sword, and of Cicero leaving his rhetorical studies to apply them patriotically to the prosecution of Cataline. The center round which the Southern political imagination gravitated was perhaps even smaller than the communities of which the South was an aggregate. In the first place, that aggregate was not a whole; and in the second, it would follow that the community itself was not a whole. The South was an aggregate of farms and plantations, presided over by our composite agrarian hero, Cicero Cincinnatus. I can think of no better image for what the South was before 1860, and for what it largely still was until about 1914, than that of the old gentleman in Kentucky who sat every afternoon in his front yard under an old sugar tree, reading Cicero's Letters to Atticus. When the hands suckering the tobacco in the adjoining field needed orders, he kept his place in the book with his forefinger, walked out into the field, gave the orders, and then returned to his reading under the shade of the tree. He was also a lawyer, and occasionally he went to his office, which was over the feed store in the county seat, a village with a population of about four hundred people.

The center of the South, then, was the family, no less for Robert E. Lee than for the people on Tate's Creek Pike; for Virginia was a great aggregate of families that through almost infinite ramifications of relationship was almost one family. Such a society could not be anything but political. The virtues cherished under such a regime were almost exclusively social and moral, with none of the intensively cultivated divisions of intellectual labor which are necessary to a flowering of the arts, whether literary or plastic. It is thus significant that the one original art of the South was domestic architecture, as befitted a family-centered society. It has been frequently noted that the reason why the South did not produce a great ante-bellum literature was the lack of cities as cultural centers. This was indeed a lack; but it is more important to understand why cultural centers were missing. The South did not want cultural centers; it preferred the plantation center. William Gilmore Simms argued repeatedly in the 1850's that no exclusively agrarian society had produced a great literature. Was this a failure of intelligence? I think not, if we look at the scene from the inside. After Archimedes had observed that, had he a fulcrum big enough, he could move the world, was it a failure of the Greek intelligence that it did not at once construct such a fulcrum? Were the Greek philosophers less intelligent than the late Albert Einstein and Professor Teller, who have found a way not only to move the world but perhaps to destroy it? But the plantation myth—and I use the word myth not to indicate a fantasy, but a reality—this myth, if Greek at all, was the limited Spartan myth. It was actually nearer to Republican Rome, a society which, like the South, was short in metaphysicians and great poets, and long in moralists and rhetoricians.

Mr. Lionel Trilling has said somewhere that the great writer, the spokesman of a culture, carries in himself the fundamental dialectic of that culture: the deeper conflicts of which his contemporaries are perhaps only dimly aware. There is a valuable truth in this observation. The inner strains, stresses, tensions, the shocked self-consciousness of a highly differentiated and complex society, issue in the dialectic of the high arts. The Old South, I take it, was remarkably free of this self-consciousness; the strains that it felt were external. And I surmise that had our Southern *persona*, our friend Cicero Cincinnatus, been much less simple than he was, the distractions of the sectional agitation nevertheless were so engrossing that they would have postponed almost indefinitely that self-examination which is the beginning, if not of wisdom, then at least of the arts of literature. When one is under attack, it is inevitable that one should put not only one's best foot forward but both feet, even if one of them rests upon the neck of a Negro slave. One then attributes to "those people over there" (the phrase that General Lee used to designate the Federal Army) all the evil of his own world. The defensive Southerner said that *if only* "those people over there" would let us alone, the vast Sabine Farm of the South (where men read Horace but did not think it necessary to be Horace) would perpetuate itself forever.

The complicated reasons for this Southern isolationism were, as I have tried to indicate, partly internal and partly external; but whatever the causes, the pertinent fact for any approach to the modern literary Renaissance is that the South was more isolated from 1865 to about 1920 than it had been before 1865. It was the isolationism of economic prostration, defeat, and inverted pride. And the New South of Henry W. Grady's rhetoric was just as isolated and provincial as the Old South of Thomas Nelson Page. For Grady's New South, the complete answer was the factory. (It was put into the less than distinguished verse of "The Song of the Chattahoochee," by Sidney Lanier.) I venture to think that there was more to be said for Page's Old South, even if we agree that, like Grady's New South, it was unreal: I take it that a pleasant dream is to be preferred to an actuality which imitates a nightmare. Neither the unreal dream nor the actual nightmare could lead to the conception of a complete society. If we want proof of this, we need only to look at the South today.

I should like now to return to the inadequacy of my speculations, twenty-four years ago, on the reasons for the sudden rise of the new Southern literature—a literature which, I have been told often enough to authorize the presumption, is now the center of American literature. (I do not insist upon this.) Social change must have had something to do with it, but it does not explain it. I do not hope to explain it now. I wish only to add a consideration which I have already adumbrated. If it seems narrow, technical, and even academically tenuous, it is probably not less satisfactory than the conventional attribution of literary causation to what is called the historical factor. No doubt, without this factor, without the social change, the new literature could not have appeared. One can nevertheless imagine the same consciousness of the same change around 1920, without the appearance of any literature whatever. Social change may produce a great social scientist, like the late Howard W. Odum, of North Carolina. Social upheaval will not in itself produce a poet like John Crowe Ransom or a novelist like William Faulkner.

There was another kind of change taking place at the same time, and it was decisive. The old Southern *rhetor*, the speaker who was eloquent before the audience but silent in himself, had always had at his disposal a less formal version of the rhetorical mode of discourse than the political oration.

Was it not said that Southerners were the best storytellers in America? Perhaps they still are. The tall tale was the staple of Southern conversation. Augustus Baldwin Longstreet's *Georgia Scenes* is a collection of tall tales written by an accomplished gentleman for other accomplished gentlemen; this famous book is in no sense folk literature, or an expression of the late V. L. Parrington's democratic spirit. It is the art of the rhetorician applied to the anecdote, to the small typical action resembling the mediaeval *exemplum,* and it verges upon myth—the minor secular myth which just succeeds in skirting round the suprahuman myth of religion. We have got something like this myth in *Huckleberry Finn,* which I take to be the first modern novel by a Southerner. We are now prepared by depth psychology to describe the action of *Huckleberry Finn* as not only typical, but as archetypal. What concerns me about it, for my purposes, is not whether it is a great novel (perhaps the *scale* of the action and the *range* of consciousness are too small for a great novel); what concerns me is the mode of its progression; for this mode is no longer the mode of rhetoric, the mode of the speaker reporting in person an argument or an action in which he is not dramatically involved. The action is generated inside the characters: there is internal dialogue, a conflict within the self. Mark Twain seems not to have been wholly conscious of what he had done; for he never did it again. Ernest Hemingway has said that the modern American novel comes out of *Huckleberry Finn,* and William Faulkner has paid a similar tribute. But this is not quite to the point.

Mark Twain was a forerunner who set an example which was not necessarily an influence. The feature of *Huckleberry Finn* which I have tried to discern, the shift from the rhetorical mode to the dialectical mode, had to be rediscovered by the twentieth-century novelists of the South. The example of Mark Twain was not quite fully developed and clean in outline. Most of the recent essays on *Huckleberry*

Finn—by Lionel Trilling and T. S. Eliot for example—have not been able to approach the end of the novel without embarrassment. (The one exception is a perceptive essay by Mr. Leo Marx.) Huck himself is a dramatic dialectician; Tom Sawyer, who reappears at the end and resolves the action externally with the preposterous "liberation" of Nigger Jim, who is already free, is a ham Southern rhetorician of the old school. He imposes his "style" upon a reality which has no relation to it, without perception of the ironic "other possible case" which is essential to the dramatic dialectic of the arts of fiction.

Here, as I come to the end of these speculations, I must go off again into surmises and guesses. What brought about the shift from rhetoric to dialectic? The Southern fictional dialectic of our time is still close to the traditional subject matter of the old informal rhetoric—the tall tale, the anecdote, the archetypal story. The New England dialectic of the Transcendentalists, from which Hawthorne had to protect himself by remaining aloof, tended to take flight into the synthesis of pure abstraction, in which the inner struggle is resolved in an idea. The Southern dramatic dialectic of our time is being resolved, as in the novels of William Faulkner, in action. The short answer to our question: How did this change come about? is that the South not only reentered the world with the first World War; it looked round and saw for the first time since about 1830 that the Yankees were not to blame for everything. It looks like a simple discovery, and it was; that is why it was difficult to make. The Southern legend, as Malcolm Cowley has called it, of defeat and heroic frustration was taken over by a dozen or more first-rate writers and converted into a universal myth of the human condition. W. B. Yeats's great epigram points to the nature of the shift from melodramatic rhetoric to the dialectic of tragedy: "Out of the quarrel with others we make rhetoric; out of the quarrel with ourselves, poetry."

1959

Narcissus as Narcissus

I

ON THIS FIRST OCCASION, which will probably be the last, of my writing about my own verse, I could plead in excuse the example of Edgar Allan Poe, who wrote about himself in an essay called "The Philosophy of Composition." But in our age the appeal to authority is weak, and I am of my age. What I happen to know about the poem that I shall discuss is limited. I remember merely my intention in writing it; I do not know whether the poem is good; and I do not know its obscure origins.

How does one happen to write a poem: where does it come from? That is the question asked by the psychologists or the geneticists of poetry. Of late I have not read any of the genetic theories very attentively: years ago I read one by Mr. Conrad Aiken; another, I think, by Mr. Robert Graves; but I have forgotten them. I am not ridiculing verbal mechanisms, dreams, or repressions as origins of poetry; all three of them and more besides may have a great deal to do with it. Other psychological theories say a good deal about compensation. A poem is an indirect effort of a shaky man to justify himself to happier men, or to present a superior account of his relation to a world that allows him but little certainty, and would allow equally little to the happier men if they did not wear blinders—according to the poet. For example, a poet might be a man who could not get enough self-justification out of being an automobile salesman (whose

593

certainty is a fixed quota of cars every month) to rest comfortably upon it. So the poet, who wants to be something that he cannot be, and is a failure in plain life, makes up fictitious versions of his predicament that are interesting even to other persons because nobody is a perfect automobile salesman. Everybody, alas, suffers a little . . . I constantly read this kind of criticism of my own verse. According to its doctors, my one intransigent desire is to have been a Confederate general, and because I could not or would not become anything else, I set up for poet and began to invent fictions about the personal ambitions that my society has no use for.

Although a theory may not be "true," it may make certain insights available for a while; and I have deemed it proper to notice theories of the genetic variety because a poet talking about himself is often expected, as the best authority, to explain the origins of his poems. But persons interested in origins are seldom quick to use them. Poets, in their way, are practical men; they are interested in results. What is the poem, after it is written? That is the question. Not where it came from, or why. The Why and Where can never get beyond the guessing stage because, in the language of those who think it can, poetry cannot be brought to "laboratory conditions." The only real evidence that any critic may bring before his gaze is the finished poem. For some reason most critics have a hard time fixing their minds directly under their noses, and before they see the object that is there they use a telescope upon the horizon to see where it came from. They are wood-cutters who do their job by finding out where the ore came from in the iron of the steel of the blade of the ax that Jack built. I do not say that this procedure is without its own contributory insights; but the insights are merely contributory and should not replace the poem, which is the object upon which they must be focused. A poem may be an instance of morality, of social conditions, of psychological history; it may instance all its qualities, but never one of them alone, nor any two or three; never less than all.

Genetic theories, I gather, have been cherished academically with detachment. Among "critics" they have been useless and not quite disinterested: I have myself found them applicable to the work of poets whom I do not like. That is the easiest way.

I say all this because it seems to me that my verse or anybody else's is merely a way of knowing something: if the poem is a real creation, it is a kind of knowledge that we did not possess before. It is not knowledge "about" something else; the poem is the fullness of that knowledge. We know the particular poem, not what it says that we can restate. In a manner of speaking, the poem is its own knower, neither poet nor reader knowing anything that the poem says apart from the words of the poem. I have expressed this view elsewhere in other terms, and it has been accused of aestheticism or art for art's sake. But let the reader recall the historic position of Catholicism: *nulla salus extra ecclesiam.* That must be religion*ism.* There is probably nothing wrong with art for art's sake if we take the phrase seriously, and not take it to mean the kind of poetry written in England forty years ago. Religion always ought to transcend any of its particular uses; and likewise the true art for art's sake view can be held only by persons who are always looking for things that they can respect apart from use (though they may be useful), like poems, fly rods, and formal gardens. . . . These are negative postulates, and I am going to illustrate them with some commentary on a poem called "Ode to the Confederate Dead."

I I

That poem is "about" solipsism, a philosophical doctrine which says that we create the world in the act of perceiving it; or about Narcissism, or any other *ism* that denotes the failure of the human personality to function objectively in nature and society. Society (and "nature" as modern society constructs it) appears to offer limited fields for the exercise of the whole man, who wastes his energy piecemeal over separate functions that ought to come under a unity of being. (Until the last generation, only certain women were whores, having been set aside as special instances of sex amid a social scheme that held the general belief that sex must be part of a whole; now the general belief is that sex must be special.) Without unity we get the remarkable self-consciousness of our age. Everybody is talking about this evil, and a great many persons know what ought to be done to correct it. As a citizen I have my own prescription, but as a poet I am concerned with the experience of "solipsism." And an experience *of* it is not quite the same thing as a philosophical statement *about* it.

I should have trouble connecting solipsism and the Confederate dead in a rational argument; I should make a fool of myself in the discussion, because I know no more of the Confederate dead or of solipsism than hundreds of other people. (Possibly less: the dead Confederates may be presumed to have a certain privacy; and as for solipsism, I blush in the presence of philosophers, who know all about Bishop Berkeley; I use the term here in its strict etymology.) And if I call this interest in one's ego Narcissism, I make myself a logical ignoramus, and I take liberties with mythology. I use Narcissism to mean only preoccupation with self; it may be either love or hate. But a good psychiatrist knows that it means self-love only, and otherwise he can talk about it more coherently, knows more about it than I shall ever hope or desire to know. He would look at me professionally if I uttered the remark that the modern squirrel cage of our sensibility, the extreme introspection of our time, has anything whatever to do with the Confederate dead.

But when the doctor looks at literature it is a question

whether he sees it: the sea boils and pigs have wings because in poetry all things are possible—if you are man enough. They are possible because in poetry the disparate elements are not combined in logic, which can join things only under certain categories and under the law of contradiction; they are combined in poetry rather as experience, and experience has decided to ignore logic, except perhaps as another field of experience. Experience means conflict, our natures being what they are, and conflict means drama. Dramatic experience is not logical; it may be subdued to the kind of coherence that we indicate when we speak, in criticism, of form. Indeed, as experience, this conflict is always a logical contradiction, or philosophically an antinomy. Serious poetry deals with the fundamental conflicts that cannot be logically resolved: we can state the conflicts rationally, but reason does not relieve us of them. Their only final coherence is the formal re-creation of art, which "freezes" the experience as permanently as a logical formula, but without, like the formula, leaving all but the logic out.

Narcissism and the Confederate dead cannot be connected logically, or even historically; even were the connection an historical fact, they would not stand connected as art, for no one experiences raw history. The proof of the connection must lie, if anywhere, in the experienced conflict which is the poem itself. Since one set of references for the conflict is the historic Confederates, the poem, if it is successful, is a certain section of history made into experience, but only on this occasion, and on these terms: even the author of the poem has no experience of its history apart from the occasion and the terms.

It will be understood that I do not claim even a partial success in the junction of the two "ideas" in the poem that I am about to discuss. I am describing an intention, and the labor of revising the poem—a labor spread over ten years—fairly exposes the lack of confidence that I have felt and still feel in it. All the tests of its success in style and versification would come in the end to a single test, an answer, yes or no, to the question: Assuming that the Confederates and Narcissus are not yoked together by mere violence, has the poet convinced the reader that, on the specific occasion of this poem, there is a necessary yet hitherto undetected relation between them? By necessary I mean dramatically relevant, a relation "discovered" in terms of the particular occasion, not historically argued or philosophically deduced. Should the question that I have just asked be answered yes, then this poem or any other with its specific problem could be said to have form: what was previously a merely felt quality of life has been raised to the level of experience—it has become specific, local, dramatic, "formal"—that is to say, *in*-formed.

I I I

The structure of the Ode is simple. Figure to yourself a man stopping at the gate of a Confederate graveyard on a late autumn afternoon. The leaves are falling; his first impressions bring him the "rumor of mortality"; and the desolation barely allows him, at the beginning of the second stanza, the conventionally heroic surmise that the dead will enrich the earth, "where these memories grow." From those quoted words to the end of that passage he pauses for a baroque meditation on the ravages of time, concluding with the figure of the "blind crab." This creature has mobility but no direction, energy but from the human point of view, no purposeful world to use it in: in the entire poem there are only two explicit symbols for the looked-in ego; the crab is the first and less explicit symbol, a mere hint, a planting of the idea that will become overt in its second instance—the jaguar towards the end. The crab is the first intimation of the nature of the moral conflict upon which the drama of the poem develops: the cut-off-ness of the modern "intellectual man" from the world.

The next long passage or "strophe," beginning "You know who have waited by the wall," states the other term of the conflict. It is the theme of heroism, not merely moral heroism, but heroism in the grand style, elevating even death from mere physical dissolution into a formal ritual: this heroism is a formal ebullience of the human spirit in an entire society, not private, romantic illusion—something better than moral heroism, great as that may be, for moral heroism, being personal and individual, may be achieved by certain men in all ages, even ages of decadence. But the late Hart Crane's commentary, in a letter, is better than any I can make; he described the theme as the "theme of chivalry, a tradition of excess (not literally excess, rather active faith) which cannot be perpetuated in the fragmentary cosmos of today—'those desires which should be yours tomorrow,' but which, you know, will not persist nor find any way into action."

The structure then is the objective frame for the tension between the two themes, "active faith" which has decayed, and the "fragmentary cosmos" which surrounds us. (I must repeat here that this is not a philosophical thesis; it is an analytical statement of a conflict that is concrete within the poem.) In contemplating the heroic theme the man at the gate never quite commits himself to the illusion of its availability to him. The most that he can allow himself is the fancy that the blowing leaves are charging soldiers, but he rigorously returns to the refrain: "Only the wind"—or the "leaves flying." I suppose it is a commentary on our age that the man at the gate never quite achieves the illusion that the leaves are heroic men, so that he may identify himself with them, as Keats and Shelley too easily and too beautifully did with nightingales and west winds. More than this, he cautions himself, reminds himself repeatedly of his subjective prison, his solipsism, by breaking off the half-illusion and coming back to the refrain of wind and leaves—a refrain that, as Hart Crane said, is necessary to the "subjective continuity."

These two themes struggle for mastery up to the passage,

> We shall say only the leaves whispering
> In the improbable mist of nightfall—

which is near the end. It will be observed that the passage begins with a phrase taken from the wind-leaves refrain—the signal that it has won. The refrain has been fused with the main stream of the man's reflections, dominating them; and he cannot return even to an ironic vision of the heroes. There is nothing but death, the mere naturalism of death at that—spiritual extinction in the decay of the body. Autumn and the leaves are death; the men who exemplified in a grand style an "active faith" are dead; there are only the leaves.

Shall we then worship death . . .

> . . . set up the grave
> In the house? The ravenous grave . . .

that will take us before our time? The question is not answered, although as a kind of morbid romanticism it might, if answered affirmatively, provide the man with an illusory escape from his solipsism; but he cannot accept it. Nor has he been able to live in his immediate world, the fragmentary cosmos. There is no practical solution, no solution offered for the edification of moralists. (To those who may identify the man at the gate with the author of the poem I would say: He differs from the author in not accepting a "practical solution," for the author's personal dilemma is perhaps not quite so exclusive as that of the meditating man.) The main intention of the poem has been to make dramatically visible the conflict, to concentrate it, to present it, in Mr. R. P. Blackmur's phrase, as "experienced form"—not as a logical dilemma.

The closing image, that of the serpent, is the ancient symbol of time, and I tried to give it the credibility of the commonplace by placing it in a mulberry bush—with the faint hope that the silkworm would somehow be implicit. But time is also death. If that is so, then space, or the Becoming, is life; and I believe there is not a single spatial symbol in the poem. "Sea-space" is allowed the "blind crab"; but the sea, as appears plainly in the passage beginning, "Now that the salt of their blood . . ." is life only insofar as it is the source of the lowest forms of life, the source perhaps of all life, but life undifferentiated, halfway between life and death. This passage is a contrasting inversion of the conventional

> . . . inexhaustible bodies that are not
> Dead, but feed the grass . . .

the reduction of the earlier, literary conceit to a more naturalistic figure derived from modern biological speculation. These "buried Caesars" will not bloom in the hyacinth but will only make saltier the sea.

The wind-leaves refrain was added to the poem in 1930, nearly five years after the first draft was written. I felt that the danger of adding it was small because, implicit in the long strophes of meditation, the ironic commentary on the vanished heroes was already there, giving the poem such dramatic tension as it had in the earlier version. The refrain makes the commentary more explicit, more visibly dramatic, and renders quite plain, as Hart Crane intimated, the subjective character of the imagery throughout. But there was another reason for it, besides the increased visualization that it imparts to the dramatic conflict. It "times" the poem better, offers the reader frequent pauses in the development of the two themes, allows him occasions of assimilation; and on the whole—this was my hope and intention—the refrain makes the poem seem longer than it is and thus eases the concentration of imagery—without, I hope, sacrificing a possible effect of concentration.

I V

I have been asked why I called the poem an ode. I first called it an elegy. It is an ode only in the sense in which Cowley in the seventeenth century misunderstood the real structure of the Pindaric ode. Not only are the meter and rhyme without fixed pattern, but in another feature the poem is even further removed from Pindar than Abraham Cowley was: a purely subjective meditation would not even in Cowley's age have been called an ode. I suppose in so calling it I intended an irony: the scene of the poem is not a public celebration, it is a lone man by a gate.

The dominant rhythm is "mounting," the dominant meter iambic pentameter varied with six-, four-, and three-stressed lines; but this was not planned in advance for variety. I adapted the meter to the effect desired at the moment. The model for the irregular rhyming was "Lycidas," but other models could have served. The rhymes in a given strophe I tried to adjust to the rhythm and the texture of feeling and image. For example, take this passage in the second strophe:

> Autumn is desolation in the plot
> Of a thousand acres where these memories grow
> From the inexhaustible bodies that are not
> Dead, but feed the grass row after rich row.
> Think of the autumns that have come and gone!—
> Ambitious November with the humors of the year,
> With a particular zeal for every slab,
> Staining the uncomfortable angels that rot
> On the slabs, a wing chipped here, an arm there:
> The brute curiosity of an angel's stare
> Turns you, like them, to stone,
> Transforms the heaving air
> Till plunged to a heavier world below
> You shift your sea-space blindly
> Heaving, turning like the blind crab.

There is rhymed with *year* (to many persons, perhaps, only a half-rhyme), and I hoped the reader would unconsciously assume that he need not expect further use of that sound for some time. So when the line, "The brute curiosity of an angel's stare," comes a moment later, rhyming with *year-there*, I hoped that the violence of image would be further reinforced by the repetition of a sound that was no longer expected. I wanted the shock to be heavy; so I felt that I could not afford to hurry the reader away from it until he had received it in full. The next two lines carry on the image at a lower intensity: the rhyme, "Transforms the heaving *air*," prolongs the moment of attention upon that passage, while at the same time it ought to begin dissipating the shock, both by the introduction of a new image and by reduction of the "meaning" to a pattern of sound, the ere-rhymes. I calculated that the third use of that sound (stare) would be a surprise, the fourth (air) a monotony. I purposely made the end words of the third from last and last lines— *below* and *crab*—delayed rhymes for *row* and *slab*, the last being an internal and half-dissonant rhyme for the sake of bewilderment and incompleteness, qualities by which the man at the gate is at the moment possessed.

This is elementary but I cannot vouch for its success. As the dramatic situation of the poem is the tension that I have already described, so the rhythm is an attempt at a series of "modulations" back and forth between a formal regularity, for the heroic emotion, and a broken rhythm, with scattering imagery, for the failure of that emotion. This is "imitative form," which Yvor Winters deems a vice worth castigation. I have pointed out that the passage, "You know who have waited by the wall," presents the heroic theme of "active faith"; it will be observed that the rhythm, increasingly after "You who have waited for the angry resolution," is almost perfectly regular iambic, with only a few initial substitutions and weak endings. The passage is meant to convey a plenary vision, the actual presence, of the exemplars of active faith: the man at the gate at that moment is nearer to realizing them than at any other in the poem; hence the formal rhythm. But the vision breaks down; the wind-leaves refrain supervenes; and the next passage, "Turn your eyes to the immoderate past," is the irony of the preceding realization. With the self-conscious historical sense he turns his eyes into the past. The next passage after this, beginning, "You hear the shout . . ." is the failure of the vision in both phases, the pure realization and the merely historical. He cannot "see" the heroic virtues; there is wind, rain, leaves. But there is sound; for a moment he deceives himself with it. It is the noise of the battles that he has evoked. Then comes the figure of the rising sun of those battles; he is "lost in that orient of the thick and fast," and he curses his own moment, "the setting sun." The "setting sun" I tried to use as a triple image, for the decline of the heroic age and for the actual scene of late afternoon, the latter being not only natural desolation but spiritual desolation as well. Again for a moment he thinks he hears the battle shout, but only for a moment; then the silence reaches him.

Corresponding to the disintegration of the vision just described, there has been a breaking down of the formal rhythm. The complete breakdown comes with the images of the "mummy" and the "hound bitch." (*Hound* bitch because the hound is a hunter, participant of a formal ritual.) The failure of the vision throws the man back upon himself, but upon himself he cannot bring to bear the force of sustained imagination. He sees himself in random images (random to him, deliberate with the author) of something lower than he ought to be: the human image is only that of preserved death; but if he is alive he is an old hunter, dying. The passages about the mummy and the bitch are deliberately brief —slight rhythmic stretches. (These are the only verses I have written for which I thought of the movement first, then cast about for the symbols.)

I believe the term modulation denotes in music the uninterrupted shift from one key to another: I do not know the term for change of rhythm without change of measure. I wish to describe a similar change in verse rhythm; it may be convenient to think of it as modulation of a certain kind. At the end of the passage that I have been discussing the final words are "Hears the wind only." The phrase closes the first main division of the poem. I have loosely called the longer passages strophes, and if I were hardy enough to impose the classical organization of the lyric ode upon a baroque poem, I should say that these words bring to an end the Strophe, after which must come the next main division, or Antistrophe, which was often employed to answer the matter set forth in the Strophe or to present it from another point of view. And that is precisely the significance of the next main division, beginning: "Now that the salt of their blood . . ." But I wanted this second division of the poem to arise out of the collapse of the first. It is plain that it would not have suited my purpose to round off the first section with some sort of formal rhythm; so I ended it with an unfinished line. The next division must therefore begin by finishing that line, not merely in meter but with an integral rhythm. I will quote the passage:

> The hound bitch
> Toothless and dying, in a musty cellar
> *Hears the wind only.*
>
> *Now that the salt of their blood*
> Stiffens the saltier oblivion of the sea,
> Seals the malignant purity of the flood. . . .

The caesura, after *only,* is thus at the middle of the third foot. (I do not give a full stress to *wind,* but attribute a "hovering stress" to *wind* and the first syllable of *only.*) The reader expects the foot to be completed by the stress on the next word, *Now,* as in a sense it is; but the phrase, "Now that the salt of their blood," is also the beginning of a new movement; it is two "dactyls" continuing more broadly the falling rhythm that has prevailed. But with the finishing off of the line with *blood,* the mounting rhythm is restored; the whole line from *Hears* to *blood* is actually an iambic pentameter with liberal inversions and substitutions that were expected to create a counter-rhythm within the line. From the caesura on, the rhythm is new; but it has—or was expected to have—an organic relation to the preceding rhythm; and it signals the rise of a new statement of the theme.

I have gone into this passage in detail—I might have chosen another—not because I think it is successful, but because I labored with it; if it is a failure, or even an uninteresting success, it ought to offer as much technical instruction to other persons as it would were it both successful and interesting. But a word more: the broader movement introduced by the new rhythm was meant to correspond, as a sort of Antistrophe, to the earlier formal movement beginning, "You know who have waited by the wall." It is a new formal movement with new feeling and new imagery. The heroic but precarious illusion of the earlier movement has broken down into the personal symbols of the mummy and the hound; the pathetic fallacy of the leaves as charging soldiers and the conventional "buried Caesar" theme have become rotten leaves and dead bodies wasting in the earth, to return after long erosion to the sea. In the midst of this naturalism, what shall the man say? What shall all humanity say in the presence of decay? The two themes, then, have been struggling for mastery; the structure of the poem thus exhibits the development of two formal passages that contrast the two themes. The two formal passages break down, the first shading into the second ("Now that the salt of their blood . . ."), the second one concluding with the figure of the jaguar, which is presented in a distracted rhythm left suspended from a weak ending—the word *victim*. This figure of the jaguar is the only explicit rendering of the Narcissus motif in the poem, but instead of a youth gazing into a pool, a predatory beast stares at a jungle stream, and leaps to devour himself.

The next passage begins:

> What shall we say who have knowledge
> Carried to the heart?

This is Pascal's war between heart and head, between *finesse* and *géométrie*. Should the reader care to think of these lines as the gathering up of the two themes, now fused, into a final statement, I should see no objection to calling it the Epode. But upon the meaning of the lines from here to the end there is no need for further commentary. I have talked about the structure of the poem, not its quality. One can no more find the quality of one's own verse than one can find its value, and to try to find either is like looking into a glass for the effect that one's face has upon other persons.

If anybody ever wished to know anything about this poem that he could not interpret for himself, I suspect that he is still in the dark. I cannot believe that I have illuminated the difficulties that some readers have found in the style. But then I cannot, have never been able to, see any difficulties of that order. The poem has been much revised. I still think there is much to be said for the original *barter* instead of *yield* in the second line, and for *Novembers* instead of *November* in line fifteen. The revisions were not undertaken for the convenience of the reader but for the poem's own clarity, so that, word, phrase, line, passage, the poem might at worst come near its best expression.

1938

V

Preface to *Reactionary Essays on Poetry and Ideas*

MODERN POETS are having trouble with form, and must use "ideas" in a new fashion that seems willfully obscure to all readers but the most devoted. The public waits to be convinced that the poets behave as they do because they cannot help it.

How have poets used ideas in the past? How are they using them today? How shall we explain the difference between the poet's situation in the past and his present situation? Or, if explanation is beyond us, as it probably is, what terms shall we call in merely to record the changes that have brought about the modern situation? It is, I think, our task to find out what the poets have done, not what they ought to have done, and to guess what it was possible for them to do in their times. But even the right guess would be a truism: what a poet wrote was alone possible for him to write. It is nevertheless a duty of the modern critic to notice the implication of the impossible, if only to warn the reader of modern verse, who is exasperated, that poets cannot write now like poets in 1579, or 1890.

Poetry in some sense has a great deal to do with our experience. Historians exhibit its general features as evidence to support still more general theories of history and society. But modern literary critics are reversing the procedure of the historian. They are using social theories to prove something about poetry. It is a heresy that has, of course, appeared before, yet never more formidably than now. We are trying to make an art respectable by showing that after all it is only a branch of politics: we are justifying poetry by "proving" that it is something else, just as, I believe, we have justified religion with the discovery that it is science.

To order our political interests is to practice one of the greater arts. Both politics and the arts must derive their power from a common center of energy. It is not certain that the old theory of art for art's sake is more absurd than its analogy—politics for politics's sake, which as an abstraction becomes Economics that we pursue as truth-in-itself. It is agreed that our political confusion is alarming. It is not agreed that it will continue to be alarming until we are able to see our belief in the absolute of a scientific society as at least a phase, if not profoundly the cause, of our confusion. Both politics and poetry, having ceased to be arts, are cut off from their common center of energy. They try to nourish each other. It is a diminishing diet. The neo-Communists are not likely to grow fatter on it than their capitalist brethren by giving it a new name. For a political poetry, or a poetical politics, of whatever denomination is a society of two members living on each other's washing. They devour each other in the end. It is the heresy of spiritual cannibalism.

This heresy is a legitimate field of modern criticism, but because it denies the traditional procedure of poets and is thus negative, it will concern the poet only in his faculty of critic, not in his job as craftsman. The poet's special question is: How shall the work be done? Why it was done and why the work is what it is, questions of first interest to readers of poetry, are of little interest to poets who are able to remain artists in a difficult age.

For poetry does not explain our experience. If we begin by thinking that it ought to "explain" the human predicament, we shall quickly see that it does not, and we shall end up thinking that therefore it has no meaning at all. That is what Mr. I. A. Richards's early theory comes to at last, and it is the first assumption of criticism today. But poetry is at once more modest and, in the great poets, more profound. It is the art of apprehending and concentrating our experience in the mysterious limitations of form.

Philosophy even in the strict sense may be the material of poetry, but poets are not chiefly philosophers. A poet whose main passion is to get his doctrine—or his personality or his local color—into his poems is trying to justify a medium in which he lacks confidence. There is a division of purpose, and the arrogance of facile "solutions" that thinks it can get along without experience. The poet had better write his poetry first; examine it; then decide what he thinks. The poetry may not reveal all that he thinks; it will reveal all he thinks that is any good—for poetry. Poetry is one test of ideas; it is ideas tested by experience, by the act of direct apprehension.

There are all kinds of poetry readers. The innocent reader and the reader till lately called the moralist, who is now the social reader, are different from the critical reader, and they are both incurably intellectual. Their heads buzz with generalizations that they expect the poet to confirm—so that they will not have to notice the poetry. It is a service that the modern poet, no less amiable than his forebears, is not ready to perform: there is no large scheme of imaginative reference in which he has confidence. He must, in short, attach some irony to his use of "ideas," which tend to wither; he may look for a new growth but with the reservation that it too may be subject to the natural decay.

The innocent reader lives in the past; he likes to see in poetry, if not the conscious ideas, then the sensibility of a previous age. Our future sensibility the social reader, wise as he is, has no way of predicting, because he ignores the one source of that kind of prophecy—the present—grasped in terms, not of abstractions, but of experience; so he demands that poets shall set forth the ideas that he, in his facility, has decided that the future will live by. The poet—and it is he who is the critical reader—is aware of the present, any present, now or past or future. For by experiencing the past along with the present he makes present the past, and masters it; and he is at the center of the experience out of which the future must come. The social reader ought to remember that the specialist worries the major works of Spenser as a hungry dog his bone, but that *The Divine Comedy* has been at the center of our minds for six hundred years. The greater poets give us knowledge, not of the new programs, but of ourselves.

1936

Preface to *Reason in Madness*

THE ESSAYS collected here were written either for an occasion or upon assignment from an editor. Only one, "Literature as Knowledge," has been written specially for this book. Every essayist—and I distinguish the essayist from the systematic literary critic—must be grateful to his editors, as I am grateful, for suggestions that led to the writing of all but three of these essays.

The reader will expect to see here only the consistency of a point of view. I hope that he will not be disappointed if he does not find it. Yet I believe that all the essays are on one theme: a deep illness of the modern mind. I place it in the mind because that is the level at which I am interested in it. At any rate the mind is the dark center from which one may see coming the darkness gathering outside us. The late W. B. Yeats had for it a beautiful phrase, "the mad abstract dark," and we are all in it together.

Few of the questions which have agitated what used to be called the "press" in the five years since the first of the papers was written, appear in this book. There are war and democracy, which are only casually mentioned. Certain features of the present war may be unique in the history of war, and if they are they may also be a symptom of our peculiar illness. What those features are this is not the place to say; yet our limitation of the whole human problem to the narrow scope of the political problem is obviously one of them. We are justified in saving democracy if democracy can save something else which will support it. That "something else," which we name with peril, so great is our distress, hovers round the periphery of these essays. Unless we consider it, everything we write will look, after a generation, when the historical irony becomes visible, like another tale of a tub.

Every writer writes within a convention which he picks up from someone else or invents for himself. The convention of this book is the attack. It asks of people who profess knowledge: What do you know? But that is only another way of asking oneself the same question. I do not hear it asked very frequently these days.

1941

Preface to *On the Limits of Poetry*

AT THE KIND SUGGESTION of Mr. Alan Swallow, who has not entirely removed my doubts that it should be done, I have put this book together from three earlier books written over a period of twenty years. Most of the articles were written in the uneasy time between the wars; whether the new age which is just beginning will be less harassed, or more, it is too early to predict. Its "problems" will seem at any rate to be different. Neo-Humanism, for example, is not likely to revive again, and I have omitted from this collection a long essay on this topic which had a little notoriety in 1930. Many of the pieces are controversial (or were); the controversies of twenty or even five years ago turn into private history, of little interest to any public. The earliest writing in the book is a part of the essay on Emily Dickinson, written in 1928 and incorporated in a longer discussion which was first published in 1932. Only two of the pieces were written without an eye to periodical publication. The book can therefore be expected to have as little unity as my previous critical volumes: if my interests of the moment happened to coincide with an editor's, an essay or a review was the result.

The temptation to revise one's early views in the light of what one would like to regard as more mature knowledge must always, I think, be resisted. I have made here and there a few changes of word and phrase which I hope will clarify without altering either emphasis or sense. The great difficulty for the critical writer (besides the insuperable frustration of learning to write) is to learn how to write for an occasion without being submerged in it. There is the greater difficulty of deciding—and this is partly a matter of propriety —how much of one's imperfect insight and small knowledge to bring to bear upon the brief treatment of a subject. I have felt that sensibility ought to remain, in an informing position, in the background; that critical style ought to be as plain as the nose on one's face; that it ought not to compete in the detail of sensibility with the work which it is privileged to report on. Criticism, unless it is backed by formal aesthetics, is at best opinion; and aesthetics frequently does well enough, for its own purposes, without attending too closely to works of literature as they are commonly known. I have tried to remember, from the time I began to write essays, that I was writing, in the end, opinion, and neither aesthetics nor poetry in prose.

There are many subjects of which I should like to have tested my perception in essays, but I never got round to them, or I didn't know enough about them, or I was not asked by an editor to discuss them. Other subjects (like Existentialism or Kafka's guilt) arrive some morning like insulting letters which, if they are not answered the same day, do not need to be answered at all. Another source of regret is the toplofty tone of some of these essays and reviews. Minorities cringe or become snobs (if they are not disciplined by the *dignitas* of St. Bernard); snobbishness, of which the explanation is not the excuse, was the unredeemed course open to me. I am told that the "school" of critics of which I have been said somewhat perplexingly to be a member is no longer a minority. If this be true, I am not sure that it is good for me or for other members of the school, whoever they are; but I think it scarcely true.

If the title of this book recalls Lessing, the reader is warned that he will find little of Lessing in it, beyond a few references to the relation of poetry and painting. On reading my essays over, I found that I was talking most of the time about what poetry cannot be expected to do to save mankind from the disasters in which poetry itself must be involved: that, I suppose, is a "limit" of poetry. Lessing says that poetry is not painting or sculpture; I am saying in this book, with very little systematic argument, that it is neither religion nor social engineering.

1948

Preface to *The Forlorn Demon*

IN ONE OF THESE ESSAYS I call Poe a "forlorn demon in the glass." It is an unhappy phrase that I had thought was entirely mine until the other day, when I remembered the rather bad poem,

> From every depth of good and ill
> The mystery which binds me still—
> From the thunder and the storm
> And the cloud that took the form
> (When the rest of Heaven was blue)
> Of a demon in my view.

The poem, which is entitled "Alone," has never been famous, and even Poe's authorship has been questioned. But I am sure that it is Poe, as I am sure that a friend is who he is without the proof of his driver's license or his social security card. If it is not by Poe, no matter; it gave me the phrase and it serves my purpose.

To the question, What would attract the attention of demons if they lost interest in us? we have no answer at present; nor can we guess how different their personalities seem to them; perhaps every demon is sure that he is unique. Poe was certain all his life that he was not like anybody else. The saints tell us that confident expectancy of damnation is a more insidious form of spiritual pride than certainty of salvation. The little we know of hell is perhaps as follows: it promptly *adjusts* and *integrates* its willing victims into a standardized monotony, in which human suffering, its purpose thus denied, begins to sound like the knock of an un-oiled piston. A famous literary critic predicted years ago that our poetry would soon echo the rhythms of the internal com-bustion engine, and he produced a short verse-play to prove it. I take it he meant that poetry would no longer move to the rhythms of the heart, which are iambic or trochaic, de-pending on whether the ear picks up the beat at the diastole or the systole, with occasional fibrillations and inverted T-waves to delight the ear and to remind us of the hour of our death. The rapidity of a piston reminds us of a machine which can temporarily or permanently break down; but it can be exactly duplicated and it cannot die. To this god, I believe, we owe our worship of *rapid* and exciting language, an idolatry that in one degree or another is the subject of most of these essays.

Sometimes I think that life is a dream, and that what I am really doing is not what I do. I sit, in doubt between waking and sleeping, on the keel of a capsized boat, eating barnacles with my old friend Arthur Gordon Pym and pre-tending that the hull is a continent.

The reader has been warned on the title page to expect in these essays a certain didacticism. It is not aimed at the reader; it is homework, the tone I take when I talk to my-self. I published my first essay twenty-five years ago. Since then, year after year, I have been conducting an unfinished education in public. All essayists seem to do this; unlike the scholars, they cannot wait until they have made up their minds before they speak. I am a little perplexed by my failure to understand why I continue to do it. The modern man of letters, if he is not a playboy, is an eccentric: he is "off center," away from his fellow citizen who is sure that he is standing in the Middle. I do not know why an eccentric should give himself away by appearing in public; he might do better to stay at home with his family and invite his friends to dinner. Yet once he appears he will appear again and again. Isn't his delighted audience convinced (as he is) that his manners are unique? He thinks he hopes that he is not like anybody else. What he really hopes is that what made him an eccentric—a committed sin, a sin desired but resisted, the musty smell of his grandmother's house, one of William Empson's "missing dates," an *intermittence du coeur*, or something else quite ordinary—will not be detected by anybody, even by his intimate friends. But it always is.

1953

Preface to *The Man of Letters*
in the Modern World

THIS IS THE FOURTH PREFACE that I have written for as many collections of my essays. Again I shrink from the task, which will be brief, and from the results, which I cannot foresee. It might have been more enlightening for myself, to write a review of an imaginary history of my literary opinions, and put it as a postscript at the back of the book, in the hope that few people would read it. On second thought, I could expect other persons to feel even less interest in my critical history than I myself feel. There was also the more ambitious possibility of a history of one's mind. But it is always a question whether one's egoism can be made to look unique, or anything but conventional and boring. To recover the secret motions of the heart, and then to testify, to bear witness, is a good thing for Christians to do; but it requires an innocence of which one can at most say that one may long ago have had it. To lay the heart bare is not at any rate the first obligation of the literary critic. As the particular virtue of the soldier is not statesmanship, and of the nuclear physicist not philosophizing, so the literary critic must not be expected to complete his nature in the public confession of mortal sin (in the French manner), or in the proclamation, rather than the exercise, of intellectual virtue. I suddenly find that I have been thinking of André Gide, who in book after book confessed and proclaimed little else.

The earliest of these essays appeared in a weekly journal twenty-seven years ago; it is nineteen years since some of them were collected in a book; the most recent book, from which I have included several essays, appeared in 1953. The present volume covers some twenty-five years of critical writing. It will be obvious to anybody who has done me the honor of reading my essays over a number of years, that I had to learn as I went along. But it was always necessary to move on, in the intervals between essays, and to think about something else, such as a room where one might write them, and whether the rent could be paid. Another matter for the mendicant poet to think about was poetry itself, and even how he might write some of it. I could echo without too much self-revelation Poe's famous (and humorless) excuse for having published so little verse: there is too much else that one must do—a distraction that frequently includes the prospect of not doing anything. I am not sure that I wanted to write more than three or four of these essays; the others I was asked to write; one can do what one does. I never knew what I thought about anything until I had written about it. To write an essay was to find out what I thought; for I did not know at the beginning how or where it would end.

Many of the opinions put forth in the early essays I no longer hold. I do not think that men can achieve salvation by painting pictures or writing poetry, or by cleaving to an historical or a social tradition; I believe I stopped short of thinking that the State could save us. Some of the early opinions that I still hold seem to be pompously or at least badly expressed. If I fail to cite examples of this fault, it is not merely because I feel responsible for my defects, and am willing to expose them; an imprecise phrase, or an illicit enthymeme, is usually implicated in a way of thinking that would be only superficially improved by a change of diction; small revisions may compound an old error with a new. I have supposed at times that I wanted to write a formal critical enquiry, on one subject, of book length, and I may write it yet (I have started one); but at present I am on record as a casual essayist of whom little consistency can be expected. I am not trying to excuse incoherence (a deeper fault than inconsistency) in the single essay or in the long development from the first essay to the latest. By development I do not mean growth, in the sense of improvement; one cannot know whether one has improved. I mean the gradual discovery of potentialities of the mind that must always have been there. Whether one is made better, or is only made aware of greater complexity, by this discovery, is a question that cannot be answered by the person who asks it about himself.

A critical skeptic cannot entirely imagine the use of a criticism in which the critic takes the deistic part of absentee expositor. To take this role is to pretend that a method can accomplish what the responsible intelligence is alone able to do. The act of criticism is analogous to the peripety of tragedy; it is a crisis of recognition always, and at times also of reversal, in which the whole person is involved. The literary critic is committed, like everybody else, to a particular stance, at a moment in time; he is governed by a point of view that method will not quite succeed in dispensing with. After the natural sciences began to influence literary criticism, scholars held that a point of view without method led inevitably to impressionism. This need not follow; it is obvious why I prefer to think that it need not. Impressionism— "what I like"—is never more intractable than when it is ordered to dine perpetually at the second table. The first table is usually an historical, or a philosophical "method"; but this is by no means the same as historical or philosophical criticism. I should like to think that criticism has been written, and may be again, from a mere point of view, such as I suppose myself to be possessed by. Of the range and direction of a point of view, and why a point of view exists in some persons, nobody can be certain. It seems to take what little life it may have from the object that it tries to see. There is surely little impropriety in describing it negatively, by what it cannot see. Whatever certainties one may cherish as a man—religious, or moral, or merely philosophical—it is almost certain that as literary critic one knows virtually nothing.

1955

Acknowledgments

WITH THE EXCEPTION OF "The Unliteral Imagination; Or, I, too, Dislike It," which was published in *The Southern Review*, Summer 1965; "Poetry Modern and Unmodern," which was published in *The Hudson Review*, Summer 1968; and "Herbert Read," which was published as the Foreword to the book, Herbert Read, *Selected Writings* (London: Faber and Faber, 1963; New York: Horizon Press, 1964), the essays in this volume were published in my previous books, as follows:

> *Reactionary Essays on Poetry and Ideas* (New York: Charles Scribner's Sons, 1936)
>
> *Reason in Madness: Critical Essays* (New York: G. P. Putnam's Sons, 1941)
>
> *On the Limits of Poetry* (New York: The Swallow Press and William Morrow & Company, 1948)
>
> *The Hovering Fly* (Cummington, Massachusetts: The Cummington Press, 1949)
>
> *The Forlorn Demon: Didactic and Critical Essays* (Chicago: Henry Regnery Company, 1953)
>
> *The Man of Letters in the Modern World* (New York: The World Publishing Company, Meridian Books, 1955)
>
> *Modern Verse in English 1900–1950* (edited with Lord David Cecil; London: Eyre & Spottiswoode, 1958; New York: The Macmillan Company, 1959)
>
> *Collected Essays* (Denver: Alan Swallow, Publisher, 1959)

A. T.

Index

Index

631